THE CREATION OF MODERN QUAKER
DIVERSITY, 1830–1937

THE NEW HISTORY OF QUAKERISM

The first historical series in Quaker studies in over a century, these volumes offer a fresh, comprehensive, up-to-date treatment of the history of Quakerism from its seventeenth-century origins to the twenty-first century. Using critical methodologies, this limited series emphasizes key events and movements, examines all branches of Quakerism, and explores its global reach.

The Creation of Modern Quaker Diversity, 1830–1937

Stephen W. Angell, Pink Dandelion, and David Harrington Watt

The Pennsylvania State University Press
University Park, Pennsylvania

Library of Congress Cataloging-in-Publication Data

Names: Angell, Stephen Ward, 1952– editor. | Dandelion, Pink, editor. | Watt, David Harrington, editor.
Title: The creation of modern Quaker diversity, 1830–1937 / [edited by] Stephen W. Angell, Pink Dandelion, and David Harrington Watt.
Other titles: New history of Quakerism.
Description: University Park, Pennsylvania : The Pennsylvania State University Press, [2023] | Series: The new history of Quakerism | Includes bibliographical references and index.
Summary: "A collection of essays examining the history of Quakerism from 1830 to 1937, tracing the resurgence of missionary work and the development of Quakerism as a global faith"—Provided by publisher.
Identifiers: LCCN 2022060949 | ISBN 9780271095028 (hardback) | ISBN 9780271095035 (paper)
Subjects: LCSH: Society of Friends—History—19th century. | Society of Friends—History—20th century. | LCGFT: Essays.
Classification: LCC BX7631.3 .C73 2023 | DDC 289.609/034—dc23/eng/20230315
LC record available at https://lccn.loc.gov/2022060949

Copyright © 2023 The Pennsylvania State University
All rights reserved
Printed in the United States of America
Published by The Pennsylvania State University Press,
University Park, PA 16802–1003

The Pennsylvania State University Press is a member of the Association of University Presses.

It is the policy of The Pennsylvania State University Press to use acid-free paper. Publications on uncoated stock satisfy the minimum requirements of American National Standard for Information Sciences—Permanence of Paper for Printed Library Material, ANSI Z39.48–1992.

CONTENTS

Acknowledgments vii

Introduction: The Remapping of Quakerism, 1830–1937 1
PINK DANDELION

1   Quakers and Empire 18
    SYLVESTER A. JOHNSON AND
    STEPHEN W. ANGELL

2   Quakers and Reform in Nineteenth-Century America: Friends' Response to Antislavery, Women's Rights, and the American Civil War 37
    JULIE L. HOLCOMB

3   The Loss of Peculiarity and the New Quaker Identity: The Outward and the Inward Life 58
    EMMA JONES LAPSANSKY

4   The Revival, 1860–1880 75
    THOMAS D. HAMM

5   Quakers and the Growth of the Pastoral System 94
    ISAAC BARNES MAY

6 Quakers and "Religious Madness" 112
RICHARD KENT EVANS

7 Quakers of the Liberal Renaissance, 1870–1930: Rediscovering the Light Within 128
JOANNA CLARE DALES

8 The Delineation of Quaker Spiritualities 149
CAROLE DALE SPENCER

9 Quakers and the Social Order, 1830–1937 173
NICOLA SLEAPWOOD AND THOMAS D. HAMM

10 Quakers and Missions, 1861–1937 191
STEPHEN W. ANGELL

11 The Peace Testimony and the Crisis of World War I 213
ROBYNNE ROGERS HEALEY

12 Quakers in Politics 232
STEPHANIE MIDORI KOMASHIN AND RANDALL L. TAYLOR

13 The All-Friends Conferences and Their Effects 248
DOUGLAS GWYN

Afterword: Rufus Jones and Quaker History 268
DAVID HARRINGTON WATT

Notes 281
Selected Bibliography 333
List of Contributors 341
Index 347

ACKNOWLEDGMENTS

Scores of people helped to create this book. We gratefully acknowledge the aid they have given us. We would especially like to note the assistance we've received from Sally Osborn, Sara Arnold, Carol Holmes Alpern, and our colleagues at the Earlham School of Religion, Lilly Library at Earlham College, the Friends Historical Library of Swarthmore College, Haverford College, the Louisville Institute, and the Woodbrooke Quaker Study Centre.

Introduction
The Remapping of Quakerism, 1830–1937

PINK DANDELION

This is volume 4 in the Penn State University Press New History of Quakerism series. The series begins with the second edition of Rosemary Moore's seminal *The Light in Their Consciences: The Early Quakers in Britain, 1646–1666*, detailing the history and theology of the first two decades of the nascent Quaker movement. Richard Allen and Rosemary Moore coedited and contributed essays to the second volume, *The Quakers, 1656–1723: The Evolution of an Alternative Community*. The third volume, edited by Robynne Rogers Healey and in press at the time of the writing of this book, looks at the eighteenth and early nineteenth centuries. A fifth volume, edited by Stephen W. Angell and David Harrington Watt, will complete the series, covering the years after 1937.[1]

The vision for this series is to provide scholars and general readers with an updated version of the Rowntree History Series, which appeared in the first two decades of the twentieth century and was overseen and largely written by Rufus Jones and William Charles Braithwaite, building on the vision of John Wilhelm Rowntree, who never lived to take part in the endeavor. These are slimmer volumes in the present series than the ones penned by Jones and Braithwaite, but we trust that they are able to make full use of the advances in scholarly thinking over the previous one hundred years and provide a fuller and more nuanced picture of the complexities of the Quaker past.²

The period from 1830 to 1937 is of great significance for the modern expression of the Quaker way. Three main tropes underpin the analysis in this volume: (1) the end of a single Quaker tradition and the development and growth of multiple types of Quaker theological emphasis, (2) the restarting of Quaker missionary work, the introduction of pastoral Quakerism, and the development of Quakerism as a global faith, and (3) the considerable change in Quaker attitudes and responses to the wider society and a cultivation of conformity as Quakers embraced citizenship and civic participation. These changes would come to alter what had counted as "Quaker" before 1830 and create a template for the following two centuries. Here, these three tropes are considered in turn, followed by an overview of the scholarly literature to date and the gaps this volume fills. This introduction ends with a dedication to Edward H. Milligan, former head librarian at the Friends House Library in London, who knew more about this period than we will ever see set down in one place.

THREE KEY ELEMENTS OF CHANGE

Multiple Quakerisms
The 1830–1937 period saw the end of a single Quaker tradition and its subsequent splintering into multiple schismatic tendencies—a splintering that occurs when counterbalancing emphases are separated from one another. As Carole Spencer's chapter in this volume attests, wholly new variants of the Quaker faith emerged during this period, with a pattern of four main groupings taking shape by the end of the nineteenth century: revival evangelical, renewal evangelical, conservative, and modernist. In the twentieth century, these solidified around umbrella organizations such as Five Years Meeting (FYM) and Friends General Conference (FGC), even as further schisms appeared and change occurred within each of these branches (see chapter 8). At the same time, Quaker groupings began to work together more, particularly on peace and social justice issues, and the decentralized nature of Quaker ecclesiology accommodated a network of cooperation that eventually led, as Douglas Gwyn's chapter in this volume charts, to the 1920 All-Friends Conference and, in time, to the formation in 1937 of a global

organization (Friends World Committee for Consultation) to help coordinate fellowship among the "world family of Friends" (see chapter 13).

Underneath this series of splits lay deep theological differences. As Emma Lapsansky explains in her chapter in this volume, the root issue was one of spiritual authority (see chapter 3). For some Quakers, such as Elias Hicks of New York, authentic spirituality lay inwardly, and any outward form, including scripture, lacked compelling religious authority. Thus, those who came to be labeled as Hicksites questioned or disregarded biblical claims at the very point in time when other Quakers were being drawn into a more scripture-centered sensibility, influenced by their work with evangelical Christians and attracted by their dynamism. For these Quakers, who became known as the Orthodox party, the faith could be renewed by this wider vision and adaptation of traditional Quakerism. During the series of schisms known as the Great Separation, many yearly meetings separated into two camps, and there were arguments over property and minute-book ownership. Each yearly meeting disowned the membership of the other. Yearly meetings that had not divided needed to decide which of the two new factions to recognize and, in particular, whose epistles to receive.[3]

Within both groups, there were some with hesitations about ecumenical cooperation, but both were invested in maintaining their interpretation of the true Quaker tradition. Indeed, in time, some Quaker practices such as plain dress fell out of favor because others (people who had previously been Quakers but who had been disowned) also adopted the practice, and thus it was now considered "worldly" or creaturely. Schism depends on both a strong sense of vision or identity and a strong sense of "othering" those in opposition to that vision or identity. Groups separating on doctrinal grounds are more prone to further schism as doctrine is debated. In the Quaker context, then, the Hicksites, who were grouped around a commitment to traditional practice, suffered only the separation of the progressives, who wished for a more radical political outlook on issues such as slavery and women's rights, as well as a congregational ecclesiology.[4]

The Orthodox, on the other hand, would splinter again within seventeen years of the Great Separation. John Wilbur of New England believed that scriptural authority needed to be balanced against the authority of revelation, whereas British traveling minister Joseph John Gurney favored the primary authority of scripture. British Quakers had experienced a schism of the "Beaconites" in 1835, led by Isaac Crewdson, who had labeled direct revelation a delusive notion, and while Gurney did not go that far, British Quakers took an increasingly scripture-centric line in the mid-nineteenth century. When Gurney traveled to America between 1837 and 1840, the seeds of a schism within the Orthodox were sown. Wilbur's own yearly meeting divided in 1845, and further schisms took place in the following decade. By 1854, there were three kinds of Quakers (Hicksite, Gurneyite, and Wilburite) in Ohio. To avoid further schism, Philadelphia's Orthodox Quakers decided not to send or receive any epistles to and from other yearly meetings.[5]

Initially the Gurneyite branch maintained traditional Quaker worship based in silence and stillness. Gurney maintained that this liturgical form helped worshippers best interpret scripture. For others, however, silent worship had become formulaic in its own way and spiritually arid. By the late 1850s, many young Friends in the Midwest were supplementing Quaker silence with prayer meetings, public tract readings, and even hymn singing. When the Holiness revival spread across the Midwest in the 1860s, many Quakers were keen to join in with the Methodist meetings and then to replicate them in Quaker settings. The first Quaker revival meeting was in 1867. Thomas Hamm offers an overview of Quaker revivalism in this volume. Within a few years, the success of these meetings had been such that pastoral committees were established to help teach the Quaker faith to the thousands of converts coming to Quaker meetings (see chapter 4). This soon translated into the decision to "release" ministers for pastoral work, and once there were Quaker pastors, the move to a form of worship led by a pastor seemed the logical next step. The first Quaker pastor was hired in 1875, and the term "Friends church" came into use at the same time. Isaac May's chapter in this book explores the development of the Quaker pastorate (see chapter 5). For more traditional Quakers, "programming," or "pastoral Quakerism," was too different from traditional Quaker understandings of the free ministry of all arising through the silence of open worship, and there was a series of antipastoral schisms in the 1880s by groups who found an affinity with Wilburite Quakers. Indeed, the Wilburite branch, together with these antipastoral Friends, would in time form the basis of modern-day Conservative Quakerism, conserving traditional theology and practice.[6]

Within the remaining Gurneyites, two main camps emerged: revival Quakers and renewal Quakers (see fig. 1). The renewal Quakers wanted to reinvigorate traditional Quaker understandings and practices with organized Bible study and "First Day" schools, whereas the revival Quakers, the subject

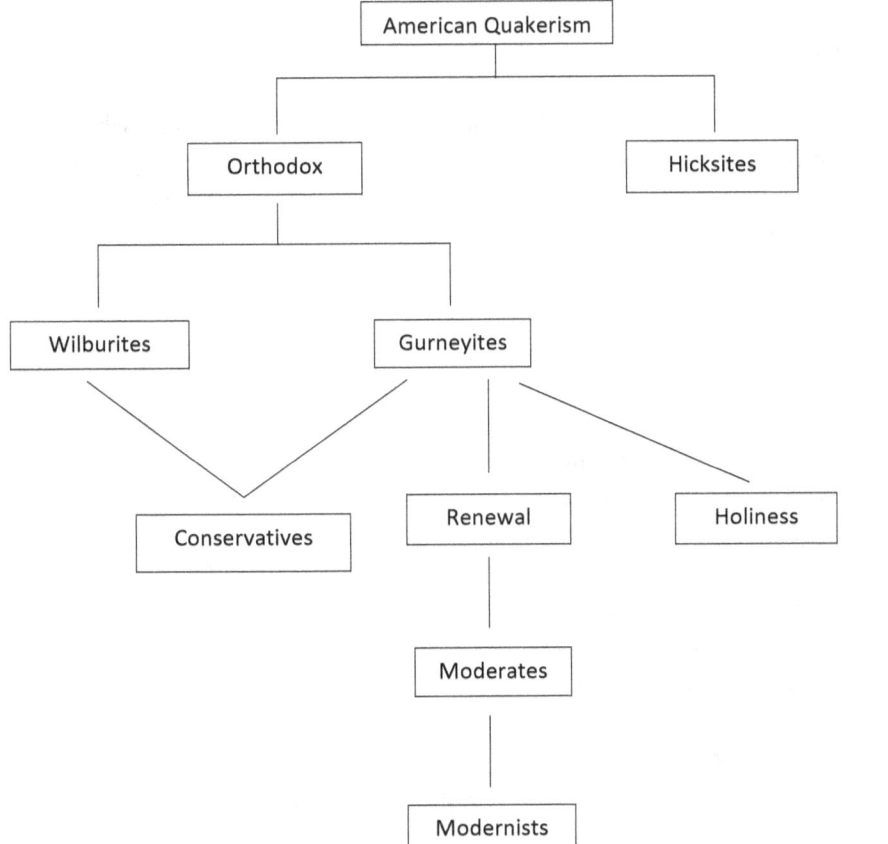

FIG. 1 The Evolution of American Quakerism, 1800–1907. From Thomas D. Hamm, *The Transformation of American Quakerism: Orthodox Friends, 1800–1907* (Bloomington: Indiana University Press, 1988), 176. © Indiana University Press.

of the chapter by Thomas Hamm, were keen to follow what they saw as the leadings of the Spirit, wherever it may take them, even if that meant a wholesale departure from previous Quaker practices. For the latter, denominational affiliation became less crucial than Christian affiliation. Revival Quakers were thus more open to spiritual innovation, and the next major division occurred around the revivalist wish for some ministers to be baptized outwardly with water instead of simply inwardly, as Quakers had traditionally held. A "water party" led by Ohio minister David Updegraff began to advocate for this option, and in 1887, all the Gurneyite yearly meetings sent representatives to a conference in Richmond, Indiana. The conference produced the Richmond Declaration, a confession of faith similar in format to a creedal statement, which specifically clarified that water baptism was not a Quaker practice.[7]

Ohio Gurneyites did not unite with the declaration, and while other Gurneyite yearly meetings held conferences every fifth year and set up an umbrella organization in 1902, FYM, other yearly meetings would leave this grouping in the first decades of the twentieth century because of perceived progressive drifts in doctrine or because of how the Richmond Declaration was seen to be optional rather than central. Oregon left FYM in 1926, Kansas, in 1937. The renewal Quakers tolerated the more radical modernists led by Rufus Jones, seen by revivalists to include FYM general secretary Walter Woodward, whereas the revival party wanted to draw a strictly evangelical Christian doctrinal line that would deprive modernists like Jones and Woodward of any leadership positions within FYM. Woodward, however, remained general secretary until his death in 1942.[8]

Revivalist Holiness yearly meetings in the first decades of the twentieth century would face two influences from wider Christianity. The first was the Pentecostal revival that began in 1905 and the question of whether speaking in tongues (glossolalia) could be part of the Quaker faith. FYM decided that it could not and gradually became more renewal centered. Yearly meetings such as Ohio, Kansas, and Oregon experienced instead the influence of the "fundamentals" movement and drew in an opposite direction. In the 1940s, a period outside the scope of this volume, as fundamentalism gave way to neoevangelicalism, they would start the Association of Evangelical Friends and later the Evangelical Friends Alliance (now Evangelical Friends Church International). Their primary affinity was with other evangelicals rather than Quakers. In 1924, Central Yearly Meeting was formed from evangelical meetings that moved out of Indiana and Western Yearly Meetings, and in 1926, Central left FYM.[9]

The Hicksite branch, in contrast, found itself increasingly shaped by modernist sensibilities in which science and faith no longer needed to be set apart. This modernism underpinned what became the "liberal" tradition of Quakerism that emerged in the 1880s, but it also influenced some renewal Gurneyites (as Joanna Dales explores in chapter 7). Quakers like Rufus Jones and Elbert Russell pioneered a modernist aspect to FYM and, in doing so, paved the way for greater cooperation between those Friends and Hicksites around service and social justice work.[10]

The liberals maintained the Hicksite emphasis on inward revelation and used it as a way to circumvent the challenges to biblical authority identified by higher criticism. They were also "renewal" in sensibility and reformed the Quakerism of their parents to adopt a more world-accepting stance. History was seen to be about progress, and, as newly minted citizens in Britain with no prohibitions facing them after 1871, Quakers wished to play a part in that progress. In Britain, the shift from Gurneyite to liberal was complete within a generation. In North America, Hicksite yearly meetings set up their own umbrella organization, Friends General Conference (FGC), to share resources and to foster fellowship. Unlike the more corporate FYM, which claimed authority over its constituent yearly meetings, FGC was more like a subscription organization, providing services to its members. Under the influence of an ecumenism increasingly defined by liberalism, many within some Hicksite, Gurneyite, and Conservative yearly meetings sought to heal nineteenth-century separations, and while this reunification movement made headway during the period up to 1937, the resulting merger or consolidation of fourteen Friends' bodies in eastern North America into five combined yearly meetings (New England, Canadian, New York, Philadelphia, and Baltimore) did not take place until later, between 1945 and 1968, outside the purview of this volume.[11]

United by the Quaker witness against war, Friends from all traditions gathered in 1920 for an All-Friends Conference in London (see chapter 13). In the one hundred years since 1827, Quakerism had gone from being a single faith tradition made up of different yearly meetings to one that included four distinct groupings along with other independent yearly meetings. By 1937, when a second world conference prompted the formation of the Friends World Committee for Consultation, fewer evangelical Friends were present, but the sense of a "world family of Friends" was nevertheless maintained across the different liturgical and theological emphases.

Mission Work and Global Quakerism
The period this book examines, 1830 to 1937, witnessed the rebirth of missionary Quakerism, which had been largely dormant since the 1670s. It saw the introduction of a pastor-led liturgical form as a response to large-scale revival recruitment, which, in turn, through mission work, became the dominant form of Quakerism. Most significantly, Quakerism became a truly global faith; it was no longer confined to the United States, the British

Commonwealth, and parts of Europe. By 1937, Quakerism was established in East and Central Africa and Central and South America. Stephen Angell's chapter on Quakers and missions gives a comprehensive overview of the different dynamics of these overseas endeavors (see chapter 10).

Mission work began again for Quakers in the form of "home mission," attempts to spread Christianity among the poor, and in "adult schools" with literacy programs. In Britain, large programmed meetings were organized on Sunday evenings in the 1850s and 1860s as part of a moral Christian crusade aimed at the working classes. In 1860, George Richardson, in a letter to *The Friend*, suggested the value of foreign mission work, and in 1866, Rachel Metcalfe became the first Quaker overseas missionary when she sailed to India. The Friends Foreign Mission Association was founded in 1870.[12]

Missionary organizations spread throughout Gurneyite Quakerism in North America as well, and newly formed educational institutions helped prepare Quakers for full-time ministry as pastors or as missionaries. Missions to Palestine and Lebanon started in the 1860s and 1870s and to Japan in 1885. In 1886, Quaker missionaries reached China. Before the end of the nineteenth century, Quaker missionaries had also worked in Mexico, Syria, Jamaica, Cuba, and Madagascar. In 1902, three Quakers based at the Cleveland Bible Institute, run by Holiness Friends Walter and Emma Malone, sailed to Kenya and then took a train from Mombasa to the far west of the country to start a Quaker mission. Thus began what would eventually become the major growth arc of Quakerism in the twentieth century, one that would outstrip the North Atlantic regional membership of its Quaker colonist missionaries. As Angell recounts, work in Kenya was followed by missionary activity in Burundi in the 1930s. Missionary activity in Central America began in earnest in 1901, and missionaries from California, Oregon, and Central Yearly Meetings started going to South America after 1902. Indigenous cultures were often disregarded by these missionaries, but there are also examples, as Angell shows in his chapter, of syncretic hybridized versions of Quakerism emerging as a consequence of the dynamic between missionaries and local converts or because of Indigenous encounters with Quaker literature such as Robert Barclay's *Apology*.[13]

As British Quakerism became liberal rather than evangelical, its home missionary activity declined in the early twentieth century, and its foreign mission was eclipsed by war relief and then by social missionary activity. The American Friends Service Committee (AFSC), founded in 1917 with participation from different yearly meetings across the separate traditions, focused far less on conversion than on general welfare, including work to improve race relations in the United States from the 1920s onward. Indeed, the lack of explicit Christian witness at the heart of social mission work led some evangelical yearly meetings to leave AFSC.[14]

Unprogrammed worship soon became shorter, and, in contrast to the development of the pastorate discussed in Isaac May's chapter in this volume, the recording of ministers was abolished in some yearly meetings in the twentieth century. In Britain, this led to a change in the seating arrangements for meeting, with less importance given to the "facing bench." The introduction of tables into the middle of meetings would see an increase in the habit of placing flowers at the heart of the worshipping group. At the very point at which parts of Quakerism were flourishing and expanding, liberal and conservative Quakerism sought new variants of stability and, in part, a sectarian identity without the aspiration or felt need for increased numbers.

Citizens and Outlaws
Wolf Mendl has described Quaker witness in terms of two contrasting strands, the prophetic and the reconciliatory. This refers to the division between absolutism and pragmatism—the decision as to whether to oppose a wrong outright, potentially as an outlaw, or work to ameliorate the injustice, perhaps even by compromising as a Godly citizen. George Fox decided to remain in jail in Derby in 1650 rather than take up a captaincy in the battle against the monarchist cause, but in 1661, a declaration of harmlessness and opposition to war was used to try to persuade the new king, Charles II, that he need not persecute the Quakers. The first action, I suggest, fits what Mendl called prophetic; the second is reconciliatory. The first made Fox an outlaw; the second presented Quakers as good citizens.[15]

In the period from 1830 to 1937, we can see Quakerism emerging from a guarded domesticity of "world-rejecting" attitudes toward an orientation, in most branches, of "world-acceptance" and of assimilation. It is a century in which conformity was both offered by the state and cultivated within the group.[16]

Critical to this process was that, from the 1830s, Quakerism stopped seeing itself as the one true church but rather as part of the true church, with each tradition having its own obvious allies in other parts of Christianity. This ecumenism became married to a greater sense of civic participation and a decreased perception of that activity as "worldly" or apostate. In general, we can view this period as one in which Quakers increasingly styled themselves as Christian citizens rather than sectarian outlaws.[17]

As Emma Lapsansky explains in her chapter on the loss of peculiarity, by 1840, Quakers were united against slavery, if not unified in terms of strategy. Julie Holcomb's chapter on Quakers and antislavery highlights the debates about slavery within each of the branches of nineteenth-century Quakerism (see chapter 2). There was, in addition to this, a growing concern for penal reform and care of the mentally ill. Richard Evans looks at the Quaker approach to mental illness, religious madness, and rational thought in his chapter in this volume (see chapter 6). Temperance and adult literacy became key social issues for Quakers in the nineteenth century. In all of these concerns, Quakers worked closely where they could with other Christians and began to question why, if salvation was available to those less set apart, Quakerism needed to be so guarded in its relationship with wider society. Driven by concern over falling numbers or geographical expansion in which Quakerism was too insignificant to endure such sectarianism, distinctive Quaker peculiarity (particularity) in dress, speech, customs, and practice gave way to a more world-accepting sensibility in which Quakers assimilated into wider society; in Britain, partly as the laws prohibiting nonconformist participation as full citizens were abolished. After 1861, Quakers in Britain were no longer obliged to wear plain dress, use the plain language, marry only other Quakers, and be buried without a headstone. Hannah Rumball's work highlights the way in which embellishments were slowly added to Quaker sartorial norms in the nineteenth century, while Brian Phillips records how hats at yearly meetings in London in the early years of the twentieth century were large enough to block the view of the clerk's table for Friends sitting behind.[18]

The shift toward denominationalism and away from sectarianism would not be smooth or wholesale (Conservatives would maintain their preference for a peculiar or particular Quakerism, and in all branches, there would be debates about whether it was appropriate to work for social justice with "the world's people"). Yet increasingly, Quakerism began to see itself no longer as the one true church but as a part of the true (Christian) church. The chapter by Sylvester Johnson and Stephen Angell and the chapter by Julie Holcomb outline how this shift impacted campaigns around slavery and issues of race (see chapters 1 and 2).

In Britain, Quakers were admitted to the Houses of Parliament after 1832. Joseph Pease famously affirmed rather than taking an oath of office, and in the 1870s and 1880s, longtime Quaker member of Parliament (MP) John Bright was part of Gladstone's cabinet but felt it made him unfit to be an Elder. This dichotomy between spiritual and civic service would disappear in the 1890s: political involvement grew alongside a sense of spiritual civic leadership to allow nine Quakers to enter the British Parliament in 1906 and Herbert Hoover to become president of the United States in 1929, as Stephanie Midori Komashin and Randall Taylor discuss in their chapter (see chapter 13). Between 1869 and 1879, US Quakers (both Orthodox and Hicksite) cooperated with President Grant's "peace policy" to administer settlements for Native Americans. This aspect of the Quaker past and its general entanglement with the mechanisms of empire is highlighted by Sylvester Johnson and Stephen Angell in the opening chapter of this volume. They find that Quaker integrity surrounding equality (particularly regarding race) and peace was often compromised by implicit and explicit cooperation with the empires of the global north. Brian Phillips has highlighted the imperial hubris and folly of British Quakers at the turn of the twentieth century in the way that they imagined themselves as global players.[19]

The chapter by Richard Evans is particularly illuminating in this regard. It is different in outlook from the other chapters in this volume but reflects well this shift in perspective and participation in wider society. Rather than offer a history of Quakers in this field, Evans illustrates how Quakers took their place on the wider playing field of developments in psychology and debates within religion more widely. He does not focus on internal denominational developments but, significantly, uses the Quakers to explore wider cultural and intellectual developments (see chapter 6). In short, Quakers became involved in the ecumenical and political order, and with civic participation came a greater openness to formal and higher education, with a concomitant growth in the number of Quaker educational institutions. In time, this involvement in education, both as students and teachers, was one of the factors that drew the group away from an earlier inclination toward business and industry.[20]

Testimony (Quaker witness) advocating plainness was adapted to the encouragement of simplicity, and testimony against war was reclaimed as a propeace stance. This diffusion of focus and intent was accompanied by a broadened theological basis for justification of particular actions and a less prescriptive attitude toward individual choice. Quakerism gave its members more freedom to choose how to live their faith, and there were fewer mechanisms to proscribe or police those choices. After 1861 in Britain, for example, a Quaker could leave Sunday morning meeting, be inaudible and invisible as a Quaker in the street, and head home to a Methodist spouse.[21]

Over the late decades of the nineteenth century, a "private life" became a possibility for some Quakers for the first time, in that what took place away from the meetinghouse was no longer seen to be the direct concern or business of the meeting. As suggested by the conversion success of revival Quakerism and the freedoms afforded Quaker children in the liberal tradition, it was also the end of dynastic Quakerism in every branch, with more joining from outside than had joined since the seventeenth century. Within the organization, women's and men's business meetings were slowly united. What counted as "worldly" or apostate shrank. In time, Quaker involvement with the arts grew, as Roger Homan's case study of Birmingham tempera revivalist Joseph Edward Southall highlights. Southall talked of involvement with craft rather than art, but Quakers became increasingly less concerned about emotion and self as enemies of the spiritual life.[22]

In only some areas of life did most parts of Quakerism maintain a countercultural position. The most obvious and enduring has been opposition to war. Quakers faced a civil war in the United States, the 1837 rebellion in Canada, and a raft of British imperial wars. In World War I, one-third of eligible British Quaker men enlisted. Others took one of four positions: joining a noncombatant army regiment such as the medical corps; joining the Friends Ambulance Unit, an unofficial Quaker organization that helped the war wounded; registering as a conscientious objector after the introduction of conscription in March 1916; or refusing to register and take alternative service (as it would enable someone else to go and serve in the military) and thus, as an "absolutist," spending time in jail. Robynne Healey's chapter in this volume looks at the Quaker response to this war (see chapter 11). Thomas Kennedy has argued that those who took the absolutist stance became the interwar leadership of British Quakerism, but in different ways, the newly styled testimony for peace was challenged. We can also see this period as one in which the nature of Quaker witness changed dramatically.[23]

Thus, Quakerism between 1830 and 1937 underwent a revolution. It split dramatically and severally and then partially gathered itself back together; it created new liturgical forms and became a global faith thanks to the missionary efforts of some Quaker branches; and, in general, it became a permissive denomination, leaving behind sectarian "true church" sensibilities and privations. It was a spreading out of the Quaker faith in many senses—a remapping of the Quaker world.

PREVIOUS STUDIES

The scholarly coverage of the 1830–1937 period is sporadic. The Rowntree History Series included this period up to the start of the twentieth century, but its authors, Rufus Jones and William Charles Braithwaite, were themselves key players in the realignment of Quakerism taking place at the time. Jones, for example, was successfully trying to unite FYM around a modernist renewal vision over and against revival Holiness—in 1907, a correspondent claimed that he had them "whipped for all time now." Later scholars would point out the ways in which these authors' own theological preferences affected the presentation of their analysis. Other histories of the movement only devote a few thousand words to this crucial century of Quakerism.[24]

National or regional studies help fill in some of the picture. Rosemary Mingins has written about the Beaconites. Elizabeth Isichei's socio-theological approach to the three types of Quakers (evangelical, conservative, and liberal) that dominated British Quakerism in the Victorian period remains a classic. Thomas Kennedy's volume on British Quakerism from 1860 to 1920, demonstrating how it so quickly and completely transformed from an evangelical to a liberal movement, has proved seminal and complements Brian Phillips's doctoral work on the way British Quakers combined their newfound identity as citizens with the ideology of empire. Martin Davie has looked at theological change within British Quakerism between 1895 and 1980 but thus covers only part of our period of concern. Anna Kett has looked at women's antislavery work in the nineteenth century. Elizabeth O'Donnell's doctoral work on Victorian British Quaker women's experience argues that in the northeast of England, the most politically radical Quaker women left the movement in order to find freedom of expression. This contrasts with the experience of women in the southwest, and O'Donnell's work sits alongside Sandra Stanley Holton's on the Priestman-Bright-Clark kinship circle, a microhistorical approach that reveals the strength of politicized women's networks. Mijin Cho's doctoral work on Isabella Ford, Isabel

Fry, Margery Fry, and Ruth Fry complements Holton's work while highlighting the elastic nature of what was permissible for women activists within early liberal Quakerism. Many of the women whom O'Donnell studies resisted the merging of women's and men's business meetings for fear of losing the agency they had gained over the centuries; meanwhile, Pam Lunn's study of attitudes toward women's enfranchisement reveals a mix of attitudes across the sexes in the first decades of the twentieth century. Julia Bush has written in particular about Caroline Stephen and her opposition to women's suffrage.[25]

As regards North America, in a deeply researched volume, A. Glenn Crothers has illuminated the dilemmas and increasing hostility from non-Quaker neighbors confronting antislavery Quakers living in Virginia, a part of the American South where slavery was deeply ingrained in society prior to 1865. There have also been book-length studies of Quakers in New York, the Delaware Valley of Pennsylvania and New Jersey, Massachusetts, North Carolina, California, Oregon, Alaska, Canada, and other regions. Some of these studies are illuminating, like Crothers's, while others are now dated and need supplementation.[26]

Biography is a further way of gaining insight into the broader Quaker picture. Clare Brown has written about the principles underlying Joseph Sturge's antislavery work. Helen Smith's work on Elizabeth Taylor Cadbury highlights the political and social capital of the great Quaker cocoa dynasty and what could be achieved by a progressive philanthropist. Sian Phillips's work on Francesca Wilson looks at another Birmingham-based Quaker, in this case, one devoted to relief work. Joanna Dales has completed extensive work on John William Graham, described as an "apostle of progress" for his advocacy of a progressive Quaker message linked to worldly advances, and she has built on that work to look at the liberal "Quaker Renaissance" more widely. Mark Frankel is currently focusing on Quaker member of British Parliament T. Edmund Harvey. Alessandro Falcetta's magisterial biography of J. Rendel Harris includes his Quaker work and role as first director of Woodbrooke College. (Harris is an intriguing character: a friend of Rufus Jones's, a prominent player in a key liberal institution, and yet cast by Carole Spencer as a Holiness Quaker.)[27]

Women's suffrage and antislavery activist Lucretia Mott has recently been the subject of an excellent new biography by Carol Faulkner, and those wanting to know more about Mott can also consult a new edition of her speeches and sermons, complementing an existing collection of her letters.[28]

A new biography of Progressive Friend Amy Kirby Post similarly illuminates a life devoted to both antislavery and women's rights but also with an interest in spiritualism, not one of Mott's causes. Carole Spencer's work on Hannah Whitall Smith is significant, given Whitall Smith's key role in Holiness spirituality within and outside the Quaker movement.[29]

The rest of Europe has also only been covered in brief. Yearly meetings began in Germany and Austria in 1925, in the Netherlands in 1931, in France in 1933, and in Sweden in 1935, often as a result of Quaker relief work and Quaker "embassies." Norway had set up a yearly meeting in 1818; Denmark did so in 1875. Hans Eirik Aarek has written about Norwegian Quaker history, and Sheila Spielhofer has researched relief work in Vienna after World War I. Farah Mendlesohn has written on relief work during the Spanish Civil War, starting in 1936.[30]

For Quaker history in the United States, we have Thomas Hamm's book *The Quakers in America*. Hamm has also written the seminal study of Orthodox Quakerism, and its companion volume on the Hicksites is in press. The Great Separation is the subject of volumes by H. Larry Ingle and Robert Doherty. Timothy Burdick has analyzed the changing theological identity of Oregon Yearly Meeting. Oregon's difficulties with FYM and AFSC were representative of how some yearly meetings in that branch of Quakerism gradually left the organization. Guy Aiken has researched the connections of AFSC's humanitarian work with "social Christianity," presenting some of the other side of that tension. Arthur Roberts has written about evangelical Friends after 1887, J. William Frost has written about the history of FGC, and Douglas Gwyn has analyzed its emblematic gatherings as an exercise in personalism.[31]

Rufus Jones remains one of the central figures in modern American Quaker history. He drew together modernist strands in FYM and Philadelphia Yearly Meeting and helped build coalitions around service work—he was one of the founders of AFSC—that, in turn, would lead to the reunification of yearly meetings in New England, Philadelphia, and Canada after World War II. However, the scholarly work on Jones is limited. Christy Randazzo and David Russell have made a start on Jones's theology. Matthew Hedstrom considers Jones's written work within a wider analysis of American liberal Christianity and, in particular, shows how Jones influenced Harry Fosdick, a prominent American liberal Protestant minister. Jones also influenced Howard Thurman, as highlighted by Stephen Angell in the volume on Quaker mysticism edited by Jon Kershner. Haverford colleague and Harvard biblical scholar Henry J. Cadbury is being researched currently by David Watt and Jim Krippner.[32]

Chuck Fager has detailed the previously under-researched role of the Progressive Quakers, with their congregational ecclesiology and radical political stance. What began as a Hicksite schism in the 1830s soon advanced ahead of their parent body on women's rights and antislavery. The last Progressive Quaker meeting closed in 1940. Thomas Hamm has explored the history of a branch of Progressive Quakers in Ohio and Indiana.[33]

Lloyd Lee Wilson has charted Conservative Quaker history in the United States, while Wilmer Cooper's autobiography highlights the temptations of revival meetings for his Wilburite father: they would ride out to the revival meetings and stay just a little way off so they could hear the proceedings without taking part.[34]

Robynne Rogers Healey has written on Quakers in Upper Canada and how they negotiated their Quaker identity in relation to the demands of frontier life. She also charts the separation of David Willson and the Children of Peace, a group that built the Sharon Temple, boasted one of the finest silver musical bands in Ontario, and endured as a counter-cultural advocate of peace until the group's dissolution in 1889. Albert Schrauwers has also written about this schismatic group.[35]

The history of Quakerism in East Africa and Central and South America remains a significant gap in the scholarship. Esther Mombo's doctoral work on the early days of the mission to Kenya is thus of crucial importance. She shows how the early Quaker missionaries to Kenya disregarded the local social fabric, enforcing monogamy on converts even though this resulted in abandonment and destitution for second and third wives. Eating chicken, previously reserved only for men, became seen as a mark of women becoming Christian. Nancy Thomas's recent work on Central and South America complements a chapter in *The Cambridge Companion to Quakerism* on Quakerism in the region by Ramon Longoria and Nancy Thomas.[36]

Thus, while there is still much to do, we believe that this collection moves us further forward in our scholarly understanding. This volume is ambitious, then: it seeks to cover the breadth and depth of one of the most dynamic periods of Quaker history and the one of greatest—indeed, seemingly perpetual—change. As editors, we have been privileged to work with such a fine set of scholars and writers, and we trust that this volume does justice to its task.

POSTSCRIPT AND DEDICATION

Edward Milligan died in August 2020, as I was preparing this chapter. Born in 1922 in Coventry to John Lloyd Milligan and Jennie E. Rowlands, "Ted" spent time at Ackworth Friends School in the 1930s and served in the Friends Relief Service from 1941 to 1946. He studied librarianship and worked at the University of Southampton library before taking over from John L. Nickalls as head librarian at Friends House, London, in 1958, a post he held until 1985. In those days, employment was no impediment to yearly meeting service, and Ted served on the 1955 book of discipline revision committee under the clerkship of Wilfrid Littleboy and on the agenda committee on three different occasions for a total of fourteen years. He also served on the Committee on Christian Relations for eleven years and Home Service Committee for twenty-one. However, for those of us interested in Quaker history, it was in his role as librarian, or in relation to his work with the Friends Historical Society for over four decades, that we most likely had the privilege to meet or correspond with him. Either was a great pleasure. Always witty, always twinkling, Ted had an encyclopedic knowledge of all things Quaker. A birthright Friend, he knew the family connections within the Quaker world firsthand, and he lived through a period of enormous change in the way Quakerism operated in Britain while becoming an expert on earlier centuries, especially the nineteenth century of his parents' youth. His letters were always humorous and kind, and he was a most generous soul and mentor. All of us who knew him will miss him, and it seems fitting to dedicate this chapter to the person who knew the most about this period—not just its outline theology and practice but also the intricate genealogical web of endogamy and its consequences—though, alas, he wrote so little of it down.[37]

CHAPTER I

Quakers and Empire

SYLVESTER A. JOHNSON AND STEPHEN W. ANGELL

Few religious sects in the English-speaking world could escape the reach of the mature British Empire or the emerging American Empire during the years from 1830 to 1937. Like most, Quakers engaged with empire in multiple ways. In fact, Quakers had been collaborators in the English imperial enterprise from the seventeenth century onward. This chapter examines the relationship between Quaker religion and empire. We look at crucial events and persons on both sides of the Atlantic Ocean. Our account traces a trajectory from the seventeenth century to the twentieth, ending with a consideration of Quaker Herbert Hoover, who served as the thirty-first president of the United States. We will examine the degree to which Quaker "testimonies" (such as their peace testimony) effectively challenged imperial powers of their time or, alternatively, supplied moral cover to imperial endeavors.

We begin with a definition of empire. We then proceed to an account, largely chronologically structured, of the various ways that British and North American Quakers engaged with empire, paying due attention to seventeenth- and eighteenth-century precedents, before proceeding to examine the period from 1830 to 1937. Given that racial formation was such a key component, much of our analysis deals directly with that dimension of empire. We examine various case studies, including the involvement of

Seneca Falls, New York, abolitionists with the economy of the emerging empire; the very different attitudes of British Quaker chocolate manufacturers toward their English and African workforces, and the contributions to the modern American Empire, or critique of empire, of two "fighting Quakers," Smedley Darlington Butler and A. Mitchell Palmer. We conclude with some consideration of various Quakers' engagement with, and embrace of, either racism or anti-racism—a crucial pillar of American imperialism—during the height of Herbert Hoover's political career. As we shall show, Hoover himself combined racist and anti-racist strategies.

UNDERSTANDING EMPIRE

What exactly is empire? And why does it make sense to examine religion through its relationship to empire? Empires have structured political power and economic systems for thousands of years, and they have done so with tremendous relevance for understanding religion. Zoroastrianism and Judaism in the ancient Persian Empire, Christianity under the ancient Roman and Byzantine Empires, and Islam within the context of the Mughal and Ottoman Empires are just a few examples. The Religious Society of Friends first emerged during the 1600s, in the heart of global empire during the ascendancy of England's overseas conquests. The ensuing decades and centuries recapitulated the historical pattern of empire's indelible influence on religion as colonial missionaries and religious activists became fully entwined in imperial networks of commercialism and settlement as well as activism targeting colonial politics and social reform. Over time, expert studies of empire have variously attended to key themes and patterns. Of special importance are "colonies," "extraction," "settlers," and the "metropole-periphery axis."

Empires have historically been constituted through the holding of "colonies," which are polities controlled by and dependent on the colonizing power. In its most familiar form, a polity becomes a colony when another sovereign state gains control over that polity. In practice, this undermines the colony's sovereignty through control of political power (the empire-state controls appointment of formal governing authorities of the colony), economic activity (monetary or natural resources), or the use of territory (settlement and displacement). The principle of "extraction" refers to empires exploiting human labor and natural resources of a given colony. Imposing slavery on a conquered population, seizing a portion of the colony's agricultural produce or profits, or controlling a polity to extract resources (uranium or oil, for instance) for cheap use by a conquering polity are representative examples. Experts have employed the term "settler colonialism" to designate a special pattern of empire whereby people from the empire-state occupy the colony chiefly to dispossess Indigenous people in order to control their land for settler habitation. Settler colonialism (examples of which include Australia, South Africa, and the commonwealths of Virginia, Massachusetts, and Pennsylvania) is not inherently at odds with aims of extraction, but it is not unusual for Indigenous peoples facing settler colonialism to be treated politically as expendable (settlers may desire neither their labor nor their presence) through wars of extermination, starvation, forced relocation, or mass slaughter (various forms of genocide).[1]

The "metropole-periphery axis" merits special explanation. It is frequently cited to highlight the hierarchy of power and physical distance separating the colony (the periphery) and the seat of power for the empire (the metropole). This emphasis has often produced the inaccurate perception that the empire-state and the colony are inherently and necessarily physically distant. The emergence of the global African slave trade and the concomitant rise of European empires, however, yielded important departures from this notion. The 1600s, in particular, witnessed the creation of multiple nonterritorial company-states that exercised colonial rule over territorial colonies. The English East India Company, created in 1601, began governing South Asia by transforming the region into a colony not of the British Crown but of the corporation. This condition obtained for approximately 250 years; not until the 1850s did the territorial state of Britain begin formal rule of South Asia. The Royal African Company, chartered in 1660, pursued the same style of colonial rule in West Africa. The Dutch East India Company (also known as the United East India Company) was established in 1602 and quickly transformed from a chiefly commercial enterprise into a company-state that established its own colonies, minted currency, exercised foreign policy, and established a global standing military. This corporate empire-state integrated multiple practices beyond those of seventeenth-century territorial states, creating the synthesis of sovereign power now commonly associated with sovereign territorial states.

There was no physical distance separating these transnational colonizing powers from their colonized polities. Even in the Americas, where possession of colonies was sometimes held by territorial states such as the empires of France, Britain, and Spain, private companies were integral to the process. The Virginia Company of London, for instance, and not the British Crown, was formally designated as the governing power in North America by the terms of its corporate charter in 1606. Finally, the United States created a reservation system to concentrate sovereign tribal nations of Native Americans onto the least arable lands of North America. This system, which achieved its zenith in the 1800s and continues today, has typified the physically proximate juxtaposition of colonized polities and the empire-state, as the United States has continually violated the putative sovereignty of Native nations through this colonial relationship.[2]

EARLY QUAKERS AND ENGLISH EMPIRE

The Quaker movement developed and matured in relationship with the English empire from its early stages. Quaker meetings developed in Ireland, without critique of empire, among the Protestant settlers who constituted an early manifestation of the British Empire. Rhode Island Quakers were expected to support the New England side in bolstering the imperium during King Philip's War (1675–76), and they largely met expectations.[3]

The settler colonies of the Delaware Valley—New Jersey, Pennsylvania, and Delaware—represented a more massive investment in English imperial concerns by Quakers. English and Welsh Quakers considered these colonies a refuge for persecuted Quakers. This standpoint obscured the realities of the displacement of Indigenous populations and exploitation of African labor that attended the mid-Atlantic forms of English colonization, just as they accompanied other English and European colonization efforts throughout the Western Hemisphere. William Penn's 1681 "Letter to the Kings of the Indians" was couched in far more respectful language than the Spanish Requerimiento of the sixteenth century, but the assertion of European sovereignty was similar. The eighteenth-century Delaware Valley colonies saw the opening of a political and cultural divide between Quakers. On the one hand, Quakers such as James Logan, architect of the infamous 1737 Walking Purchase, tended to be quite uncritical of the demands of empire. On the other hand, reformers such as Anthony Benezet and John Woolman launched critiques against some of the most severe depredations resulting from empire, including enslavement. The reformers managed to gain control over much of the organizational heft of Quakerism, but both parties—the reformers and the cultural Quakers—remained important throughout the nineteenth century, including in the various branches after the separation of 1827–1828, and subsequent separations.[4]

As a result of agitation from radicals such as Benjamin Lay and reformers such as Benezet and Woolman, the Society of Friends committed to freeing itself from slaveholding, in a process culminating in disownment of slaveholders between about 1772 and 1782, and to scrutinizing the treaty-making process with Native Americans, implicitly raising the question whether the empire inhabited by Quakers could be one grounded on principles of justice. The reform impulse coincided with a partial withdrawal from political involvement when, in 1756, at the beginning of the French and Indian War (as it was known in the American colonies; it was called the Seven Years' War in Europe), enough Quaker legislators resigned from the Pennsylvania Assembly that Quakers would never again constitute the majority of legislators in that body. Consequently, reform, as advocated by Benezet and Woolman, was based on a perceived divine leading toward purification that was incompatible with such worldly stratagems as providing funds for military purposes.[5]

AFRICAN AMERICAN QUAKERS AND THE GAMBIT OF RACIAL EMPIRE

A commitment, advocated strenuously by the reforming Quakers, to ending Quaker involvement in the most egregious form of colonial oppression—slavery—did not translate into a society-wide commitment to rooting out injustice in all its forms. Significant barriers guarded against African Americans becoming members of the Society of Friends in nearly all regions of the country. An African American in Philadelphia who long discerned an intimate connection with Quakerism, Sarah Mapps Douglass (1806–1882), was, with her family, made to worship on a "Negro bench" in the rear of the Arch Street Meetinghouse because of the racism that grounded White religious norms. Eloquent protests such as those raised by Douglass made clear, not for the last time, the extent to which the White Quaker world would be willing ultimately to be profoundly complicit in the racist oppression of burgeoning North Atlantic English and White American empires.[6]

Paul Cuffe was a man of African American and Native American descent whose family had a long association with Friends, and he applied and was accepted into membership in a Friends Meeting in Westport,

Massachusetts, in 1808, at the age of forty-nine. Cuffe was a fighter for human rights in the emerging United States, serving jail time in his home state for refusing to pay taxes while deprived of the right to vote and later setting up an interracial school on his property when his children were denied access to local schools because of their race. He amassed a considerable fortune as a seaman and a merchant. Notably, however, his main interest was in building commercial connections between the United States and West Africa and encouraging African American settlement in Africa. During the War of 1812, he petitioned the US Congress for financial assistance in building settlements and supporting commerce. Cuffe had strong connections with free African Americans in Philadelphia and Quaker philanthropists, such as William Allen, in Great Britain who were interested in his ventures in commerce and settlement. Given the commitment by Britain and the United States to ending the international slave trade, a policy adopted on both sides of the Atlantic in 1808, this complex African American Quaker initiative tied together a mature empire in Britain and an emerging one in the United States through transplanting principles of "civilization" to a third region of the Atlantic world.[7]

Both houses of Congress narrowly defeated Cuffe's proposal, deeming it outside their constitutional powers, and instead gave widespread endorsement to the establishment of a private benevolent society, the American Colonization Society (ACS), founded in 1817 for the purposes of civilizing and Christianizing Africa through Black American settlers. Cuffe endorsed the society before his death the same year. While some Quakers supported the American Colonization Society, other Quakers strongly opposed this effort that one of their members had such a large part in promoting.

Cuffe's life and work has multiple significations. Many have revered him as a founder of Black nationalism. Liberia was a main project of the ACS.[8] The role of diplomacy by military force that resulted in the formation of the state of Liberia received insufficient attention from Quakers. The violent origins presaged the continued and sustained violence between African American settlers in Liberia and the native African population in that part of West Africa. Some African Americans who were formerly held by Quakers accepted ACS settlement in Liberia in 1825 and 1836. Orthodox Quaker Benjamin Coates, a strong supporter of the ACS, corresponded extensively with Liberia's first president, Joseph Jenkins Roberts, after independence in 1847. Quaker missionaries such as Eli and Sybil Jones ministered among the Baptists and Methodists in Liberia in 1851. Liberia's commodity-based export economy struggled for traction in world markets and largely faltered. One wonders what Cuffe would have made of Liberia's travails over the decades.[9]

ANTISLAVERY ACTIVISM AND WORLDLY ENTANGLEMENT

The economics of colonization, rooted in imperial methods of extraction and settler colonies, was intertwined with ecumenical friendliness. Given the small, and sometimes shrinking, size of the Society of Friends in the midst of a vastly expanding Anglo-American North Atlantic seat of empires, it would be hard to visualize an alternative, even though a substantial portion of both Hicksite and Orthodox Quakers in North America still wished to hold themselves apart from the "world" and from entanglements with other religious sects. The inter-Christian cooperation was even more pronounced in the immediatist abolitionist community, which was smaller than the community of colonization advocates during the first half of the nineteenth century, so more sectarian Quakers in both branches looked at the abolitionists' engagement with the world with great suspicion. In New York State, to choose one crucial example, the abolitionist agitation of Quakers and other antislavery advocates was enabled, in part, by Presbyterian Gerrit Smith's quiet deployment of his substantial fortune, gained from the purchase and resale of large tracts of land in New York during the first three decades of the nineteenth century. The land occupied by antislavery forces, as well as those not involved with the movement, had been violently wrested from the Haudenosaunee people during the American Revolution, something that weighed on the conscience of Quakers like Lucretia Mott enough that she explored justice for Native American peoples on her visits to the region.[10]

Mott's visit in 1848 resulted in the successful planning of an epochal women's rights convention—the Seneca Falls Convention, the first in the country endorsing women's right to vote—by five women, four of them Quaker, in the Seneca Falls and Waterloo region of New York. The economic well-being of these convention planners stemmed largely from the burgeoning industrial economy. The wealth of Elizabeth Cady Stanton's husband, Henry, had come largely from textile manufacture; in the 1810s, her father-in-law, Joseph, had manufactured both woolen and cotton goods. Lucretia Mott's husband, James, who by the 1820s had established himself comfortably in the sale of cotton goods, had decided by 1830, for reasons of conscience, to forgo dealing in cotton fabrics and to sell woolens instead—a further extension of the strong ethical foundation for Quaker capitalism, which included setting a fair price and full payment of one's debts. James's merchandising of woolens was something he pursued diligently throughout the 1830s and 1840s until his eventual retirement in 1852. Many Quakers in the Seneca Falls area had embraced the "free produce" movement (eschewing consumption of all slave-made goods) by the mid-1840s.[11]

Perhaps the wealthiest among the planners of the Seneca Falls Convention was Quaker Jane Hunt, whose husband, Richard, had taken the proceeds of his land dealings and invested them in woolen manufacture. Like James Mott, he avoided owning any business in cotton manufacture so that he would not have to buy and sell slave-produced goods. His modern woolen factory was "the second largest shawl factory in the United States." Those whose convictions prevented them from buying, even in small retail quantities, slave-produced goods like cotton or sugar were faced with buying free produce, which was often inferior in quality. The lack of attractive goods to spend money on surely encouraged investment rather than consumption. As the history of Seneca Falls in this period illustrates, abolitionists played their own part in shaping the economy of the emerging American Empire.[12]

CONTESTED IDEALS IN THE IMPERIAL FRAME

The Society of Friends often sought to apply ethical principles to Quaker involvement with empire, but imperial entanglements were so pervasive that it was difficult to achieve any consistency in that endeavor. At the start of the twenty-two-year war with France, the Quaker meeting in Birmingham, England, began disciplinary proceedings against a father and son, Samuel Galton Sr. and Jr., in 1793, because they would not cease the manufacture of guns for sale to the British military. The meeting had expressed no opinion on the Galtons' production of guns earlier in the century, when, for example, they were used (either by barter or by live fire) to procure Africans for the slave trade. It was only at the start of the war with France that the meeting took a definite stance. The elder Galton repented, but the son mounted a determined defense, noting that his family's seven-decade involvement with gun manufacture had never been at issue before the meeting and contesting the meeting's advice that he could readily convert his factory to a different line of production. Galton Jr. disclaimed his and his firm's responsibility for the use of the firearms, placing ethical responsibility on the British government or the taxpayers, who included Quakers remitting their war taxes. Nevertheless, Galton Jr. was disowned and prevented from participating in meetings for business. He remained a Quaker attender for life, but his descendants became Anglicans. In North America, Hicksite Quaker Joseph Wharton participated in the manufacture of ammunition for the Union Army during the American Civil War, apparently without any condemnation from his meeting.[13]

Generally speaking, when Britain or the United States went to war against another European empire, or a people descended from Europeans, Quakers were solidly opposed to that military conflict. Quakers took an outspoken position against the Mexican War (1846–48), sending numerous petitions to the US Congress and reprinting antiwar pamphlets. The clash of British, French, Russian, and Ottoman imperial aspirations during the Crimean War produced the same overwhelming opposition from British Quakers, and a Quaker delegation to Czar Nicholas in 1854 failed to forestall the war. However, the extent to which Quakers should abstain from active involvement in the military divided the Society of Friends during the American Civil War (1861–65), given the central role of the struggle against slavery in that conflict.[14]

Quaker reactions to the consolidation of the British and American Empires at the expense of people of color in the last third of the nineteenth century often represented much murkier and more ambiguous applications of the Quaker antiwar testimony, in accordance with patterns of racial capitalism. In 1869, US president Ulysses S. Grant pioneered a peace policy, sometimes called the "Quaker policy," in which religious leaders, including both Hicksite and Orthodox Quakers, were put in charge of Native American reservations. Quakers had previously introduced ways of Western civilization to the Seneca in New York, beginning in 1795, and other American Indian nations. This arrangement positioned Quakers at the crux of the metropole-periphery axis of power that defined the United States' imperial relationship with Indigenous nations. William Penn's dealings with the American Indians were complicated, as his commitment to settler colonialism coexisted with his advocacy for strict compliance with treaties and his humble, peaceful comportment in European–Native American relations.[15] His diplomacy was perceived as a model for US relations with the

Plains Native Americans. In 1869, Samuel Janney, a Quaker biographer of Penn, was appointed as an agent to the Ho-Chunk, Pawnee, and Omaha nations, and other Quakers assumed similar posts with other American Indian nations. In the early 1870s, Quaker agents, especially Iowan Lawrie Tatum, worked in tandem with the US military to encourage Native American peoples like the Kiowas and Comanches to cease raiding White people's horses and livestock and to stay on their reservations, sometimes withdrawing rations (that had been guaranteed by treaty) as punishment for what was perceived as violence, or as coercion for good behavior. The Quaker committees that oversaw these agents sometimes second-guessed their more forceful actions, such as withholding rations, but also considered advocacy of far-reaching dispositions, such as removal of these nations from their lands, to ensure (as they saw it) quicker progress in civilization. In short, during the 1870s, Quakers who were involved with Grant's peace policy, working ecumenically as "friends of the Indians," became active, if also sometimes uneasy, collaborators in the internal American imperial consolidation, through a process of forcing submission of Native American peoples on the Great Plains.[16]

ASSIMILATION AND EXPANSION IN QUAKER RELIGION

Quakers, both Hicksites and Orthodox, also strongly supported the efforts to assimilate the Native American nations after all armed resistance on the Great Plains had been subdued in the 1870s. In the late nineteenth century, Quakers supported the American Indian boarding schools, especially the famous Carlisle Indian Industrial School in Pennsylvania, where young Native Americans were stripped of their language and culture. Beginning in 1883, Hicksite Quaker Albert Smiley, proprietor of a hotel on Lake Mohonk in New York, sponsored a series of influential conferences on the proper methods of assimilating Native American peoples (and later, on international arbitration). Smiley aimed at a moderate neutrality on the sensitive issue of imperialism, guided by the Quaker peace testimony but also informed by his perspective on race as a hierarchy with White Anglo-Saxons at the pinnacle. When Smiley died in 1913, a peace publication memorialized him as "a most effective champion of the Indian, the Negro, and any backward peoples."[17]

In Great Britain, Quakers failed to mount any effective opposition to late nineteenth-century imperialist ventures such as the Egyptian campaign, although John Bright did resign from Prime Minister William Gladstone's cabinet in protest of the shelling of Alexandria (see chapter 12). One of the period's leading young Friends, John William Graham, opined that Quaker pacifists could be pleased by the expanding influence of the presumably beneficent (despite resistance from the Zulus and others) British Empire throughout the world. Influential Quaker committees expressed unease with the violent conflicts spawned by British imperialism. Perhaps, some thought, they were not doing enough to live up to the Society's testimony against war. A few Quakers were outspoken. John Stephenson Rowntree thought that the British policy toward Black South Africans was "as despicable as it is wicked." While British Friends thought their mission work in Pemba in the aftermath of emancipation was benevolent, the writings of Friends involved with the mission, notably Henry Stanley Newman, clearly envisioned this work in the context of empire and a definite racial hierarchy (see chapter 10). At least one British Friend of the era proposed that William Penn's example be seen as the prototype for a benevolent trustee relationship with the people of color who were subjects of the British Empire, just as Penn was also the prototype for Grant's peace policy in dealing with Native Americans.[18]

When, in 1898, American involvement in imperialist ventures became more overt with the conquest of Cuba and the Philippines as a result of the Spanish-American War, Quakers in Philadelphia deplored the war but offered only muted criticism of President William McKinley in its aftermath. The war itself was a defining point in American imperialism, as the United States established its own possessions overseas to advance colonial extraction from Cuba and the Philippines while asserting that the true purpose was defending Filipinos and Cubans from Spanish rule. Albert Smiley guided the Lake Mohonk Conference to a middle path, refusing to engage in "any acrimonious anti-imperialistic discussion. . . . The conference has without exception always declared itself strongly in support of the general policy adopted by the U.S. Government." Smiley urged that altruism be made one of the goals of US imperialism.[19]

The Boer War revealed divisions among British Friends on such matters as pacifism and imperialism. While such influential Friends as recent convert Caroline Stephen and Thomas Hodgkin argued strongly for defeating the Boers, John Wilhelm Rowntree drew the conclusion that every generation of Quakers needed to relearn the core principles of their faith, including the testimony against war. Rowntree foreshadowed twentieth-century developments by not contenting himself with decrying the taking up of arms but also arguing that Friends needed to "cut at the roots of war." Toward the end of the Boer War, Quaker disgust at the concentration camps in which Boers were held intensified the opposition to war among British Friends. However, equally poor conditions in camps holding Black South Africans were ignored by British Quakers and non-Quakers alike.[20]

RELIGION AND COMMERCE ON THE WORLD STAGE

This application of military might by the mature British and emerging American Empires paved the way for an increase in a variety of Quaker activities. One of these was missionary activity by Orthodox Quakers in Asia, Africa, and the Americas (see chapter 10). Another was increased global economic acquisition, securing of supply chains, and building of a customer base. A primary example of this was Britain's chocolate industry, dominated through the late nineteenth century by three Quaker families: the Cadburys, the Rowntrees, and the Frys. Their competition was cutthroat, even involving industrial espionage to find out trade secrets of other chocolate firms. But slave labor among cacao workers in Portuguese colonies in Africa, especially São Tomé, where the Quaker firms bought many of their beans, caused them much concern, as the growing efficacy of European corporations was leveraged to extract labor from non-White people in the colonial peripheries of Western imperialism. Portugal had formally abolished slavery throughout its dominions in the 1870s, but investigators for the Cadburys were able to establish beyond a doubt that slavery, while carefully hidden, was still widely employed in harvesting the cacao beans. Rather than simply boycotting beans produced by the Portuguese colonies, the Cadburys approached the British Foreign Office to pressure the Portuguese to truly end slavery. But the Liberal Party government needed Portuguese cooperation to maintain Britain's own unjust labor practices in South African mines, so they put off the Cadburys and chocolate manufacturers. At last, the Cadburys, Frys, and Rowntrees decided in 1909 to boycott cacao beans from the Portuguese colonies, and they then began to work with producers from other regions of Africa to produce the quality of beans they required. Meanwhile, however, the British press had begun to unearth the Cadburys' activities and paint an unflattering portrait in print. The Cadburys sued for libel, asserting that they, as philanthropists, had been seeking real reform in this part of their supply chain all along. The jury nominally entered a judgment on behalf of the Cadburys but assessed the defendants only one farthing in damages. The resulting publicity, while damaging to the Cadburys and Quaker chocolate manufacturers, did bring sufficient attention to the issue of slavery that the Portuguese authorities began to take substantive steps to address the international concern.[21]

While few people saw the chocolate firms' actions in the São Tomé episode as evidence of philanthropy and benevolence, the chocolate manufacturers could make a more convincing case in other areas. George Cadbury built model housing for his workers in Bournville, and Joseph Rowntree did the same in New Earswick, as well as opening soup kitchens and financing charity medical care. Seebohm Rowntree, son of Joseph, became an influential sociologist and social reformer, influencing actions to alleviate poverty by David Lloyd George's Liberal government and also by later Labour Party governments. The younger Rowntree improved wages and working conditions of his own chocolate firm's workforce in accordance with his scholarly findings. In general, the Cadburys and Rowntrees showed more solicitude for their White English workers than for the people of color who harvested their cacao beans.[22]

While conscientious philanthropy and benevolence mixed with profit-making made up one major aspect of late nineteenth-century Quaker business activity, an embrace of efforts to rationalize the workforce was another. Seebohm Rowntree was a member of the Taylor Society, named after the American social engineer and efficiency guru Frederick Winslow Taylor. Taylor, from Philadelphia, had Quaker parentage. As a consultant to such firms as William Wharton's Bethlehem Steel, Taylor was interested in a variety of engineering methods to improve the efficiency of the industrial workplace, including the implementation of new and better tools, but he was most famous for his time-motion studies, which aimed to speed up the accomplishment of repetitive tasks. Taylor's rationalist approach to business efficiency held widespread appeal for heads of industry throughout the Anglo-American world and even outside of it (Taylor's methods were utilized in Communist Russia, for instance).[23]

"FIGHTING QUAKERS" AND THE NATIONAL SECURITY STATE

As we have seen, the division between religious, observant Quakers and political and cultural Quakers had been a feature of the Quaker impulse at least since the eighteenth century, and this persisted in the nineteenth century. Observant Quakers such as the Cadburys, the Rowntrees, and Lawrie Tatum helped drive the development of the British and American Empires, but so did those on the margins of Quakerism, like Frederick Winslow Taylor. Among the latter were "fighting Quakers," a term bestowed on a wide variety of Friends. Fighting Quakers had been known before 1800; for example, the Free Quakers, a group that included flag-maker Betsy Ross, formed during the American Revolution to actively support the American patriot cause and survived until 1836. The "fighting Quaker" was a matter of fascination and humor for literary magazines during the Civil War, as many Quakers volunteered to fight in that conflict in the 1860s.[24]

Smedley Darlington Butler, a notable figure who fit this category, had a Hicksite Quaker mother; his father, Thomas Butler, a US congressman, came from a long line of "fighting Quakers." (Smedley's grandfather had fought in the American Civil War.) Butler went to a Friends school in West Chester, Pennsylvania, and found Quaker meetings boring. In 1898, at age sixteen, he enlisted in the Marine Corps, and he served in the military for thirty-three years, eventually rising to the rank of major general. Butler helped suppress the Boxer Rebellion in China and also fought in France during World War I, but most of his military career was taken up with lower-profile interventions in Mexico, Central America, and the Caribbean—actions that he would attribute, quite plausibly, to the subservience of US administrations of both parties to the interests of large American corporations. He resigned from the military in 1931, and, sympathetic to the Bonus Marchers (veterans seeking payment of their bonuses in 1932, at the height of the Great Depression), he opposed Herbert Hoover's reelection. Disenchanted with the military and with American big businesses, which he feared were fomenting a coup against the US government, Butler returned to Quaker antiwar roots, and, addressing Quaker meetings and antifascist organizations in the 1930s, he memorably delivered scathing critiques of the military and its close ties with US businesses. In 1935, Butler confessed to being a "racketeer": "I helped make Mexico and especially Tampico safe for American oil interests in 1914." His participation in interventions in

Haiti and Cuba helped National City Bank. His fighting in Nicaragua benefited Brown Brothers banking, and his presence in the Dominican Republic assisted American sugar companies. He said: "I helped make Honduras 'right' for American fruit companies.... I feel I might have given Al Capone a few hints. The best he could do was to operate his racket in three city districts. We Marines operated on three continents." Butler died in 1940; he would not witness the realization of his fear that the United States would formally intervene in another world war.[25] But his denunciations of the imperialistic fruits of his own military service inspired generations of antiwar activists.

Another major figure from this period who earned the "fighting Quaker" name was A. Mitchell Palmer. Of Quaker parentage, Palmer graduated from Swarthmore College and pursued a political career as a progressive Democrat. He was elected to the US Congress in 1908. In 1913, Palmer refused Woodrow Wilson's offer to nominate him as secretary of war, stating that since he was a Quaker, "the United States requires not a man of peace for a war secretary, but one who can think war." This statement was actually somewhat disingenuous, as Palmer was angling for a different position in Wilson's cabinet. His maneuvering did not achieve immediate success, but in 1919, Wilson did appoint him as attorney general. The bombing of Palmer's Washington, DC, townhouse by an Italian American anarchist on June 2, 1919—the bomber blew himself up, but Palmer was not hurt—stirred Palmer to vigorous action, and it was at this point that he became known as the Fighting Quaker. He created an Intelligence Division and appointed as its head J. Edgar Hoover, who would proceed to head the Federal Bureau of Investigation until 1972. And in the fall of 1919, Hoover, under Palmer's direction, launched widespread raids to arrest thousands of anarchists and socialists. At a time when racists promoted the claim that Europeans consisted of multiple White races of unequal status, Palmer cast his White radical-left targets as racially inferior, asserting that "out of the sly and crafty eyes of many of them leap cupidity, cruelty, insanity and crime" and decrying the radicals' "lopsided faces, sloping brows and misshapen features." The thousands arrested in the Palmer Raids were often beaten badly, but only a small fraction were charged with any crimes or subject to deportation. From the thousands of arrestees, only four pistols were confiscated, and it is not clear that any bombs were uncovered. Palmer hoped to ride his newfound fame to the Democratic Party's nomination for US president in 1920, but when his opponents from labor union and civil liberties factions effectively publicized the excessive violence and the extreme miscarriage of justice resulting from his raids, his political prospects collapsed. Palmer soon returned to private life and to his law practice—leaving behind, as his legacy, a vastly expanded modern security state. He died in 1936.[26]

HERBERT HOOVER AND THE "AMERICAN CENTURY"

Of all the Quakers who achieved political fame during the period of military and economic ascendancy of the United States in the years following the First World War, the one who went the furthest was Herbert Hoover (see chapter 12). Hoover was born to Quaker parents in Iowa, but both died by the time he was nine years old, so he went to live with his Quaker uncle in Newberg, Oregon. After earning a geology degree from Stanford University in California, Hoover made his fortune administering mines in Australia, China, and other locations. Hoover styled himself as an "engineer," in the manner of Frederick Winslow Taylor, finding and profiting from efficiencies. However, much of Hoover's impact was in rearranging the finances of the mines he took over. Hoover would be subject to political attacks on this basis during his term as president. Decades after he was defeated for reelection, private diaries of a subordinate would disclose that Hoover authorized at least one Watergate-style burglary in an unsuccessful attempt to silence a critic. The public, however, knew nothing about this action during Hoover's presidency.[27]

In 1914, Hoover's fortune was estimated at four million dollars, but he retired from for-profit business in order to administer humanitarian ventures during World War I and in its immediate aftermath. He also set in motion the child-feeding initiatives of the American Friends Service Committee, programs for which the organization (along with its British counterpart) would later receive the Nobel Peace Prize in 1947. Hoover was one of the few political figures to emerge from the World War I period with a heightened reputation. As secretary of commerce for the Harding and Coolidge administrations in the 1920s, Hoover further burnished his humanitarian credentials with relief and recovery efforts for those affected by the devastating 1927 floods in the Mississippi River Valley. Herbert Hoover was influential in shaping numerous dimensions of American imperialism. As a consequence, American imperialism would come to be perceived as intensely business oriented, often involving unscrupulous exploitation of the poor at home and abroad awkwardly combined with an idealistic humanitarian dimension.[28]

Friends had a range of orientations toward race-relations issues in the 1920s. Quaker and Haverford College graduate L. Hollingsworth Wood continued his service as president of the National Urban League, a civil rights organization advocating for economic justice and empowerment for African Americans. This was a position he would fill from 1916 to 1942. Wood had participated in the founding of the National Association for the Advancement of Colored People (NAACP) in 1909. Rufus Jones taught at all-White Haverford College, which graduated a Black Jamaican student in 1926 but would not graduate an African American student until 1951, three years after Jones's death. However, Jones welcomed a budding African American mystic and activist with the Young Men's Christian Association (YMCA), Howard Thurman, to study with him in 1929 as a "special student." Although Jones and Thurman never discussed issues of race relations, to Thurman's recollection, Jones's mentorship profoundly shaped Thurman's mystical interests and output. Quaker educator Rachel Davis DuBois was active with the NAACP and the Women's International League for Peace and Freedom in that decade, having been moved to activism in race relations by Wood's speech to the 1920 All-Friends Conference in London (see chapter 13). Subsequently, she worked diligently to build interracial understanding, paving the way for the multicultural approaches to education in a later era. Gay civil rights activist Bayard Rustin, an African American man, was raised by his Quaker grandmother in West Chester, Pennsylvania, not far from Haverford. In the 1930s, Rustin would attend college not at Haverford, where his presence was precluded, but at Wilberforce University, an African Methodist Episcopal college in Ohio, and then move to New York and enter into a life of activism. As a youth, Rustin witnessed Ku Klux Klan (KKK) rallies in West Chester; if he had grown up six hundred miles to the west, he might have witnessed the women's phalanx in the KKK rallies led by Quaker Daisy Douglas Brushwiller Barr. In the Wesleyan-Holiness-inflected Quakerism of Indiana, Barr first earned renown as a pastor with a magnetic pulpit presence in Muncie and New Castle, Indiana. She was also a temperance activist and an advocate for reclaiming prostitutes with the Young Women's Christian Association (YWCA), but by 1923, she had transferred her energies to the rapidly burgeoning Klan, which combined opposition to liquor and prostitution with a strong anti-immigrant platform. Barr's involvement with the KKK was very controversial among

Friends in Indiana. Such varied attitudes and actions concerning race from leading Quakers were key concomitants of the structuring and operationalizing of—and building mitigation and resistance toward—the burgeoning American Empire.[29]

When Herbert Hoover was elected president of the United States in 1928, he seemingly presented a perfect balance of concern between business, philanthropy, and race relations. In regard to race relations, he maintained strong connections with both the "lily white" and "black and tan" factions of the Republican Party. (Some state Republican parties in the American South were all-White, while others had mostly African American members, and the few White people willing to be Republicans in the states which had mostly African American members were dubbed "tans," not for their skin color but for their readiness to associate closely with African Americans.) When Hoover nominated North Carolina native John J. Parker, a vocal opponent of African Americans in politics, for a seat on the US Supreme Court in 1930, the NAACP campaigned against Parker's confirmation and prevailed, deriding Hoover as the "man in the lily-White House." Hoover never appointed African Americans to high office in the federal government during his administration. To the extent that he concerned himself with racial issues, Hoover likely intended to balance his support for White supremacists with support for African Americans. As secretary of commerce, for example, he had abolished racial segregation within his department. He proposed a land redevelopment program to increase the affordability of land ownership for African American farmers. While Hoover was thus capable of racially progressive action, the contemporary African American press tended to be harshly critical of him for a variety of reasons, especially as president. One Black newspaper, the *Pittsburgh Courier*, described the attitude of Hoover and his administration toward the concerns of African Americans as one of "studied indifference." Hoover did agree to accelerate the return of sovereignty to the Haitian people by two years, and, responding to critiques of American imperialism by those like Smedley Darlington Butler, he was far less ready to intervene throughout the hemisphere at the behest of American businesses or for any other reason. Hoover, as a noninterventionist, was notably restrained in his deployment of US military forces during his four years as president, and he was vigorous in pursuing treaties for disarmament and settlement of differences by means of arbitration between the United States and other nations.[30]

While the numerous crises associated with the Great Depression necessarily preoccupied Hoover during his presidential term, it would be interesting to conduct a more thorough study of the degree to which Quaker tenets affected his attitudes and actions throughout that term. His actions, or lack thereof, on the economic crisis ultimately doomed his reelection. The imperial contradictions (racial, economic, and social) that Herbert Hoover, with Quaker influences, exemplified had contributed in key ways to landing the American Empire (and others, such as the British) in the midst of the most profound crisis since the American Civil War.

CONCLUSION

Over roughly three centuries, various communities of Quakers put their stamp on the contours of Western empire. From the heart of the British metropole and American Empire to the various peripheries of colonized regions, Quaker religion was both conditioned by the exigencies of colonial regimes and engaged in determining the direction and destiny of imperial power. If empire was the larger frame for action on the global stage, racism and the practice of slavery were major pillars, connecting the conditions of elites and colonial riches with those whose lives and bodies were subjected to the most extensive forms of domination and marginalization. It was within this high-stakes context that Quakers lived out their ideals and made complicated efforts to extract a faith of simple devotion and justice. The results, not surprisingly, were far messier than those ideals. Across dimensions of piety, commerce, race, gender, slavery, and national security, the story of Quaker religion and its entanglement with empire emerges as a foundational one, supplying outspoken humanitarian articulations while often actively bolstering, or quietly complying with, burgeoning imperial structures. Without the Quaker story, it becomes difficult, if not impossible, to account for the modern forms of faith and ruling power in national and transnational contexts.

CHAPTER 2

Quakers and Reform in Nineteenth-Century America
Friends' Response to Antislavery, Women's Rights, and the American Civil War

JULIE L. HOLCOMB

In April 1875, as members of the Pennsylvania Abolition Society prepared to celebrate their centennial, invitations were sent to leading abolitionists, including Frederick Douglass and William Lloyd Garrison, as well as Quaker activists Lucretia Mott, Sarah Pugh, George W. Taylor, John Greenleaf Whittier, and Passmore Williamson. At the event, Douglass and Mott occupied prominent seats near William Still, who served as chair of the arrangements committee. Pugh, Taylor, Williamson, and other selected guests "whose services won the honor, were grouped on the stage in the sight of a large audience." Quakers "were conspicuous everywhere," it was noted in the centennial proceedings, "temper[ing] the brilliant colors of the assembly by the sedate tone of their attire." Quakers were also highlighted in the historical overview of the organization provided by Dr. William Elder, who began his oration with Philadelphia Yearly Meeting's decision in 1776 to disown Quaker slaveholders who did not free their enslaved people.[1]

Quakers were among the most committed advocates of abolition, as evidenced by their prominence at the centennial celebration; however, Quakers' support for the antislavery and other reform movements varied widely. Among Hicksites, antislavery activism ranged from the radicalism of Mott, who also advocated racial and gender equality, to the conservatism of George Fox White, who denounced both slavery and Quaker participation in organized reform movements. Similar divisions could be found among Orthodox Quakers like Whittier and Taylor. Whittier supported Garrison; Taylor, on the other hand, remained aloof from Garrisonian abolitionism. Mott, Whittier, Taylor, and other like-minded Quakers embraced reform, associating with Quakers and non-Quakers alike in organizations that supported antislavery, free produce, temperance, nonresistance, and women's rights. For this diverse group of Quakers, reform advanced Quaker testimonies against social ills into the wider society. In contrast, Friends like White worried that joining with non-Quakers, even in good causes such as antislavery, jeopardized Friends' testimonies and undermined their faith. As Friends debated the relationship between Quakerism and social reform, their definitions of appropriate religious activism became both more explicit and more diverse.[2]

Even as Quakers disagreed about participation in worldly antislavery societies, Friends continued to play an outsized role in social reform. Abolitionism, and the women's rights movement it helped birth, relied on the labor of Quaker men and women. Friends were also prominent in other social justice campaigns, such as prison reform and American Indian rights. In 1860, Quakers supported Abraham Lincoln's election to the presidency, believing he would further the antislavery cause. During the American Civil War, Quakers struggled to reconcile their traditional testimony against war with the bloodshed of combat for emancipation. Rather than actively support the war, many Quakers supported the cause of emancipation by appealing to Lincoln to abolish slavery and by providing aid to recently freed slaves. Other Quakers traveled south to establish schools for freedmen and their children. Still, some young Quaker men chose to enlist even though they risked criticism from their coreligionists and disownment by their meeting. As before the war, in making these decisions, Quakers weighed their individual consciences against the religious teachings and responsibilities of the Society of Friends. Although nineteenth-century Quakers failed to resolve the tension between religious belief and social reform, their efforts laid the foundation for modern Quaker diversity.[3]

This chapter focuses on American Friends' struggle to balance Quaker discipline and individual conscience when confronted with social evils such as slavery and gender and racial inequality. Beginning with the development of Garrisonian abolitionism in the 1830s, this chapter explores Quaker participation in the antislavery and "free produce" movements, as well as the

Underground Railroad. The varied responses of Quakers to reform movements divided Friends, who, by the 1850s, had separated into four distinct groups: Gurneyite Orthodox, Wilburite Orthodox, Hicksite, and Congregational or Progressive. The presence of abolitionists in each of these groups suggests Quakers' ongoing commitment to the abolition of slavery. Exploring these divisions, this chapter highlights Friends' lack of unity about Quakers' involvement in popular reform movements. The chapter concludes in the 1860s with Quakers' response to the election of Abraham Lincoln, the onset of the Civil War, and the abolition of chattel slavery.

ABOLITIONISM

In January 1831, William Lloyd Garrison published the first issue of his antislavery newspaper, *The Liberator*, an event that is often cited as the beginning of the movement for the immediate abolition of slavery. Garrison worked with Quaker Benjamin Lundy, editor of the *Genius of Universal Emancipation* newspaper, in the 1820s. Garrison and Lundy had met as a result of their shared interest in the American Colonization Society, organized in 1817 to promote the establishment of an American colony in Africa for freed slaves and free Black people (see chapter 1). In his paper, Lundy published news from the British abolitionist movement, including reprints of British Quaker Elizabeth Heyrick's *Immediate, Not Gradual Abolition*, as well as reports from the American free produce societies that formed in this period. A women's column featured antislavery and free produce poems and essays written by the American Quaker Elizabeth Margaret Chandler. By 1830, Garrison abandoned the idea of colonization. Influenced by the anticolonization efforts of Black abolitionists, including David Walker, author of *Appeal to the Colored Citizens of the World*, Garrison embraced immediate abolitionism. In language that echoed the evangelical fervor of the Second Great Awakening, Garrison denounced slavery as a sin against God and all slaveholders as sinners. The abolition of slavery, Garrison argued, had to begin without delay. The inaugural issue of *The Liberator* marked the end of the movement for the gradual abolition of slavery and ushered in an interracial, radical movement that demanded both the immediate abolition of slavery and racial equality.[4]

Quaker sympathizers joined with Garrison in establishing abolition societies, such as the New England Anti-Slavery Society (NEASS), founded in 1832 by Garrison and Whittier along with New England Quakers Effingham Capron and Arnold Buffum. The NEASS was the first American association committed to the immediate abolition of slavery. In 1833, when delegates gathered in Philadelphia to establish the first national abolition group, the American Anti-Slavery Society (AASS), one-third of the delegates were Friends. The gathering included prominent White abolitionists, such as Garrison, Theodore Weld, and Lewis Tappan, and Black abolitionists, including James McCrummell, Robert Purvis, and James Barbadoes, a reflection of the interracial character of the immediatist movement. A committee that included Garrison and Whittier drafted a Declaration of Sentiments. The final declaration affirmed the delegates' commitment to moral suasion and their rejection of physical resistance. Prejudice was to be overthrown "by the power of love." Members of the AASS agreed that slaveholders should receive no compensation for freeing their slaves. The declaration also included a statement supporting the use of free produce: "We shall encourage the labor of freemen rather than that of slaves, by giving a preference to their productions." Four days after the AASS organized, Mott called on McCrummell to assist in the founding of the Philadelphia Female Anti-Slavery Society (PFASS). By seeking McCrummell's help, Mott and the women of the PFASS explicitly linked the two organizations, including their shared commitment to racial equality.[5]

To promote their cause, abolitionists used several tactics. Believing that once convinced of the world's hostility to slavery, slaveholders would voluntarily end the institution, activists organized a postal campaign. The thousands of pieces of abolitionist literature that flooded the South sparked a wave of mob violence. Abolitionists also organized petition campaigns, drawing on their constitutional right "to petition the Government for a redress of grievances." Again, the abolitionists' tactics drew strong protests. In Congress, the petitions went unread as a result of the "gag rule." Adopted by the House of Representatives in 1836, the gag rule automatically tabled, or postponed action on, all petitions relating to slavery without hearing them. The gag rule was intended to quell sectional tensions by refusing to debate any antislavery petition in Congress. Instead, the rule fueled both sectional tension and abolitionist resistance.[6]

Quakers joined these efforts, forming pockets of radical antislavery activism within the Philadelphia and New York Yearly Meetings. For example, in November 1835, the Hicksite Caln Quarterly Meeting, in Chester County, Pennsylvania, sent a petition to the United States Senate asking

Congress to act against slavery in Washington, DC. The quarterly meeting included several abolitionists among its membership, such as Lindley Coates, Thomas Whitson, and Moses and Elizabeth Whitson. The Caln petition arrived in January 1836 as the Senate was debating two antislavery petitions from Ohio. Senator James Buchanan of Pennsylvania presented the Caln petition, asking the Senate to accept the petition but reject the attached prayer. South Carolina senator John C. Calhoun reacted strongly against the Ohio and Pennsylvania petitions. Though the Caln petition was more respectfully worded, Calhoun claimed "the same principles were embodied in [all three petitions], and the innuendoes conveyed [in the Caln petition] were as far from being acceptable as the barefaced insolence" of the Ohio petitions.[7]

Defenders of the Quaker petition made a clear distinction between Quakers and abolitionists. New Jersey senator Garrett Wall demanded that the Caln petition be heard. The Caln petition, Wall claimed, did not "come from the great laboratory of abolition *incendiarism*. It [did] not spring from the *heated* atmosphere produced by the contention of men struggling for political power; nor [did] it come from men, who under pretense of conscience, cloak worldly, selfish, or unholy designs." Friends were not seeking "to destroy the Constitution or endanger the peace and permanency of the Union." Rather, by using "the calm, mild, and dispassionate voice of *reason*," the Caln petitioners had exercised their political rights in a manner consistent with the principles of the Constitution and the discipline of their society. Opponents of the Quaker petition, however, condemned the Society of Friends for agitating the slavery question. On March 9, the Senate voted to receive the Quaker petition and to reject the petitioners' prayer. Afterward, the Senate adopted the rule to lay all antislavery petitions on the table, a practice that had the same practical effect as the "gag rule" passed in the House. After the Caln controversy, *The Friend* of Philadelphia warned against petitions to Congress and suggested that Friends' actions "in behalf of oppressed humanity, ought ever to be characterized by mildness, by prudence, by a proper regard to fitness as to the time and the occasion."[8]

Of the eleven quarterly meetings that comprised New York Yearly Meeting (Orthodox), Farmington Quarter was the most active in promoting antislavery measures. In 1836, for example, in an "Address to Its Members," the meeting suggested that Friends had failed to make a thorough exertion of "moral influence" in the "cause of emancipation" and, as a result, manifested "a degree of apathy." Farmington Quarterly Meeting urged its members to reject indifference and to exercise "active virtue" on behalf of the slave. It also urged New York Yearly Meeting to prepare petitions to the national government and to establish a standing committee on slavery. New York Yearly Meeting, however, continued to limit Friends' antislavery activism to making public statements—such as those issued by the yearly meeting in 1837, 1844, and 1852—and to abstaining from the products of slave labor. When Farmington suggested the yearly meeting prepare a petition to Congress for members of subordinate meetings to sign, it was not adopted by New York Yearly Meeting.[9]

As the case in New York Yearly Meeting (Orthodox) makes clear, many Quakers—Hicksite and Orthodox—were leery of Garrisonian abolitionism. Still reeling from the aftermath of the Hicksite-Orthodox split in 1827–28, Quakers were wary of Garrison and other radical abolitionists. Garrison was "strong on denunciation rather than persuasion, a prophet rather than a healer." He advocated disunion, which many Friends believed would lead to war, a violation of Quakers' testimony. Garrison and other radical abolitionists also encouraged mixed gatherings, bringing together men and women and Black and White abolitionists, an action that sparked anti-abolitionist mob violence. For these Quakers, radicals like Mott who joined with Garrison and other abolitionists undermined traditional Quakerism.[10]

In the 1830s, yearly meetings warned Friends against joining antislavery societies. Philadelphia Yearly Meeting (Hicksite) refused to take any action as a corporate body other than to encourage its members "to embrace every right opening, to maintain & exalt our righteous testimony against slavery." The members of the Meeting for Sufferings, Philadelphia Yearly Meeting (Orthodox), noted in September 1839 their desire to "stand open, individually and collectively, to the tendering influences of that Spirit which breathes peace on earth and good will to men ... [and] be prepared to take such measures as Divine Wisdom may point out to clear our own hands and to espouse [the slaves'] cause whenever the way may clearly present." In the 1840s, that yearly meeting issued its own statements on slavery. These debates reveal Friends' efforts to discern the limits of Quaker antislavery action.[11]

Those activists who defied their yearly meeting's admonition were forced to defend their actions. Orthodox Quaker merchant William Bassett of Lynn, Massachusetts, a member of New England Yearly Meeting's Meeting for Sufferings, came to believe that Quakers had "lost the spirit of Him who was no respecter of persons and who came to 'preach deliverance to the captive.'" In the late 1830s, Bassett came out in support of the AASS. He presided at the Requited Labor Convention in 1838, was active in the American Free Produce Association, and helped found the New England Non-Resistance Society. When he was criticized by Quakers for his antislavery activism, Bassett responded by publishing several pamphlets and articles condemning New England Quaker leaders for closing the meetinghouse to antislavery lecturers and for their objections to reform societies. He also attacked Quaker meetings that segregated seating for White and Black members. Bassett published a "Letter to a Member of the Society of Friends" defending his participation in antislavery societies. In 1840, after several years of tension between Bassett and the New England Quaker leadership, Bassett was disowned. Bassett eventually drifted away from Garrisonian radicalism and toward political abolitionism. He later became a Unitarian.[12]

Friends' reluctance to take collective action against slavery led a group of Philadelphia Hicksites to organize the Association of Friends for Advocating the Cause of the Slave, and Improving the Condition of the Free People of Color in May 1837. Organized as a Quaker antislavery society, the group had more than one hundred charter members who saw in the association an opportunity to work for the abolition of slavery without joining worldly societies. Nonetheless, the presence of Quaker abolitionists, including James and Lucretia Mott, Caleb Clothier, Daniel Neall, and Emmor Kimber, gave the association a decidedly abolitionist slant. The group made free produce a central tenet of their activism, forming the Committee on Requited Labor in September 1837. The committee compiled a list of free-labor stores, supported the American Free Produce Association after its establishment in 1838, and wrote addresses for the association.[13]

FREE PRODUCE

In advocating free produce as an antislavery strategy, the Association of Friends for Advocating the Cause of the Slave, and Improving the Condition of the Free People of Color relied on an established Quaker antislavery tactic, one that was used by eighteenth-century reformers like John Woolman and Anthony Benezet to end Friends' dependence on slave labor. As a traditional Quaker practice, abstention provided a seemingly apolitical solution for Quakers who wished to pursue what one *Friend* editorialist described as a "noiseless path" while promoting the "general good." The Hicksite yearly meetings in New York (1837) and Philadelphia (1839) advised against the use of slave produce. The latter also, in response to the sixth query asking Friends to remain clear of prize goods, among other things, noted that some members "consider the use of slave goods . . . a departure." In the early 1840s, many Quaker meetings issued statements on free produce. For example, in its 1842 statement on free produce, Farmington Quarterly Meeting (Orthodox) reiterated Quakers' traditional stand against the products of slave labor, describing abstinence as a moral duty. New York Yearly Meeting (Orthodox) issued a similar address on free produce in 1845, while the Hicksite Friends of Genesee Yearly Meeting advised that Quakers consider, as part of their discipline, "whether by dealing in, or consuming the produce of the labor of slaves, we are not encouraging the system of slavery."[14]

In 1838, supporters of free produce organized the Requited Labor Convention, bringing together three hundred delegates representing more than twenty antislavery societies, with the goal of establishing a national free produce association to promote the movement. The Clarkson Anti-Slavery Society of Chester County, Pennsylvania, and the PFASS organized the event. They had hoped to draw a broad cross section of the abolitionist community; however, most of the attendees were Hicksite and Orthodox Quakers. Delegates adopted a resolution forming the American Free Produce Association and appointed Quaker Lewis C. Gunn to prepare an address on the duty of abstinence from slave-labor goods. The delegates elected reformer and philanthropist Gerrit Smith, though absent, as president. Businessman and AASS founder Lewis Tappan was selected as one of the vice presidents.[15]

In the early 1840s, Orthodox Quakers Samuel Rhoads, George W. Taylor, and Abraham Pennock established the Free Produce Association of Friends of Philadelphia Yearly Meeting, a Quaker-only free produce society. Rhoads had authored a tract on free produce for Philadelphia Yearly Meeting in 1844, challenging Friends to examine their testimony on slave-labor produce. Citing the example of Woolman, Rhoads argued that Friends had practiced individual abstinence from slave-labor products for more than a century, yet Quakers as a sect had failed to adopt abstinence, despite the Society's stance against slave trading and slave owning. "We are told that we shall have no reward for attempting *to do good in our own wills,*" Rhoads wrote, quoting New York Quaker Charles Marriott. "Would it not be as well to inquire what our reward will be for persisting *to do evil in our own wills*," he asked, countering Conservative Friends' claims that joining antislavery societies was an attempt to correct that which was better left to divine guidance. The association maintained close ties to Taylor's free-labor store in Philadelphia and Levi Coffin's store in Cincinnati. Orthodox Quakers in New York (1845), Ohio (1846), and New England (1848) Yearly Meetings organized similar associations. Although these associations focused on increasing supplies of free-labor goods, the organizations also reminded Friends of their moral duty to the slave.[16]

For all its deep history as a form of Quaker antislavery, abstention from the products of slave labor also held radical potential, as female abolitionists and Black abolitionists linked the strategy to gender and racial equality. In the late 1830s, at the annual conventions of antislavery women, the female delegates endorsed free produce resolutions, urging women to refuse "participation in the sin" of slavery and encouraging them to maintain "a pure example." The women of the Buckingham Female Anti-Slavery Society urged women to combine the moral and the political in their daily lives: "Take [your principles] also to the grocers, and dry-goods store, to the tables of our friends, and into every social circle and thus make them have a moral bearing on the social and commercial interests of the whole community." The boycott of slave-labor goods, the women asserted, formed the foundation of equal rights for all.[17]

Black abolitionists made similar links between the boycott of slave labor and equal rights. In his *Appeal to the Colored Citizens of the World*, David Walker reprinted a letter by Richard Allen, the founder of the African Methodist Episcopal Church, in which Allen claimed that African tears and blood had watered the land, which was the means by which Black people would claim civil and political rights. In his pamphlet, Walker elaborated on Allen's image of blood-stained soil, claiming that "America is more our country, than it is the whites." For Black abolitionists like Allen and Walker, boycotting slave-labor goods would end the theft of African labor and restore to Black people the fruits of that labor.[18]

QUAKERS AND THE UNDERGROUND RAILROAD

Resistance to slavery by enslaved people predated Quaker antislavery. Black resistance to enslavement took many forms, including armed resistance, escape, and legal suits. Quakers aided these efforts by establishing schools, providing legal and economic assistance to enslaved and free Black people, and aiding Black freedom seekers. In the 1830s, Black and White activists established vigilance committees to aid enslaved freedom seekers and to protect free Black people from being kidnapped and sold into slavery. These committees formed the organizational structure that would become the Underground Railroad.

The first vigilance committee was organized in 1835 in New York by Black abolitionist David Ruggles. The committee assisted enslaved and free Black people, hired lawyers to represent African Americans in court, and advocated for equal rights, including education, suffrage, and economic opportunity. Vigilance committees were soon formed in other Northern cities, including Philadelphia, where Black abolitionist Robert Purvis organized the Vigilant Association in 1837. John Greenleaf Whittier, who had moved to Philadelphia to edit the *Pennsylvania Freeman*, assisted Purvis in founding the association. The following year, Philadelphia women organized the Female Vigilant Association to assist in fundraising. Abolitionists from the Pennsylvania Abolition Society and the Pennsylvania Anti-Slavery Society, many of them Quakers, assisted in the work of the committee. One of the more dramatic episodes in the committee's history was the rescue of Jane Johnson and her children in 1855. The family had been brought to Philadelphia by her owner. Johnson approached local free Black people about her wish to gain her freedom. Having learned of Johnson's plight, William Still, Passmore Williamson, and several Black dockworkers helped Johnson escape. Williamson, who by this time had been disowned by the Society of Friends, spent more than three months in Moyamensing Prison for refusing to reveal Johnson's whereabouts.[19]

Elsewhere, Quakers like Levi Coffin and Thomas Garrett helped thousands of enslaved people gain their freedom. Born in North Carolina, Coffin was part of the massive migration of Quakers from North Carolina to Indiana in the early nineteenth century. In Newport (now Fountain City), Indiana, Levi and Catharine Coffin lived near a settlement of free African Americans. The Coffins provided shelter, clothing, and food for the freedom seekers before sending them to the next stop. In 1847, when Coffin moved to Cincinnati to open a free produce store, the Coffins continued to assist freedom seekers. For twenty years, "seldom a week passed without our receiving passengers by this mysterious road," Coffin wrote in his autobiography. "We knew not what night or what hour of the night we would be roused from slumber by a gentle rap at the door." Garrett was a businessman who worked in iron, coal, and hardware in Wilmington, Delaware. In Delaware, Garrett was on the dividing line between the North and the South. Working with Black and White abolitionists, Garrett helped move enslaved people through Delaware and on to locations farther north. In 1848, Garrett, along with fellow Quaker abolitionist John Hunn, was arrested and convicted of aiding enslaved Black people in their quest for freedom. Undaunted, Garrett returned to work. In 1849 he assisted Harriet Tubman's escape from slavery. In the 1850s, Tubman guided more than three hundred enslaved people out of slavery.[20]

WOMEN'S RIGHTS

In the mid-1830s, as women sought a more equal and public role in the antislavery movement, radical men like Garrison supported their efforts. In 1836, Garrison hired Angelina and Sarah Grimké as lecturers for the AASS. The Grimkés were members of a well-known South Carolina slaveholding family. The popularity of their lectures soon drew mixed-sex audiences, which challenged traditional views of appropriate female behavior. In 1837, the Congregational clergy of Massachusetts issued a pastoral letter publicly rebuking the Grimkés, stating that when women assumed the public role of men, they risked shame and dishonor: "The appropriate duties and influence of women are clearly stated in the New Testament. Those duties and that influence are unobtrusive and private, but the sources of mighty power. But when she assumes the place and tone of man as a public reformer, our care and protection of her seem unnecessary, we put ourselves in self-defense against her, she yields the power which God has given her for protection and her character becomes unnatural." That same year, Catharine Beecher, eldest daughter of the famous minister Lyman Beecher, published an essay criticizing the Grimkés and condemning antislavery societies and petition campaigns. According to Beecher, women should not enter the public political sphere in their opposition to slavery. Rather, their influence should be limited to the domestic sphere. In 1838, Angelina Grimké published her response to Beecher, in which she compared women's historically and socially constricted position to that of the enslaved. She argued for women's political rights, a position that placed her among the more radical of abolitionists.[21]

Through the late 1830s, activists debated the proper role for women in the abolitionist movement. At the national gatherings of antislavery women in the late 1830s, women gave speeches and passed resolutions, including a call for women to assume a more public role in the abolitionist movement. Many men and women opposed a public presence for women. In 1840, when Abby Kelley was nominated to the business committee of the AASS, several hundred members walked out in protest. Under the leadership of the evangelical abolitionist Lewis Tappan, these protestors formed the American and Foreign Anti-Slavery Society. That same year, male and female delegates from the AASS, including Mott, Pugh, and Garrison, traveled to London to participate in the first World's Anti-Slavery Convention. However, the conservative British abolitionists refused to recognize the women delegates. That rejection is often cited as the origin of the women's rights convention held eight years later in Seneca Falls. However, other factors helped shape the debate about women's rights.[22]

After the financial panic of 1837, federal and state governments began passing laws to protect the assets of debtors. The first married women's property act, passed in Mississippi in 1839, exempted a married woman's real and personal property from the debts of her husband. In New York, a new state constitutional convention was organized in 1846. Two years later, after several petitions from women and much public pressure, New York passed a married women's property law. Similar laws were passed in other states. Married women's property laws did little to change women's subordinate position in marriage, however. And, often, married women's property laws did not extend protection to women's earnings.[23]

Reformer Elizabeth Cady Stanton believed the passage of the Married Women's Property Act in New York created an environment favorable for a women's rights convention. Stanton was one of the Americans who had attended the World's Anti-Slavery Convention in 1840, traveling with her husband, Henry, a political abolitionist associated with the American and Foreign Anti-Slavery Society. After her return from London, Stanton balanced reform work with her growing family and Henry's legal and political career. In July 1848, a tea party hosted by Quaker Jane Hunt brought Stanton and Mott together again. Joined by Mott's sister Martha Coffin Wright and Quaker Mary Ann McClintock, the women decided to "do and dare anything," as Stanton later recalled.[24]

Ten days later, three hundred men and women gathered at the first women's rights convention. The two-day meeting focused on the writing and signing of the movement's founding document. Delegates called the document the Declaration of Sentiments, consciously creating a link with the founding document of the AASS. The declaration outlined women's civil and political grievances, namely the failure of men to grant women the elective franchise; legal discrimination against women, especially married women; the limitations on women's rights in relationship to work, education, and participation in the church; the sexual double standard; and the exclusion of women from the public sphere. It was a comprehensive critique of women's social role in the antebellum period. Significantly, the Declaration of Sentiments did not address whether these rights were intended for all women regardless of race. The declaration also reflected the differences between Stanton and Mott. Stanton defined women's inequality as a political and legal problem. Mott, in contrast, believed women's subordination was one of many threats to individual liberty. Once convention delegates agreed to the wording of the declaration, the document was offered for signature. Sixty-eight women signed the document and thirty men signed a separate document, representing a compromise that allowed women to make their own demands yet still give men a voice on the issue. In the 1840s and 1850s, as opposition to antislavery and women's rights deepened, both within the Society of Friends and in American society, Quakers experienced another series of separations.[25]

QUAKER SCHISMS IN THE 1840S AND 1850S

Orthodox Quakers
Between 1837 and 1840, British evangelical Quaker minister Joseph John Gurney traveled among American Friends. Gurney supported Quaker efforts to work with non-Quakers in a variety of reform movements, including antislavery, temperance, Bible reading, and prison reform. Rhode Island Quaker John Wilbur, who is described by one scholar as "a model of the quietist Friend," attacked Gurney's teachings, claiming the British minister's views were unsound.[26]

The supporters of Wilbur and Gurney held distinct theological views that shaped their response to social reform. Wilburites emphasized the writings of early Friends, investing them with a sort of infallibility in the belief that "early Friends had been given a greater measure of understanding than others in grasping the truths of Christianity." Those Wilburites who were committed to the complete guidance of the Holy Spirit refused to read the Bible unless they felt a special leading. Wilburites emphasized disengagement with the world, participating in exclusively Quaker organizations. For Wilburites, the impulse for reform work originated in self-will and drew Quakers into the spirit of the world. Ohio Quaker Joseph Edgerton warned Friends that by "joining with those who do not believe in the immediate direction of Christ in such matters, and therefore do not wait for it, you will very likely become like them." One of the most influential ministers in Ohio Yearly Meeting and one of the foremost opponents of abolitionism, Edgerton described abolitionism as an "overactive, restless spirit" that "like the locust, the cankerworm, and the caterpillar" was "ready to eat up every green thing." Thus, by participating in reform, Wilburites believed Quakers would be unable to discern the moving of the Holy Spirit.[27] In contrast, Gurneyites were active in reform and frequently joined with non-Quakers in social reforms such as antislavery and free produce. "What a pity! What a pity! That for the abolition of slavery, and the spreading of the Bible, people should be turned against Christ," a voice in a dream warned Indiana Quaker Charles Osborn. For Friends like Osborn and Gurney, good works were an essential part of Christianity. The Gurney-Wilbur conflict led to formal separations in New England and Ohio Yearly Meetings and exacerbated divisions in the Philadelphia Yearly Meeting.[28]

Hicksite Quakers
In the 1840s and 1850s, Hicksites experienced similar divisions as disaffected Friends left their established meetings to form independent associations of Congregational, or Progressive, Friends. As it did in the Orthodox split, social reform played a role in the Hicksite division. Hicksite Quakers were as divided as the Orthodox on the issue of Friends' participation in popular reform movements, particularly abolitionism. One area of conflict centered on the use of Quaker meetinghouses for antislavery lectures. This prohibition applied equally to all advocates of reform, including antislavery and temperance. "To open our meetinghouses to lecturers whose opinions and principles on many subjects that *we* consider of primary importance are widely different from ours ... will have a tendency to draw off the minds of our members from an establishment in the Truth of those principles which have ever been maintained by us," New England Yearly Meeting warned.[29]

One of the more dramatic closures came in East Fallowfield, Pennsylvania, where a riot broke out during a meeting of the Chester County

Anti-Slavery Society. On the second day of the meeting, a large crowd gathered for the evening lecture. Quaker Joseph Pennock, who was present, noted the presence of "half a dozen or dozen mobocrats, and a few loose fellows of the baser sort." Just as Quaker physician Edwin Fussell commenced speaking, a riot broke out. Pennock described what ensued:

> [A] mobocrat, in the back part of the house, cried out, "There, you have talked enough, you talk as if you were going to talk all night." Then came the din of war. Whistling, shrieks, cries of "drag him out, clear the house," resounded on all sides. The stove-pipe was knocked down: brimstone was flung on the stove; panes of glass were knocked out; the women rushed from the house. . . . Some others leapt out the windows; and all was delightful confusion. . . . Benjamin Jones stood up on a bench in the midst of the disturbers, and asserted to good purpose the right of every human being to utter his free thoughts upon any question.[30]

In the wake of the riot, Fallowfield Preparative Meeting debated whether the meetinghouse should be closed to any meetings other than those of worship and discipline of the Society of Friends. After extensive discussion, Friends decided to close the meetinghouse, even though most of the membership supported keeping the meetinghouse open for antislavery lecturers. That summer, the more radical among the local Quakers opened the "People's Hall." Located next to Fallowfield Meetinghouse in Ercildoun, the People's Hall would serve as a "Free Hall wherein to discuss any and every subject of Interest in Religion, Morals, Physics, Politics, or any subject of interest to the family of man irrespective of clime, class, cast, sex, sects, or party."[31]

The closure of meetinghouses to antislavery activists exacerbated theological conflicts among Hicksite Quakers. Like the divisions among the Orthodox, divisions among the Hicksites centered on theological questions as well as concerns about Quakers' involvement in popular reform movements. This is particularly evident in the ministry of New York Hicksite George Fox White, who is described by historian Thomas Hamm as "the most controversial, most polarizing figure in Hicksite Quakerism."[32]

In the 1840s, White's crusade against popular reform movements "help[ed] fracture every Hicksite yearly meeting except Baltimore and change the course of Hicksite Quakerism." White's theological views were consistent with the positions espoused by leading Hicksites in the 1820s. White's "antireform argument was a logical and consistent outgrowth of the Hicksite Reformation," Hamm argues. "Its roots lay in a quietism that eschewed undertaking any action without a clear divine leading, in worries about the impact that joining with non-Friends even in good causes would have on Quakers, and in fear of the ambitions and influence of evangelical Protestant reformers, especially the clergy, in American society." White was an opponent of slavery who could sometimes denounce it in terms consistent with the most fervent of abolitionists. He also abstained from the products of slave labor. Yet White vehemently opposed nonsectarian reform societies, believing they were a threat to Quakerism. Non-Quaker abolitionists, notably Oliver Johnson, who was editor of the American Anti-Slavery Society's newspaper, the *National Anti-Slavery Standard*, criticized White. In 1840, Johnson and White exchanged a series of letters in which Johnson took White to task for a range of failures. In February 1841, Johnson published the exchange. The following month, Johnson published "A Rare Specimen of a Quaker Preacher," an even more scathing attack on White. Johnson's conflict with White led to charges being brought against Quakers Isaac T. Hopper, Charles Marriott, and James S. Gibbons, who as members of the board of directors of the AASS were held responsible for promoting discord and disunity among Friends. When Hopper, Marriott, and Gibbons denied any wrongdoing, they were disowned. White also attacked Lucretia Mott for her participation in antislavery and nonresistance organizations.[33]

White's crusade against worldly reform contributed to the polarization among Hicksites over the issue of antislavery. In the late 1840s and early 1850s, Hicksite Quakers in New York, Michigan, Ohio, and Pennsylvania withdrew from their respective yearly meetings. In New York, the separation came in 1848 when about two hundred members of the Genesee Yearly Meeting withdrew and established the Congregational Friends. The Congregational Friends rejected creeds, rituals, and ministers and embraced cooperation with non-Quaker abolitionists. Moreover, they rejected any hierarchical meeting structure. As Lucretia Mott described it, "Three yearly mgs. [meetings] will be formed this autumn on radical principles—doing away with select mgs. & ordaing [ordaining] ministers, men and women on perfect equality. . . . What a wonderful breaking up there is among sects." The Yearly Meeting of Congregational Friends rejected the structure of the Society of Friends; they also embraced reform causes such as antislavery and temperance. That same year witnessed similar divisions among Hicksites in Michigan and Ohio. In Pennsylvania, the split came later, in 1851, in Kennett Monthly Meeting. That split culminated in 1853 with the formal establishment of the Pennsylvania Yearly Meeting of Progressive Friends.[34]

Indiana Yearly Meeting of Anti-Slavery Friends
In Indiana, when the yearly meeting disowned a group of abolitionists, those disaffected Friends formed their own yearly meeting. Quakers in Indiana had led opposition to slavery in the state in the 1830s. Levi Coffin and his distant cousin, Elijah Coffin, were among those Quakers who petitioned the state legislature for repeal of the state's infamous Black Laws, which limited Black immigration to Indiana and denied citizenship to Black people already living in the state. Radical Quakers such as Levi Coffin advocated for immediate emancipation and full racial equality. In contrast, Elijah Coffin and other conservative Quakers favored gradual emancipation through colonization. As clerk of the Meeting for Sufferings, Elijah Coffin was also among the powerful elite of Indiana Quakers. Until 1839, these two groups, conservative and radical, maintained an uneasy truce.[35]

That year, Arnold Buffum arrived in Indiana. An agent of the AASS, Buffum had been disowned by the Society of Friends in the East. His arrival in Indiana was followed by letters and traveling ministers who denounced Buffum as an infidel and a deceiver. While in Indiana, Buffum established antislavery societies, edited the abolitionist journal the *Protectionist*, and organized antislavery lectures throughout the state. Levi Coffin, Walter Edgerton, Charles Osborn, and other radical abolitionists welcomed Buffum's efforts.[36]

Two years later, tensions among Quakers reached a boiling point when presidential candidate Henry Clay appeared in Richmond, Indiana, during the yearly meeting. His warm reception by conservative Friends stood in sharp contrast to the "stinging rebuke" of abolitionist Quakers, who publicly demanded Clay free his slaves. As a result, the Meeting for Sufferings removed eight of its members for their abolitionist sympathies, including Coffin and Osborn. Indiana Yearly Meeting also warned its subordinate meetings not to appoint abolitionists to positions of power and continued to caution against the "excitement and zeal" of the antislavery movement. In the end, nearly two thousand Friends, or about one-tenth of the yearly meeting's membership, left to form the Anti-Slavery Friends.[37]

The Indiana Yearly Meeting of Anti-Slavery Friends sought to transform abolitionist practice into enforceable doctrine, the only corporate body of Quakers to do so. Anti-Slavery Friends required their members, who were primarily Orthodox Quakers, to support the Liberty Party and to adopt free produce. In 1849, the Anti-Slavery Friends revised their discipline, making the boycott of slave-labor goods a requirement. Deficiencies reported by subordinate meetings prompted the group to issue epistles in 1853 and 1855 reminding the quarterly and monthly meetings as well as individual Quakers of the importance of "a faithful testimony against Slavery." Anti-Slavery Friends did not receive widespread support from American Quakers and dissolved in 1857 for lack of members.[38]

QUAKERS AND THE CIVIL WAR

Not surprisingly, Quakers' response to the election of Abraham Lincoln in 1860 was mixed. Some Quakers, such as Elizabeth Newport, a member of the Hicksite Green Street Monthly Meeting in Philadelphia, lauded Lincoln's desire to preserve the Union. Others were more cautious. An editorial in the Orthodox *Friend* described Lincoln's inaugural address as "mild and peaceful, and evidenced that he appreciated the serious difficulties of his position." Lucretia Mott, however, denounced Lincoln's inaugural address as "infernal and diabolical." Lincoln's promise not to interfere with slavery where it already existed was evidence of his "willingness to strengthen the pro-slavery parts of the Constitution," Mott fumed. Quaker meetings expressed concern over the "serious commotions now agitating the community" and the "threat of civil war."[39]

With the fall of Fort Sumter, South Carolina, in April 1861, and Lincoln's call for troops to put down the rebellion, Friends faced a dilemma. Quaker meetings affirmed their loyalty to the federal government and their support for antislavery but cautioned against taking up arms in defense of either cause. Nonetheless, some Quaker men enlisted. The decision to enlist was not an easy one even for the most enthusiastic Quaker recruit. In September 1861, James Parnell Jones, oldest son of Quaker ministers and missionaries Eli and Sybil Jones, enlisted in the Seventh Maine Infantry. Prior to the war, the family had been active in the abolitionist movement. Jones attended Haverford College briefly but left in 1852, frustrated by what he saw as the conservatism of Pennsylvania Quakers. Jones had been silenced at Haverford when he tried to speak out against slavery. In a letter home, he criticized Philadelphia Quakers: "My opinion of Philadelphia is that there is little religion but that is hypocracy [sic], but little charity but that is pride and almost no morality for I do not think I saw a friend in P. that would dare attend a temperance meeting." Jones spent the next several years in Michigan. In 1861, he and his wife returned to Maine, where he enlisted. Describing his decision to enlist to his mother and sister, Jones wrote, "I am treading a path dictated by duty and above all for the best welfare of the human race." Like many Quakers, he wrestled with the tension between Quakers' testimony and a bloody civil war for the abolition of slavery. "Many of us," Jones wrote in December 1861, "would break our swords and retire from the service with disgust were it not for the prospect it opens for the emancipation of the negro race in this country." In the days before his death in 1864, Jones told his commanding officer that he remained "a Quaker still. In their religious beliefs they are the nearest correct, I believe. I only differ as to the present contest." Indiana Quaker Daniel Wooton also struggled to reconcile his Quaker beliefs and what he saw as his need to defend the Union. After Union victories at Gettysburg and Vicksburg, in the summer of 1863, Wooton became convinced that he had made the right choice. "There was my duty to my country, to my God and my friends at home, and the object was which should I serve first," Wooton wrote home. "I came to the conclusion by serving my country I would be serving my God and friends also, there fore [sic] I resolved to enlist." Perhaps as many as three hundred Quakers enlisted in the Union army, although there is no accurate record of the number of Quakers who participated.[40]

More often, Quakers provided direct assistance to soldiers and to freedpeople. From the beginning of the war, Northern yearly meetings sent delegations south to provide aid to freed slaves. As the Union Army captured Southern territory, thousands of slaves were freed, many in need of food, shelter, and clothing. Levi Coffin collected bedding, clothing, and money from Friends in Ohio and Indiana. "We had no facilities to send them to the various camps of the freedmen, or for properly distributing them," Coffin later recalled in his *Reminiscences*. "It seemed necessary to have some regular organization here on the border, to receive and forward the supplies." In 1863, Coffin helped establish the Western Freedmen's Aid Society to do just that. He also visited contraband camps in Helena, Arkansas, petitioned the government to form the Freedmen's Bureau, and traveled to Britain to seek additional funding for newly freed slaves. Most Quaker meetings, regardless of theological orientation, had freedmen's aid committees and sewing groups. On occasion, Hicksite and Orthodox Quakers worked together to aid freedmen.[41]

Quakers also worked to help freedmen become independent. To that end, Quakers established freedmen's schools throughout the South. Philadelphia Friends established the first school, appropriately named the Penn School, on South Carolina's Sea Islands in 1862. Within three years, the school was sending African American teachers into the surrounding area to establish schools of their own. In 1864, Philadelphia Friends provided for the education of nearly four thousand students and more than twenty thousand Sunday school students. New York Yearly Meeting helped build a system of industrial and elementary schools throughout the South, while New England Yearly Meeting concentrated their efforts in Washington, DC, and Tennessee.[42]

In another effort to help freed slaves become self-sustaining, Quakers raised funds to establish stores where the formerly enslaved could purchase clothing, shoes, household goods, and food supplies. Philadelphia Quakers raised six thousand dollars to open a store in Hampton, Virginia, in 1864, using half the funds to purchase goods to sell and the other half to construct the building. Similar stores were established in the Mississippi Valley in what *The Friend* called "the store movement." The stores were not established as profit-making enterprises. Rather, according to historian Amy Murrell Taylor, "the stores promised to transform the refugees from recipients of charity into consumers, and thus, the missionaries believed, to harness the allure of consumption in order to instill certain virtues, such as hard work, saving, and prudent decision making, that were considered essential to free labor and good citizenship." Although such ideas overlooked freed slaves' experiences—"many were already seasoned consumers," Taylor notes—the refugees patronized the stores.[43]

In September 1862, after Union victory at the battle of Antietam, Lincoln issued his preliminary Emancipation Proclamation. One month later, Eliza Gurney and three other Quakers visited Lincoln in Washington, DC. Eliza, the widow of Joseph John Gurney, expressed her gratitude to Lincoln for his proclamation and offered her sympathy and a prayer that Lincoln would be sustained through the trials that emancipation would bring. When Lincoln signed the Emancipation Proclamation on January 1, 1863, freeing the enslaved people in the states still in rebellion, he transformed the war into a war for emancipation. This change in war aims intensified the dilemma for Quakers, who sought to reconcile their antislavery principles with their pacifist religious beliefs. For many Quakers, the dilemma was resolved by recommitting themselves to aiding those most in need, freedpeople and soldiers.⁴⁴

CONCLUSION

The end of the Civil War and the ratification of the Thirteenth Amendment ended the fight for the abolition of chattel slavery in the United States. For thirty years, Quakers had debated the relationship between religious belief and social activism. Although this process of discernment made Quakers' definition of appropriate religious activism more specific and more diverse, it did not resolve the tension between Quaker discipline and individual conscience.

CHAPTER 3

The Loss of Peculiarity and the New Quaker Identity
The Outward and the Inward Life

EMMA JONES LAPSANSKY

What might it mean to live a life of religious commitment that countenanced no distinction between secular and sacred life? Writing in 1823, Benjamin Ferris, clockmaker, surveyor, and a revered member of Philadelphia Yearly Meeting, had the start of an answer: "Let us set the candle in our own candlestick before we attempt to enlighten others." With this advice, counseling British and American Friends to clarify and solidify their own theology before seeking to recruit or enlighten new converts, Ferris's concern encapsulated what would become a bewildering era of Western Protestantism. Over succeeding decades, much of the day-to-day secular world would evolve with unnerving rapidity. Inexpensive mass communication, the ascendancy of canals and railroads promising efficient land transportation, and expanding transatlantic trade provoked both optimism and anxiety about the accessibility of new people, exotic luxuries, and tantalizing ideas. Anxiety also arose from volatile monetary markets, which could bring unprecedented wealth but which also led British bankers to be skittish in the early 1830s. In addition, disturbing international economic instabilities periodically crested in crushing economic depressions, such as the ones in 1819 and 1837.[1]

The religious upheavals and realignments that would become known as the Second Great Awakening among American religions—fueled, in part, by Congress's "Civilization Act" in 1819, which offered subsidies for religious organizations to "civilize" Native Americans by recruiting them to Christianity—called into question, for all American denominations, many of the foundational mainstays of Protestant faith and practice. What were the best ways to conceptualize, verbalize, teach, publicize, and model Christian beliefs, doctrines, creeds, and spiritual practices? What was the best way to understand and interpret the Bible? Quakers in Britain and America were not exempt from this crisis of self-examination that swept across Christianity in the first half of the nineteenth century. Indeed, as individual Friends found it tempting to survey—and to connect with—the economic and political world around them, many Quakers found it increasingly difficult to keep their candle firmly set in their own candlestick.

The world was just a *very* different place from America's postrevolutionary era of excitement and promise into which Ferris was born and grew to adulthood. And it was certainly a very different place from the seventeenth-century British world in which Quaker founders like George Fox, Margaret Fell, William Penn, Robert Barclay, James Nayler, and Elizabeth Hooton had attempted to identify and codify their mystical version of modern Protestantism: a Christian path illuminated by an "Inward Light" that would outshine all other religious authority. What might the fast-changing era of the mid-nineteenth century portend for Quakers, who had spent two centuries proudly proclaiming—and trying to visibly manifest—their uniqueness among Christians? Ferris and his New York friend Elias Hicks were concerned that some Quakers' association with "Bible societies and missionary societies" would lead Friends to lose their distinctive theology of the Inward Light.[2]

Though by 1830 there were pockets of Quakerism scattered as far north as Norway and as far south as Australia, the most vibrant energies of Friends' faith and practice were centered in Britain and in the eastern regions of North America, including Canada. It was from these latter regions that mid-nineteenth-century Quaker theological upheavals emanated, eventually reverberating across the globe and across nearly two centuries.

Focusing on Britain and the United States, which by 1830 had become the epicenters of dynamic Quaker leadership, this chapter considers the context in which some provocative thinkers and ideas helped reshape

Quakers' religious definitions, cultural currents, secular experiences, and spiritual mindsets in the succeeding century. The reshaping—a blurring of some of what early Friends had considered to be Quaker uniqueness—was steeped in controversies that swirled around the lives of such Americans as Elias Hicks (1748–1830) and Hannah Barnard (1754–1825), both of New York; Benjamin Ferris (1780–1867) of Wilmington, Delaware; Joel Bean (1825–1914), who made his Quaker career in Iowa; Rufus Jones (1863–1948), a New Englander active in Philadelphia Yearly Meeting; women's suffrage leader Alice Paul (1885–1977) of New Jersey; and racial justice activist Bayard Rustin (1912–1987). British contemporaries include abolitionist Joseph John Gurney (1788–1847); his sister Elizabeth Gurney Fry (1780–1845), a stalwart prison-reform advocate; pioneering social reformer Joseph Rowntree (1836–1925); and Joseph Bevan Braithwaite (1818–1905), a staunch believer in the authority of the Bible over individual Quakers' Inward Light. Though one might identify a much longer list of Quaker characters who influenced the contours of Quaker thought in the decades following the 1830s, the contributions of these men and women are representative of concerns that were central to Quaker thought during the ensuing century.

NEW CHALLENGES TO QUAKER IDENTITY: TECHNOLOGY, COMMERCE, AND CONSUMERISM

The convulsions that catapulted Benjamin Ferris to prominence began as early as the 1790s, when several young people from rural areas of New York Yearly Meeting began to question whether their coreligionists were placing undue emphasis on external evidence—particularly the Bible or the words of earlier Friends—instead of on their own immediate experience of Christ. In the 1790s, Hannah Barnard, a middle-aged wife and mother and a respected "recorded minister" from the Hudson Valley near Albany, left home on a mission to London and Ireland, professing her perceptions of the supremacy of the "inward" manifestation of the Divine Spirit. Her preaching was welcomed in parts of Ireland. However, among London Friends, Barnard's emphasis on prioritizing individual "inward" authority over biblical scripture got her censured for heresy and banished. When Barnard returned to New York, her home meeting disowned her in 1802.[3]

But Barnard was not just a lone voice. For example, Elias Hicks, a carpenter from Long Island who was just a few years older than Barnard, disseminated similar notions. Like Barnard, Hicks was a "recorded minister" with a charismatic style. Among other concerns, Hicks—a farmer's son—worried that the distractions and ill-gotten gains of the modern technological world were clouding some Quakers' vision, diverting their attention from the mystical and elusive inward essence of Friends' theology. Hicks opposed building the Erie Canal, a waterway that could speed up the transfer of trade goods from coastal ports into America's interior. "If the Lord had intended there should be internal waterways," Hicks insisted, "he would have placed them there." And he advised that "such low and groveling concerns ... [as] ... the railroad business, principally belongs to men of this world, but not to the children of light, whose kingdom is not of this world." Some of Hicks's renowned coreligionists—including Josiah White and William Norris—were making their fortunes as innovators in American canal and railroad development, often supported by investments from British Quaker bankers. But Hicks's anxieties about the pitfalls of modernizing technology and capitalism were symbolized by the experience of Jeremiah Thompson, whose economic speculation in the emerging transatlantic transport of luxury goods led to his plummeting from a revered position in New York Yearly Meeting to being disowned for bankruptcy in 1828.[4]

Anxieties about capitalism, consumerism, and technological innovation were among a cluster of tensions for Quakers of this period. Scholars debate the degree to which the alleged moral concerns of Hicks and his followers paralleled friction between rural Friends and their wealthier, more sophisticated urban compatriots—tensions that also troubled New England Unitarians and transcendentalists. However, the controversy clearly took the form of disagreements about sacred rituals (baptism and other sacraments), hired or paid church authorities, and the proper understanding and uses of the Bible. Disputes over the sequencing and techniques of salvation sometimes contributed to the turmoil. But for Hicks and many of his followers, slavery, and the associated profits from transportation, exploitation, corruption, violence, and consumerism, represented an irresoluble incompatibility with Friends' testimonies. Indeed, argued Hicks, corruption and violence—or the temptation of these—was also an inevitable by-product of governments, and therefore Friends should avoid taking any part whatsoever in "the government and policies of this world, which are all supported and defended by the Sword."[5]

Hicks, who by 1811 had widely publicized his condemnation of slavery, inspired not only Ferris but also thousands of other Friends to follow the practical implications of the faction that would come to bear his name. The rising factionalism erupted in a confrontation in 1827 at Philadelphia's Green Street Meeting, where the growing tensions between what would become known as "Orthodox" and "Hicksite" Friends exploded into irreconcilable division. But in the months before, Quakers across New York, Pennsylvania, Delaware, Maryland, Indiana, and Ohio had already been solidifying contentious divisions about the nuances of Quaker faith and what behaviors should flow from that faith. And across parts of New England, an additional faction developed, spearheaded by the teachings of John Wilbur (1774–1856), a New England schoolteacher who worried that both Hicksites and Orthodox Friends were too casual about religious discipline. The Hicksites, Wilbur argued, paid too little attention to biblical scripture, while Gurney's followers had become too intellectual to embrace Quakerism's mystical dimensions. Wilbur recommended that Friends reconnect with the writings of seventeenth-century Quaker founders. Nevertheless, Orthodox Quakers agreed that it was important to stay connected to their Christian beginnings, and if a hard choice needed to be made, preserving a robust *Christian* community as the "Life" might need to take precedence over protecting the uniqueness of *Quaker* lifestyles and behaviors.

FAITH INTO PRACTICE: "MEANINGFUL LIVES"

If one important aspect of Hicksite Quaker faith was its emphasis on the supremacy of the Inward Light over the Bible, another defining characteristic was that part of Hicksite Quakerism soon came to be associated with "immediatist" abolitionism, an antislavery movement that embraced any group, regardless of religious affiliation, that would focus its energies on ending slavery immediately—even if this might mean inviting non-Friends and secular political gatherings into Quakers' sacred meetinghouses or breaking civil laws (see chapter 2). By the 1850s, Progressive Friends, the most aggressively activist wing of the Hicksite faction, included many Friends who had been banished from their Hicksite meetings. Some of the earliest agitation for this immediatist strategy had arisen from a set of crusading British Quakers who were frustrated by the fact that the 1807 termination of the British slave *trade* had not led to the ending of *slavery* in the British Empire.

In 1823, Elizabeth Heyrick (1769–1831) published her blueprint for the "shortest, safest, and most effectual means of getting rid of West Indian slavery": organize a boycott of products created by slave labor. By 1827, crusading American Hicksite reformers Thomas McClintock and James Mott had coalesced a Free Produce Society in Philadelphia, aiming to demonstrate that, indeed, a community-wide abstinence from slave-made products would encourage growers to use free labor, thereby forcing slaveholders out of business. In 1829, Benjamin Lundy (1738–1839), Maryland's strident Quaker publisher of the *Genius of Universal Emancipation* (the nation's first antislavery newspaper), reported that the boycott of Southern slave-grown produce had resulted in a measurable loss for Southern slaveholders; by this time, antislavery action had become part of the faith for both Orthodox and Hicksite Quakers (though the two factions disagreed about the proper way to translate that faith into action). The instigation of Heyrick and others had also helped the "free produce" strategy take hold in England (where the 1833 Emancipation Act began to free slaves in the British Empire) and the British India Society adopted a free produce strategy against purchasing products from British-colonized India.[6]

By 1840, under pressure from their meetings, most American Friends had renounced slavery and were taking a stand against other forms of human exploitation. And increasingly, by midcentury, many Friends—particularly Hicksite Friends—judged themselves and each other not just by the depth of their piety but also by the vigilance and integrity with which they and their comrades confronted the ills of the secular world. At the extreme liberal wing of Hicksite Quakerism, Progressive Friends stood shoulder to shoulder with some of the most radical of abolitionists, including Unitarians and others who actively and openly defied government authority.

Nevertheless, as international capitalism put consumer goods within easy reach of an ever-widening consumer base, some Friends had to work harder to remind themselves of the value of their "simple" or "plain" living, which eschewed fashion, theater, music, fiction, and other distractions of the material word so as to leave themselves open to hearing and heeding God's "leadings" or instructions. Advertising, producing, distributing, and consuming commercial goods were the cornerstones of modernizing capitalism, with temptations that presented enormous challenges to Quakers' commitment to abstemiousness. Pennsylvania sign painter Edward Hicks (1780–1849), who struggled to reconcile his desire to be a fine-arts painter with his calling to be a Quaker minister, poured out his anguish that one of the "formidable obstacles" to becoming "a consistent and exemplary member of the Religious Society of Friends" was his "excessive fondness for fine painting." Hicks—a cousin of the controversial Elias Hicks and a sympathizer with his cousin's emphasis on the inward, personal nature of religion—could not support his family by painting utilitarian signs. However, since he *could* earn an adequate living painting what Friends derisively labeled "ornamental" art, he eventually—after a bankruptcy, much soul-searching, and the encouragement of another Friend—returned to his fine-arts career in order to support his five children.[7]

It seemed that Quakers in all sectors struggled, like Hicks, to align their behavior with Friends' spiritual guidelines. Historian Abigail Corcoran writes of "contradictory and confusing standards" by which young Hicksite and Orthodox Quaker women were advised to design "meaningful lives." Examining the writings of several young Quaker women, Corcoran concludes that Orthodox women were encouraged to turn "inward" to piety, while Hicksite daughters were steered more toward religious "performance" (that is to say, toward "outward" activist reform work). These women struggled to assuage a rigorous inner taskmaster. Even as scholars deliberate over the nuances of Hicksite versus Orthodox religious dictates, it is clear that nineteenth-century Friends—like their Protestant contemporaries in the English-speaking world—were at pains to define a belief structure in the context of their rapidly globalizing world. Local and international missionary work (see chapter 10), religious instruction, liturgy, social reform, navigating political alignments (see chapter 9), and advocating for members' (or nonmembers') secular needs—for example, hunger, health, or education—were among the concerns that many denominations pondered. As a Christian sect that lacked a central authority to set denomination-wide policies and to designate a durable and stable leadership, Quakers found themselves particularly vulnerable to the turbulence of the times. Intervisitation among Friends' scattered communities, the dissemination of "epistles" (written exchanges between distant meetings suggesting doctrinal standards), and the regional yearly meetings' publication and periodic revising of "disciplines" were no substitute for the denomination-wide directives issued by the anointed leaders of other denominations.

Thus, individual Quakers were allowed—even encouraged—to chart their own paths, or to "follow their leadings," under the watchful eye of local meetings. In England, Joseph John Gurney's sister, Elizabeth Gurney Fry, set her path toward a "meaningful life" by spearheading the establishment of the British Ladies' Society for Promoting the Reformation of Female Prisoners. This enterprise, like the antislavery work of other British Quakers, brought her and her cohort into contact with reformers from other cultures and religious traditions. Such intermingling for social causes surely contributed to the fact that, by midcentury, many British Quakers had loosened restrictions on some of the long-hallowed Quaker directives, including "plain speech," clothing styles, "marrying out" (i.e., marriage across denominational lines), celebrating Christmas, and placing decorative gravestones.[8]

Thus, concern about what to believe—and about how to operationalize those beliefs—ricocheted among Friends across the Atlantic and beyond the Appalachians as traveling Quaker-practice spokespersons disseminated their views. By 1830, Elias Hicks had completed sixty-six religious trips, totaling some six years of travel, crisscrossing New York, the Ohio Valley, Pennsylvania, New Jersey, Maryland, Virginia, and south-central Canada. Mesmerizing Quaker audiences with his passion and conviction, Hicks had spread his message that Friends should shield themselves from the temptations of the modern world, even as they sought to improve that world. Seventeenth-century Quaker William Penn, speaking with the authority of his comrades in consolidating the Quaker faith, had left a daunting directive: "true religion don't [sic] turn men out of the world, but enables them to live better in it, and excites their endeavors to mend it." Animated by that call to mend the world, Hicks—and the ensuing generations who would support, oppose, or amend his ideas—encountered a world filled with new ideas, new questions, new challenges, and new uncertainties.[9]

"SIMPLICITY" IN A MODERNIZING WORLD: MUSIC, LITERATURE, GRAVE MARKERS, AND SHIRRING

Some of the resistance to Elias Hicks's interpretation of the best relationship for Quakers to the new uncertainties was inspired by wealthy British Friend Joseph John Gurney. Descended from—and deeply embedded in—a family of influential Quaker bankers and social reformers, Gurney had internalized the admonition that one should actively "endeavor to mend" the world. Sharing Hicks's belief that Quaker energies needed revitalizing, Gurney traveled widely, arriving in America in 1837 as part of a British delegation to help calm the theological conflagration among American

Friends. In the 1820s, previous British ambassadors—revered ministers Anna Lloyd Braithwaite (1788–1859) and Thomas Shillitoe (1754–1836)—had made similar (unsuccessful) attempts to cool the feverish confrontation between the warring American Friends. Modern scholars believe that this peacemaking tour of the evangelical Gurney only fanned the flames.[10]

Gurney shared Hicks's revulsion for slavery and slaveholding. And Gurney shared the Hicksite focus on turning one's faith into social action. But Gurney enjoyed music and poetry: he believed young people could benefit from these forms of communication. And his recipe for reawakening the "real" Quaker spirit was at odds with Hicks's. Whereas Hicks's followers privileged the individual spirit over printed gospel, Gurney's supporters stressed the importance of biblical scripture. Was Gurney the embodiment of a backlash against Hicks's emphasis on personal charisma and individualistic mystical experience? Or was the appeal of Gurney's more visible form of worship—focusing on the Bible, some organized worship forms, and a move toward clearly articulated theology—the result of an inchoate fear among Friends that Quakers' worship services had become so formless and undemonstrative as to be stagnant and lifeless? Another way to frame the question is this: if there had been no Elias Hicks and no Joseph John Gurney, might some other version of crisis in Quaker communities have resulted from the waning of Quaker membership?[11]

Though Gurney was one of the most vocal Friends, the 1830s and 1840s saw the emergence of an increasingly evangelical cadre of Friends whose presence influenced Quaker communities in Britain and the United States. Many Quakers were acutely aware that their communities—so animated in previous decades—were watching members drift away. What to do about it? The resulting anxiety—symbolized by the establishment of Philadelphia's Bible Association of Friends—was especially noticeable west of the Appalachian Mountains, where Quakers were surrounded by the more theologically systematic, demonstrative, and Bible-focused Baptists, Presbyterians, and, especially, Methodists on the American frontier. These other Protestant congregations—with their prescribed repetitive rituals such as baptism and communion, their "camp meeting" celebrations, and their designated church officials who were paid to study, interpret, and dramatize religion—were more visible and more numerous, and they attracted the attention of isolated frontier Friends (see chapter 5).

Indeed, Hicks was right that the "internal improvements" designed to unify the sprawling American continent under one federal government challenged the regionality that had been a staple of Friends' tight-knit-community traditions. Thus, even as many Gurneyite Friends took leadership roles in developing those internal improvements that scattered their constituency, these same Gurneyites often encouraged Sunday schools, organized Bible recitations, and formalized creeds, and they cheered the 1847 inauguration of the Philadelphia periodical *Friends Review* (facilitated by the decreasing costs of print and paper), established to publish conservative Orthodox American Quaker voices. Similarly, *The Friend*, which began publication in London in 1843, aimed to disseminate the voices of greater theological consistency among British Quakers. Biblically inspired religious language and symbolism—taken for granted by George Fox and other seventeenth-century Friends and by other Protestant sects—had, by the nineteenth century, dropped out of the daily experience of many Quakers. However, by the 1830s, a cadre of American Friends—especially those who were in close contact with Baptists, Methodists, and Presbyterians—advocated a reconnection to biblical authority. American Friends moved west into the Ohio River Valley and Iowa, where, in the early 1850s, evangelical Quakers Joel and Hannah Bean had begun developing their "renewal" theology. In the shadow of Iowa's structured and demonstrative denominations, "renewal Friends" (as they came to be known) revisited the meanings of Christ's life, death, and resurrection, of the Bible, and of such concepts as "justification" and "sanctification" that sought to delineate the sequencing and process by which an individual could seek and confirm a personal relationship with God. A few American Quakers, such as Ohio's David Updegraff, even advocated water baptism (see chapter 4), and British evangelical minister Helen Balkill, who visited the United States in 1879, agreed with this idea (though Updegraff later recanted).[12]

Though less frenzied than American Friends, Quakers in Britain, too, were reconsidering their benchmarks for measuring themselves against non-Friends. In addition to a wide-ranging reexamination of Protestant concepts and language, one manifestation of this self-reflection was the ongoing debate among nineteenth-century British and American Friends about the value or dangers of literature. Attentive to their long-standing concern that "worldly" imaginings might dilute members' attentiveness to what Friends valued as the "still, small," mystical inward voice of God, many Friends were wary of fiction, theater, poetry, and music. But by the early decades of the nineteenth century, in both England and America, a few tentative and surreptitious Quaker voices could be heard in the margins of literary circles.

In America, novelist Charles Brockden Brown (1771–1810) and poet John Greenleaf Whittier (1807–1892) used their literary talents to illuminate matters of sin and corruption, while in England, novelist and art promoter Amelia Opie (1769–1853)—encouraged in her abolitionist sympathies by her friend Joseph John Gurney—joined the Religious Society of Friends. Gurney, in turn, increasingly championed the spiritual value of music and literature.[13]

Quakers also experimented with the new and inexpensive technologies that expedited the broadcasting of ideas. A few, like British novelist Sarah Stickney Ellis (1799–1872), aimed to use the new popular media to lure wayward Friends back to the fold. Ellis's 1858 novel *Friends at Their Own Fireside* was enticingly subtitled *Pictures of the Private Life of the People Called Quakers*. Fully conscious of her controversial mission, Ellis wrote in an introduction to her novel:

> Music being to [Friends] a forbidden indulgence, and until very recently the arts of design being rather discouraged . . . there was nothing but reading left available to them [Quakers] in their leisure hours; and that resource was often so limited in its range as to afford but little attraction. Hence, there has probably never yet been in any society such greedy and indiscriminate devourers of novels as . . . might be found among the Friends; so that the most vehement, spasmodic, and highly-wrought productions of the poet, the dramatist, and the novel writer, have been seized upon, *perhaps by stealth* and read with an avidity seldom known to those who are accustomed to occasional indulgencies of this kind under the careful supervision of some judicious parent or friend.[14]

Hoping to interject a broader perspective into what she viewed as overly conservative Quaker minds, Ellis went on to note that music was no longer "so rare a thing to the members of this Society" and that an "ear for music was a natural gift" against which "rigid" discipline need not be so strict. Eventually, however, apparently frustrated by what she viewed as Friends' limited vision, Ellis moved away from Quakerism to Unitarianism.

Ellis's novel, prompting Friends toward a greater acceptance of the arts, appeared the same year as an essay contest inviting young British Friends to speculate about how to prevent young Quakers from abandoning the faith of their forebears. The winning essay, composed by twenty-two-year-old

Joseph Stephenson Rowntree (1836–1925), the son of a wealthy chocolate manufacturer in York, criticized Quakers' tradition of turning their backs on "the love of the beautiful in art or song." Rowntree's essay reflected the tenor of the times: within a few years, according to Nancy Cho, several of the prohibitions separating Quaker practice from other denominations began to melt away. Cho asserts that the contest was a harbinger of the acquiescence of British Quakers—and subsequently American Friends—to the diversity of the modernizing world. Over ensuing decades, Cho argues, strictures against the arts loosened, though the process was slow and lurching. For example, as late as the 1920s, Pennsylvania's Haverford College—founded in the 1830s expressly to provide a "guarded" education to shield young Gurneyite Quaker men from the pollution of Hicksite viewpoints—refused to stock fiction in the college library.[15]

J. William Frost has analyzed other aspects of the relaxation of Quaker discipline in America, as the early nineteenth-century guidelines of "plainness" in clothing, architecture, household furnishings, and even grave markers evolved into less stringent twentieth-century rules for Quaker "simplicity" in lifestyle and material culture. And, building on Frost's analysis, costume historian Mary Anne Caton has investigated the evolution in Quaker women's wardrobe choices as modernization widened the possibilities of fabric, dyes, sewing techniques, and country of origin. At the end of the eighteenth century, suggests Caton, American Quaker fashion was shaped by three concepts: "practicality," a disdain for "vanity," and the concern that Friends should not "waste" time in creating and caring for elaborate clothing. (White clothing, for example, was discouraged, since it required additional care to keep clean.) The late eighteenth-century guidelines for this clothing were framed in terms of vague suggestions of what to *avoid*: ornaments (including collars) and fabric with flowers, stripes, or bright colors. Thus, Quakers' "plain" clothing—drab colors and unadorned design—became the target of many stereotypical nineteenth-century satirical images. But Caton explains that by 1900, though the focus on practicality remained, the guidelines about clothing design—both more relaxed *and* more explicit—included some detailed concessions: figures, stripes, and plaids were allowed as long as the patterns were "small and inconspicuous. Collars were to be without tucking or shirring." Caton notes that there was an ever-narrowing distinction between Quaker "simple" clothing and the prevailing fashions of non-Friends. By the end of the nineteenth century, she argues, many Quakers were no longer recognizable by their distinctive clothing.[16]

QUAKER FAITH IN ACTION: VISIONS OF BUILDING COMMUNITY

As early as the 1840s, various visionary Quaker individuals and groups experimented with practical applications of living their faith. One dramatic manifestation was the Society for Universal Inquiry and Reform, an Indiana-based Hicksite utopia aiming to resist all government "coercion" and to erase the inequities of capitalism by instituting "a perfect system of equitable commerce by making cost the limit of price." The Nicholson and Wattles families, who were among the leaders of this group—which included some politically radical non-Friends, as well—initiated dynasties of Quaker "alternative community" leaders. Other Quakers put their faith into other kinds of practical work. Blending her New England Methodist background into her Quakerism, Sybil Jones pursued missionary work in the American Midwest before moving to the Middle East in 1869 to establish a school for girls in Palestine (see chapter 10). Later in the nineteenth century, Emma Brown Malone, another Midwestern American Quaker, also brought her Methodist experience to inform her Quaker vision as she spearheaded education-building for Kenyan women (see chapter 10). Each of these initiatives reflected a particular interpretation of the "Quaker" commitment that would become known as "evangelicalism," which involved broadcasting and modeling Quaker faith and practice beyond the narrow confines of established Quaker communities. As with the antislavery work, none of these projects proceeded without controversy both at home and abroad.[17]

The doctrinal tensions reached their most strident proportions in the United States, where the followers of Hicks subdivided along the lines of local politics and Orthodox Friends subdivided over fine points of theology. Efforts to impose sacrament conformity culminated in a conference of American Gurneyite Friends in Richmond, Indiana, in 1887, where representatives from more than a dozen Gurneyite yearly meetings met to craft a "declaration" of their faith. This conference attempted to knit together a statement of belief upon which all Orthodox Friends could agree. Though the delegates returned home with a document that none of their local yearly meetings would support, a publication, *The American Friend*, was one outcome of the deliberations. Edited by Rufus Jones, the journal helped preserve connections between various cadres of Friends who eventually united into the Five Years Meeting (1902) and then the Friends United Meeting (1963). Joseph Bevan Braithwaite, a British Friend who had attended the

Richmond Conference and helped author the "Richmond Declaration," was subsequently part of a conference for British Friends at Manchester in 1895. However, in Britain, the focus and the outcome of the conference were quite different: British Quakers did agree to modernizing their doctrines and practices. Braithwaite was joined in this endeavor by John Wilhelm Rowntree, nephew of the 1859 essay winner. Many British Friends, whose numbers had increased by nearly 25 percent since 1871—perhaps accelerated by British Friends' high-profile peacemaking and relief efforts in the 1850s Crimean War—seemed less wary of Christian denominational diversity and were content to embrace both an intellectualized religion and a mystical focus. Hence, the Manchester Conference has been seen by some scholars as "the watershed moment where modernist thought and liberal theological views won out over evangelicalism."[18]

Over succeeding decades, organizations such as Friends "service committees" formalized some peace initiatives in England and the United States, as an overwhelming majority of Friends around the globe identified their community life as synonymous with local, national, and international peace. Individuals such as Elizabeth Pease Nichols, a veteran of the British antislavery movement in the early nineteenth century, later turned their attention to international peace projects. In the United States, Quaker scholar and activist Alice Paul did the same. And in 1917, Rufus Jones was among the initiators of what would become the American Friends Service Committee, which had among its aims the healing of Hicksite-Orthodox divisions by bringing diverse Quakers together around an undertaking upon which all could agree: relief efforts and resistance to war. Thus, by the early decades of the twentieth century, Friends on both sides of the Atlantic increasingly focused their energies on the one tenet of their communities that was nearly universally shared: peace is good; war, with its attendant violence and suffering, is bad (see chapter 11).[19]

CONCLUSION

One way to define the changes in nineteenth-century Quakerism is to envision modernizing technology and traditional Quaker practices as spawning a Hydra-headed offspring, with some outgrowths closely resembling other Protestant groups in beliefs and rituals, others emerging more heavily colored with the markings of "worldly" capitalism, and still others defined by what might be termed philosophical or "lifestyle" choices such as resistance to worldly governments or by a nostalgic clinging to old-style elements of austere "plain" style. Despite this diversification, and even as doctrinal fissures have periodically erupted, Friends around the world have apparently focused on three foundational, unifying aspects of their faith: (1) tracing their origins, beliefs, and behaviors to the model and experiences of a few dozen seventeenth-century British Friends—though Friends sometimes vehemently disagree about the emphases, meaning, and legacy of those seventeenth-century models and experiences; (2) focusing energies on eradicating suffering and violence in themselves, their communities, and the world around them; and (3) mounting stiff resistance to what they perceive as corrupt governments.

In the late nineteenth century, Friends from the United States and Britain were among the religious sects that fanned out across the world to offer assistance—and to proselytize—in places where there was famine, war, or other human suffering (see chapter 10). In every place Quakers carried their message, the message was influenced by the local culture of the people there. In Alaska, Bolivia, Japan, China, Mexico, Lebanon, Jamaica, and India, what had been a predominantly British-influenced religion culture found its cultural boundaries subtly transformed as charismatic Quaker missionaries lived among, learned the ways and languages of, and sometimes even married into local families. When Cleveland Friends Meeting's Willis Hotchkiss (1873–1948) went to Kaimosi, Kenya, in 1902 to help establish the Friends Industrial Mission, he could hardly have known that they were launching what would become the world's largest concentration of Quakers, which—among other things—would include some British and American Quakers becoming permanently embedded in the regions, languages, and cultures of East Africa. Similarly, when Inazo Nitobe, a young Japanese scholar studying in the United States in the 1880s, encountered Quakerism and then married a Philadelphia Quaker, another incidence of what might be called "cultural infusion" occurred, as he and Mary Patterson Elkinton built a cross-cultural life (see chapter 12). And the three American yearly meetings that sponsored missionaries to the Aymara people in the Bolivian Andes in 1919 launched a cultural partnership that has grown stronger in the ensuing decades, adding to the broadening of Quaker theological and cultural diversity. Into the twentieth century and beyond, Quaker men and women in Britain and the United States availed themselves of ever-easier international travel to deliver missionary zeal and practical assistance such as modern technology—often including literacy programs and a printing press—to isolated corners of the world. In return for these "deliveries," Friends sometimes learned—and learned to appreciate—the value of envisioning themselves as global citizens. And gradually, as increasing numbers of Friends have become comfortable with a true blending of cultures, leadership in mission-founded Friends meetings has been ceded to local residents.[20]

The struggle Friends faced in Hicks's time—and continue to face in the twenty-first century—is the problem of what might be called "authority." Writing in the 1670s, founding Quaker Robert Barclay described Quaker worship as a gathering of like-minded believers awaiting divine wisdom as it is received by individual members of the gathering: "Our *Work* then and *Worship* is, when we meet together, for every one to *watch and wait upon God in themselves*, and to be *gathered* from all Visibles thereunto." While such a system has worked well for many Quaker groups' *worship*, especially among Friends whose geographic, familial, and economic experience was similar, it has worked less well for enduring consistency in Quaker *governance* for Friends whose experiences carry them across the world, into contact with new peoples and cultures, and into myriad varieties of the printed word.[21]

What can be achieved, and how can conflict be adjudicated, if individuals within the group receive differing realities and different divine messages? How can it be discerned whether an individual's message is adding new information, in the time-honored Quaker process of "continuing revelation," or obfuscating and challenging what longtime Friends know to be clearly established truths? Unlike the Jewish, Catholic, or many other Protestant bodies, Quakers have never established a formal hierarchy of authority or a standardized system for training, certifying, or anointing "leaders." Lacking such a hierarchy, and lacking a universal, agreed-upon creed, text, or leader, "Quakerism," as defined and practiced, has been dependent upon the interpretations of whatever individual carries a convincing message to a given group or region, in the context of whatever else is happening—politically, economically, sociologically, or theologically—in the region where that particular charismatic Quaker chooses to locate. The challenge of remaining true to received tradition while remaining open to exploring new theological possibilities became, in the context of nineteenth-century modernization, the challenge all Quaker communities faced—and continue to face in the twenty-first century. In the closing decades of the nineteenth century and the early years of the twentieth, several initiatives—the American Friends

Service Committee and the Friends World Committee for Consultation—have, with mixed success, sought to ameliorate those challenges through organizations that focus on Friends' shared commitments to peace, philanthropy, and justice.[22]

Thus, many Friends sought, and continue to seek, to balance paradoxical challenges; to understand, interpret, and remain faithful to their seventeenth-century "roots"—roots that include openness to "continuing revelation"; to negotiate a truce with the ever-changing world as they encounter it, as they "endeavor to mend it"; and to carve out a distinctive niche. The latter, for some, includes remaining both "Christian" *and* "unique," while for others the goal is to embrace a universalism among *all* belief systems, including atheism. Approaching the middle of the twentieth century, individual Friends and individual monthly and yearly meetings adopted multivariate strategies to "set the candle in their own candlestick."

CHAPTER 4

The Revival, 1860–1880

THOMAS D. HAMM

In the fall of 1858, Dougan Clark, a Quaker physician lately moved to Indiana from North Carolina, was invited to give a lecture before the faculty and students of Friends Boarding School, soon to become Earlham College, outside of Richmond, Indiana. At the time, Clark was best known as the son, grandson, and great-grandson of eminent Quaker ministers. Only later would he emerge as a recorded minister in his own right. Clark's theme was "The Society of Friends in the Mississippi Valley." His outlook was optimistic, almost triumphal. "To George Fox . . . were revealed clearer ideas of Gospel Truth, loftier visions of human destiny, nobler ideas of human perfectibility, and more accurate ideas of human duty, than had before been communicated to any of our race since the days of the Apostles," Clark asserted. Indeed, Quakerism was "the great precursor of political Republicanism, and the pioneer of religious liberty." Friends were leaders in all the great reforms that had advanced the welfare of humanity. In the Mississippi Valley, Clark concluded, Friends had a splendid opportunity. If they held fast to their distinctive doctrines of simplicity, unprogrammed worship, peace, and direct revelation, they would be a power for righteousness.[1]

Two decades later, Dougan Clark not only was a recorded minister among Friends but had won an international reputation as an exponent of second-experience holiness. Attending London Yearly Meeting in 1879 and intervening in a debate on the temperance movement, he evinced quite a different outlook. He saw most of the distinctive beliefs and practices of Friends as unnecessary for salvation. He regarded direct revelation as derogating the authority of the Bible. For reform movements he now had little use. "This Society is a religious Society and a Christian Church: it is not an association for the promotion of certain moral reforms," he told British Friends. The duty of Friends was to save souls and to embrace the means that most effectually did that. For Dougan Clark, that meant an end to silent meetings and unpaid ministers. Clark had come to see Friends as simply being part of a larger community of evangelicals committed to soul-saving revivalism.[2]

Dougan Clark was a central figure in the revival movement that transformed much of American Quakerism between 1860 and 1880. The changes were by all accounts dramatic, as the full panoply of evangelical revivalism—mourners' benches, music, prayer groups, extreme outbursts of emotion—were introduced into meetinghouses. Their impact was specific to the Gurneyite branch of Friends—Wilburites and Hicksites generally viewed revivalism as confirming their worst fears about the tendencies of Gurneyism—and to North America. London Yearly Meeting, while it certainly contained sympathizers with American developments, never experienced a revival in the American model. But because most of the world's Quakers in the nineteenth century were Americans and because a majority of them were Gurneyites by 1860, the revival movement would have a profound impact on the future of Quakerism.

GURNEYISM AND WILBURISM

"Gurneyite" was a label that the revivalists embraced; indeed, many said that it was the English minister Joseph John Gurney (1788–1847) who had, through his ministry and writings, reinvigorated Quakerism after a century and a half of Quietism and decline. Gurney was at the forefront of the movement to articulate Quakerism in terms of commonality with contemporary evangelicalism. Gurney emphasized the authority of scripture over the leadings of the Inward Light, saying that the difference between the two was that the former was like the noonday sun and the latter like twilight. He urged Friends to become more open to working with other Christians in reform and philanthropy. Further, he took issue with 150 years of Quaker theology about the nature of salvation. Friends had long seen justification (acceptability to God) as inseparable from sanctification (a state of sinlessness or holiness). Earlier, Friends had taught that obedience to the leadings of the Seed or Light Within would lead gradually, through baptisms of suffering and mortification, to the holiness that made a person acceptable to God. This did not take place in an instant; salvation, for Friends, was a matter of growth rather than the "new birth" of evangelicals. Gurney, however, argued that justification and sanctification were distinct experiences, with justification preceding sanctification. Many of Gurney's followers by the 1850s were experiencing justification as an instantaneous experience, although conceding that it, like sanctification, could be gradual. While Gurney did not reject the idea of Friends as a "peculiar people," called by God to manifest to the world a form of worship based entirely on the leadings of the Holy Spirit and, through the plain life, rejection of vain adornments, he modeled a life that was comfortable with learning, political activity, and ties with non-Friends. And the evidence is considerable that by 1860, most American Friends shared that comfort.[3]

Such change did not come without resistance from more conservative Orthodox Friends. They found their most articulate leader in the Rhode Island minister John Wilbur (1774–1856). Traveling in the British Isles early in the 1830s, Wilbur found the direction of London Yearly Meeting disturbing, and Gurney's writings even more so. When Gurney came to the United States in 1837, Wilbur was outspoken in his criticism. The leaders of New England Yearly Meeting sided with Gurney, and the result was a separation in 1844. Most Orthodox Friends sided with Gurney, but the Wilburites were a majority in Ohio and Philadelphia Yearly Meetings. Ohio experienced a bitter separation. Philadelphia avoided one only by suspending correspondence with all other yearly meetings.[4]

Conservatives feared that openness to contacts with non-Friends endangered Quaker peculiarity. They also found Gurney's apparent dismissal of the writings of early Friends disturbing. But it was Gurney's view of justification and sanctification that most upset them. It offered, in Conservative Friends' view, an easy way to salvation, a false hope that implicitly undermined a century of Quaker practice. As Wilbur put it: "Instead of submitting, therefore to die with Christ, and to abide the painful struggle of yielding up the will and wisdom of the flesh," they had "fashioned to themselves a substitute, by professionally extolling and claiming the faith of

Christ's incarnate sufferings and propitiatory sacrifice upon the Cross." So "trusting in this alone for justification, without its essential concomitant, the true obedience of faith," they no longer felt it necessary to go on to "the work of sanctification wrought in the heart." And this was unsurprising: "If barely believing in Christ, and that his death and sufferings *alone*, would save men," then who would not choose to avoid "the painful endurance of the baptism of fire and the Holy Ghost in themselves"? Gurneyites, in this view, were making salvation a matter of words and intellectual profession, rather than the hard, tried experience that it truly was.[5]

THE RENEWAL MOVEMENT

By 1860, most Gurneyites embraced a different vision. They were committed to what they viewed as a renewal of Quakerism, one that would affirm much that was distinctive but that would put aside features that had become archaic or hindered Quaker witness. The leaders of this movement were mainly, although not all, recorded ministers born after 1815. They were better educated than the masses of Friends, sharing experiences as students or teachers in schools like Providence, Haverford, and Earlham. Many were bound together by ties of blood or marriage. They were also more likely to live in towns or cities and to be professionals. They included both men and women. Indeed, ministers like Rhoda M. Coffin in Indiana, Hannah E. Bean in Iowa, and Elizabeth L. Comstock in Michigan would be central figures.[6]

The renewal-oriented Gurneyites began with the discipline. They affirmed simplicity in dress and address but argued that this did not always require wearing distinctive plain dress or avoiding the use of *you* in speaking to a single person. As one advocate put it, since plain dress had become an "obsolete costume" and plain language "an ungrammatical peculiarity," there was a need for "recalling the principle of simplicity to more enlarged and consistent applications" (see chapter 3). A particular target of these reformers was the rule that disowned those members who married "out of meeting." Reformers argued for the repeal of that regulation entirely, or at least a softening of its enforcement.[7]

The "renewal" leaders also called for changes in the experience of worship, particularly preaching. By the early nineteenth century, Quaker ministers were distinguished by speaking in what was known as the "sing-song," a kind of chant "without any regard to proper pauses or proper emphasis." Fluency, even eloquence, became something desirable. Renewal leaders also criticized the assumption that only recorded ministers, or those who showed signs of the development of a gift in the ministry, should speak in meeting. "To be able to tell what the Lord has done for us is a happy privilege," argued an Indiana minister. The problem was, as an Iowa Friend asserted, that "a large proportion of the Society of Friends seldom, if ever, confess Christ with their lips. They seldom, if ever, speak a word on the subject of *personal* religion." Such critics hoped to hear more Friends relating their spiritual experiences. The result was often preaching that broke with the Quaker past. The comment of a Hicksite drawn by curiosity to attend an Orthodox quarterly meeting in Clinton County, Ohio, in 1861 is revealing: "There was an abundance of what I would call excellent Methodist preaching & praying."[8]

The renewal leaders embraced new ideas about education. It is significant that many were connected with Haverford and Earlham, the first two Quaker colleges in the world. Friends had long regarded higher education with suspicion out of a sense that it existed largely to prepare "hireling ministers." But by 1860, there was a growing conviction that Friends should not remain aloof from "keeping pace with the progress of knowledge." While these reformers affirmed the venerable Quaker conviction that any gift in ministry came from God, they saw nothing irregular in cultivating that gift through reading and scholarship. Some even argued that it was not inappropriate for ministers to ponder or think in advance about what they might say in a meeting for worship, as God might lead the faithful in advance of meeting as well as during it. An astonished visitor to Indiana Yearly Meeting in 1870 heard Friends advocating that "we should *have a better educated ministry and if possible a college preparation*."[9]

Finally, the advocates of reform continued Gurney's push for openness to working with other Christians, consistent with his belief that Friends were *part* of the true church rather than the *only* true church. While they regarded Unitarians and Universalists with horror, "as they would serpents and venomous snakes," the advocates of renewal argued that Friends should be lights in their communities. Indeed, in the progress of reform and humanitarianism, many saw evangelicals embracing truths Friends had long held. On certain theological matters—the divinity of Christ, the authority of the Bible, and salvation through the Atonement—they saw themselves as one with the larger evangelical culture of the United States.[10]

By the early 1860s, Gurneyites were beginning to use the word *revival* to describe the events they saw taking place among their branch of Friends. "We continue to hear of *awakenings & revivals*," wrote a weighty English Friend in the fall of 1860. In early 1861, another said: "From the reports which have reached me, I should judge that a great awakening had begun amongst the Friends in America." What did these observers have in mind?[11]

One event attracted considerable attention. It took place during the sessions of Indiana Yearly Meeting in October 1860. Sybil Jones, a visiting minister from Maine, after consultation with some leading renewal Friends, including Charles F. and Rhoda M. Coffin, John Henry Douglas, and Murray Shipley, sought and received permission to hold an evening meeting for young Friends. It was understood that older Friends who were accustomed to speaking would defer to younger Friends. Perhaps two thousand people attended the meeting, which went until 1:30 a.m., and hundreds spoke, most for the first time in their lives. A particularly striking moment came when Richard J. Hubbard, a middle-aged Friend, broke into a hymn. "It is the general opinion that we never before had such evidences of the prevalence of real, vital religion amongst us," one Indiana Friend wrote. "It has been spoken of as a genuine revival." At the Gurneyite Ohio Yearly Meeting, although there was no comparable special meeting, a similar spirit of enthusiasm was felt.[12]

Over the next few years, this spirit manifested itself in a growing interest in what became known in different places as tract-reading meetings, social circles, or prayer meetings. One began meeting at the home of Charles F. and Rhoda M. Coffin in Richmond, Indiana, immediately following the 1860 Indiana Yearly Meeting. Attenders agreed on common readings, sometimes a Quaker work and sometimes a non-Quaker evangelical one. Meetings included silent worship and opportunities for prayer. They became spaces where younger Friends could discuss their spiritual lives and concerns apart from older members.[13]

Not all members of Indiana Yearly Meeting were pleased with these developments. Writing about the 1860 meeting, an elderly Richmond Friend in attendance, William Bell, asserted that "in my estimation and that of many others, a great deal of creaturely excitement [was] displayed.... The whole affair reminded me very much of a camp meeting." He claimed: "*I have heard a great many express their disapproval of it, and among them* both ministers and elders." In Philadelphia, the Wilburite editors of *The Friend* were critical when they surveyed "the lauded reforms and revivals said to have taken place within the pale of our religious society." They concluded that there was "little doubt in the mind of any serious, consistent Friend, that this is a day of much weakness and degeneracy among the members." Such disapproval may have helped squelch the impulse behind the 1860 meeting. Bell claimed in 1863 that "Friends generally are ashamed of it" and that attempts to replicate it as yearly meetings in 1861, 1862, and 1863 had failed. Bell also pointedly noted that many of the participants in the 1860 meeting often attended prayer gatherings with non-Friends. Referencing Bell's account, the Philadelphia *Friend* editorialized: "It must be a source of sorrow to every true-hearted Friend, that such things are going on within our shattered Society."[14]

The start of the Civil War doubtless deflected energy that might have gone into such activities. The response of Friends to the war is largely separate from the development of revivalism, save in one respect. Many Gurneyites saw a natural "field of labor" for Friends, who could not bear arms, in work among the freed slaves in the South. John Greenleaf Whittier summed up this view: it was a "blessed privilege for Friends," protected from the worst ravages of the war, to do "all in their power to aid in the good work of educating and caring for the free people." And hundreds of Gurneyites, male and female, went south as teachers and camp superintendents (see chapter 2).[15]

The "freedmen's work" is significant because of a debate that developed. Most Quaker work was humanitarian. But some Friends wondered why no attempts were being made to make converts among the freedpeople. John Henry Douglas, after a tour of the South in 1865–66, wrote emphatically: "I most earnestly say that if we *would* we *can* make living Quakers of them." Friends did establish a school and monthly meeting for former slaves at Southland, Arkansas, but it was unique. Many of those who advocated evangelism among the freedpeople were leaders of the later revival movement.[16]

The 1860s also saw a growing interest in missionary work among Gurneyites. Since the rise of the Quaker movement, ministering Friends had felt led to travel, often holding meetings among "the world's people." But Friends had initially held themselves aloof from the great Protestant missionary movement that developed in the British Isles and North America after 1815. Many saw it as inextricably entangled with support of a hireling ministry. By 1860, that was changing. Two Iowa Friends, Joel and Hannah E. Bean, felt led to visit the Hawaiian Islands in 1860, and that was widely perceived as missionary labor. Indiana Yearly Meeting formed a foreign missionary society in 1864, and by 1870, American Friends were working as missionaries in India and Madagascar (see chapter 10).[17]

THE REVIVAL

Thus the word "revival" had entered the vocabulary of Gurneyite Friends by 1865. But it was still used in the general sense of "new life" or "awakening," and the procedures were not radical. As Rhoda M. Coffin noted, "there was no confusion, no haste, no urging or calling on anyone for prayer."[18] But other forces were at work that would introduce just such practices—and others even more radical.

Contact with non-Friends was one force for more radical innovations. There are accounts of Friends being caught up in non-Quaker revivals in the 1860s. In Bangor Quarterly Meeting in Iowa, for example, a few Friends who had attended a Campbellite revival "became impatient of the healthful restraints of church discipline" and embraced "the strangest and wildest fanaticism." In Mooresville, Indiana, early in 1866, an observer noted that some Friends had "taken a very active part" in a Methodist revival and that "several of the old Quakers professed religion and shout as loud as the Methodists." Similarly, near Winchester, Indiana, in the summer of 1868, it was reported that Friends "in connection with prominent members of the Methodist church, are holding tract readings and prayer meetings for the benefit of those not members of any society."[19]

Early in 1867, what is widely regarded as the first "modern revival" among Friends took place at Bear Creek Meeting in Dallas County, Iowa. Two ministers from eastern Iowa, John S. Bond and Stacy E. Bevan, held a single night meeting "in which many hearts were reached and all broken up, which was followed by sighs and sobs and prayers, confessions and great joys for sins pardoned and burdens rolled off." But meeting elders refused to allow the meetings to continue, and nothing similar took place for seven years at Bear Creek.[20]

Better known are events at Walnut Ridge Meeting in Rush County, Indiana, later the same year. Prayer meetings held in a schoolhouse included both Quaker and Methodist young people. Jane Jones, a minister of Walnut

Ridge Meeting, began to attend and exhort those present, and attendance grew so much that a local Methodist minister offered his church, Gilboa, for the meetings. Under the Methodist minister's guidance, a number of "seekers" professed conversion. Young Friends began to attend, and so Jones, fearing that they would leave the Society of Friends, appointed a series of meetings at Walnut Ridge. As one somewhat bemused observer later reported, there was "such singing, praying, preaching and exhorting [as] had never been heard within those walls." Dozens, often after publicly emotional, agonized experiences, professed to be "born again." One participant emphasized that "our members conduct themselves in all our meetings very much as Friends are accustomed to do, but the exercises are much distributed over the meeting." Another observer offered a different account:

> Some of our old men "saw visions," and our young men "dreamed dreams." One who seemed especially favored, went into a trance, and claimed to have made a complete geographical survey of heaven. Others claimed to have been permitted to take a good square look into hell, and would give vivid and startling descriptions of the manner in which his Satanic majesty treated his subjects, saying, "thus would their hearers be treated unless they likewise engaged in the great work." Others claimed to see angels flying through the air, with drawn swords, threatening destruction upon all who did not at once repent of their sins.... Some, again, claimed to be able to heal the sick by prayer and laying on of hands; others that they could raise the dead, and one actually made the attempt at a funeral before a large congregation.... One brother declared that he was commanded, like Abraham of old, to sacrifice his son, and began the religious duty by knocking the boy down; but the boy, fearing the Lord might not provide a ram for the occasion, ran off to hunt one, and failed to return. Some wives claimed to receive commands to leave their husbands, and husbands, also, claimed that duty required them to abandon their wives.... Many claimed to be able to perform miracles, and numerous attempts to were made.

That winter, the revival fever spread to nearby Raysville and Spiceland, but as reaction to excesses grew (one Walnut Ridge farm family left its fields unplanted for several years because of a special revelation) and some participants had second thoughts, it died down.[21]

Many historians have seen Walnut Ridge as the beginning of the "Great Revival"; Rufus Jones later wrote that it was the source of a "contagion." In fact, it received limited attention at the time. We do have evidence of other "revivals" from 1867 to 1870. Almost invariably, however, they were events taking place in prayer or tract meetings or Friends becoming caught up in the revivals of other denominations. They were common enough that some Friends were worried, but leaders of the renewal movement dismissed such fears. "I think that we may no more conclude that the religious movement out of which they have sprung, is all wrong, than that the rise of Quakerism was wrong, because of the ranterism that followed it," Joel Bean concluded in 1870. "What Reformation has not been attended by some excesses? How rare the vigorous growth that needs not the pruning hand."[22]

Meanwhile, a movement had begun in Indiana Yearly Meeting that became a vehicle for "the revival." In 1867, the yearly meeting formed a committee to hold what it called "general meetings." These would be a combination of teaching and preaching. They grew partly out of a concern on the part of leaders of the renewal movement, such as Charles F. Coffin, that many Friends had only superficial understandings of Quaker beliefs and doctrines. Indiana Yearly Meeting, which included a large membership in southwestern Ohio, also faced a desire from Friends there to form their own yearly meeting. At that time, Indiana Yearly Meeting rejected the request but saw general meetings as a way that the yearly meeting could show its concern for Friends there.[23]

The general meetings brought leading ministers to the more distant parts of the yearly meeting. They included lectures on Quaker doctrines, such as peace, worship, ministry, and the sacraments. Significantly, the early general meetings had "chairmen," implying that they were not purely occasions for worship. But they did include significant periods of worship, and by 1869, leaders found that attenders were most interested in the topic of the new birth. Some observers thought that the general meetings were failing to meet such needs. "We well remember many times, when we would have responded gladly to an invitation to come forward and unite in earnest prayer for an immediate blessing," wrote the editors of a new Chicago Quaker periodical, the *Herald of Peace*, "but we were coldly turned away, and sent to our homes to dissipate the influence of the occasion." The problem, they asserted, was that Quaker ministers could preach the Gospel but were not leading sinners to Christ. "A practical ministry," they concluded, was needed. Within two years it had emerged. Ultimately, it would revolutionize Quakerism.[24]

A full-blown revival movement developed through the leadership of a group of ministers who shared a common experience, that of second-experience holiness or sanctification. The Holiness movement had considerable influence on American Protestants in the 1850s and 1860s. Its advocates argued that perfection, or freedom from sin, was possible for all believers. It was a second experience, following conversion or the new birth, and it was instantaneous, achieved through belief in the efficacy of the Blood of Christ. Evangelicals of all denominations embraced Holiness teachings, although those with a Wesleyan heritage were most prominent in the movement.[25]

By the early 1870s, a number of young Quaker ministers had experienced second-experience sanctification. They included some who had been prominent in the renewal movement, such as John Henry Douglas and Dougan Clark. Others were newcomers to Quaker leadership.[26]

Of Quaker Holiness revivalists, the most influential was David B. Updegraff of Mount Pleasant, Ohio. Born in 1831 into a fervently Gurneyite family, Updegraff attended Haverford College. By his own account, he was only a nominal Christian and Quaker until he underwent conversion at a Methodist revival in 1860. In 1869, John S. Inskip, a Methodist minister and head of the National Camp Meeting Association for the Promotion of Holiness, led Updegraff to instantaneous sanctification. "'Every vile affection was nailed to the Cross. . . . The Holy Ghost fell upon me,' just as I supposed He did at the beginning. Instantly I felt the melting and refining of God permeate my whole being," Updegraff wrote later. "I was deeply conscious of the presence of God within me, and His sanctifying work." Soon Updegraff emerged as a minister.[27]

Updegraff was an aggressive and uncompromising advocate of Holiness teachings. His converts included Clark and Douglas. In Clark's case, all that was necessary was for Updegraff to tell him that just claiming it publicly through faith could sanctify him. "Oh it filled me," Clark remembered. "All my being was filled with this wonderful peace." He was "dead to self and sin, alive to Christ, and filled with the Holy Ghost."[28]

By 1871, the general meeting movement had spread from Indiana to other yearly meetings. Holiness enthusiasts like Updegraff seized control of it and changed its focus. As Updegraff put it, "Many could not see that the blessing of God rested upon an attempt to convey to perishing sinners 'accurate *information*' about our 'distinctive *tenets*.' I was one of that number and joined with others in imploring that 'the dead' might be left to 'bury the dead,' and that we might unite in preaching the gospel and getting converts to *Jesus*. In the providence of God such counsel prevailed, and then it was that our General Meetings became 'Revival Meetings.'" John Henry Douglas agreed, writing many years later that the general meetings failed because "we tried to explain Friends doctrines by lectures and discussions" and succeeded when they turned to "salvation of souls." By 1872, the Holiness revivalists had introduced all the techniques of classical evangelical Protestant revivalism into Quaker worship: the mourners' bench or "anxious seat," fire-and-brimstone preaching, encouragement of displays of extreme emotionalism, singing, and calling on individuals in a congregation to speak or testify. Worshippers were told that both conversion and sanctification were instantaneous experiences and could be experienced simply by "claiming" them. "Jesus saves me and saves me now, Jesus sanctifies me and sanctifies me now," was the formula that many used. A newspaper in Richmond, Indiana, in the spring of 1873 wrote of the scenes in a local Friends meeting: "For enthusiasm [it] beats any protracted meeting that even the Methodists of that benighted section ever conducted." By 1875, yearly meeting sessions themselves were the scene of such events. Attending Indiana Yearly Meeting in 1875, a Methodist minister wrote: "It resembled one of our best *love feasts* at a *National Camp Meeting* [more] than anything else to which I could liken it."[29]

How did such a dramatic change take place so quickly? The simple answer is that Holiness revivalism unquestionably met a deeply felt spiritual need of many Friends. For generations, they had heard that they should experience justification and sanctification. But older Friends had always taught that these experiences came through baptisms of suffering and tribulation; beyond that, seekers must wait and be led by the Inward Light and the Holy Spirit in ways that were not immediately clear or even perceptible. Illustrative is the experience of Hannah Whitall Smith, a Philadelphia Gurneyite who became both a prominent proponent of Holiness teachings and a skeptic about revivalism. Her book *The Christian's Secret of a Happy Life* remains an evangelical classic. She remembered of her youth: "The most we ever heard was how to walk and live, how to be good." Such teachings "failed to tell the secret by which this holiness could be realized." And one should not underestimate the attraction of a life in which the power of sin over the believer was destroyed for people who fervently believed in the reality and power of sin.[30]

The revivalists also brilliantly employed traditional Quaker language and concepts. It was easy to fit traveling revivalists like Updegraff, the Douglases, or Nathan and Esther Frame into the venerable framework of Friends "traveling in the ministry." Similarly, Friends had long spoken of justification and sanctification. The revival simply showed an easier, more direct way. And Quaker worship, with its lack of structure and set program, lent itself to being used—or hijacked, depending on one's perspective—by ministers with a burning message to share. Holiness advocates had little use for silence as the basis of Quaker worship: preaching saved souls and sanctified believers.[31]

A court case in Canada in the early 1880s produced revealing testimony about how the revival transformed worship and ministry in one meeting there. A visiting revivalist declared that there was no such thing as silent prayer. Another said that "he thanked God he didn't have to wait for the anointing of the spirit" in order to preach, for "he was always ready and full." Revival-style preaching was different from older ways; the sermons of a visitor from Indiana were described as "often interspersed with anecdotes, a thing that Friends were never used to be in the habit of doing; sometimes they would be rather on the ridiculous, so as to have the meetings almost in laughter, and at other times it would take them to tears." But most of all, there was a new message: "Christ had finished the work of man's salvation on the cross on Calvary, and therefore it is only necessary that a man believe that fact to be saved."[32]

The revivalists, moreover, were not content to revolutionize Quaker worship. They took determined aim at the plain life. For them, plainness was a variety of "dead works." It served only to distinguish Friends from other believers, a distinction that Holiness Friends wanted to obliterate. In the 1870s, the last vestiges of marriage regulations disappeared, as did any requirements of plainness of speech and dress. Long sections of doctrinal statements replaced them in the books of discipline. The revivalists wanted to demolish anything that marked Friends as sectarian or separated them from the larger community of sanctified believers (see chapter 3).[33]

By 1877, revivalism had spread into all the American Gurneyite yearly meetings except Baltimore. Generally, revivals did not arise spontaneously among Friends. Instead, they were the work of ministers committed to Holiness, often working in teams. Cyrus W. Harvey, a critic of revivalism, left a pointed narrative account of how it came to Kansas Yearly Meeting. Before 1877, he claimed, only four Kansas ministers had revival sympathies. But then "all at once we were literally overrun by this class of ministers from abroad. They swarmed into the yearly meeting in 1877." After controlling the worship during yearly meeting sessions, "they scattered into all parts of the yearly [meeting] to break up the old way of worship and ministry." The tendency of Friends to settle in discrete communities, and the relatively small number of them, made it possible for revivalists to visit almost every Quaker neighborhood in a few years.[34]

Once they had revolutionized Quaker life, the revivalists did not lack for new fields of labor. Many, such as Updegraff and Clark, became fixtures in the larger Holiness movement and its summer camps and parks. After 1875, revivalists held revivals and established new meetings in places where Friends had earlier died out or had never lived: Surry County in North Carolina, Jay and Adams Counties in Indiana, Van Wert and Mercer Counties in Ohio, and Saline and Cumberland Counties in Illinois. The circumstances of their founding, and the fact that few, if any, of the new members had experience of traditional Quakerism, meant that the old ways found little support in such places.[35]

After the revival took hold, Gurneyites were on a path toward lasting change. The music that was part of revivals gradually found its way into regular worship. So did an expectation of regular preaching, which from the late 1870s led to the pastoral system. Gradually, musical instruments were introduced, usually first in Sunday schools and then into meetings for worship. By the 1890s, observers found little difference between most Gurneyite meetings and other evangelical churches (see chapter 5).[36]

Signs of change were also apparent in meetinghouse architecture, although the most radical changes came after 1880. Elbert Russell, who was born in 1871 and lived through the transition, provided a convenient summary in a 1921 article. The rise of the pastoral system, he concluded, led to "remodeling of meeting houses to get rid of partition and gallery. Naturally chapel and church styles were affected in the new meeting houses, at first hesitantly, as for example in those at Glens Falls, New York; Brooklyn, New York; Baltimore, Maryland, and Richmond, Indiana. Then came a perfect riot of new types with belfry towers, pulpits, and platform railings, and a few with Greek temple architecture, with choir lofts or with pipe-organs." The first departures, in the cities Russell named, came in the form of gable-front buildings and arched windows. When Friends in West Milton, Ohio, built a new meetinghouse in 1881, it included a small steeple and bell. These exterior innovations were not signs of theological innovation but rather a loosening of older understandings of plainness and peculiarity. The great changes in interiors, with pulpits, platform railings, and choir lofts, came with the spread of pastoral Quakerism after 1880 (see chapter 5).[37]

Initially, the revival had little impact on women's ministry among Gurneyites. Some leading revivalists were women, such as Esther Frame in Indiana Yearly Meeting, Mary H. Rogers in Kansas Yearly Meeting, and Caroline E. Talbot of Ohio Yearly Meeting. Supporters of the revivals uniformly affirmed women as ministers, and it is clear that sometimes ministering women Friends used the novelty of women preaching to their advantage with non-Quaker audiences. However, while the revival led to the loss of distinctiveness, it ultimately also led to the demise of women's meetings for business. And in laying the foundations of the pastoral system, it undoubtedly weakened the opportunities for women's ministry.[38]

The revival shaped the development of world Quakerism after 1880. The overwhelming majority of Quaker missionaries would come from yearly meetings that the revival movement had transformed. And the Quakerism that missionaries shaped in Africa, Asia, and Latin America would be an outgrowth of the revival: pastoral, with forms of worship similar to those of evangelical churches, and with theological directions deeply influenced by larger evangelical and fundamentalist movements (see chapter 10).

RESPONSES

Unsurprisingly, the revival movement was controversial. While a majority of Friends in the yearly meetings that it touched embraced it, other responses ranged from wary acceptance to outright opposition.

The most extreme response was separation. Western, Canada, Iowa, and Kansas Yearly Meetings experienced splits between 1877 and 1882, with the separatists calling themselves Conservative Friends. A few monthly meetings in other yearly meetings were affected, as well. Typical of the justification for separation was that issued by a conference at Bear Creek, Iowa, in 1877. Perceiving "the sorrowful condition of our beloved and once favored society," those present saw two fundamental problems. The first was "the running into great activity in religious and benevolent undertakings, showing an untempered zeal by taking up one particular truth, and carrying that to an extreme to the exclusion of other important truths." The other was making religion a "product of the intellect and imagination . . . without wearing His yoke, and undergoing the humiliating baptisms which He appoints for His truly dependent and obedient followers." The revivalists had dismissed the value—indeed, the necessity—of Quaker peculiarity. And in embracing instantaneous conversion and sanctification, the revivalists taught that "mere belief constitutes conversion." Lacking this deeper, inward experience, such converts "long for vocal service," the editors of *The Friend* argued. Thus, one Conservative saw "the rapid approach in many places of the manner in which our meetings are held to that practiced by other religious professors. One step follows another. The singing of hymns, at first, by a single individual, is followed by many joining in concert; the reading of the Scriptures, at first only occasionally practiced, becomes a customary thing; the feeling grows that silence is time wasted, and this leads to arrangements for supplying meetings with ministers; the idea more and more prevails that outward ministry is almost, if not quite, essential to any convincement or awakening of the people." The new Conservative yearly meetings quickly formed ties with the older Wilburite bodies and Philadelphia Yearly Meeting, although some Wilburites feared that the Conservatives had tarried too long amid Gurneyite errors. One staunch Wilburite in Ohio demanded that before that yearly meeting recognized the Conservatives, they formally condemn the writings of Joseph John Gurney.[39]

Ultimately more influential were Friends who chose to remain in the main Gurneyite bodies and work to moderate what they saw as the excesses of the revival. One example of this impulse is Allen Jay, who was at the center of the revival in North Carolina in the 1870s and helped put it on a relatively moderate course. Significantly, Jay never embraced second-experience sanctification. He refused to introduce practices that the entire meeting could not embrace, and he eschewed judgmental preaching. "No doubt it is right to preach at times the terrors of the law," Jay wrote to his wife in 1875, "but there is so much danger of getting a little bit of self in with it—wishing to bring everybody to our idea of what is right—that I often think it is safer for me to leave the judging with my heavenly father." Revivalists counted Jay as one of their own, but his course increasingly diverged from theirs after 1880.[40]

Others who had been involved in the renewal movement in the 1860s also fall into this group, including such Friends as Timothy Nicholson and

Charles F. and Rhoda M. Coffin in Indiana Yearly Meeting, Barnabas C. Hobbs in Western Yearly Meeting, William Nicholson in Kansas Yearly Meeting, Nereus Mendenhall in North Carolina Yearly Meeting, Elizabeth L. Comstock and John Butler in Ohio Yearly Meeting, James Wood and Thomas Kimber in New York Yearly Meeting, and the leaders of Baltimore Yearly Meeting. They found their organ in the *Friends' Review*, which became increasingly critical of revivalism after 1875. These Friends continued to embrace gradual justification and sanctification and the value of silent worship. They were relatively few in number, but they held positions of authority and influence as clerks of yearly meetings and of yearly meetings of ministers and elders.[41]

Of the old renewal group, the most prominent opponent of the revival after 1875 was Joel Bean in Iowa. He had been clerk of Iowa Yearly Meeting most of the time from 1867 to 1878. He had welcomed the early stirrings of revivalism as new life. But after 1877 it deeply worried him. Bean rejected instantaneous sanctification and affirmed the Inward Light as the "root" of Quakerism. When his own meeting in West Branch was deeply divided by a revival led by Updegraff in March 1880, Bean felt that he had no choice but to challenge the revival openly. A year later, he published an essay, "The Issue," in *The British Friend*. It was a devastating analysis of revivalism's impact on Quakerism. Revivalists, through their dismissal of the Inward Light and insistence on instantaneous conversion and sanctification, Bean claimed, had fundamentally broken with historic Quakerism. Indeed, they were open in their contempt for what had long distinguished Friends from other Protestants. Their converts often drifted away. Meanwhile, the revivalists had displaced experienced and committed Friends. The results were clear. "Disorganization and disintegration are confessedly making rapid progress," Bean concluded, "and most rapid where protest is silenced and conservatism most inert." Moderate Friends praised Bean, but such attitudes made him a marked man in the eyes of the revivalists and completed his marginalization in his own yearly meeting.[42]

The response of British Friends to revivalism was complicated. On the one hand, London and Dublin Yearly Meetings were never "revived" in the way that most North American Gurneyite yearly meetings were. On the other hand, revivalism did find supporters among British Friends—often enthusiastic supporters who urged the introduction of revival methods into British meetings. Additionally, Dublin and London

Yearly Meetings uniformly recognized the revived bodies as the legitimate yearly meetings when separations took place in North America.

As early as 1860, a member of London Yearly Meeting had noted with concern that "Quakerism has no revival machinery to put in motion, either on its own account or for the conversion of the world." This, argued Reigate Friend Robert Barclay (a descendant of the apologist) in 1868, was deplorable. Friends needed to become an "aggressive" organization, dedicated to "the conversion of sinners" and the "propagation of the Gospel." A convinced Friend, J. G. Hine, agreed two years later: "What struck him forcibly was that the Society ... was doing nothing for those in sin and misery around it."[43]

Between 1860 and 1883, London Yearly Meeting took some steps in this direction. It set up "adult schools" where, on Sunday mornings, the illiterate working classes learned reading, writing, and Christianity, with the Bible as a textbook. By 1883, the yearly meeting had a Home Mission Committee whose purpose was avowedly evangelistic. Adult education was combined with meetings for worship aimed at converting sinners, where hymn singing and Bible reading were very different from the way they were in regular meetings for worship. In 1875, London Yearly Meeting had established a Committee on General Meetings, clearly modeled on the American practice. One enthusiast described a scene in 1876: "Strong men bowed before [God], and shook as aspens; depraved sinners listened eagerly to and drank in the glad tidings." Many left "feeling that they had been washed in the precious blood of the Lamb." Visiting American ministers, such as Caroline E. Talbot and Dougan Clark, took part.[44]

Yet, ultimately, British Quakers would reject the revival. The reasons for that rejection are beyond the bounds of this chapter. More conservative British Friends were vocal in their scorn for what they called "Methodistical manifestations" among American Friends. The emerging liberal movement in British Quakerism was equally unenthusiastic. Critically, the adult schools and mission meetings were kept separate from regular meetings for worship. And the Holiness movement never found the support among British Friends that it did among American Gurneyites.[45]

The significance of the moderates is twofold. First, they kept alive a vision of a distinctive Quakerism in the midst of revolutionary change. And second, in their lack of dogmatism, they opened the way for the emergence of a new generation of modernist Gurneyites, akin to those in London Yearly Meeting in the 1880s and 1890s. Rufus Jones was a product of New

England Yearly Meeting, nurtured by Haverford and the group around the *Friends' Review*. Timothy Nicholson and Allen Jay defended Friends like Elbert Russell as they made Earlham a modernist bastion.[46]

CONCLUSION

Between 1860 and 1880, the Gurneyite majority of Quakers in the United States experienced rapid change. Indeed, few religious groups have ever been transformed so dramatically in so short a period of time. The Holiness movement gave rise to the revival, and that revival transformed American Quakerism and, ultimately, Quakerism across the world. By removing the theological foundations for the plain life among most Friends and by laying the foundations for the pastoral system that most of the world's Quakers now employ, this became one of the most dramatic turning points in Quaker history. Revivalists saw themselves as part of a larger Holiness movement that hardened into fundamentalism in the twentieth century. That, in turn, would lay the groundwork for conflicts that continue even into the present day.[47]

CHAPTER 5

Quakers and the Growth of the Pastoral System

ISAAC BARNES MAY

The late nineteenth century saw radical changes to Quaker polity and liturgy. Among the most visible of these shifts was the introduction of a paid, professional ministry among American Gurneyite Quakers, the theologically moderate branch of Quakerism headquartered in the Midwest. When Friends missionaries spread Quakerism internationally, the Quakerism that they brought with them typically included pastors (see chapter 10). American Hicksites and British Quakerism resisted this movement, opting to have silent meetings for worship with no division between clergy and laity. The result of this transition is that contemporary Quakerism is now split between a large number of "programmed" or pastoral Friends, who have paid ministers and whose worship resembles that of other Protestants, and a much smaller community of "unprogrammed" Friends who have largely eschewed paid ministry and who worship in silence except when individuals feel moved to speak. The split between these groups on the topic of ministry and liturgical practice is coextensive with a deep gulf on the question of theology; typically, programmed Friends are evangelical, while unprogrammed Friends are theologically liberal.[1]

Both programmed and unprogrammed Friends were religious innovators who changed what ministry meant among Quakers in order to respond to demographic and social pressures. There would be significant changes to the system of "recording" ministers that had prevailed among earlier generations of Friends, where meetings recognized the ministerial gifts of an individual without providing formal ordination or a salary. While programmed meetings continued to avoid formal ordination, they did in many cases provide a salary and often recording to ministers engaged in pastoral service. Nearly all unprogrammed Friends associated with Hicksite yearly meetings or Britain (then London) Yearly Meeting came to abolish or ignore the recording of ministers altogether, and they did not replace it with ordination. While the two camps came to starkly different conclusions about how best to adapt Quakerism to remain viable, each was convinced that to simply maintain past practices was not an option.[2]

EARLY QUAKER ATTITUDES TOWARD MINISTRY

One of the features that most clearly distinguished early Quakers from their Puritan counterparts was their rejection of a specially trained clergy. George Fox believed that he had received a divine revelation that education was not a necessary prerequisite for ministry, writing that "the Lord opened unto me that being bred at Oxford or Cambridge was not enough to fit and qualify men to be ministers of Christ." Early Quakers denounced what they termed the "hireling ministry" of the established Church of England.[3]

Quakers could at times sound anticlerical, but their rejection of a separated ministry was not total; for most of their history, Friends still conceived of the role of a minister as distinct and reserved for a few people. Quakers understood ministers as being directly "led" by God, speaking words that God provided them, rather than acting under their own volition. Ministers were thus understood more as conduits of the divine than as human agents. Meetings believed they were providing public recognition of ministry by recording it in their minutes, but they did not conceive of themselves as conferring a new status.

The Quaker theologian Robert Barclay was representative of Quaker views on ministry. Barclay stated that the leading for ministry must come directly from God rather than any human organization. Minsters, Barclay wrote, had to preach freely "without hire or bargaining." Above all, they should not turn their religious calling into a trade, as ministry was not supposed to be a full-time occupation. Yet Barclay also included an important caveat. If ministerial work prevented a Friend from earning a livelihood, they should be allowed to receive goods from those to whom they ministered. Barclay specified that ministers could be provided "what may be needful to them for meat or clothing." The position of Barclay and other early Quakers on the ministry left a number of important questions unanswered. There was little clarity on how much remuneration, or what kind, a minister could receive without becoming a "hireling." Because the leading for ministry came from God, there were no universally agreed-upon criteria by which the Quaker community could evaluate and recognize it. These ambiguities would generate considerable debate in the nineteenth century.[4]

From its beginnings, Quaker ministry was open to both men and women, a gender egalitarianism that was exceptionally rare among other Christian groups. Quakerism's founder, George Fox, wrote in defense of women's ministry in his 1656 pamphlet *The Woman Learning in Silence*. Quaker leader Margaret Fell, who eventually married Fox, produced a 1666 pamphlet, *Women's Speaking Justified*, that made a scripturally based case for women's suitability to be ministers. Fell vociferously denounced those who believed that the apostle Paul had categorically forbidden women's ministry, arguing that when Paul had commanded women to "learn in silence with all subjection" (1 Timothy 2:11), he had meant only to condemn the small group of wayward women about whom he was writing. Fell also argued that when Jesus rose from the dead, he appeared first to Mary Magdalene, signifying that "Lord Jesus hath manifested himself and his Power, without Respect of Persons," and showing that there were no restrictions to the ministry on account of gender. For women, involvement in Quaker ministry could be a path to social advancement and status. Because most Christian denominations forbade the ministry of women, until the twentieth century, Quakerism was nearly unique among religious groups in Britain and the United States for having a substantial number of female ministers.[5]

Quakers began the process of formalizing and codifying the requirements for ministers fairly early in their history. Beginning in 1683, Friends who were engaged in ministry in the London area were expected to participate in the Second Day Morning Meeting, which not only controlled matters pertaining to ministry but acted as a censorship board to vet Quaker publications and served as a central committee that helped govern the London Yearly Meeting. In 1722, a dispute over the status of a Friend named William Gibson led the Morning Meeting to begin to require traveling ministers to present certificates of their status from their home meetings and to start submitting lists of all recorded minsters to them. As such regulations spread beyond London, Quaker ministry stopped being a purely congregational affair; ministers' status was also recognized by yearly meetings.[6]

While paid pastoral ministry would only be introduced among American Quakers in the last quarter of the nineteenth century, the debates within the Religious Society of Friends about the role of paid ministers dated to the early nineteenth century. What was at stake originally was not whether Quakers themselves would have a paid ministry but how much Quakers should tolerate the clergy of other Christian groups. One of the issues in the schism between Hicksite and Orthodox Quakers in the United States was that the Orthodox favored fostering connections with evangelicals and collaborating on shared projects like promoting Bible reading and temperance. The Orthodox found that maintaining such close connections with other denominations was not easily compatible with being openly critical of their clergy.[7]

The English Quaker minister Joseph John Gurney, who was widely influential among American Orthodox Friends, defended Friends' prerogative not to provide salaries for "hired" ministers but was particularly apologetic for implying that other denominations were in error: "I must beg my readers to understand that, in using the word 'hiring,' it is wholly foreign from my intention to express anything in the least degree offensive to Christian ministers of any denomination. That a considerable portion of these persons are truly the servants of Lord Jesus ... and are incomparably, more intent on the winning of souls than upon their own temporal advantage—I both know and am happy to acknowledge." Gurney pointed out that many clergymen he knew were too poorly paid for anyone to reasonably believe they were motivated by the expectation of financial reward. While Gurney did not want to completely give up Quaker teachings on the ministry, he hoped to stress the ways in which Quakers and other Protestants were in agreement.[8]

GURNEYITES AND THE INTRODUCTION OF THE PASTORAL SYSTEM

It was the Gurneyites, successors of the Orthodox, that introduced paid ministry into Quakerism. Proponents of paid ministry argued that it was a necessary measure to allow Friends to welcome in new members as meetings responded to a series of revivals in the 1870s and 1880s that attracted many new converts (see chapter 4). This boom was especially visible in the Midwest; during the 1880s, for example, Indiana Yearly Meeting's membership increased by a third.[9]

The revivalists embraced Holiness theology, emphasizing the need for believers to have the experience of sanctification, and they were closely affiliated with the movement that would later be called fundamentalism. The revivals they conducted were not considerably different from those done by evangelists from other groups. These revivals could be raucous; one account of preacher David Updegraff describes how he kept exhorting a woman who was praying for sanctification to pray louder until she began to weep and shout. After such passionate encounters, new converts often arrived in unprogrammed Friends meetings without a sense of how silent worship worked or clarity about how to become oriented to their new community. Gurneyites considered several options in responding to this surge of new members. Thomas D. Hamm observes that theological moderates suggested introducing a probationary period for new converts and ministering to them with pastoral committees arranged by monthly meetings. Proponents of the revival, however, held out for the creation of paid pastorates.[10]

The vast majority of Gurneyite Quakerism accepted the new way of worshipping. In Western, Iowa, Kansas, and Indiana Yearly Meetings, the embrace of paid ministry was an important factor in the choice of some Gurneyite Quakers to join with another faction, the Wilburites, now known as Conservative Quakers. These Friends sought to preserve traditional worship practices and customs such as plain dress, fearing that the revivals were endangering such conventions.

The advocates for paid pastorates also had theological reasons for advocating this form of ministry. Their involvement in the Holiness movement often meant that they nurtured close sympathies with other denominations, and so they began to copy their neighbors in referring to their local religious communities not as meetings but as churches. The Holiness movement was particularly linked with Methodism. Nathan and Esther Frame, two prominent Quaker evangelists, were representative of Friends' involvement in the Holiness movement. Both had contemplated going into the Methodist ministry before deciding that there would be less of a barrier on account of gender to Esther's ministry among Friends. Revivalists saw Quaker rejection of paid ministry as harmful, a way that Quakerism failed to nurture the religious gifts of its members.[11]

A number of the revivalists began to argue that ministers were clergy, who held a different religious status from laity. Evangelist Luke Woodward, for example, derided the notion of the ministry of all believers as a "dangerous abuse" that threatened to "nullify that respect, honor, and authority which God himself has assigned to the office of Gospel ministry." Woodward and other revivalists argued that pastors must exercise leadership over their congregations, guiding them just as shepherds cared for their flocks.[12]

Even among the most zealous advocates of the pastoral system, however, the notion persisted that a divine prompting led some individuals to ministry, which was distinct from merely holding the professional job of pastor. In 1895, Holiness Quaker leader Dougan Clark Jr. and his ally, Methodist evangelist Joseph H. Smith, declared: "Many are disqualified for ecclesiastical office who are efficient Gospel ministers. Upon the other hand, many have buried ministerial talents in the ambitions and cares of ecclesiastical office. The ministerial gift is a direct energy of the Holy Ghost working through and sometimes beyond the faculties of the man (or woman)." The ideal, they implied, would be a minister imbued with this "direct energy" who also received professional recognition.[13]

A paid pastorate meant the decline of itinerant ministry. Whereas Quaker ministers had previously been financially and materially supported only while traveling on ministerial visits, the emergence of the pastoral system meant that ministers began to operate more like the clergy of other denominations, staying close to home and ideally serving only one congregation. Individual churches took charge of paying the salaries of these ministers. If a single church could not financially support them, ministers might serve several churches in geographic proximity.

The churches that adopted paid pastors almost always abandoned the traditional Quaker way of worship, which featured extended periods of silence, and began to use programmed liturgies that closely resembled those of nearby Protestant churches. These Friends abandoned Quakerism's long-held aversion to music and introduced organ playing and hymn singing into services. Ministers would deliver prepared sermons because the belief that speaking had to be extemporaneous to evidence that it came from the Spirit was no longer operative. When future Friends churches were built, they would typically have stages or pulpits for their ministers, as was common in many American churches, rather than the distinctive row of facing benches that had been common in Quaker meetinghouses.

For the ministers, working in the pastoral system often meant a financially precarious existence. Some proponents of the pastoral system even advertised the low salaries of ministers as a sort of virtue. Just as Gurney had once argued that Anglican ministers were too impoverished to count as hirelings, now the same argument was being employed to suggest that Fox's condemnation would not have applied to Friends ministers. In 1888, J. H. Douglas, the general superintendent of Evangelistic, Pastoral, and Church Extension Work for Iowa Yearly Meeting, claimed, "We hear but little now of hireling ministry, for all know that no one is making money by preaching, and no one is preaching for money."[14]

Douglas was only exaggerating slightly; pastoral ministry in most American denominations was not a path to riches or even financial stability. Between 1890 and 1900, on average, American ministers across all denominations made $574 annually, which spurred reformers to complain that the low pay would drive qualified men away from the work. Quaker ministers were poorly compensated even compared to the standard of other denominational clergy. As Thomas D. Hamm has observed, "In 1890 the average annual salary of a pastor in [Iowa Yearly Meeting] was $136, less than the wages of an unskilled factory worker."[15]

One consequence of the introduction of the pastoral system was that it curtailed women's ability to become ministers wherever it was implemented. There was no formal prohibition on women serving as minsters, but over the next few decades, women's ministry would become less common. In 1920, Emma Cook Coffin, a recorded Friends minister and evangelist from California, published an article lamenting the decline in women's ministry among the Five Years Meeting of the Religious Society of Friends. She wrote to various officials of yearly meetings and asked them about the issue.

Responses to Cook's query varied. A few of the respondents saw the lack of women in ministry as a problem that needed to be addressed, but the majority were relatively unconcerned. One wrote Cook that men could not stand to see a woman minster, while another claimed that women simply were not interested in ministry, and a third argued that the time occupied by motherhood would take women away from congregations. These answers clearly failed to explain why Quakerism had a robust tradition of women in ministry prior to the introduction of the pastoral system but not once it was in place. The most persuasive response suggested that Quaker churches almost universally preferred hiring men and rarely considered hiring women.[16]

Now that ministry was understood by some American Friends as a career, it would also be seen as a way for a man to earn a living and provide for a family, whereas the societal expectation was that women should be provided for by their fathers and husbands. Further, whereas Quaker meetings in the past might have had multiple people recognized as ministers, Friends churches typically could only afford to hire one pastor. If there was only going to be a single minster, then the presumption was that it would be a man.

Rhetorically, Gurneyite revivalists continued to maintain a commitment to the ideal of women's ministry, even if this rhetoric was increasingly distant from reality. Dougan Clark made the case in his writing that both the Bible and early Christian history clearly showed that women were allowed to serve in ministerial roles and that the Holy Spirit could provide both sexes with the gift of ministry. David Updegraff argued that, if properly understood, the apostle Paul had approved of women's ministry. Gurneyites were more open to the prospect of women's ministry than most religious groups in the United States. In an era when only a few mainline denominations ordained women at all, some exceptionally determined women, including Esther Frame, did manage to become ministers, but they made up an increasingly small fraction of the ministry.[17]

Curiously, one negotiable factor among Friends ministers in this system was their Quakerism. Often, Friends churches were willing to hire men from other Protestant denominations who had the necessary education and qualities for ministry. Reflecting on the faults of the pastoral system, in 1960, theologian D. Elton Trueblood lamented how such ministers treated Quakerism like any other Protestant denomination: "Often he has come from another tradition, and is so ignorant of Quaker history as not to know that for the two hundred years of Quaker life *there was not one pastor.*"[18]

The acceptance of paid ministry among Gurneyite Friends also raised the question of how ministers should be trained. Mainline Protestants in the United States had begun to professionalize their clergy and aspired to have college- and seminary-educated ministers. Quakers had to choose whether they wanted to do the same. The revivalists were often skeptical of the value of college and seminary education because it was costly and could involve studying the historical critical approach to the Bible, which saw the

Bible as a cultural product of ancient societies. Instead, like many other denominations that were part of the Holiness and emerging fundamentalist movements, they favored the creation of Bible colleges and missionary training schools to prepare ministers. That style of education emphasized an inerrantist and devotional study of scripture and often lacked rigorous academic standards. Friends founded a number of these institutions. Later in the twentieth century, many of these would become colleges and universities; Cleveland Bible Institute became Malone College, Haviland Bible Training School turned into Barclay College, and the Training School for Christian Workers evolved into Azusa Pacific University. Existing Gurneyite Quaker institutions also tried to contribute to the education of ministers. In 1888, Earlham College began to operate a Bible Institute, a two-year program designed to train pastors.[19]

Those Gurneyite Friends who were critical of revivalism and the turn toward paid pastoral ministry sometimes paradoxically found that the introduction of paid ministry opened up new educational and career avenues for them, since the creation of the pastoral system had removed many of the taboos surrounding Friends attending or teaching at seminaries and divinity schools. Because seminary admission was largely closed to women, the Gurneyites who could take advantage of these new opportunities were predominantly men. Elbert Russell was part of this emerging group of theological modernists. Russell had been hired to teach in the Biblical Department at his alma mater, Earlham College, where proponents of the revival expected him to uphold an inerrantist view of the Bible. Instead, Russell defied expectations and went to the University of Chicago Divinity School, where he worked with modernist theologian Shailer Mathews and eventually earned a PhD. Later in his career, in 1928, Russell would become dean of Duke Divinity School. Biblical scholar Alexander C. Purdy came from a similar background. The son of a Quaker minister without any formal training, Purdy earned a PhD from Hartford Theological Seminary in 1916 and spent well over two decades on its faculty. Another biblical scholar, Henry J. Cadbury, worked at Harvard Divinity School and in 1934 became the Hollis Professor of Divinity, the oldest and one of the most prestigious endowed academic chairs in the United States. Through their seminary attendance, these Friends were influenced by the thought of mainline Protestants, and, as faculty, they worked to train a new generation of ministers from the mainline.[20]

Though Gurneyite modernists tended to gravitate toward working in academia rather than in the ministry, they had few principled objections to paid preaching. Haverford College philosophy professor Rufus Jones, one of the most eminent Quaker leaders in the early twentieth century, usually worshipped in the unprogrammed meeting near Haverford but would regularly visit the summer residence of his friend and patron John D. Rockefeller Jr. at Seal Harbor in Maine and be paid to guest preach in a local church. Rockefeller even described Jones as being "the parish's best friend."[21]

The aggressive mission work of Gurneyite Friends (who eventually became Five Years Meeting and, later, Friends United Meeting) and the evangelical Friends meant that the pastoral system was exported worldwide as they spread Quakerism. Missions had great success in Bolivia, Burundi, Cuba, Guatemala, Honduras, and what is now Kenya. Elsewhere, missionaries managed to attract smaller communities to the Religious Society of Friends (see chapter 10).

In Kenya, for example, programmed pastoral worship was the norm from the arrival of the first American missionaries in Kaimosi in 1902. The missionaries held daily services at the mission's station with the staff and larger worship services on Sundays. The rapid spread of the Friends church was made possible by Kenyan Friends, who would attend a lecture at the mission station on Sunday mornings and then fan out to preach in the area. Friends Bible Institute (later renamed Friends Theological College), which was established in the 1940s, provided a way to educate and train local ministers.[22]

Missionaries, like pastors, were financially supported in their work. They often served as pastors for local Christian communities, ideally being replaced with local pastors when clergy could be trained. Missions work was more open to women than pastoral employment, so many women were involved in both going abroad as missionaries and leading missionary organizations in the United States, a calling that they often saw as a kind of ministry.[23]

CHANGING HICKSITE VIEWS ON THE PROFESSIONAL MINISTRY

Hicksites sustained hostility toward paid ministry longer than the Orthodox did. Elias Hicks ranked paid ministers with "the worst of mankind" and strongly suggested that their salvation was in grave doubt. Yet, in the midnineteenth century, as a vocal faction of Hicksites began to work with non-Quaker social reformers on antislavery efforts, they had to become more tolerant because many of their closest allies were in the clergy (see chapter 2).[24]

Any acceptance of the validity of paid clergy could be a fraught process. Hicksite leader Lucretia Mott greatly admired the preaching and writing of Unitarian minister William Ellery Channing, but she was troubled by the fact that he was paid for his religious work. Mott eventually came to the conclusion that even though Channing's career violated the teachings of the Religious Society of Friends, he nevertheless possessed valuable religious insights. Mott herself was accused of being a "hireling minister" because of her work for the American Anti-Slavery Society as a lecturer. If such work was paid, her Quaker critics argued, then it was a form of ministry that violated Friends' discipline. Such criticism was not enough to deter Mott.[25]

The most theologically and politically radical Quakers, the Progressive Friends who began to separate from the Hicksites in the late 1840s, took the position of tolerating paid clergy from other denominations while vigorously opposing Quaker ministers. At the Pennsylvania Yearly Meeting of Progressive Friends held in Longwood, clergy from other faiths were often present, and that yearly meeting even appointed a Unitarian minister as clerk of the gathering. Progressive Friends prized personal liberty of conscience, and if clergy felt like worshipping with Quakers, they were supportive of this choice. Yet Progressive Friends feared that recording their own ministers and elders would result in them wielding too much authority in Quaker meetings, arguing that through the mechanism of Meetings of Ministers and Elders, they could exercise almost despotic powers. Progressive Friends opted to abolish the recording of ministers, effectively ending the distinction between a separate "recorded" ministry and other Quakers. Gatherings that had previously been Meetings of Ministers and Elders were renamed Meetings of Ministry and Counsel, and all interested Friends were now invited to attend. While they were numerically small, Progressive Friends would have an outsized influence on the rest of unprogrammed Quakerism, which, starting in the twentieth century, began to phase out the recording of ministers in many yearly meetings.[26]

Hicksites also felt compelled to eliminate recorded ministry for practical reasons. By the late nineteenth century, in smaller unprogrammed meetings suffering from demographic decline, there were often no recorded ministers. Because people other than recorded ministers were heavily discouraged from offering messages during meeting for worship, this meant that in many meetings without ministers, there was often complete silence. By the 1890s, the situation seemed desperate, as even a sizable community like Indiana Yearly Meeting (Hicksite) had only a handful of recorded ministers, and there was active concern about whether it would begin having to lay down its constituent meetings (effectively declaring them permanently closed) due to the lack of ministry. In their desperation, a few Hicksites even considered whether it would be viable to pay recorded ministers, adapting their own version of the pastoral system, but this seemed to them too extreme a break with tradition. Eventually, they decided on eliminating the distinction between the ministry and other Friends by ceasing to formally record ministers, in the hope that it would actually encourage a broader range of people to give ministry. While this was not a panacea, it does seem to have at least allowed many meetings to eliminate absolute silence during worship, and it allowed younger Quakers to express and cultivate their ministerial gifts.[27]

Yet even as they moved to eliminate the formal recording of ministers, by the early twentieth century, Hicksites (who would become part of Friends General Conference) still gravitated toward certain practices that once would have been derided by Friends as "hireling ministry." Hicksites did not hire pastors but instead created a paid denominational bureaucracy. They felt that in the twentieth century, the demands of administration were so intense that they could no longer be filled by part-time volunteers. In 1904, Henry Wilbur became the first paid staff member of Friends General Conference (FGC), accepting a salary to work as the organization's general secretary. Hicksite yearly meetings also began to employ staff. In 1911, Philadelphia Yearly Meeting (Hicksite), for example, formed the Friends Central Bureau as an office to carry out the work of the meeting and hired Jane P. Rushmore to work as its head, with a salary of one thousand dollars annually. While Hicksites saw these activities as distinct from paid pastoral ministry, it had nevertheless become possible in all branches of Quakerism to earn a living doing religious work. Hicksites and FGC kept the practice of having silent, unprogrammed worship, however, and paid pastors never gained authority over individual meetings.[28]

BRITISH FRIENDS' EXPERIMENTS WITH PASTORAL MINISTRY

British Quakers did not adopt paid pastors or employ ministers to preside over church services, but they did experiment with various kinds of Quaker ministry. They created First Day schools (the Quaker equivalent of Sunday schools), which taught the non-Quaker poor. By the latter half of the nineteenth century, these efforts increasingly dovetailed with the "adult school" movement and focused on imparting basic literacy and religious lessons to adult learners. Quaker adult schooling was a considerable undertaking; there were over 29,000 students in 191 schools by 1900. The schools themselves often began to resemble churches, with hymns, prayer, and even sermons. The content in the schools was an evangelically infused, broad form of Christianity rather than lessons specifically based on Quaker doctrines. Despite this, the adult students sometimes referred to themselves as "Quakers," even though the Religious Society of Friends showed little interest in formally admitting the poor and socially marginal students to its membership.[29]

The teachers at these schools were Quakers. These instructors were selected by virtue of their education, and they were appointed by Quaker meetings to the positions, though they were not typically paid. Their role was often similar to that of dissenting ministers, in that their jobs involved teaching their students about the Bible and leading them in worship on Sundays. In many ways, it was a radical revision in how Quakers had conceived of ministry, because these First Day school teachers claimed no direct guidance from God to work in their positions, and they could use fixed liturgical forms rather than waiting for inspiration of the Spirit. Yet the fact that teachers were not officially considered ministers, and did not work among Quakers, seems to have prevented controversy.

The First Day school movement led to the formation of home missions meetings. These meetings were originally intended to be religious services for the benefit of the students at the schools, but they became fully developed, programmed religious services held for poor non-Quakers, conducted by Quaker leaders. In a few cases, the missions meetings actually did become independent churches, although most continued to operate under the care of Quaker meetings. Historian Elizabeth Isichei writes that by the late 1870s, there may have been as many mission meeting attenders as there were English Friends. As they experimented with these new ministerial forms directed at others, British Quakers struggled to maintain the traditional system of unpaid recorded ministry.[30]

By the late nineteenth century, many Friends in Britain and Ireland felt that they were in the midst of a crisis and decline. In 1886, a visitor to Dublin Yearly Meeting reported that the meeting had only recorded a single minister that year. While it had thirty-five ministers altogether, "the number of recorded ministers looks a good many on paper, yet several are very aged, and comparatively few are able to take part in ministry beyond their own monthly meetings." The situation was not better among British Friends. In 1899, London Yearly Meeting sent out a letter on "Worship and the Ministry" to all its constituent congregations urging young people to become more involved in ministry. At times, the message from the yearly meeting sounded positively desperate: "We sympathize with those who are craving for a ministry that feeds their minds and souls who do not find such in their own meeting.... [We] believe much of the want might be supplied by our younger members themselves, if instead of deserting a meeting, they would under the fresh anointing of the Holy Spirit, throw their spiritual energy to its help."[31]

Despite that plea, it does not seem that young people were easily persuaded to remain among Friends. By the end of the nineteenth century, some British Friends began to believe that something like ministerial training might help spur more young Friends to be involved in ministry and improve what they said when they contributed in meetings for worship.

In 1897, chocolate manufacturing scion George Cadbury began collaborating with John Wilhelm Rowntree, a rising and theologically progressive leader among British Quakers. The two sought to create a series of summer schools in England, designed as short training programs to be conducted over a few weeks that would expose Friends to lectures on religious topics such as church history and the origins of the New Testament. Though they wanted to retain unprogrammed worship, they worried that a lack of seminary training meant that Quaker ministers might be less prepared to deal with modern developments in science and biblical criticism than ministers from other denominations. The summer schools allowed them to provide an extremely abbreviated version of a seminary experience to a large number of Friends. The idea spread across the Atlantic, and in 1900, philosophy professor Rufus Jones began to convene summer schools in the United States at Haverford College.[32]

British Friends decided in 1903 to try to extend the work of summer schools to a full year by creating Woodbrooke Settlement for Religious and Social Study, an educational center that had its own faculty and could provide regular instruction to students. Aside from the fact that it did not formally grant degrees and it offered only a short course of instruction, Woodbrooke strongly resembled a seminary, something that concerned even some of its supporters, who feared routinizing Quaker ministry rather than having it led by the divine. American Friends attempted to establish an American equivalent to Woodbrooke. In 1918, Hicksite Friends set up the John Woolman School at Swarthmore College, while Orthodox Friends eventually created a short-lived graduate school at Haverford specializing in Quakerism. The most enduring of these American efforts was Pendle Hill, founded in 1930, which served as both a retreat and a center for the study of Quakerism. None of these institutions, however, provided professional training in ministry in the same way that a seminary or divinity school did, though they continued to be places to experiment with spirituality and pursue the academic study of Quakerism. The founding of Earlham School of Religion in 1960 meant that, for the first time, Friends had a seminary like other denominations.[33]

For British Friends, providing education to future recorded ministers turned out not to be the path they ultimately pursued. It would take longer, but London Yearly Meeting would come to follow the same route as Hicksites in the United States, and in 1924, they would discontinue the practice of recording ministers. Their logic was the same as that of the Hicksites: they wanted to universalize ministry so that more people would be inclined to speak, which they felt could best be done by abolishing the distinction between recorded ministers and other Friends. For almost a century, British Friends were ostensibly connected with American Gurneyite Quakers, and they had accepted the Gurneyite disownment of the Hicksites as legitimate; but by the early twentieth century, they had reached almost identical conclusions as the Hicksites had regarding the future direction of Quaker ministry and were becoming much closer to them in practice.[34]

REASONS BEHIND THE LIBERAL QUAKERS' REJECTION OF THE PASTORAL SYSTEM

One intriguing question is why the pastoral system failed to take root among Hicksites and British Quakers. This seems particularly remarkable because many religious groups in the early twentieth century, such as Buddhists and Reform and Conservative Jews, faced intense cultural pressures to model themselves more on Protestantism. They frequently adopted measures that made their clergy seem more like mainline ministers, such as having clergy give sermons, and in some cases, they even began using titles like "reverend." In contrast, liberal Quakers resisted the professionalization of the ministry, and by ending the recording of ministers, they took concrete steps to universalize the call to ministry, trying to include all participants in Quaker meetings for worship.

One key reason for their opposition to paid pastors lay in the liberal theological outlook that these Quakers fully embraced at the end of the nineteenth century. Many of the positions espoused in liberal theology tended to undermine the status of ministers. Religious liberals were skeptical of any claimed authority outside of religious experience and rational knowledge, so appeals to the Christian tradition to buttress the legitimacy of paid ministry held little appeal.

Liberal Protestants frequently aspired to an ideal of the priesthood of all believers. Unitarian minister James Freeman Clarke, for example, built on the writing of Martin Luther to argue that all men and women held the same priestly authority and that ministers were justified in being employed by congregations only for the sake of "convenience" in making churches run smoothly. Clarke held up Friends as the most successful group in realizing the Protestant "principle of equality" by making no distinction between clergy and laity. Despite the strong rhetoric of figures like Clarke, however, few liberal religious communities actually tried to eliminate ministers. Unitarians ultimately retained their paid clergy, but their support would help reinforce liberal Quaker perceptions that they already had an admirable style of church polity and there was no benefit to adopting paid ministry.[35]

Liberal Friends were also aware that their evangelically minded coreligionists in Friends United Meeting (FUM) were adopting the pastoral system, and they sometimes conflated paid pastors with Holiness and evangelical theology. Pastors became the most obvious distinctive mark between these different kinds of Friends, and the choice to reject or accept the paid pastoral system took on partisan dimensions. For liberal Quakers—who faced the charge that they were abandoning traditional Quaker theology by accepting biblical criticism—the choice to continue to worship in silence, without the aid of a pastor, become a critical component of their claim to be the authentic heirs of the early Quaker movement. Evangelical and FUM Friends maintained that they were in continuity with the beliefs of the early Friends about God and Christ, while, in contrast, the liberals felt that they had kept intact many traditional Quaker liturgical practices.[36]

Another factor in the rejection of pastoral systems both in Britain and among American Hicksite Friends was the issue of social class. The fact that in London Yearly Meeting the missions meetings and evangelical preaching were directed at the poor may have helped prevent the pastoral system and more conventional Protestant styles of worship from spreading. Organ playing, hymn singing, and sermons began to be perceived as things that good Quakers provided for non-Quakers who were in financially and socially desperate circumstances, not liturgical practices that should be used among Friends, who felt themselves to have a dignified and historically grounded style of worship.

British Quakers were also reluctant to deal with converts from outside their social milieu. In 1895, at the Manchester Conference, a farm laborer rose and spoke to the assembly, explaining that, though he believed in the tenets of Quakerism and had found that the experience of unprogrammed worship resonated with him, he had been socially excluded by middle-class Friends. He had attended Quaker meetings for months and only a single person had spoken with him, because other Friends would not condescend to speak to someone of such low social status. The class divide between American Gurneyites and the converts they made in the revivals, in contrast, was narrower. While there were wealthier Gurneyites, they were still a heavily rural and agricultural population, as were their new converts. Gurneyites were eager to assimilate as many people as they could into their faith in a way that would have been unfathomable to British Friends.[37]

Hicksite Friends in the United States faced different issues related to status and social class. They had an unusually high percentage of well-educated laity, some of whom expressed reluctance to yield authority to professional ministers. To cite one example, during the 1920s, Roscoe Pound, the dean of Harvard Law School, was able on occasion to leverage his prominent status as a legal scholar to publicly weigh in on Hicksite theology and argue for an antisupernatural, rational religion (see chapters 6 and 7). In a mainline denomination, a figure like Pound would likely have had less influence. Pound's distaste for ministers was almost a point of pride, and he once threw a young Unitarian Harvard Divinity School student out of his office, citing his Quaker aversion to abetting "hireling priestcraft."

Hicksites and Friends in FGC already had an educated leadership, working in careers beyond the ministry, and they saw little need to radically innovate in this regard.[38]

THE CHANGING NATURE OF MINISTRY

The distinction between programmed and unprogrammed Friends was firmly established by the mid-1920s, but there continued to be attempts to innovate on ministerial practice. Several meetings, mostly affiliated with Hicksite Quakerism, experimented with creating "executive secretary" positions. Often this paid role was conceived of as a middle ground between pastoral Quakerism and the unprogrammed tradition, allowing leadership over administrative affairs and providing pastoral care to meetings while not fully directing meetings for worship. Gurneyite D. Elton Trueblood held this position in Boston Monthly Meeting from 1924 to 1927 and described the ideal: "The theory is [the executive secretary] earns his living six days a week and not on Sunday. He is not a conspicuous leader, but rather the hidden servant." Some unprogrammed Quaker meetings and institutions (such as colleges and nonprofits) would eventually adopt the practice of having a "Friend-in-residence," a position that typically fulfilled many of the roles of executive secretary.[39]

By the mid-twentieth century, the ways that ministry had changed probably would have been unimaginable to early Friends. Unprogrammed Friends had paid denominational staff, but they had abolished recorded ministry. Pastoral Friends not only had paid clergy but, in 1960, even established a seminary, Earlham School of Religion, the first Quaker institution of its kind. Other seminaries would follow. Though their visions of ministry within the Religious Society of Friends were incompatible, both groups were convinced that they had managed to adapt to the needs of the contemporary world while still maintaining the essential core of Friends' practices.

CHAPTER 6

Quakers and "Religious Madness"

RICHARD KENT EVANS

It took only a few minutes into the first of his 1901 Gifford Lectures at the University of Edinburgh for William James to declare that George Fox was a "psychopath or détraqué of the deepest dye." James, the father of both religious studies and American psychology, meant it as a compliment. The Religious Society of Friends was, in James's view, "impossible to overpraise." Early Friends had preached "something more like the original gospel truth than men had ever known in England," and by the start of the twentieth century, the word "Quaker" had become synonymous with religious liberality and rationality. To James, Quakerism was a thoroughly modern religion, bound by a firm commitment to the limits of reason. But, James conceded, despite the fact that twentieth-century liberal Quakers were the embodiment of healthy, modern, rational, and reasoned religion, there seemed to be something about Quakerism that once drove Quakers mad. William James's pronouncement about the relationship between Quakerism and insanity—that Early Friends were frequently insane but that turn-of-the-twentieth-century liberal Quakerism was the quintessence of a healthy, reason-bound Protestantism—was not at all controversial when he said it in 1901. But it would have been seven decades prior. Until around the 1830s, European and American theorists of the mind—including medical practitioners, natural scientists, theologians, and philosophers—believed that Quakerism was an inherently dangerous religion that frequently drove Quakers insane.[1]

Beginning in the 1830s, however, Quakers—many of them on the cutting edge of the emerging field of psychiatry—convinced theorists of the mind in Europe and North America to reverse their position on Quakerism's relationship to insanity. Friends such as American alienists Pliny Earle and Amariah Brigham and certain British Friends, including James Cowles Prichard and three generations of Tukes, the family that founded and ran the famous Quaker asylum at York, argued that Quakerism was not a particularly dangerous religion; that other religions (Methodism and Spiritualism, especially) were far more dangerous to the mental health of their adherents; and, further, that Quakerism in fact protected its adherents from insanity more than any other religion. The effect of this intellectual work was that by the middle decades of the nineteenth century, psychiatrists and theorists of the mind in the Western world had almost entirely reversed their positions on Quakerism's relationship to insanity.

More importantly, nineteenth-century Quaker theorists of the mind encoded their version of Quakerism as the only safe religion for mental health and turned psychiatry's attention to the dangers posed by other religions. Quaker theorists of the mind, defending Quakerism against charges that it drove Quakers insane, described American Protestant practice, marking emotional, experiential forms of Protestantism and post-Protestantism as unhealthy and disordered. Before the 1830s, Friends were the embodiment of the dangers to mental health caused by false religious ideas. By the end of the century, if one wanted to observe a healthy religious mind—a mind immune to the charms of premodern superstition—one needed, so the Quaker theorists of mind claimed, to look no further than the Quakers. This remarkable transformation is the subject of this chapter.

QUAKER THEORIES OF THE MIND

Given that Quakers were once so frequently suspected of madness, it is ironic that Quaker theorists of the mind played such an outsized role in transforming the way their colleagues thought about the relationship between religion and insanity.

In their influential work, *Description of the Retreat*, published in 1813, Samuel Tuke, his son Henry, and a group of Yorkshire magistrates and Quaker lunacy reformers described how the "very horrid and filthy condition" at York Asylum, an eighteenth-century county hospital, had inspired Samuel Tuke's grandfather, William Tuke, a wealthy tea merchant, to create an alternative in the York Retreat, a private asylum that opened in 1796 with the backing of York Quarterly Meeting. The York Retreat was both a place for the long-term care of insane Quakers and a comfortable place for local Friends to recover from bouts of religious melancholy, a standard feature of Georgian Quaker spirituality. At York, William Tuke and his descendants pioneered an approach to the care of the mentally ill that they called moral treatment, a mistranslation of Philippe Pinel's *traitement moral*.[2]

British Quakers built upon the early success at the York Retreat to effect nothing short of a revolution in English psychiatry. After forcing the reluctant leadership at York Asylum to allow them in using legal maneuvers, the Tukes discovered mentally ill patients chained to excrement-covered walls. The scene was so revolting that members of the Tukes' investigating group vomited. They learned that attendants at York Asylum had murdered, raped, and defrauded patients and that officers forged medical records to cover up their abuses and embezzled funds. The following year, Quaker reformer Edward Wakefield led a separate investigation into Guy's Hospital, St. Luke's Hospital, and Bethlem (also known as Bedlam) Hospital and discovered that the horrors of York Asylum were the rule, not the exception. Wakefield convinced Parliament to open an investigation into English facilities for the treatment of the mentally ill, which found inhumane care and conditions at most of England's public and private psychiactric hospitals and workhouses and forced many of England's leading physicians to resign in scandal. The parliamentary commission praised the Quakers of York Retreat, however, for having proved that such inhumane treatment was not only unethical but medically counterproductive.[3]

After the parliamentary commission issued its report, the Quaker approach to the treatment of the mentally ill became the standard for psychiatric care in Britain and beyond. As we know from Charles L. Cherry's definitive histories of Quakers and mental illness, York Retreat set the template for a new kind of private insane asylum, run by Quakers or based on the Quaker model of treatment, that quickly took root on both sides of the Atlantic. Quaker and Quaker-inspired asylums opened in rapid succession in the United States. Friends Hospital opened in 1813 in Philadelphia;

McLean Asylum, in 1818 near Boston; Bloomingdale Insane Asylum, in 1821 in New York City; and Hartford Retreat, in 1824 in Connecticut. Moral treatment soon became its own reform movement in North America, Britain, Germany, France, and Italy, complete with its own journals and professional associations. In the United States, Quaker asylum keepers dominated intellectual discourse about mental illness from the 1830s on. Six of the thirteen founding members of the Association of Medical Superintendents of American Institutions for the Insane were Quakers, including the president, or ran Quaker asylums. (In 1921, that association changed its name to the American Psychiatric Association.) By the 1830s, Quakers led the psychiatric profession both in England and America, and Quaker ideas about the relationship between the brain and the mind, about the immortality or materiality of the soul, and about the nature of mental illness itself gained widespread acceptance among non-Quaker theorists of the mind.[4]

With Friends leading the way, theorists of the mind in the 1830s turned with renewed vigor to the debate over Quakerism's relationship to insanity. The question had become more pressing since the invention of a new mental illness called "religious madness." Religious madness was the creation of French psychiatrist Philippe Pinel, whose Salpêtrière Hospital in Paris overflowed with Catholics driven mad by the anticlericalism of the Jacobin dictatorship. Pinel thought his patients' psychiatric symptoms were caused by their now-antiquated commitment to Catholicism. He theorized that they suffered from a disease of the brain that began when false religious ideas entered the body through the sensory organs (such as heard from a sermon or read in a book). Once inside the body, these ideas inflamed the brain tissue, leaving behind something akin to a scar. This injury of the brain, Pinel argued, caused a wide variety of psychological symptoms that, if left untreated, progressively worsened until the patient suffered a psychotic break from which it was very difficult to recover. Those suffering from religious madness were "swelled up with morbid pride" or might be thinking of themselves as "a privileged being, an emissary of heaven, a prophet from the Almighty, or even a divine personage." These false ideas made it particularly difficult to treat the disease, for "what measures are likely to counteract the influence of mystic visions or revelations, of the truth of which he deems it blasphemy to express a doubt?"[5]

Pinel's theory of religious madness quickly became a standard diagnosis in the burgeoning field of psychiatry. Pinel presented his fullest theory of religious madness in his *Treatise on Insanity*, which was published in French in 1800 and became the world standard after it was translated into English in 1806. By 1809, Mexican psychiatrist Joseph Roxas was diagnosing patients with religious madness at his hospital in Mexico City. The influential Spanish psychiatrist Ramón López Matias published a monograph on religious madness in 1810. In 1812, America's leading physician, Benjamin Rush, introduced Pinel's theory of religious madness to American medicine. Soon, 10 percent of patients admitted to his Pennsylvania Hospital were there because they held "erroneous opinions on religion." By 1818, religious madness had entered the psychiatric textbooks in Germany, and German psychiatrists would become leading theorists of the disease in the 1840s. As the theory of religious madness spread throughout the Western world, its purported symptoms, causes, etiologies, and names were changed to match local contexts, but the core claim of religious madness stayed consistent: some religious ideas drove people insane.[6]

To theorists of the mind, religious madness was both terrifying for its metaphysical implications—how could religion ever lead to madness?—and tantalizing for the religious controversies it could solve. If Catholics, Quakers, Anglicans, and Methodists alike could contract the disease, how could any one form of Christianity claim to be the true religion? What did religious madness mean for religion and for humanity's relationship with God? The stakes of the religious madness debate were even higher for Quaker theorists of the mind. Quakers had long worried over the prevalence of insane Friends—a concern, no doubt, originating in both Quaker theology and history (it was George Fox, after all, who first suggested building a retreat for Friends wrestling with mental illness). The usual explanation for why Friends seemed to lose their reason so regularly was intermarriage, though by the first half of the eighteenth century, Friends prohibited the practice. But if the theory of religious madness was right—if religious ideas could drive people insane—and if Quakers were indeed overrepresented among those patients, religious madness portended something more ominous: what if it was Quakerism itself that drove Quakers mad?[7]

In hopes of answering both the physical and metaphysical questions raised by religious madness, psychiatrists and theologians on both sides of the Atlantic began arguing over which religion most frequently drove its adherents insane. They found that the most dangerous religion was Quakerism. Statistics from York Retreat—based on an exceedingly small sample size—seemed to show that three out of every thousand Quakers suffered from insanity, a rate that far outpaced any other religion's, or indeed any other population group's. George Man Burrows, a leading English physician and member of the Royal College of Physicians who ran the private asylum in London, believed that Quakers lost their minds more frequently than non-Quakers, but he remained ambivalent about whether the cause was Quaker beliefs and practices or too frequent intermarriage. As Charles L. Cherry has shown, anti-Quaker writers continued to attack Quakerism as dangerous to mental health well into the 1820s, and anti-Quaker polemicists used the phrase "mad Quaker" well into the nineteenth century.[8]

THE RELIGIOUS MADNESS DEBATE

By the mid-1830s, the religious madness debate had erupted in both Europe and North America. Carl Wigand Maximilian Jacobi, rightly considered the father of psychiatry in Germany, designed a clever experiment where he combed through the records of the over two thousand patients admitted to his asylum in Siegburg, near Cologne, with the goal of determining which religion correlated with higher rates of insanity. Jacobi thought his asylum provided the proper balance between the rich and the poor and between Catholics and Protestants, given its location in a region famous for its religious disputes. According to his calculations, among the four categories recorded by his asylum—Catholics, Lutherans, Mennonites (a category that might have included Quakers, if there had been any), and Jews—it was the Catholics who had the highest rate of insanity.[9]

Yet Jean-Pierre Falret, who had replaced Philippe Pinel as both the head of the famous Salpêtrière Hospital in Paris and the leading psychiatrist in France, came to a different conclusion: he was certain that the unusually high rate of suicide in England, as compared to countries in Europe, could be explained by the rise of Methodism. William Hallaran, a leading Irish psychiatrist who ran a public asylum in Cork, also observed that religious madness only affected Protestants. Though Catholics outnumbered Protestants at his asylum ten to one, he had never seen a Catholic contract the disease. Hallaran's findings were confirmed by the famous Belgian psychiatrist Joseph Guislain, who argued that religious madness only affected Protestant dissenters. The Italian psychiatrist Vincenzo Chiarugi split the difference: he argued that Catholics and Protestants both contracted religious madness at roughly the same rate but that Catholics experienced different symptoms than Protestants. According to Chiarugi, insanity affected the weak-minded, and the strength of one's mind correlated directly with one's social standing. Theorists of the mind should spend less time looking at rates of insanity among sects of Christianity, Chiarugi argued, and more time comparing rates of insanity between the rich and the poor.[10]

Quakers eager to defend their faith in the religious madness debate began combing through asylum records, hospital and poorhouse statistics, and census data in search of proof for their claim that Quakerism was at least as safe as any other form of Protestantism. Samuel Tuke published statistics from York Retreat showing that very few patients there suffered from mental illnesses originating in religion. The data puzzled Tuke's colleagues around the world, some of whom wondered how an asylum hosting so many Quakers could have so few instances of religious madness. In 1835, another prominent Quaker psychiatrist, James Cowles Prichard, asked Tuke to clarify his statistics. Tuke responded that only eight patients had been treated for mental illnesses related to religion between 1796 and the end of 1811—about 2 percent of all cases. And of those eight cases, none had been "excited by any special religious means or occasion." So, technically speaking, no one had ever been diagnosed with religious madness in the history of York Retreat. Those eight patients whose mental illness related to religion were "generally persons of rather weak and of contemplative minds," and several of them were not even Quakers.[11]

To press his argument even further, Tuke published, in 1841, a full collection of statistics gathered from the records kept at York Retreat since its opening in 1796 with the goal of proving that Quakers were not nearly as mad as everyone thought. Beginning in 1820, York Retreat had begun taking on wealthy patients who were not Quakers, and there were on average ten non-Quaker patients at York Retreat in any given year. Compared to non-Quakers, Tuke determined that Quaker patients at York recovered more often, lived longer, abused fewer substances, suffered fewer relapses, and had experienced fewer psychotic episodes prior to their admission. The difference between the outcomes of Quaker patients and non-Quaker patients wasn't large—and by no means was it statistically significant—but Tuke's readers (and there were many on both sides of the Atlantic) were convinced that the Tukes of York Retreat had concrete proof that Quakerism was not, in fact, the most dangerous religion.[12]

One of Tuke's most prominent allies in the religious madness debate was the aforementioned English Quaker physician James Cowles Prichard, who argued that Quakers were immune to religious madness and asked

Tuke to clarify his statistics. Prichard, who ran a public hospital in Bristol, suspected that religious madness was far less common than other theorists of the mind suggested. He had no doubt that religion could lead to insanity in those predisposed to mental illness, but he worried that psychiatrists and asylum keepers overdiagnosed religion as the cause of insanity in cases where disordered religion was only a symptom. "The mind of a lunatic," he wrote in his 1835 *Treatise on Insanity*, is frequently drawn to "ideas and feelings connected with an invisible world." But just because an insane person seemed preoccupied with certain religious ideas or practices did not mean, to Prichard, that those religious ideas and practices caused the insanity in the first place. Prichard was certain that religious madness did exist, but he thought Quakers were immune. "It seems," Prichard wrote, "that religious insanity so termed is a disorder from which the Society of Friends [is] in a great measure exempt."[13]

American alienist Amariah Brigham, superintendent of the Quaker-influenced Hartford Retreat in Connecticut, ignited a controversy in 1835 when he suggested that, among all the religions of the world, only the Society of Friends had developed a religious practice that kept its adherents safe from harm. Although Brigham came from a long line of Quakers, he attended an Episcopal church in Hartford to uphold, as he saw it, social expectations and lived most of his life as a skeptic with a Unitarian bent. That skepticism comes through in his *Observations on the Influence of Religion upon the Health and Physical Welfare of Mankind*. The book was Brigham's attempt to use his knowledge of the human mind to purge Christianity of religious practices he deemed dangerous to the physical and mental health of American Protestants.[14]

Brigham believed that the religious practices of everyday Americans contributed to an epidemic of insanity and other physical diseases. He saw American churches as shoddily built, poorly ventilated disease incubators outfitted with painful wooden pews designed, seemingly, for the purpose of human suffering. He had "no doubt" that the constant ringing of church bells had proved "fatal" and contributed to this epidemic. He believed that Christians should spend their Sabbaths resting and studying their Bibles in the comfort and safety of their own homes because the constant travel back and forth between home and church exposed Christians to dangerous temperature fluctuations, traveling accidents, animal attacks, and other terrors of the night. Even if one did manage to make it to church safely, dangerous preachers subjected their congregations to anxiety-inducing sermons, "mental agony," dangerous "excitements," and "contagious" zeal—all of which contributed to an alarming increase in insanity that, Brigham worried, was poisoning the heredity of future generations.[15]

Amariah Brigham's finding of danger in Christian practice struck many readers as overblown at best, heretical at worst. He thought that Christians should stop partaking of the Eucharist because the bread or the wine could contain impurities, because some people might be tempted to drink too deeply from the communion cup, and because in some denominations the Eucharist required contorting the body into positions—kneeling, for example—that led to injury. Brigham thought that baptism was downright deadly, that Jesus did not require it, and that "the practice ought to be abandoned." Given that American Protestantism seemed designed to drive people insane, Brigham remarked that one should not be "surprised at the number of the insane being so great, but rather that it should be so small."[16]

To Brigham, only one religious group struck the right balance between maintaining their proper duties to God and protecting their physical and mental health: the Religious Society of Friends. Brigham cited throughout his book the writings of both George Fox and Robert Barclay (whose thoughts on the appropriateness of Christian sacraments Brigham deemed "irrefutable" and whose interpretation of the Christian scriptures struck him as "unanswerable"). The Quakers, Brigham noted approvingly, did not celebrate any sacraments. Unlike other Protestant sects, Quakers did not claim the "special influence of [God's] Spirit to a few individuals and at particular times" but believed God's Spirit was accessible to all, regardless of sectarian divisions. Quakers did not have to worry about preachers driving them to madness with "vivid descriptions of hell." Most importantly, Quakers understood that, in the words of Brigham, "God has no supernatural dealings with men," so they were not tempted to bounce from one revival to the next, following the sensational and emotional outpourings of the Spirit, as other Protestants did. To Brigham, Quakerism was a religion fit for the modern world—sublimated to "reason, calm and enlightened."[17]

Though Brigham's defense of Quakerism in the religious madness debate bordered on the ridiculous, he and his Quaker colleagues successfully convinced the burgeoning field of psychiatry that Quakerism was not the most dangerous religion for the mental health of its adherents but among the safest. Carl Wigand Maximilian Jacobi was convinced. After translating Tuke's work into German, Jacobi determined that Quakers seemed to be mostly immune to religious madness and that the Quaker patients at the York Retreat seemed to be exempt also from mental illness originating in "pride, ambition, jealousy, rage, debauchery." Jacobi believed that Quakers avoided these diseases because of their strict moral code and the seriousness with which they took religious education. John Haslam, one of England's leading psychiatric writers, was also among the theorists of the mind convinced that Quakers were immune to religious madness. Haslam's is a somewhat remarkable position to take given the role that Quakers played in getting him dismissed from his post as apothecary at Bethlem Hospital in London in 1816. (He was one of several officers at that institution who resigned in scandal after having been found "wanting in humanity.")[18]

Assured of Quakerism's safety—and newly confident in their abilities to heal the mentally ill—Quaker activists spread moral treatment throughout Europe. Elizabeth Gurney Fry, the pioneering theorist of prison discipline, was also devoted to asylum reform. (There was much overlap between those two social causes.) In 1838, Fry—who as a young woman worried that she had tendencies toward religious madness—toured Salpêtrière, the famous women's asylum in Paris where Pinel had first formulated his theory of religious madness four decades earlier. Fry found the patients well cared for but worried over their lack of religious instruction. She became an advocate for "the universal circulation of the Scriptures" in asylums and used her fame to urge governments throughout Europe to supply asylum patients with the Bible. Fry believed that Bible reading was the "only means capable . . . of controlling the power of sin, and shedding light upon the darkness of superstition and infidelity."[19]

To Quaker theorists of the mind like Elizabeth Fry, Victorian domesticity was central to the treatment of the mentally ill. Fry urged asylum keepers to treat their patients, as much as possible, as they would sane people. All patients and staff were to dine together at one large table, as a family. Most Quaker asylums modeled on York Retreat employed women as nurses and maids and in other nonmedical positions; most Quaker-influenced asylums had more women on staff than men. At most York-influenced asylums (including Friends Hospital in Philadelphia and Bloomingdale Asylum in New York), the wife of the superintendent held a post as matron of the asylum and would have been involved in the day-to-day life of the institution. Friends Asylum, later Friends Hospital, divided its facilities by gender, which was typical. Women patients had their own library, replete with books written by women, which had been vetted by hospital staff.[20]

By the middle of the nineteenth century, Quaker theorists of the mind had exerted control over the burgeoning field of psychiatry. But the theory that Quakers were more susceptible to insanity did not go away entirely. In 1844, the London *Globe* published an article that used census data to argue that the frequency of insanity among members of the Society of Friends (by the paper's count, slightly less than three per thousand) far outpaced the rate in the British population at large. As the editors of the *Globe* reasoned, Quakers placed too much emphasis on upholding moral standards. When Friends inevitably failed to live up to their own ethical expectations, the article suggested, the weaker among them succumbed to madness. The London *Globe* article was controversial, and it threatened to undo the victories that Quaker theorists of the mind had won over the previous decade. No less an authority than Samuel Tuke again rose to Quakers' defense. Responding in the *Globe*, Tuke argued that the paper's findings had been based on a misreading of his statistics—the frequency of insane Quakers was actually slightly *more* than three per thousand. But, Tuke continued, the apparent high rate of Quakers in insane asylums testified to the concern that Quakers showed their fellow Friends who suffered from mental illness. Quakers knew the signs of mental illness, so ill Friends received care promptly. Quaker-run asylums ranked among the best in the world, so Friends admitted to asylums lived long enough to be counted in the census—unlike pauper asylums and other public hospitals, which were more effective at killing their patients than curing them. Most critical, Tuke argued, was that the *Globe* had dramatically underestimated the rate of insanity among the general population. If it were possible to accurately count the number of mentally ill Britons—an unlikely task, given that many of them were incarcerated in poorhouses, prisons, or pauper asylums—Quakers would look quite sane in comparison. To Tuke, the *Globe* had gotten it exactly wrong. The data were clear: when compared to the general population, Quakers were less likely to suffer from insanity, not more. Still, the idea that Quakerism drove Quakers insane with great regularity persisted. As late as 1870, American Quakers worried that Quakerism drove people mad with its mystical ideas and "habits of introverted silence and self-examination." The editors of *Friends' Review* believed that there was "no question" that Quakerism drove some Friends insane and that asylums like York Retreat and Friends Hospital were filled with Quakers whose religious beliefs or practices put them there.[21]

On the whole, however, Quaker theorists of the mind won the religious madness debate. They did so not by critiquing the central claims of religious madness—that certain religious ideas cause insanity—but by arguing that the real danger lay in the ideas being spread by other religions. Amariah Brigham, who suggested that only Quakers had found the right balance between duty to God and mental health, thought that Methodism was the most dangerous form of Christianity, that fire-and-brimstone preachers frequently drove Methodists insane, and that Methodist camp meetings "gave rise to alarming epidemics," both physical and mental. In 1845, Samuel Woodward, the president of the Association of Medical Superintendents of American Institutions for the Insane, raised the alarm about a new epidemic of religious madness caused by the apocalyptic teachings of the American preacher William Miller. Woodward's asylum was full of new patients diagnosed with religious madness who seemed to have been driven insane by Miller's ideas, and there was no sign of the epidemic abating. Woodward worried that American psychiatrists had "yet seen only a small part of the evils this doctrine has produced." His Quaker colleague Pliny Earle, who began his psychiatric career at Friends Hospital before taking charge of Bloomingdale Asylum in New York, agreed that Millerism was fueling an alarming epidemic of religious madness. He considered Millerism a "grotesque mask" of "fanaticism" and "zeal untempered with prudence" that covered the face of "true religion," which was "pure religion and undefiled." In the 1850s, American Quakers helped stoke new concerns that Spiritualism had triggered an epidemic of religious madness of alarming proportions, and in 1864, a patient was admitted to Friends Hospital because of religious madness caused by having attended a Spiritualist séance.[22]

Quakers also won the religious madness debate because they held the power to determine which religious experiences were healthy and which religious experiences were insane. The era of asylums, roughly the 1820s to the 1850s, was a period in which Quakers dominated intellectual discourse about the relationship between religion and insanity. The Tuke family remained atop British psychiatry for three generations: Daniel Hack Tuke, grandson of York Retreat's founder, Samuel Tuke, published in 1858 the landmark *Manual of Psychological Medicine*, a comprehensive guide to the diagnosis, treatment, classification, and legal implications of insanity. Tuke's *Manual* soon became the standard work on psychiatry in the Anglophone world and went through three editions before 1875. American psychiatry, too, was dominated by Quakers in the middle decades of the nineteenth century. Quakers and superintendents of Quaker asylums held the presidency of the Association of Medical Superintendents of American Institutions for the Insane fairly consistently through the 1870s. During the era of asylums, Quakers went from the object of study to the ones doing the observation. A chapter of Tuke's *Manual* listed various religious groups throughout history that were supposed to have suffered from religious madness, including the Mormons, Spiritualists, and the Agapemonites. Notably missing from Tuke's list: the Quakers.[23]

RELIGIOUS MADNESS IN THE INVENTION OF LIBERAL QUAKERISM

The distinction forced by religious madness—between sane and insane religious experiences—is key to understanding the emergence of liberal Quakerism in the last decade of the nineteenth century. As we have already seen, William James famously adopted that distinction in his *Varieties of Religious Experience* (1902), a text that was important to the first generation of liberal Friends. James was particularly interested in the inner lives of those few "geniuses" whose "nervous instability," "discordant" inner lives, and "abnormal psychical visitations" imbued them with higher truths that stirred the masses to follow them on their path to God.[24] The key to understanding religion, James believed, was to account for its "pathological aspects"—religious insanity chief among them. Insanity, disordered minds, mystical raptures, intoxicated trances, and other forms of unreason were not aberrations from true religion but alternative epistemologies.[25] Using George Fox as his prime example, James argued that religious madness and religious genius are often difficult to discern, even within the same individual.

William James, evoking earlier Quaker theorists of the mind, believed that the healthiest religion looked a great deal like rationalistic, mystical, liberal Quakerism. Several of James's lectures were devoted to advocating what he called "the religion of healthy-mindedness." His ideal theology had its origin in the "fact"—which James believed to be universally true—that "man has a dual nature," one that is concerned with natural matters and another that responds to a higher sphere of being that we might call the divine. Through mystical experiences, one can gain access to this higher sphere of being, and the purpose of religion is to train the mind to habitually reside in this higher sphere. Mystical experiences, as James read them, seemed to confirm the validity of this theology and point toward an optimistic view of human nature. James's religion of healthy-mindedness was a nondogmatic, rationalistic form of Christian mysticism, and he believed that it had, since the middle of the nineteenth century, begun to exercise its influence in American Protestant circles under the banner of liberalism, New Thought, and mind cure. He recognized his ideal religion in the lives of Ralph Waldo Emerson, Walt Whitman, the New Thought philosopher Ralph Waldo Trine, Thomas Ellwood, John Woolman, and George Fox, among others. The religion of healthy-mindedness was to be the true inheritor of the Christian tradition of inward-looking submission to the divine, which, in James's telling, "consisted in little more than the greater and greater emphasis attached to this crisis of self surrender."[26]

We recognize in James's religion many of the hallmarks of liberal Quakerism because the first generation of liberal Quakers responded to James's influential theory of religious madness—and his religion of healthy-mindedness—with great enthusiasm. John Wilhelm Rowntree and Rufus Jones endeavored to bring William James to lecture to British Friends. *The British Friend* suggested that a copy of *The Varieties of Religious Experience* ought to be in every meetinghouse and made available to every Quaker minister. James's interpretation of Quaker history, as an essentially mystical religion, found acceptance in the Rowntree History Series, the intellectual foundation for liberal Quakerism. In sociologist Stephen A. Kent's judgment, "No single non-historical work, in fact, can rival James's book for its influence on early 20th century interpretations of emerging Quakerism, even among members of the Society of Friends itself."[27]

Few Friends thought more deeply about the difference between sane and insane religious experiences than the American psychologist, philosopher, and activist Rufus Jones. Jones deeply admired William James and taught his *Principles of Psychology* at Haverford for decades.[28] With James's ideas, Rufus Jones transformed the old distinction forced by religious madness—between healthy and unhealthy religious experiences—into a theory of positive and negative mysticism. Jones agreed with James that all mystical experiences "are abnormal and pathological," and, like James, he believed that these disordered states could contain promising insight into the deeper truths of human experience. "The *real* mystic," Jones explained in his 1909

Studies in Mystical Religion, is one who has "realized his life upward in full union with God" but has done so without the dramatic and "abnormal" psychic manifestations associated with religious madness. But there is another tradition that goes by the name of "mysticism." This "negative mysticism" manifests as "trances, losses of consciousness, automatisms, visions of lights, audition of voices, 'stigmata,' and such-like experiences" and is "in no way distinguishable" from mental illness. Through his voluminous and influential public writing, Jones warned against religious experiences that he and James associated with religious madness and advocated for a rational mysticism that protected the mental health of its practitioners.[29] Like prior theorists of the mind, Rufus Jones believed that such a thing as religious madness existed and that liberal Quakerism was a particularly effective prophylactic against it. With William James, Rufus Jones ensured that a concern for the limits of religious experience would become a hallmark of liberal Quakerism in the twentieth century.

CONCLUSION

Before roughly 1830, theorists of the mind believed that Quakerism was an unusually dangerous religion for the mental health of its adherents. By the second half of the nineteenth century, theorists of the mind generally agreed that religious madness was a real disease, that it seemed to originate from false religious ideas, and that it was a disease to which Quakers were particularly resistant. The longer legacy of this transformation is that it was Quakers who decided which religious experiences were healthy and which were disordered. Daniel Hack Tuke explained in his *Manual of Psychological Medicine* what he viewed as the difference between normal, healthy religious experience and unhealthy religious insanity. Healthy religious experience—"true religion"—was unemotional, unceremonial, Quietist, and liberal. Disordered religious experience was emotional, ecstatic, and sectarian. To Tuke, a healthy mind was marked by "weakness, humility, and sincerity." A diseased mind saw angels, heard the voice of God, or uttered prophecy.[30]

In order to create a modern form of Christianity, one safe for an age of reason, Quaker theorists of the mind had to narrow the range of experiences that counted as authentic religious experience. What may have passed for authentic religious experience in previous centuries—seeing and conversing with angels and uttering prophecy, for example—became, over the course of the nineteenth century, proof of insanity. For Quaker theorists of the mind, if Christianity were to survive the modern world—if belief could coexist with reason—then Christianity had to change. If Christianity was to be made fit for an age of reason, it had to look more like liberal Quakerism.

CHAPTER 7

Quakers of the Liberal Renaissance, 1870–1930
Rediscovering the Light Within

JOANNA CLARE DALES

This study focuses mainly on liberal Quakerism in Britain, but developments among American Friends are not ignored. In both communities, liberalism defined itself against the evangelicalism that dominated the Quaker movement during the nineteenth century, but the progress of liberalism was different in each country. The differences were not softened by the considerable amount of intervisitation, and Quakers of all shades of opinion were keenly aware, not to say wary, of each other's proceedings.

For the purposes of this essay, "liberal Quakerism" means, in the first place, the appeal to reason as the basis of religious authority. It is significant that the document that rudely broke in upon the evangelical Quaker consensus in Britain in 1884 was called *A Reasonable Faith*: its authors demanded that beliefs be subjected to rational inquiry. Thus, liberal Quakers accepted the need for biblical criticism and faced the challenges presented by scientific discoveries. In this acceptance, they were heirs of the eighteenth-century Enlightenment. Liberal Quakers, however, believed that there was more to life than was evident to the outward senses as interpreted by the rational mind. Like William Blake, William Wordsworth, Samuel Tayler Coleridge, Ralph Waldo Emerson, and Margaret Fuller, they sought wisdom through feeling and intuition, but above all through the divine gift of the "Light Within."[1]

Liberal Quakers believed that science and religion could work together to produce a sense of human nature widely different from that prevailing in seventeenth-century Puritan England, where Quakerism began. At that time, Christian thinking was dominated by the belief that humankind had fallen, through disobedience, into a state of corruption from which it was powerless to extricate itself, hence the necessity for Christ's sacrifice. Nineteenth-century evangelical Christians continued to emphasize the Cross as the only remedy for the corruption of human nature. Liberal Christians, Quakers among them, thought instead in terms of a human nature evolving from its animal past to become steadily wiser and more humane. With this optimistic outlook came an emphasis on the loving nature of a God working with and within His most favored creature to bring about this end. The necessity of Christ's suffering the penalty due to human sin was questioned, while the idea of a punitive God and of Hell for the unrepentant was rejected: a loving God could no more punish His creatures with eternal torment than could a loving human father so treat his children.[2]

Liberal Quakers, no longer able to accept a literal reading of the Bible or evangelical views on God and atonement, turned to inwardness and, by extension, to mysticism. They brought into the perennial mystical tradition Romantic subjectivity and individualism. In Coleridge's influential *Aids to Reflection*, they could find the statement: "That which we find within ourselves, which is more than ourselves, and yet the ground of whatever is good and permanent therein, is the substance and life of all other knowledge." The American Quaker Rufus Jones (1863–1948), who conducted extensive studies in the history of mysticism and insisted that Quakerism was an inherently mystical religion, incorporated in his philosophy the Romantics' sense of the divine potential within the human subject, especially as he found it in American Romantics like Ralph Waldo Emerson (1803–1882), who declared, "God in us worships God."[3]

The result was a religion in which mysticism shaded into humanism. Hugh Rock has argued that Jones "never did establish that Quakerism is a mystical religion," because his "affirmation mysticism" does not fit the classic view that the mystic's goal is annihilation of the self in God. Liberal Quakers like Jones, Edward Grubb (1855–1939), and John William Graham (1859–1932) based their claim that Quakerism was mystical on George

Fox's conviction that Christ was present in the hearts and minds of human beings, but they knew that the psychology of their time was different from that prevailing in the seventeenth century. The new psychology, said Jones, had to be accommodated in twentieth-century interpretations of the "Inward Light," just as liberal Christianity had had to come to terms with nineteenth-century geology, biology, and sense of history. This meant, for Jones, rejecting the idea of the Light as a supernatural essence injected from without. Instead, he insisted that God and human nature were "conjunct"—or, as Edward Grubb said: "'The Light Within' is just as much a human faculty as is 'Reason' in its widest sense; it is the power of a self-conscious person to enter into communion with God. It is also Divine; for it is God revealing Himself within us."[4]

Jones was the principal architect of liberal Quakerism in the United States, and his impact on Quakerism in Britain was hardly less decisive. He and others who thought like him also insisted that Quaker mysticism was inseparable from active engagement in society and endeavors to improve it. The history of liberal Quakerism in both America and Britain is in large part a history of social activism, from abolitionism in America to housing reform in Britain. This chapter, however, focuses on the theological aspects of the subject.[5]

Liberal Quakers of the nineteenth century, while necessarily influenced by the climate of opinion in their day, cultivated a sense of their unique history and "peculiar" way of approaching the divine. This was no longer the peculiarity of a people sheltered from the "world," with a special dress code and antiquated modes of speech. Rather, it was an insistence on the reality and authority of the Inward Light as they found it in the teachings of Early Friends, interpreted according to their own ideas about human nature. For most liberals, this entailed retention of the meeting for worship based in silence, enabling participants to focus on the Inward Light, which might then become the source of inspired words.[6]

Even in the seventeenth century, emphasis on the "Light" within the individual conscience led to divisions. To alleviate the dangers of individualism, a system was devised whereby "concerns" were brought before a meeting to test whether they were indeed in accordance with God's will. The quest for an elusive unity was a recurrent theme, as disagreement and division plagued the movement during the nineteenth century, leading, in America, to proliferating separations along with various attempts to promote unity. Among evangelical Quakers, unity might be sought by appealing to the authority of the Bible as against the Inward Light, but this was no adequate remedy. The British Quaker Edward Grubb noted, with a sidelong glance at Quakers in America, that the divisions among "those who ground themselves most unreservedly on 'the plain declarations of Scripture' as their only guide" were especially numerous and bitter.[7]

The crucial occasion at which British Quakers became irreversibly set on course to become the nonprescriptive religious body that they have become was the Manchester Conference of 1895. From today's perspective, the trajectory from evangelicalism to liberalism seems inevitable. It is quite possible, however, that British Quakers might have split, as happened in the "Beaconite" separation of the 1830s, with several Friends leaving the Society, because they distrusted reliance on the Inward Light rather than scripture. That the great majority of Quakers in Britain remained united at the time of the conference and after was largely due to the determination, skill, and conviction of a few individuals.[8]

AN AGE OF DOUBT

During the Victorian age, many in Britain, both upper and working class, left the Church because they could no longer accept its authority or that of the Bible, whether intellectual or moral: an example is James Anthony Froude, author *The Nemesis of Faith* (1849), whose attack on the morality of the Bible, especially the New Testament threats of eternal punishment and the cruel and illogical doctrine of atonement, anticipated the views of the authors of *A Reasonable Faith* of 1884.[9]

With the publication of Charles Darwin's *Origin of Species by Means of Natural Selection* in 1859 and of the multiauthored *Essays and Reviews* in 1860, choices between faith and doubt became starker. The freethinking Harriet Martineau hailed Darwin's book for its antireligious implications: "What a book it is! Overthrowing (if true) revealed Religion on the one hand, & Natural (as far as Final Causes and Design are concerned) on the other." "Revealed" religion was threatened because the sacred story, beginning with Creation and the Fall of Adam and finishing with the Last Judgment, was incompatible with the story of the gradual emergence of different species through natural selection. Equally, natural religion, whereby God is to be known through His works, was for some thinkers ruled out by the spectacle of the cruelty and randomness inherent in the evolutionary process.[10]

Essays and Reviews was the work of seven scholars, soon dubbed "Seven against Christ," all of them Anglican, six of them ordained priests. Each expressed disbelief in the literal veracity of the Bible; they shocked their readers by retaining their positions in the Church. The Reverend Rowland Williams pleaded for the Coleridgean idea of the "verifying faculty"—something within the human subject that makes it possible in reading the Bible, as in other spheres, to distinguish truth from falsehood. "We are to have the witness in ourselves," he said, quoting from the Bible. Early Quakers likewise insisted that the Bible is to be understood through the "Spirit that gave it forth"—that is, the Bible is to be understood by means of the Inward Light.[11]

What became known as "Broad Church" theology developed among individuals who chose to remain Christians but felt unable to cling to an unaltered faith in the Bible. This type of thinking had a profound effect on liberal Quakerism. The most prominent figure in the Broad Church movement was Frederick Denison Maurice (1805–1872), who famously lost his Chair at King's College London for questioning the doctrine of everlasting punishment for sinners. Herbert George Wood (1879–1963), second director of studies at Woodbrooke, the Quaker college near Birmingham founded after the Manchester Conference, wrote an admiring biography of Maurice. Some representatives of the Broad Church theology also admired the Quakers: Dr. Alexander McLaren, for instance, the Baptist preacher who led the "deputation" of non-Quaker ministers at the Manchester Conference, praised the Quakers for their "emphatic recognition of the Inner Light and guiding Spirit."[12]

LIBERAL QUAKERISM IN AMERICA: BACKGROUND AND DEVELOPMENT

British Quakers as a body eventually made the transition from evangelicalism to liberalism over a single generation with surprisingly little friction and no major split. Despite the "Duncanite" rebellion in the 1860s, the Society as a whole retained an evangelical, Bible-based faith until it was ready to change definitively during the late nineteenth and early twentieth centuries. In America, by contrast, moves toward liberalism took place among Quakers throughout the nineteenth century alongside ever-stronger currents of evangelicalism (see chapter 4). The differences gave rise to branching separations, reflecting the diverse strands of religious thought and practice coexisting in a country with no established church and a passion for independence.[13]

Outside the Quaker fold, powerful liberalizing trends existed among New England Unitarians early in the nineteenth century. The Unitarian preacher William Ellery Channing (1789–1842) preached a liberal reading of the Bible informed by German criticism; he denounced traditional views of atonement as presenting a false, "unscriptural" view of a harsh God requiring sacrifice for sin. His pronouncements had distinctive liberal Quaker resonances. Channing wrote of the "Light Indwelling: the Divine Likeness," which he said was deducible from nature and apprehended through experience: "The Infinite Light would be forever hidden from us did not kindred rays dawn and brighten within us." As liberal Quakers in both America and Britain turned to Early Friends' teachings on the Light Within as their guide in life rather than the Bible, their understanding of the Light had at least as much in common with Channing's sense of it as with George Fox's.[14]

The idea of "light" inherent in human personality informed Ralph Waldo Emerson's insistence on "self-reliance" as the only basis for authentic living. Emerson began his career as a Unitarian pastor, in Channing's shadow, but he soon found even Unitarianism too constricting. In his controversial "Divinity School Address," Emerson spoke to his audience of budding Christian leaders about the "Indwelling Supreme Spirit" that could be reached only by intuition, not by instruction. Emerson's teaching paved the way for the transcendentalist movement, with its emphasis on individual spiritual enlightenment free of religious institutions.[15]

Rufus Jones studied Emerson in college. He found affinities between Emerson's teaching and that of George Fox that enabled him to begin his identification of Quakerism as a mystical religion. Emerson and Fox helped him gain a liberating sense of human nature as possessing within itself the means to mystical transcendence, rather than as lost, ruined, and incapable of redemption except through the undeserved and arbitrary mercy of God, as John Calvin taught. Jones thought that the sense of human potential that he found in Early Friends' thinking had been endangered or lost by Quakers under the sway of evangelicalism. He praised the liberal-minded Quaker poet John Greenleaf Whittier (1807–1892) for resisting this trend—"the shifting of base from the ancient position of the Light Within to a theology kin to that of Calvin"—and went on to quote Whittier's words on the Light as "disclosing the law and the prophets in our own souls."[16]

Elias Hicks (1748–1830), the American Quaker who gave his name to the Quakers who separated from the "Orthodox" in 1828 (the Hicksites), was as "self-reliant" in his theology as Emerson could desire. His sense of the Light Within gave him a license to express views that many Quakers saw as dangerously heterodox. The Great Separation may not have been brought about by doctrinal variance alone, but differences on the relative authority of scripture and the Light certainly played a part. Hicksites were defined by one among them in 1825 (before the Great Separation) as "those who choose to read the Bible and think for themselves."[17]

The course followed by Orthodox Friends was much influenced by the English Quaker Joseph John Gurney (1748–1847), who traveled as a Quaker minister in America in the years 1837 to 1840; his followers became known as Gurneyites. Then, during the 1840s, a number of Friends, under the leadership of John Wilbur (1774–1856), became so disturbed by trends in the Gurneyite meetings that formal separations took place in several yearly meetings. The Wilburites considered the Gurneyites as having departed from the essential truths of Quakerism, especially in placing the authority of scripture above that of the Inward Light. Toward the end of the century, some other Orthodox Quakers who had become dissatisfied with Gurneyite trends sought a return to traditional Quakerism. They became known in time as "conservative" Friends. The conservatives were not necessarily liberal in their theology, but there was a bridge between them and liberal Quakerism in their rejection of the Bible as the ultimate authority in favor of the Light Within, just as there was between the Quietist Friends in Britain and the new liberalism. In contrast, the radically evangelical Ohio Yearly Meeting in 1878 went so far in the opposite direction as to declare the doctrine of the Inner Light "dangerous, unsound, and unscriptural."[18]

Hicksites and Orthodox alike experienced further divisions and much mutual bitterness within their own ranks over the course of the century, with differences as to the authority of the Light playing an important part. Among the Hicksites there arose, in the years following 1843, various separatist groups calling themselves Progressive or Congregational Friends. The immediate cause of these separations had to do with slavery: all Friends were at least theoretically in favor of abolition, but opinions varied as to pace and tactics (see chapter 2). In addition, the Progressive Friends also stood unequivocally for intellectual and religious freedom.[19]

The career of Lucretia Coffin Mott (1793–1880) illustrates the connection between liberalism in political and social affairs and in theology. Mott remained within the main body of the Hicksite branch despite tensions and threats of disownment. Although she is best known now for her campaigning zeal in the causes of abolition and women's rights, she deserves to be remembered too for her rejection of doctrinal rigidity and her defense of the Inner Light—a term she used to denote the Light's presence within as a part of human personality, just as Emerson and the transcendentalists taught, and not an alien infusion.[20]

By 1870, according to Thomas Hamm, the Hicksites, as a whole, were liberal. At the end of the century, liberal Friends like John William Graham found them far more congenial than the Orthodox and were infuriated by London Yearly Meeting's refusal to acknowledge the Hicksites' credentials by rejecting correspondence with them.[21]

Meanwhile, Orthodox Friends were increasingly dominated by evangelical tendencies. During the 1860s and 1870s, they embraced the revivalist movement that was sweeping American Christendom under the impact of skilled preachers like Charles Grandison Finney (1792–1875). Evangelicals were still subject to further disagreements among themselves. In an attempt to secure unity, a conference of Gurneyite Quakers was held in Richmond, Indiana, in the autumn of 1887. The impetus was the question whether to "tolerate" the optional use of outward sacraments—especially water baptism, something Quakers had opposed from the beginning—but the agenda expanded into an attempt to reach agreement on essential Quaker beliefs and practices. During the conference, the English Friend Joseph Bevan Braithwaite (1818–1905), who was there representing London Yearly Meeting, was asked to put together a declaration of faith as the grounds for unity. Braithwaite, Gurney's disciple and memoirist, was the most powerful opponent of liberalism in Britain. He was for many years "drafter in chief" of the London Yearly Meeting epistles, from which he drew largely for his declaration.[22]

The Richmond Declaration glanced at the Inward Light in terms that effectively denied its universality: "We own no principle of spiritual light, but the influence of the Holy Spirit of God, bestowed on mankind in various measures and degrees, through Jesus Christ our Lord." Rufus Jones called the declaration "a relic of the past"; for him, Quakerism was a "dynamic faith" and not to be confined within the rigid boundaries of a "creed." The declaration was adopted by most of the yearly meetings represented at Richmond (agreeing to reject outward sacraments), but when Braithwaite brought it to London Yearly Meeting in 1888, expecting Friends there to endorse it, there was vigorous opposition. Two men who were to become prominent in the liberal renaissance, John William Graham and Edward Grubb, each spoke against its adoption, and they were supported by some evangelical Friends who saw it as a "creed" and could not accept such a departure from Quaker norms. The upshot was that London Yearly Meeting declined either to accept or reject the declaration.[23]

Most yearly meetings represented at Richmond accepted the declaration, with its emphasis on biblical authority and sound doctrine. However, some liberal and modernist voices within those same Gurneyite yearly meetings were already raising doubts about the most extreme claims other Friends were making for biblical authority and instantaneous sanctification. They included such Friends as Nereus Mendenhall, with his condemnation of "bibliolatry." Liberal Quakers were also wary of the teaching on salvation promoted by evangelical leaders like David B. Updegraff. According to this teaching, the sinner was "justified" in an instant when he or she came to faith in the redeeming blood of Christ and was subsequently "sanctified," or made perfectly holy, through the work of the Holy Spirit. There was continuity between the Holiness movement among nineteenth-century Quakers and the perfectionism of the earliest Friends, as Carole Spencer has shown, but for modernist Friends, the process promoted by the revivalists could seem mechanical and contrived. They found among Early Friends evidence for the belief that sanctification was a gradual process. Nereus Mendenhall's daughter Mary Mendenhall Hobbs, who became a notable spokesperson for modernist Quaker values, came to repudiate her early experience at the hands of Updegraff himself, when she was "put through all the paces" and declared sanctified.[24]

Rufus Jones did not repudiate the conversion experience he underwent as a boy at a revival meeting, feeling it to be a valuable step in his spiritual progress, but his mature faith was quite different from any doctrine of immediate justification and sanctification. He taught that the whole of life could and should be a process of striving toward an ever-expanding ideal. Jones did not suffer the purgatory of doubt so common among nineteenth-century British Christians. Edward Worsdell, Edward Grubb, John William Graham, and John Wilhelm Rowntree all had to shed the evangelical teaching they had been brought up with before they could reach a faith they felt to be real. Jones, who hated quarrels and divisions, was keen to incorporate into his vision of Quakerism what he found most valuable among evangelical Quakers: their fervor, their intense quest for holiness, their sense of mission, their ecumenical outlook, and their readiness to cooperate with other Christians. But for Jones, evangelicals "had no new stock of ideas"; it was necessary to move beyond them to the future but also to revisit the past. Like other liberal Quakers both in America and in Britain, Jones sought inspiration for the future through a new appreciation of the "ancient" ways.[25]

BRITISH QUAKERS: STEPS TOWARD LIBERALISM

In Britain, the most significant attempt to break the evangelical mold in the mid-nineteenth century was that led by David Duncan in Manchester. Duncan (1825?–1871), a convinced Quaker, first gave offense to powerful evangelical Friends in 1861 with a lecture on the newly published *Essays and Reviews*. Controversy erupted. A yearly meeting committee dominated by Joseph Bevan Braithwaite was sent to Manchester to impose discipline. Braithwaite, in a move foreshadowing his activity at Richmond, persuaded other members of the committee to issue a "declaration" of the doctrinal position of the Society. Duncan was asked to "moderate his views," at which point he declared that "he would die for what he felt to be the truth" and continued to give offense to evangelical Friends by inviting Friends to meet a controversial Anglican clergyman, Charles Voysey. This further provocation brought about his disownment; then, before the arguments could be resolved, Duncan suddenly died. A supporter of his, Edward Trusted Bennett, was subsequently expelled from the Society, a victim of "the last great heresy hunt in London Yearly Meeting," according to John William Graham. An eloquent protest was voiced by Mary Jane Hodgson, contrasting Braithwaite's attitude to "heresy" with that of Christ: Christ, "the greatest heretic of his time, would welcome me to his society and not excommunicate me." The Duncanite remnant was soon dispersed, and doctrinal rigidity won out over freedom of thought and expression—for the time being.[26]

After the defeat of the Richmond Declaration, British Friends still had to contend with another perceived threat from across the Atlantic: the large-scale abandonment of the meeting for worship based on silent waiting. Many Quaker meetings in America had become "Friends' Churches," led by pastors, with prepared services (see chapter 5). Fears that the old-style meeting for worship might succumb to transatlantic contagion were exacerbated by the activities in Britain of the Home Mission Committee (HMC). The HMC was set up in 1882 with two main aims: (1) to support attempts that were already being made to encourage students at adult schools to attend Quaker meetings, and (2) to enliven small and struggling meetings. Anxiety arose in response to the evangelical spirit in which both these aims were carried out. "Mission" meetings were set up specifically for adult school students. Their leaders were evangelicals, and they were paid. To put a paid pastor at the head of a Quaker meeting seemed to Joseph Bevan Braithwaite Jr. (1855–1934) tantamount to dethroning Christ, the only Head of the Church. Similarly, paid mission workers sent to support struggling meetings were seen as endangering the Quaker ideal of direct access to the Divine Spirit. There were, however, Friends who argued that rigid adherence to the prohibition of payment amounted to a "property qualification," since those who had to earn a living could not afford to give their time to the ministry. John Stephenson Rowntree argued strenuously for a relaxation of the prohibition, noting that payment was already made for missionaries working overseas; John William Graham responded by associating the practice of the HMC with that of the western yearly meetings in America. Both, he claimed, violated the principles of Early Friends.[27]

A special conference on home mission took place in the autumn of 1892, where younger Quakers like Joseph Bevan Braithwaite Jr. and John William Graham spoke on behalf of old Quaker ways. The opponents of the HMC gained a qualified victory. A strong perception remained, however, that Quaker meetings were not always, or often, the spirit-filled occasions that their apologists wished for. Edward Grubb complained of the mismatch between the "noble" ideal of "reverential silence," in which individuals approach the "perfect purity and justice" of God without human mediation, and the actuality, where "many of us are positively afraid to invite our friends, because of the spiritual poverty they are likely to find when they come."[28]

The problem was seen to lie in the spoken ministry, or lack of it: how was the ministry to be improved without recourse to professionalization? The ideal was "prophetic ministry," God speaking through His chosen vessel, yet Friends agreed that ministry required dedication and training as well as "that spiritual insight, vigor and tenacity, which communion with the Unseen can alone supply." Restoring the ideal, some felt, was crucial to the life of the Society. John Wilhelm Rowntree wrote in a letter to Graham, "I feel that on the solution of the problem our future as a church depends." Graham later complemented this assertion with a statement on the "prophetic ministry, for the preservation of which the Society of Friends now chiefly exists as a separate Church."[29]

THEOLOGICAL CHALLENGES

Many Quakers in the 1880s and 1890s were in Graham's position of "being compelled to dig up [their] beliefs and see what they grow from." Some young Quakers gave up, such as Graham's university friend Harry Rawlings, who became an agnostic and abandoned the Society of Friends. Others, like Graham and Grubb, succeeded in finding a nondogmatic faith that could accommodate Darwinism and modern attitudes toward the Bible.[30]

In addition to the challenges driving individuals into agnosticism, liberal Quakers had to contend with a type of evangelicalism that arose in British religious circles toward the end of the nineteenth century in reaction to the doctrinal looseness of the Broad Church party. It was characterized by extreme emotionalism, an emphasis on a standardized conversion experience as a necessary rite of passage, Bible literalism, and a theology of atonement that seemed to many thoughtful people both irrational and immoral. All this evangelical practice and doctrine was sanctioned by the threat of eternal punishment for nonbelievers. At the forefront of this movement was the immensely popular Baptist preacher Charles Haddon Spurgeon (1834–1892), who, in 1888, left the Baptist Union rather than tolerate the view then gaining ground there, as elsewhere, that there might be "future probation" for sinners after death rather than an eternity of punishment.[31]

The Richmond Declaration contained the words, "We believe that the punishment of the wicked and the blessedness of the righteous shall be everlasting." Joseph Rowntree (1836–1925), father of John Wilhelm Rowntree, objected particularly to this sentence. Liberal-minded Friends believed that the God who made such threats could not be the object of their devotion. Rufus Jones, in his college years in America in the 1880s, was moved by George MacDonald's novel *Robert Falconer* (1865), which dramatized revolt against the doctrine of a punitive God. Among British Quakers, a milestone in the move away from an "angry God" was marked by the publication of *A Reasonable Faith* in 1884. Thanks to progressive revelation, according to its three authors, humankind had come by stages to ever more adequate ideas of what God is like, moving from a "revengeful, almost diabolical" image through the deist picture of a distant, unconcerned Creator, and then to that of a "ruler & Judge, holy indeed, but stern & relentless," until now He could be seen as "Our Father" indeed. They argued that the Bible itself contained conceptions of God that had to be outgrown.[32]

Edward Worsdell's *The Gospel of Divine Help* treated the subjects broached by these "three Friends" in more depth but in the same vein. Worsdell, like Jones, approved of George MacDonald's plea for a gentler concept of God. His *Gospel* contained a moving autobiographical account of growing up under the evangelical dispensation and then being cast into despair by the impossibility of loving a God who threatened him with Hell because he could not love Him. He went on to claim that God seeks to free humankind from the bondage of sin rather than from its consequences. Salvation means personal transformation rather than escape from pain. Hellfire preachments cannot have a good effect: "Selfish terror cannot nurture the higher life." It was entirely fitting that John Greenleaf Whittier should provide a prefatory note.[33]

The elder Joseph Bevan Braithwaite was, unsurprisingly, troubled by these developments. John William Graham described a conversation with him concerning Worsdell's book: "JBB . . . is greatly distressed about E. Worsdell's book; can't make out, poor man, why people find anything wrong with what seems to him good gospel; & wanted me to tell him what was the real difficulty. I have never seen him so moved before. I tried to explain, & to minimise differences & to show that the change from JBB to EW was not so great, & certainly not terrible, & to get it clearly into his mind that EW had written under a sense of religious duty, and in a heroic self sacrificing way." For all Graham's attempts to soothe his older friend, he could not cover over the generational gap between them.[34]

During the early 1890s, to judge from the *British Friend*, there was, in meetings and in Quaker schools, something of an upsurge of emphasis on blood as necessary for redemption. An anonymous article of 1893 complained that children were being taught that Abel's sacrifice was more acceptable than Cain's "*because he shed blood.*" The writer quoted from Whittier's poem "The Eternal Goodness" the words "nothing can be good in him / Which evil is in me." The distinguished physicist and influential Friend Silvanus P. Thompson lamented the recourse in some ministry to imagery of bloody sacrifice to appease the vengeance of an angry God. In this opinion, he was typical of liberal Friends reacting against remnants of evangelical preaching.[35]

THE MANCHESTER CONFERENCE (1895)

It was a religious society much exercised about its faith and its duty in the world that gathered at Mount Street Meetinghouse in Manchester on

November 11–14, 1895. The conference was set up following the reconstitution of the Home Mission Committee in 1893. Its remit was "to dispel the ignorance that, more or less, exists in the public mind with regard to the principles and practices of the Society, and to strengthen the attachment of its younger members to its work." The best-remembered session of the conference, that on "the attitude of the Society of Friends towards modern thought," took place on the fourth day. Thomas Hodgkin, chair of the session, declared that Charles Lyell's and Charles Darwin's discoveries could be accepted among educated people without detriment to their Christian faith: once the idea of an "infinite Maker" was grasped, the age of the earth and the ancestry of humankind were of scant importance. J. Rendel Harris (1852–1941), expert in early biblical texts, pleaded for the free exercise of the intellect in matters of faith; he declared that "the internal discords of all Scriptures, and of all explanations of Scriptures, ought to be enough to convince us that we have no infallibility in the house, not a drop!" Silvanus P. Thompson spoke in favor of "honest, fearless, sacred doubt" in all matters accessible to scientific investigation, yet still maintained that "the illumination of the divine life within the soul, the Christ within, the witness of the Spirit, is a fact that science can neither explain nor investigate." Thus, all three were willing to countenance large holes in the edifice of traditional, Bible-based Christian belief. John William Graham rejoiced that Quakers could now take the leading place among Christians that they had earned through their time-honored resistance to fixed doctrines: "Men have got down to the bed rock of faith, so that the religious world has come round to the Indwelling Voice as its central conception, and so essential Quakerism holds the future in the hollow of its hand."[36]

The only paper in this session to urge caution with respect to modern thinking was presented by Joseph Bevan Braithwaite Sr. According to Braithwaite's daughter, when in old age he was asked about his response to new developments in religious thinking, he replied: "My dear, *my* views on all these subjects were settled more than sixty years ago." His conference paper made a gesture toward modern thought in referring to the work of Samuel Rolles Driver (1875–1914), one of the team responsible for the new "Revised Version" of the Old Testament and author of *Introduction to the Literature of the Old Testament* (1891). Yet Braithwaite insisted that Driver's conclusions "imply no change in respect to the Divine Attributes recorded in the Old Testament; no change in the lessons of human duty to be derived from it; no change as to the general position . . . that the Old Testament points prophetically to Christ." "No change" was the message inscribed on the barrier he attempted to set against the inroads of liberalism, but it was too late.[37]

The most arresting speech at the conference was probably that of twenty-seven-year-old John Wilhelm Rowntree in the session headed "Has Quakerism a Message for the World To-day?" Rowntree did not spare his elders: he accused Friends of "spiritual pride, false respectability, and unmanly deference to mere wealth or title," leading to an "invertebrate Christianity, which in its sluggish self-complacency is even ignorant of its weakness." He mentioned challenges to Christian belief as incentives to present "the ideal of the Christ in the thought-form of the age." Friends, he said, were well placed "to go beneath form and convention, and strike the deep springs of actual communion with the Father," but in practice they were so much given to formality and complacency that they disabled themselves from responding to the "perplexity and skepticism" of the age. If Quakers were to deliver a message to the world of their day, they had to wake up.[38]

AFTER THE CONFERENCE

John Wilhelm Rowntree (1868–1905), the Sir Galahad of the Quaker Renaissance, was a scion of the famous chocolate-making family in York. As well as ably serving the business, he directed his formidable intelligence and energy to addressing the intellectual, spiritual, and practical challenges facing the Religious Society of Friends. After the Manchester Conference, despite deafness and encroaching blindness, he became the undisputed leader of the liberalizing movement until his death in 1905 at the age of thirty-six. His active and intelligent enthusiasm, his charm, and his managerial ability gave Friends the impetus and guidance they needed for their renewal.[39]

Two of the most important developments fostered by Rowntree in the years following the conference were the Rowntree history project and the summer school movement, leading up to the Woodbrooke Settlement. A call for Quakers to consider their history was sounded by Matilda Sturge (1829–1903) in the opening address at the Manchester Conference, on "Early Quakerism—Its Spirit and Power." "Early Friends," she asserted, "bore witness against a blind, almost idolatrous, faith in the Bible and Bible texts"; they proclaimed that all of us possess a "witness to truth in our hearts"; and, moreover, they rejected the Calvinist doctrine of the utter depravity and helplessness of each human being who was not arbitrarily elected to escape Hell. All this, Sturge maintained, was of great help to their descendants who were struggling with the "difficulties which have arisen out of the growth of the scientific and critical spirit."[40]

John Wilhelm Rowntree was fully in accord with such claims, and he wanted to give them substance. He conceived the idea of a great work of scholarship that would provide the Society with a truthful account of the rock from which they were hewn. Some pioneering work had been done by Norman Penney, first full-time librarian to the Society of Friends and custodian of manuscripts, on which historians could build. Rowntree intended to carry out much of the work himself (planning it in consultation with his close friend Rufus Jones), but his early death prevented him from fulfilling his plan. Jones accepted as a sacred trust the task of carrying on with Rowntree's project. His main partner in this task was William Charles Braithwaite (1862–1922), second son of Joseph Bevan Braithwaite Sr. The work had the moral and financial backing of John Wilhelm's father, Joseph Rowntree.[41]

Braithwaite and Jones, with a good deal of help, realized the vision in the seven-volume work that bears Rowntree's name. Alice Southern has shown in detail how they used their findings to support the liberal Quakers' agenda. Notably, the authors brought to their historical work their late nineteenth-century sense of the potential for goodness in human nature. This had consequences for the doctrine of the Inward Light, as will be discussed. Contentious elements identified by Southern include the historians' sharp distinction between early Quakerism and Puritanism, resulting in misrepresentation or oversimplification of seventeenth-century Puritanism. Jones insisted that Early Friends' religious origins were to be found not in English or Scottish Puritanism but in Continental Christian mystical traditions, both Catholic and Protestant. Attempts have since been made to confute this thesis, one of the earliest (and perhaps the best) being the account of Quaker origins in Geoffrey F. Nuttall's 1946 book *The Holy Spirit in Puritan Faith and Experience*. Nuttall found that Early Friends are best understood as being at the radical end of a Puritan continuum, with thinkers like Richard Baxter at the conservative end.[42]

The educational potential of the Rowntree History Series, along with that of the Friends Historical Society and its journal, founded in 1903, was supplemented by the summer school movement and the foundation of Woodbrooke—both to a large degree dependent on the initiative of John

Wilhelm Rowntree. The first of these British national summer schools took place in Scarborough in 1897 and was followed by five more.[43]

There was a focus at the first school on new biblical research, with Rendel Harris speaking on newly discovered manuscripts. In the second summer school, which took place in Birmingham in 1899, Joan M. Fry (1862–1955), one of the many formidable women who helped further the Quaker Renaissance, spoke on the medieval mystic Johannes Tauler. She bade her auditors be like Tauler: "ready to go out into the ways of sadness and poverty" while keeping "the power of being alone with God." Tauler was already a favorite with Caroline Stephen; another woman Friend, Frances Cooke, quoted Tauler's advice on discerning the guidance of God "by a careful looking at home and abiding within the gates of thy own soul." The summer schools thus reflected not only the flourishing of paleographic biblical studies in which Harris played a distinguished part but also the contemporaneous fascination with mysticism seen also in the work of such Anglican luminaries as William Ralph "Dean" Inge and Evelyn Underhill. Jones's studies of the mystics followed an established Quaker trend of substantiating claims to the reality of the Light Within by reference to an earlier mystical tradition.[44]

Woodbrooke was conceived as a "permanent settlement" for serious study in order to give weight and authority to a ministry that would yet remain spontaneous and open to all, in accordance with the ideal of the "priesthood of all believers." Graham later insisted, "As priests ourselves, we ought to aim at being as well educated as the clergy. We should not prepare sermons, but we should prepare ourselves to be ready to preach when bidden to do so." It was an impossible requirement and rather far from George Fox's disparagement of human learning as part of the equipment of ministers. Thomas Kennedy has unearthed some misgivings among renaissance Friends on the score of a perceived threat to the freedom of the ministry from too much emphasis on intellectual attainment; Graham addressed such fears in three essays of the 1890s. At the dawn of the twentieth century, the urgent need for realization of the ideal was felt as keenly by the evangelical George Cadbury, the Birmingham chocolate magnate, as by the Rowntrees.[45]

Cadbury was moved to offer the use of his large house near Birmingham for the purposes of the new institution. Woodbrooke was established in 1903. The key position of director of studies was offered to Rufus Jones, but he did not feel able to leave his post at Haverford College in Pennsylvania.

The post went instead to Rendel Harris. The emphasis was on the Bible to begin with, but at the suggestion of John Wilhelm Rowntree's brother Seebohm, a lecturer in social studies was appointed in 1906; a lectureship in international relations was added in 1919.[46]

THE INWARD/INNER LIGHT

The term "Inner Light" was not used by Early Friends; its use by Friends of the modernist period may be held to suggest that it is innate, which is not what Early Friends intended. Liberal Quakers in fact felt a need to moderate the teaching of Early Friends on this crucial point. They believed that Early Friends had bequeathed to them their precious insight that Christ, the Light, was their Teacher Within. Yet Braithwaite ascribed to Early Friends "a very imperfect doctrine of human nature" and hence of the Light. He realized that Early Friends assumed, along with nearly everybody at the time, that the image of God in Adam had been radically corrupted at the Fall, so humankind lacked any natural goodness; therefore, the "Light" or the "seed" of God or Christ in the human soul had to be a supernatural essence infused from outside. Jones could not accept that the "Inner Light" was "a mysterious way by which ideas or truths or words were to be communicated by God to the passive mind of man as a gratuitous gift from above." Rather, Jones said, "It means ... that God as Spirit and man as spirit are inherently related and that there is something in man which is unsundered from God."[47]

Caroline Stephen (1834–1909) was one of the first among Friends in Britain to examine the meaning of the Inner Light. She linked it to the extraordinary visions of the mystic in that "inner sanctum" of which most people are unconscious, but she insisted that it is also an ordinary part of daily life and that those who heard George Fox and the others would have recognized it as such. For her, there was a continuum between conscience and the mystic vision: we are all capable of growing in our capacity to recognize and respond to the Light if we attend to that which is within us instead of looking to others for help, just as Fox taught. This may look like Emerson's self-reliance, but for Stephen, recognition of and submission to the Light was necessarily bound to belief in God and devotion to Christ crucified; to submit to the guidance of the Light required courage to accept the way of the Cross as leading to the "deep things of God."[48]

Stephen did not concede that the first Quakers' view of the Light was inadequate. Before Braithwaite's first volume appeared, however, Edward Grubb worked on the problem of Early Friends' dualism, especially in the theology of Robert Barclay (1648–1690). Barclay, he said, convinced of the total depravity of human nature occasioned by the Fall, assumed that "God and man were wholly out of organic relation with one another. Since they had nothing in common, the Light must be one of two mutually exclusive things—human or divine. Either it was wholly supernatural and non-human, or else a mere 'light of nature' by which man could save himself without Divine intervention. The Quakers recoiled in horror from the latter view, and found themselves shut up in the former, with all its consequences."[49]

Modern Quakers, Grubb thought, were more fortunate: "We are now returning," he said, to the concept of "'Divine Immanence,' which was strong in the days of early Christianity." According to Grubb, "The 'Light Within' is just as much a human faculty as is 'Reason' in its widest sense; it is the power of a self-conscious person to enter into communion with God. It is also Divine; for it is God revealing Himself within us."[50]

In a later essay, Grubb wrote of the "subconscious" as a way of understanding something of mystical experience. For John William Graham, the thought of the "subliminal soul," the seat of the Inward Light, opened up the exhilarating possibility of access to a spiritual world: "[We] know that our minds communicate in a spiritual world, and we can fill in the rest. If we are creatures with a spiritual environment, drawing life from it and following its non-material laws, anything most glorious is possible. A new dimension is added, a wholly different perspective becomes ours. It forms an epoch in thought and opens windows out of the prison-house of the flesh." Thus, Graham brought together seventeenth-century Quaker religious insights and the "science" of the paranormal (the "psychical," to use the term then current) that was fashionable in his day.[51]

Herbert George Wood took a different approach. He warned against a "too facile optimism" with respect to human nature: "George Fox's belief in the possibility of moral victory has little in common with Godwin's belief in the perfectibility of man." He conceded that Early Friends made too sharp a distinction between "intuition" and reason, not fully appreciating the extent to which the conscious and unconscious mind affect one another. Wood considered that Early Friends might have learned from the

Cambridge Platonists, contemporaries who could have taught them to find God within themselves without Barclay's sharp dichotomy between natural and supernatural. Henry More (1614–1687), one of the Cambridge Platonists, identified the Light Within with "reason and conscience," rather than seeing it as a supernatural infusion. This suggests that an integrated concept of the natural and divine elements in humankind was (pace Grubb) available to seventeenth-century Quakers. There were in fact connections between the Quakers and the Cambridge Platonists, as F. J. Powicke has pointed out. In the end, Wood, following Stephen, indicated that the philosophical or psychological status of the Light was less important than its relation to the devotional life: "The light," he said, "is not so much a normal element in human nature as an experience of a transforming friendship."[52]

CONCLUSION

The Quaker Renaissance resulted from the successful efforts of liberalizing Quakers to reimagine themselves not only through embracing aspects of the intellectual movements of their time but also, and crucially, through renewing the traditional Quaker emphasis on the Inward Light as the final authority. Evangelicalism could be combined with a progressive outlook: the great scholar J. Rendel Harris retained some typically evangelical traits along with his dismissal of biblical infallibility and his conviction of the reality of the Guiding Light. In Violet Hodgkin Holdsworth's Quaker Christianity, there was no incompatibility between the evangelical emphasis on the gospel of redemption and the liberal exaltation of the Light; in Fox's teaching, she said, they were inseparable: "The Inward Light was not thought of as something antagonistic to, or a substitute for, the redeeming power of the Gospel, but as the redeeming power itself." Although some liberal Quakers were aware of difficult dichotomies, amid the crumbling of old religious certainties and the inroads of agnosticism and materialism, they still found themselves thrown back on the defining tenet preached by those others who had experienced a "world turned upside-down": "Christ has come to teach His people Himself" by means of the Inward Light in the hearts and minds of His followers. Reason demanded escape from the bondage of "sound doctrine," from theories of atonement that made no sense to these liberal Quakers; moral feeling demanded abandonment of belief in a punitive deity prepared to consign multitudes of human beings to eternal punishment in order to satisfy an abstract "justice." Instead, the remaking of the original Quaker idea of the Light enabled liberal Friends to face down a world of doubt and disbelief: "About the beams of the Light Within, the waves of materialism and pessimism and a narrow naturalism might rage on the rocks and suggest dark things, but the lighthouse stood."[53]

CHAPTER 8

The Delineation of Quaker Spiritualities

CAROLE DALE SPENCER

In Elizabeth Gray Vining's preface to *Quaker Spirituality: Selected Writings*, a volume in the Classics of Western Spirituality series, she writes: "In relation to their short history . . . and their small numbers, Friends have produced an extraordinary amount of religious and spiritual writings, many of which . . . have moved out of the sectarian orbit into the realm of religious classics, valued by many who have no further interest in Quakerism itself." This chapter compares, contrasts, and examines some of the representative Quaker religious writers and the diversity of their publishing in the area of spirituality, from Holiness and evangelical to conservative and liberal, in the nineteenth and early twentieth centuries. Quaker spirituality in its beginnings in the seventeenth century was contemplative and charismatic, mystical and evangelical, and political and missionary oriented. All these threads are evident in the schisms and exploding diversity of the Quaker tapestry after 1800.[1]

This chapter will trace how these themes have been reflected in the complex forms of Quaker spirituality as it burst into new expressions and formed new branches in the tumultuous period from 1830 to 1937. The tendency to divide over the freedom of the spirit and the formalism of a unifying faith and practice existed from the beginnings of Quakerism, and this chapter will show how the strong forces of sociocultural and intellectual movements in the nineteenth century amplified those tendencies. The first major division in the United States led one branch to adopt a more establishment-oriented religion and the other to embrace an openness toward Enlightenment thought. Subsequent division led many Friends seeking religious renewal toward evangelicalism and the enthusiasm of the Holiness revival. Quakers in the United States became separated by two divergent forms of worship that created two distinct traditions of corporate spirituality (see chapters 4 and 5). The diversity of Quaker spirituality will be presented as differing reinterpretations of the essence and spirit of the early movement. While the bitter conflicts over expressions of spirituality in this time period were painful, they were necessary adaptations to a changing culture and resulted in transformations that accommodated the needs of a broad spectrum of religious seekers, both innovators and traditionalists. Ultimately, this generated the richness of Quaker spiritual writing that this chapter will describe.

By 1828, the tensions between a Quietist mystical faith of deep introversion and cultural separatism and an emerging evangelicalism became too strong, and the Society of Friends, which had maintained an almost seamless faith for nearly two hundred years, split forcefully into two branches, the Orthodox and Hicksite. Each side championed a somewhat different version of Quaker spirituality, and each claimed to be the authentic, true heirs of George Fox and Early Friends. Both spiritual traditionalists and spiritual innovators helped tear the fabric of Quietist Quakerism, each conserving and reinterpreting differing principles and practices of the Quaker tradition. The Orthodox tended toward a doctrinally and biblically centered spirituality, and the Hicksites looked to the Inward Light as the wholly sufficient authority. Both branches valued a nurturing of the inward life and traditional silent worship, but Quaker spirituality became more individualistic within both branches as time went on.[2]

HICKSITE AND ORTHODOX FRIENDS

The leader of the Hicksite branch, self-taught Quaker minister Elias Hicks (1748–1830), embraced a type of spirituality with primary emphasis on the "Light of Christ within" over any other authority. Almost all Quaker ministers kept a journal, following the example of founder George Fox, who created a style of autobiographical writing that detailed spiritual experiences and travels in ministry, and volumes of such journals were published as the primary spiritual reading of Quakers, after the Bible. Hicks's journal was published soon after his death. In many respects, Hicks was a traditional Quietist who emphasized the death of self and the direct guidance of the Holy Spirit for every action. Hicks was suspicious of most cultural and social trends of the time, and yet the rationalism of the Enlightenment found expression in his journal: the Light of Christ, he wrote, was "the most rational" that "no man of right reason could doubt or dispute." Hicks's strong appeal to individual reason attracted the more radical thinkers, and liberals, transcendentalists, Spiritualists, Unitarians, and freethinkers would later interpret Hicks within their own frameworks.[3]

Hicksites are often associated with radical reform movements, especially abolition and women's rights, and a few of the most progressive thinkers spearheaded these movements. But most Hicksites were sectarians opposed to participation in reform movements, and those who did participate, such as Lucretia Mott (1793–1880), faced stiff opposition (see chapter 2). Mott was a recognized minister within her Hicksite yearly meeting, a follower of Jesus, and a radical activist who believed supremely in the equality of all persons, which she based on her interpretation of Jesus's ethics and an egalitarian reading of scripture. Following the Hicksite emphasis on the Inward Light, which gives humans a direct connection to God, she sought to assert its prominence over dogma and literal, authoritarian, unreflective use of scripture. For Mott, guidance of the Inward Light emerged when people engaged in both quiet, prayerful reflection and spirit-guided reason, and it led not to passivity but to active engagement in good works, a conviction that propelled her spirituality into the political realm. She was an early spiritual leader in women's rights and a radical abolitionist, preaching that both women and Black people should have civil rights. She often preached publicly and drew large crowds. Yet, because of her radical activist spirituality, her relationship with her Hicksite Philadelphia Yearly Meeting during her lifetime was a combative one. Her meeting often tried to silence her; she was accused of being a heretic and of undermining traditional Quakerism. Yet she remained within the fold on the radical fringe of her meeting, feeling she could do the most good by being a prophetic voice within her own community. Mott was the rare Quaker minister who did not keep a journal, and she rarely wrote for publication; but her sermons, spoken extemporaneously as was the Quaker tradition, were often recorded in shorthand and published in newspapers. Many other radical Hicksites split off and formed their own associations, called Congregational Friends or Progressive Friends, holding tenaciously to Quaker principles that they felt had been compromised.[4]

Another leading figure of the time, but an opponent of the Hicksites, was Stephen Grellet (1773–1855), a revered evangelical Quietist who traveled more extensively in the ministry than any of his Quaker contemporaries. Prior to the schism, he and Elias Hicks had, at times, traveled together. Both men were powerful and influential preachers, but the style and themes of their preaching took different trajectories. Grellet had a high view of scripture and expressed concerns about Hicks devaluing the Bible and the atonement of Christ. Grellet preached an evangelical message of conversion and sanctification, but with an irenic and sensitive spirit. Hicks was a controversialist and bold in his critique of the Quaker establishment and authority of the elders. As early as 1808, Grellet could see that a bitter clash was on the horizon, and the schism of the Society of Friends toward the end of his ministry was deeply traumatic for him, the darkest night of his soul.[5]

Like Hicks, Grellet was a self-taught Quietist minister without formal theological training. He kept a journal of his spiritual experiences, his convincement, his calling to ministry, his travels, and his observations. His memoirs were published as spiritual reading for Quaker edification in 1862 (two volumes of over eight hundred pages). Grellet's journal may have been widely read by Quakers in the nineteenth century because it is a fascinating narrative in its own right. Grellet, the son of French aristocrats, was a Voltairian atheist who admired William Penn as a political thinker and began reading his works. His reading prompted a mystical encounter with God, and soon thereafter, he visited a Quaker meeting and had a dramatic conversion experience. Within a few years, he joined Philadelphia Yearly Meeting and was soon recognized as a minister. He was known for his heartfelt preaching and the breadth of his listeners, gaining audience with Pope Pius VII and nobles of many countries as well as speaking to enslaved persons, prisoners, and the poor and sick. In 1888, Frances Anne Budge wrote a popular biography called *A Missionary Life: Stephen Grellet*.[6]

A well-known Quaker saying first circulated in 1869 has been widely attributed to Grellet: "I expect to pass through this world but once. Any good thing therefore that I can do, or any kindness that I can show to any fellow creature, let me do it now. Let me not defer or neglect it, for I shall not pass this way again." While the sentiment reflects the spirit of his preaching, the statement cannot be found in any of Grellet's published works.⁷

GURNEYITE AND WILBURITE FRIENDS

In American Quakerism, the Orthodox body of Friends who maintained traditional Christian doctrines became polarized once again in 1845 and formed two separate branches, the Gurneyites and the Wilburites (see chapter 4). The Gurneyites were named after their most influential leader, Joseph John Gurney (1788–1847). Gurney, an Oxford-trained biblical scholar from a wealthy banking family, was one of the few Quaker ministers who had formal theological training. In 1837, he felt called to leave England for the United States and traveled widely for three years, making a decisive impact on Friends drawn to more ecumenical and mainstream evangelical views of the day. Gurney, though Orthodox in doctrine, was not in any sense a modern evangelical; he was more of a Quietist who had been influenced by Anglican evangelicalism. He wore plain dress, spoke in plain language, and, after a long period of struggle over abandonment of the sacraments, accepted traditional, nonsacramental Quaker worship. But Gurney introduced Quietist Quakers to new theological trends and set the stage for the opening of Quakerism to the wider Christian world of religious education, Bible study, and missions, and he encouraged joining with others in reform activities. Most evangelical Friends today consider him their greatest proponent and trace their heritage through him.

Gurney's memoirs were published in 1854, edited by prominent British Quaker Joseph Bevan Braithwaite. Ironically, though he was British and highly influential in his day, Gurney had no lasting impact on British Quakers and was virtually forgotten by 1900. His ministry in America, however, brought lasting change. In 1824, he published *Observations on the Distinguishing Views and Practices of the Society of Friends*, followed a year later by *Essays on the Evidences, Doctrines, and Practical Operations of Christianity*. These works placed Quakerism as one particular body of Christianity within the universal church, one that had developed certain practices and testimonies as a witness over time—an ecumenical view that challenged the spiritual elitism and sectarianism of the Quaker culture. Gurney also questioned what he perceived as the vagueness of the meaning of the Inward Light and preferred to use the language of the Holy Spirit. He placed a strong emphasis on biblical authority and the need for Bible study. He developed a rational defense of scripture, a different approach to the Bible than the contemplative reading of scripture that characterized earlier Friends. His most widely read devotional work was *Essays on the Habitual Exercise of Love to God*, published in England in 1834, reissued in Philadelphia in 1840, and translated into both French and German.[8]

A response to the robust evangelicalism of Joseph John Gurney and his followers came from a traveling minister named John Wilbur (1774–1856). Wilbur became a staunch opponent of both Gurney and the Hicksites. He was committed to orthodox Christian doctrine and the traditional Quaker practice of "plainness" in dress and speech, and he resisted any innovations or adaptations that borrowed from mainstream religious culture. Wilbur was a primitivist who maintained an undiluted Quietist spirituality, emphasizing the Christ within, holiness, and obedience, which included strict adherence to Quaker discipline. His followers split from the Orthodox in New England in 1845, and by 1858, other separations of Wilburite sympathizers from various Orthodox meetings resulted in a third branch of Quakerism called the Wilburites, later called Conservative Friends. The spirituality of the Wilburite Friends found its source in the defense of Quaker theology written by Robert Barclay, *Apology for the True Christian Divinity*, in which holiness is realized through the experience of "Christ in you, the hope of glory" (Col. 1:27). Much of the spiritual writing of the nineteenth-century Wilburites is found in journals of the period, the most important of which is the *Journal of John Wilbur*.[9]

HOLINESS FRIENDS IN AMERICA

A new vision of holiness spirituality emerged in the late 1860s when many Quaker leaders found powerful inspiration in the interdenominational Holiness movement. They began preaching a second instantaneous experience of sanctification subsequent to conversion, comparing it to George Fox and Robert Barclay's doctrine of perfection (see chapter 4). They became leaders of a radical Holiness movement, often labeled "Fast Friends," among the Orthodox Gurneyites.

The Holiness revival began in the 1830s among the Methodists and reached its peak in the 1870s, though it had continual influence throughout the first half of the twentieth century. It influenced almost all American denominations, but none were transformed to the degree of American Quakers, whose meetings, especially from Ohio westward, adopted new forms of worship, ecclesiology, and a Wesleyan-shaped theology and spirituality (see chapters 4 and 5). The Holiness movement had deep similarities with the Christ-centered mystical vision that sparked the early Quaker movement, where sanctification and perfection, often referred to as the "baptism of the Holy Spirit," were normative experiences of Early Friends.

For many younger Quakers, the long periods of silence had begun to feel numbing and barren. They were drawn to gospel music, emotionally charged testimonies and prayer, and the dramatic preaching that led to altar calls and spiritual highs that characterized the popular revival meetings. The quest for personal and social perfection of the Holiness movement resonated with a new generation of Quaker ministers, both male and female. The traditional practice of a traveling ministry directed by a spiritual call, rather than clerical qualifications, easily shifted to the role and style of a Holiness evangelist. In less than forty years (between 1860 and 1895), two-thirds of American Quakers evolved from traditional, apophatic Quietism to an evangelistic, kataphatic spirituality more akin to that of the "singing Methodists." Meetings, especially in Ohio and westward, became Quaker churches with settled pastors, hymn singing, and revival-style altar calls to sanctification and renewal. The practice of silent worship gradually diminished in these new evangelical meetings. The adoption of these mainstream forms brought hundreds of new attendees into Quaker meetings and led to the establishment of a settled pastoral ministry to meet the pastoral-care needs of new converts (see chapter 5).

Almost all Gurneyites desired renewal, but some were more moderate in their approach, hoping to retain traditional Quaker practices such as silent waiting while incorporating such new innovations as pastoral preaching, congregational singing, and public testimonies. Controversies erupted over many of the changes, as well as the physical manifestations of revival meetings. For many, the enthusiasm and emotionality of tears and trembling seemed to be signs of a return to the spiritual power of Quaker beginnings. But other renewal Friends were vocal opponents of the excesses and emotionality of the revivalists and tried to steer a more moderate course. Some leaders, such as Joel Bean (1825–1914), who initially supported revivals, later became outspoken opponents, and fiery debates raged in Quaker journals between revivalists and antirevivalists. The most widely read critique of the Holiness revival among Friends was published by Bean in the *British Friend* in 1881 and republished in 1883. It created a storm of controversy in both England and America. Bean later founded a new Quaker meeting in San Jose, California, that worshipped in traditional silence, later called "unprogrammed" worship, and was distinct from other western Quaker meetings established at the time that were influenced by the revival. Bean drew up a brief "five-point statement of faith" for his independent meeting that represented a liberal wing of Gurneyite spirituality in the West: "Friends believe in the continuing reality of the living Christ, available to all seeking souls ... and ... recognize their oneness with humanity everywhere, regardless of race or nation, abstaining from all hatred." The most widely read of Bean's writings was "Why I Am a Friend," published as a prize essay in the new *American Friend* in 1894. It was republished in 1895 in the *Saturday Review* as a pamphlet and has been reprinted numerous times by Quakers over the years. Bean claimed that Friends' principles express a broad ecumenical orientation that "unite us to a fellowship with all the good in every religion and every race of mankind."[10]

In many Holiness Quaker meetings, the devotional literature of the Wesleyan tradition and the Methodist-led National Holiness Association replaced the writings of Fox, Barclay, and Early Friends. The leading theologian of the Holiness wing of the Gurneyites was Dougan Clark (1828–1896). His *Theology of Holiness*, published in 1893, became the standard work of theology and spirituality among the radical Holiness factions, a Quakerized version of the Methodist doctrine of holiness. Clark taught that "entire sanctification" was an instantaneous gift of God through faith and defined it as "an act of God's grace by which inbred sin is removed and the heart made holy." His influence was short-lived, as he lost his faculty position at Earlham College in 1895 because of his support for baptism by water. The public water baptism of several leading Quaker ministers in the 1870s had shocked the Orthodox establishment. The "waterite crisis" arose as the more radical Holiness leaders such as David B. Updegraff promoted "toleration" and "liberty of conscience" in the practice of water baptism. Allowing the inward baptism to be expressed outwardly became the most threatening new practice to disrupt the historic Quaker tradition of inward spiritual experience. This breach of the Quaker tradition of interiority exposed the limits of the accommodation of mainstream religious practice.[11]

The ordinance controversy, along with other hotly debated issues such as "hireling pastors," the role of scripture, the meaning of the Light Within, and the doctrine of sanctification, led to the organization of a groundbreaking conference in 1887 in Richmond, Indiana, of representatives from all Orthodox bodies, including London Yearly Meeting, still the historic center of power in the Quaker world. The conference brought about the creation of a uniform "Declaration of Faith" in an attempt to balance tradition with innovation and restore a sense of unity of mission, purpose, belief, and practice to shattered late nineteenth-century Orthodox Quakerism in America. The resulting document was written by a committee led by British Quaker Joseph Bevan Braithwaite, an evangelical moderate, and was received by the majority of Gurneyite Friends as the Richmond Declaration of Faith. It tried to balance historic Quaker tradition with the emerging revival impulses. The declaration did not address all the controversies within the Society of Friends, but it attempted to restrain the more extreme Holiness faction and maintain the inward sacraments, much to the chagrin of the radical Holiness stronghold of Ohio Yearly Meeting, which failed to endorse it. And although written primarily by an influential British Friend, it was not endorsed by London Yearly Meeting or Irish Friends. Although it did not please all Gurneyite moderates, it nevertheless managed to produce an evangelical mainstream shaped by historical Quaker principles but open to a changing culture. The Richmond Conference ultimately led to the creation of Five Years Meeting in 1902, a diverse network of Quaker meetings and churches that aspired to be a mainstream Quaker Christian body. Through its renewed emphasis on missions, especially in Africa and South America, evangelical spirituality became characteristic of the majority of Quakers worldwide (see chapter 10).

By the end of the nineteenth century, three different approaches to spirituality could be discerned among American Quakers: (1) the Wilburites, or primitivists, traditional Quietist sectarians who maintained the strictest ties to Early Friends' faith and practice; (2) an evangelical wing of renewal-oriented Gurneyite and Holiness Friends who adopted a more doctrinally oriented theology; and (3) a liberal-oriented wing of Hicksites who maintained traditional Quaker silent worship and the notion of the Inward Light as the central belief of Quakerism. Each faction kept within its own orbit, rarely interacting with each other. They published separate periodicals to promote and maintain their approach to spirituality and theology.

THE ENDURANCE OF QUIETIST SPIRITUALITY

Spiritual reading for most Quakers in the first half of the nineteenth century would have been the Bible, journals, and extracts from Early Friends. Yet Quaker spiritual life was also distinctly shaped by some mystical writings outside that of Friends. In 1813, extracts from the writings of Jeanne Guyon, François Fenelon, and Miguel Molinos, Catholic Quietist mystics, were compiled and published anonymously as a devotional manual for members of the Society of Friends, called *A Guide to True Peace*. According to Howard Brinton, the *Guide* was written "to nourish the spiritual life . . . and passed through at least twelve editions from 1813 to 1877." The *Guide* left a deep impact on Quaker spirituality throughout its history, though it fell somewhat out of favor in the early twentieth century. It focused on contemplative prayer, silence, suffering, and death of self—characteristic elements of Quietist Quaker spirituality. The writings of Guyon and Fenelon were also read and appreciated by Methodists and adherents of various Pietist movements. While it could be claimed that *A Guide to True Peace* is the most representative text of Quaker devotion and spiritual guidance in the nineteenth century, there were differing attitudes toward this mystical spirituality. Some Holiness Friends were eager to point out the difference between Quaker silent waiting and the contemplative prayer of Guyon and in other mystical writings. Yet the most influential theologian of the Quaker Holiness movement, Dougan Clark, recognized the parallels between Guyon and other earlier mystical writers and Quakerism, despite the strong anti-Catholic prejudice of the time: "Every denomination has had its witnesses. Some of the most holy men and women of whom we have any account, have been Roman Catholics. Such were Tauler and the Friends of God, Thomas a Kempis, Fenelon, and Lady Guyon."[12]

A MEDIATING VOICE

Although most Quakers by the latter half of the nineteenth century had separated into their own branches, a few bridged the divide. One such Friend was John Greenleaf Whittier (1807–1892), an Orthodox Gurneyite from New England, writer, editor, and political activist, often called "the Quaker Poet." Whittier, one of the most popular American poets of his day, was an ardent abolitionist and a strong advocate of peace. Some of his religious poems are sung as popular hymns today in various Protestant churches. But they were never meant to be hymns, as Whittier worshipped in traditional Quaker silence, without singing or music, as many Gurneyites in New England, in Philadelphia, and on the East Coast continued to do. The hymn "Dear Lord and Father of Mankind" is taken from his 1872 poem "The Brewing of Soma," based on a passage in the Hindu Vedas. Soma was a mystical drink that led to ecstasy. The poem has been interpreted as a polemic against excessive liturgy and ritualism as well as the excesses of revivalism then rising among Friends, and it concludes with his ideal of Quaker silent worship and a contemplative spirituality.[13]

Whittier's poetry reflects his deep regard for traditional Quaker principles and practices but also his commitment to a renewal of Quaker spirituality wedded to politics and social justice. He partnered with William Lloyd Garrison in the radical abolitionist movement, writing a poem every week for *The Liberator*. He wrote many pamphlets, articles, and poems advocating the immediate and unconditional emancipation of slaves, a highly unpopular and even dangerous position at the time. Most Quakers of all three branches judged slavery to be evil but were opposed to the "immediate emancipation" espoused by the radical abolitionists and their breaking of laws to aid people who had escaped from slavery (see chapter 2).[14]

After the Civil War, Whittier became a national hero. With the publication of his poem "Snow-Bound" in 1866, he became the most famous Quaker in America. Whittier's antislavery poetry reflects a prophetic Quaker spirituality of politics, persuasion, and transformation. He could be considered nineteenth-century Quakerism's one and only public theologian and moral philosopher. By his own estimation, he was always an abolitionist first and a poet second. And despite his identification with the Orthodox wing, he was one of the few Quakers (perhaps the only Quaker) of his time to be read and respected by all Quaker branches, Hicksite, Gurneyite, and Wilburite, and non-Quakers as well, and his poems were published in the periodicals of all three Quaker factions.[15]

Whittier's hero was the seventeenth-century Quaker minister, prophet, and mystic John Woolman. Woolman's *Journal* was first published in 1774 by Philadelphia Yearly Meeting two years after his death. But Whittier's edition of the *Journal*, with his introduction and notes, published in 1871, helped give it national exposure far beyond the confines of Woolman's own generation and the small circle of the Society of Friends. More than any

Quaker journal, it seemed to transcend its age, as Woolman's prophetic spirituality spoke even more strongly in the nineteenth century and was read more widely than in his own day. His *Journal*, as well as his other writings on injustice and oppression, reflected the highest Quaker ideals of humanitarianism, nonviolence, simplicity, the unity of all humanity and creation, and justice and mercy to all oppressed and marginalized people. His *Journal* was appropriated widely by Ralph Waldo Emerson, Walt Whitman, and other writers in transcendentalist circles, even though theologically, Woolman "stood in the mainstream of the Christian evangelical tradition." Liberals claimed that Whittier embodied "a new type of devotional literature," and transcendentalists celebrated Whittier as "the poet of Inner Light liberalism," even though Whittier identified with the Orthodox.[16]

TRANSCENDENTALISM

A countervailing trend to revivalism in the nineteenth century was transcendentalism, which also had a marked influence on Quaker spirituality. As revivalism began to transform the Orthodox, transcendentalism began to impact the Hicksites, and, conversely, Quaker spirituality influenced transcendentalism.

Ralph Waldo Emerson, when asked about his religion, said he was "more of a Quaker than anything else" and believed in the Christ within. He also wrote that the best of Quakerism came closest to the ethics and genius of Christ. In 1832, Emerson resigned his Boston pulpit because he could no longer administer the communion rite, a decision clearly influenced and supported by Quaker belief. He found many Quaker beliefs that paralleled his own thinking, such as the doctrine of the Inward Light of Christ, which he called the Inner Light, as well as silent prayer and nonresistance. God, for Emerson, was the Over-Soul discerned by the Light in the individual conscience. Frederick Tolles writes that "Emerson's 'spiritual religion' is entirely at one with Quakerism in this respect. Religion for him ... was an intuitive and personal experience, completely divorced from traditional forms and authority."[17]

Transcendentalism also paralleled Quaker theology in the belief that matter is the shadow and spirit is the substance. In the 1830s and 1840s, while revival fires burned through New England, transcendentalism spread among intellectuals, writers, poets, and skeptics. Quaker spirituality in its emerging Hicksite forms, pared of its puritanism and sectarianism, had great idealistic appeal and was assimilated and updated into transcendentalism. When Henry Thoreau heard the Quaker Hicksite minister Lucretia Mott preach, he called it "Transcendentalism in its mildest form." Emerson, too, was a great admirer of Mott, calling her "the Flower of Quakerism."[18]

Walt Whitman (1819–1892) was raised in a Quaker family with Hicksite leanings. As a child of ten, he was spellbound when he heard the aged Quaker minister Elias Hicks preach, and he sometimes referenced Hicks with sincere admiration in his poetry. While Whitman never joined with Friends, he too, like Emerson, appropriated progressive Quaker ideals that he selectively blended with his ideas of individual freedom and self-realization.

The more mystical heterodox Hicksites tended to come under the spell of the transcendentalists, while the more rational Hicksites were attracted to the rationalist Unitarians. But some of the most radical and progressive Hicksites were drawn to Spiritualism, such as Amy and Isaac Post, who were abolitionists and women's rights advocates who became strong supporters of Spiritualists such as Margaretta, Kate, and Leah Fox.[19]

Many of the most radical of the women's rights activists split off from the Hicksites and formed their own associations. Many of the revival Gurneyites assimilated into Wesleyans or became Pentecostals, such as Holiness Friend A. J. Tomlinson, one of the leading figures in the Pentecostal movement who cofounded the Church of God, Cleveland, one of the largest Pentecostal denominations in the United States. The charismatic element that existed within Quakerism in its beginnings remained a strong thread, particularly among Holiness and evangelical Friends.

OTHER EXPRESSIONS OF QUAKER SPIRITUALITY
IN A TRANSITIONAL TIME

Hannah Whitall Smith (1830–1911), born into a wealthy Philadelphia Orthodox family, was one of the most widely read devotional writers in the last half of the nineteenth century, more renowned and celebrated beyond Quaker circles than within them. Her book *The Christian's Secret of a Happy Life*, published in 1875, was an instant bestseller; it was translated into many languages, was reprinted numerous times, and is still read by spiritual seekers today. It is the most enduring book to emerge from the literature of the nineteenth-century Holiness movement of which she was a part.[20]

Smith had a wide circle of friends from all walks of life and religious contexts, including a surprising friendship with the Harvard philosopher and pioneer in psychology William James. Smith sent him a copy of her book, and his interest in religious experience, despite his agnosticism, may have prompted him to read it. James sent Smith a note on May 11, 1886, from Cambridge, Massachusetts, where he was teaching at Harvard:

> I am not a Christian after the pattern you have in mind; your book has not made me one; and I doubt if I ever become one.... And yet... I find that something in it peals through and through me and awakens the liveliest response.... I suppose it is the rare unsentimentality and practicality of the attitude of mind your pages so clearly work out. If I were a Christian, I should like to be one of that sort.... I have got a fresh source of edification of a most unexpected kind, and the book will be one of my lifelong treasures.

He added, tongue in cheek, "I may become a revivalist ere I die—who knows!" He also referenced her book in his psychology lectures as an example of practical, healthy, unsentimental religion.[21]

Smith's 1903 spiritual autobiography *The Unselfishness of God and How I Discovered It*, though less well known, described her spiritual journey from youth to old age as she wove in and out of Quaker circles, and it critiqued both Quaker Orthodoxy and her Holiness sympathies. She published numerous popular devotional books, such as *Everyday Religion* (1893) and *The Open Secret* (1885), as well as books on how to study the Bible. Like Mott a generation before her, Smith was a passionate advocate of women's rights and often gave speeches on suffrage, which her Orthodox Philadelphia Yearly Meeting never supported. She resigned her membership in the Society of Friends in 1858 to explore the wider religious world. She became a popular speaker at camp meetings and in churches that allowed women to speak, in meetings of the Woman's Christian Temperance Union, and, later in life, for unions and the labor movement.[22]

Smith observed the splintering and gradual enculturation of a large portion of the Society of Friends in her lifetime. Her autobiography details, sometimes with humor, that changing landscape. Although she always identified as a Quaker, she happily identified as a "heretic" on the outside edge of the Quaker world on both sides of the Atlantic. She embodied multiple identities (devoted mother, outspoken feminist) and contradictions (evangelical, universalist) as she sought to expand her horizons and find a public voice and vocation within the constraints of the Victorian age.

Smith and her husband, Robert Pearsall, helped spark the Keswick Movement, an interdenominational spiritual renewal movement in England. As David Bebbington has pointed out, "Quaker spirituality was one of the foundations of the Keswick Movement." Quakers were both participants and leaders in the movement. Smith incorporated some Quaker elements into the early movement, such as contemplative periods of silence, and shaped into it what was called a spirituality of "the Higher Life."[23]

Smith maintained an evangelical piety throughout her life, yet she broke with Christian orthodoxy in her embrace of universalism. (Always a current in Quaker spirituality, universalism is rooted in the founding principle of the concept of the universal Light that enlightens everyone.) She explored many of the new spiritual movements of the time, including Spiritualism, mind cure, and faith healing, and recorded her experiences, observations, and analyses of these new movements. This material was published posthumously in 1928 by her granddaughter, who titled it *Religious Fanaticism*. Smith wrote in her final reflections that she was nurtured as a Quaker in a culture inclined toward mysticism, which she called "the mystical way of approaching God," and was taught a life of introspection and self-abandonment. She admitted that Quakerism contained a degree of fanaticism, with divine guidance sometimes taken to extremes, but she valued the principle nonetheless, which she felt was "mostly kept in check."[24]

Another woman who became a leading voice of Quaker spirituality in this transitional period was a convert to Quakerism from the Church of England named Caroline Stephen (1834–1909). Her *Quaker Strongholds*, published in 1890, has become a Quaker classic and is considered one of the most articulate expressions of Quaker spirituality, especially her descriptions of the practice of worship in silence that drew her into the Society of Friends in midlife from the Church of England. Stephen described a mystical approach to God, which she claimed is the principal truth upon which Quakerism was built: "the conviction that God does indeed communicate with each one of the spirits he has made, in a direct and living breathing of some measure of the breath of his own life ... and that in order clearly to hear the divine voice thus speaking to us, we need to be still; to be alone with him in the secret place of his presence." Stephen contended that

Quakerism is a mystical movement, and she was one of the early voices in reinterpreting Quakerism in terms that would appeal to a new generation of modernist Quakers. Stephen's niece, the novelist Virginia Woolf, kept copies of her aunt's books in her private library.[25]

Although Stephen and Smith were contemporaries, and prominent spiritual writers living in England at the same time, there seems to be no evidence (to date) that they knew each other or ever corresponded. Although they described Quaker spirituality in a similar way, their lives represented very different trajectories of practical living. Smith, a broad-minded evangelical who hoped for renewal and revival among Friends and embraced the enthusiasm of the Holiness movement, was nevertheless a progressive, even a radical, on social issues—an outspoken feminist with strong ecumenical sympathies. Stephen represented the conservation of traditional Quaker worship and practice, but reinterpreted in a modernist context. Unlike Smith, Stephen was conservative on many social issues, and she was a publicly outspoken antifeminist and a founding member of the Anti-Suffrage Society. Stephen was one of the first modern Quakers to interpret historical and contemporary Quakerism as a mystical movement. Rufus Jones would soon follow that trend and interpret mysticism in a way attractive to twentieth-century spiritual seekers. Stephen defined a mystic as "one who has, or one who believes in, a certain illumination from within." And she was willing to go one step further and identify herself as a mystic, albeit, as she called herself, "a rational mystic."[26]

MYSTICISM AND MODERNISM

At the turn of the twentieth century, new scholarly studies of mysticism were flourishing, beginning with William James's pioneering phenomenological study *The Varieties of Religious Experience*, which included a section on George Fox and Quakers. Rufus Jones (1863–1948), an Orthodox Quaker born into a devout Quaker family in South China, Maine, studied at Harvard and was strongly influenced by William James's analysis of religious experience, which he applied to Quakerism. Jones taught at Haverford College, a Quaker school outside Philadelphia, for most of his career. He was the author of over fifty books and thousands of articles. Jones taught and wrote on philosophy, theology, history, and mysticism, and he essentially defined Quaker spirituality for modern liberal Quakers at a time when Protestants were embroiled in the modernist-fundamentalist controversy. Matthew Hedstrom claims that Jones's mysticism "offered life-transforming religious experience not confined to the evangelical paradigm" and fueled with "spiritual energy" the Social Gospel. Jones tirelessly joined mysticism to social reform and political activism.[27]

All his books, including his historical studies, had a devotional aspect. They were meant to both inform and inspire. They all contained themes of mysticism, which Jones defined as the reality of the direct experience of God—a democratized mysticism available to ordinary people, not only for rare saints. He wrote in an accessible, engaging style that appealed to a nonscholarly but literate readership, and his books were marketed beyond Quaker circles and read by all types of spiritual seekers.

In the tradition of early journal-keeping Quaker ministers, Jones also wrote his memoirs, which comprised five volumes. His defining book may be one of his earliest, *Social Law in the Spiritual World*, heavily based on James's psychological and philosophical theories that Jones learned at Harvard. Through his prolific writing and speaking, Jones, more than any other Quaker writer, changed the way outsiders perceived Quaker spirituality. When it came to mysticism, he was as pragmatic as James: the test for authentic "affirmative" mysticism was in its empowerment for service.[28]

Jones captivated Quaker historians with his innovative theory of Quaker origins in Christian mysticism. He declared, "No other large, organized, historically continuous body of Christians has yet existed which has been so fundamentally mystical, both in theory and practice, as the Society of Friends." He helped shape the spirituality of numerous theologians in the twentieth century, among them Harry Emerson Fosdick, a close friend of Jones, and the African American religious leader Howard Thurman, who studied with Jones at Haverford. Jones also had protégés in two preeminent Quaker spiritual writers of the later twentieth century, Douglas Steere and Thomas Kelly, both students of his at Haverford. Jones's biographer, Elizabeth Gray Vining, writing in 1958, lauded him as "the greatest spiritual philosopher living in America since William James." His view of the Society of Friends as a fundamentally mystical religion became the dominant understanding of Quaker spirituality throughout his lifetime.[29]

However, by the mid-twentieth century, critics of Jones's "modern invention of mysticism" arose, and his historical theory of Quaker mysticism was largely rejected by a new generation of Quaker scholars who claimed that Early Friends were not mystics, at least not in the way Jones described. Jones's theories of mysticism continue to be debated, but as a leading Quaker scholar has recently concluded: "On a popular level among liberal Quakers the tendency to see Quakerism as a fundamentally mystical religion endures."[30]

AMERICAN HOLINESS IN THE EARLY TWENTIETH CENTURY

The leading Holiness voices at the turn of the century were J. Walter Malone (1857–1935) and his wife, Emma (1860–1924). Walter and Emma Malone were the quintessential religious entrepreneurs, creating new kinds of Quaker social, spiritual, and educational institutions. They were cofounders of the Friends Bible Institute and Training School in 1892, later called Cleveland Bible Institute, modeled on Dwight L. Moody's Bible Institute in Chicago. Despite the Malones' own lack of higher education or any training in biblical studies, their capable teaching and administration of the school enabled it to grow and thrive and to graduate scores of Quaker ministers, missionaries, and social workers. Like many Bible institutes, it eventually evolved into a Christian liberal arts college, now Malone University.

The Malones were Bible teachers, evangelists, and publishers. They were also Quaker mystics, though they would not have used that term. From their Quaker roots, they brought egalitarian and pacifist values and a mystical spirituality into the evangelical milieu. They challenged conventional views concerning the role of women and racial minorities. According to John Oliver, their Bible school admitted African Americans fifty years before most other American Quaker schools, and the Malones' lack of class and racial prejudice contrasted sharply with the racist and classist attitudes of the wider society that infected much of Victorian Quakerism.

Walter Malone's reminiscences, which he titled "Lifestories," were written in the 1920s, but the manuscript was never completed. They provide a fascinating history of how traditional Quaker spirituality could flow easily into Holiness mysticism and missional evangelicalism, though not without strong resistance from some quarters. The Malones adopted the new-style language and methods of early twentieth-century evangelicalism—they were not merely Quaker ministers but "soul-winners" who preached and witnessed one on one so that souls would be "saved" and "sanctified." The Malones, like many Holiness Friends, believed in faith healing, exorcism of demons, and miraculous interventions through prayer.[31]

Walter Malone was editor of *The Christian Worker*, a thriving western-based Holiness journal, which had the largest circulation of all Quaker journals in the 1880s and 1890s. In 1893, the editorship of the much smaller Gurneyite journal *The Friends' Review* was offered to Rufus Jones. Malone and Jones had a friendly relationship at the time, and Jones convinced Malone to merge the two journals into one new journal, renamed *The American Friend*. Malone seemed confident that Jones, as an Orthodox Friend, had at least moderate evangelical sympathies. Jones and Malone's 1894 collaboration in creating and editing the journal *The American Friend* may represent one of the last partnerships between two leaders of the rapidly diverging transformations of Quaker tradition in America. By 1898, Jones was receiving significant criticism from Holiness Quakers in the Midwest for his editorial choices. Then, as Jones steered *The American Friend* toward liberal perspectives, Malone published a journal specifically as a vehicle for Holiness readers, *The Soul Winner*, in 1902, which was renamed *The Evangelical Friend* in 1905. Malone was a fervent pacifist and humanitarian, but like most evangelicals of his time, he held evangelism as his top priority.[32]

THE QUAKER RENAISSANCE IN GREAT BRITAIN

At the end of the nineteenth century, British Friends metamorphosed within a generation from evangelicalism to a theologically liberal and activist Society. They also reaffirmed their pacifist testimony, which had been challenged by World War I. British Friends never developed a paid pastoral ministry, any type of programmed meeting, or a unifying doctrinal statement, which many evangelical Friends had argued was necessary in a changing culture.

The catalyst for the liberal turn in Great Britain was John Wilhelm Rowntree (1868–1905), the visionary hero of a young Friends movement who would save the Society from "two centuries of backwater." Rowntree planned to write a new narrative of Quakerism that would uncover the spiritual history of the movement, but, tragically, he died young, not long after beginning work on the project. After his sudden death, his dear friend Rufus Jones said that "his life in some sense went into mine" and vowed to carry on his vision. Jones and William Charles Braithwaite (1862–1922) went on to produce the multivolume project from 1909 to 1921, and it became the standard history of Quakerism, reinterpreting that history from a liberal perspective. Rowntree published little in his short life, but in his many addresses and essays, he helped instigate religious and spiritual reforms to awaken British Quakers from their theological slumbers. Evangelicals, Rowntree argued, had revived Friends by casting off Quietism but had abandoned the Inward Light in their eagerness to fit into the "narrow light of scriptural infallibility." His critiques of the failures of the Society of Friends and his solutions for their revival were published soon after his death in *Essays and Addresses*.[33]

The turning point in the break with evangelicalism came with London Yearly Meeting's rejection of the Richmond Declaration of 1887. The Manchester Conference of 1895, often referred to as the beginning of the Quaker Renaissance, ushered in the turn to liberalism. Over a thousand Quakers gathered to hear from scholars and expert teachers from many fields on how the best of Quaker faith and practice could adapt itself to modern thought and new scientific knowledge. The architects of the Quaker Renaissance were a combination of young, well-educated modernist thinkers, including Rowntree, Braithwaite, Edward Grubb (1854–1939), and the American theologian Jones, along with influential progressive evangelicals such as George Cadbury (1839–1922), the chocolatier. Cadbury funded a series of "summer schools" from 1897 to 1902 that led to the newly established Woodbrooke in 1903. Woodbrooke was a non-degree-granting college where Quakers could study new research in biblical thought, theology, science, and practical ministry under a new generation of educated religious scholars. British Quakers had long been opposed to seminaries and religious schools, but the new generation of liberal Friends felt that anti-intellectualism had long hindered Quaker growth and ministry, and academic training of its leaders was needed to emerge from the obscurantism and isolationism of the past.[34]

London Yearly Meeting, the historic center of the Religious Society of Friends, endured many of the same doctrinal controversies as American Friends faced. While they never split into separate branches, they suffered from generations of declension and decline. Less influenced by the religious revivalism of the nineteenth century, British Friends evolved fairly rapidly from evangelical Quietism into theological liberalism. Today, Quakers in England, where the movement first arose, are represented by the umbrella organization of Britain Yearly Meeting. Worship is silent, nonsacramental, and nonpastoral, and spiritualities are diverse and often post-Christian and nontheistic, with a strong focus on social activism.

The first director of Woodbrooke was one of the key speakers at the Manchester Conference, prominent modernist and biblical scholar J. Rendel Harris (1852–1941). Harris was a study in paradox, combining progressive thought with Holiness piety. Theologically, he was a robust modernist voice and a defender of evolutionary theory but also a Christocentric mystic with a deep affinity for the Holiness tradition of the early Keswick Movement. Harris wrote dozens of scholarly works, including pioneering studies of textual and higher criticism, and he discovered and translated many ancient Christian and pre-Christian texts. But he also published devotional works based on homilies given extemporaneously in Quaker meetings for worship that were popular with a general audience.[35]

Harris and Rufus Jones were friends and scholarly colleagues (Harris had taught for a time in the United States at Johns Hopkins University and Haverford College). Both were in many ways Victorian romantics, but Harris maintained his grounding in the Holiness milieu even as Jones distanced himself from his earlier evangelicalism. Harris was often viewed as a "true mystic," whereas Jones was instead a scholar of mysticism. Both published prolifically, but Harris's influence declined among Friends after his retirement from Woodbrooke, and his writings in time fell into obscurity, while Jones pioneered the twentieth-century evolution of liberal Quakerism.

Harris, though a modernist in biblical studies who embraced evolution, could also be called British Quakerism's last Holiness Quaker. His ability to integrate holiness, evangelicalism, and mysticism into his certainty of faith was soon challenged by William Littleboy, a teaching colleague at Woodbrooke. Littleboy was a rationalist with no taste personally for mystical experience. He wrote a popular pamphlet—in contrast to Harris's exuberant, heartfelt, embodied spirituality—called *The Appeal of Quakerism to the Non-mystic*, published in 1916. While he reaffirmed Jones's interpretation of Quakerism as appealing to those souls who find themselves in "a love-relationship with the Living God," Littleboy claimed that only a small minority of Quakers, primarily its ministers, experienced that kind of personal divine presence. Thus, he was questioning Jones's contention that direct experience of God could be felt by everyone, positing that, counter to the idea of a practical mysticism for the masses, mystical faith was reserved for the few and was, in a sense, an abnormal experience. Littleboy emphasized instead duty, service, and obedience, which gradually took hold of the majority of liberal Quakers. He separated the two ways—the inner life of mystical experience and the outward life of social activism—that had been of one piece for the early Quakers and for such prophetic figures as John Woolman. An ethical idealism based in the recovery and reformulation of the peace testimony after World War I and the strengthening of humanitarian activities took hold among modernists, for which the Society of Friends has often been commended, but a decline in the integration of mysticism into resistance also resulted (see chapter 11).[36]

TOWARD INTERSPIRITUALITY

Howard Brinton (1884–1973) was one of the leading voices of liberal Quakerism and spirituality in America throughout much of the twentieth century. Brinton, who had a PhD in both philosophy and physics, was a student of Rufus Jones's at Haverford and studied at Harvard with William James. Brinton was sympathetic to Jones's modern understanding of mysticism and continued to propagate Jones's perspectives on Quakerism. Brinton's first widely read publication was *Creative Worship* in 1931.[37]

In his 1940 book, *The Nature of Quakerism*, Brinton summed up the essence of liberal Quaker spirituality: "The primary doctrine of the Society of Friends declares that the Presence of God is felt at the apex of the human soul and that man can therefore know and heed God directly, without any intermediary in the form of church, priest, sacrament, or sacred book." He believed that the best type of religion combined the mystical, the evangelical, the rational, and the social. All four balanced and restrained the others, but he also declared that the mystical was foundational.[38]

In the United States, the integration of Brinton's four elements was actualized in the establishment in 1930 of a spiritual retreat center near Philadelphia, called Pendle Hill. The vision for Pendle Hill began with Rufus Jones and the American Friends Service Committee's desire to create a Quaker educational and spiritual center in the Woodbrooke model. In 1929, Rufus Jones, Henry Cadbury, and Henry Hodgkin envisioned a new direction for "a vital center for spiritual culture" and a training place for Quaker leaders. It was to be an inclusive, intentional community modeled on the Benedictine rhythm of work, worship, and study. It opened in 1930, with Henry Hodgkin (1877–1933) as the director. Hodgkin was a British doctor, missionary, ecumenist, and active pacifist. He cofounded the International Fellowship of Reconciliation. Hodgkin was also a religious writer, and he published his first book, *The Message and Mission of Quakerism*, with William C. Braithwaite in 1912.[39]

As he narrated his spiritual journey, Hodgkin reflected on the momentous shift in Quakerism from evangelism to interfaith dialogue in twentieth-century liberalism. He wrote, "I find myself wanting to learn from people whom I previously would have regarded as fit objects for my 'missionary zeal' . . . to discover another way in which God is operating . . . and the deliberate attempt to share the life and interests of others who are not in my circle . . . and through that reach, maybe, fresh truths about God."[40]

Hodgkin envisioned Pendle Hill as a place of spiritual depth, reconciliation, and social concern. After Hodgkin's untimely death, Howard and Anna Cox Brinton became the directors and carried on the vision. They created a community of Quaker contemplatives, activists, artists, and spiritual seekers, a culmination of early twentieth-century liberal spirituality embodied in an institutional form. In 1934, the retreat center began publishing a series of booklets known as Pendle Hill pamphlets, essays and meditations that reflected the breadth of liberal and mystical spirituality.

Rufus Jones and other liberals reshaped the modern Society of Friends as a movement of spiritual seeking. Leigh Schmidt astutely points out that Jones recast Quakers as "'archetypal seekers' in part by resurfacing that category from the seventeenth-century literature of sectarians and applying it in a universalized way to the modern religious world." Thus, the mystical seeker spirituality of Rufus Jones, his influence on others across the boundaries of the Society of Friends, and the embodiment of his worldview in the retreat center at Pendle Hill made Quakers "disproportionally influential in the shaping of a contemporary American spirituality of seeking" and helped spawn today's "spiritual but not religious" generation.[41]

Although Rufus Jones and modernism overshadowed evangelicalism in the early decades of the twentieth century, the Friends Church, spawned by the Holiness revivals of the nineteenth century, continued to attract those who desired a more certain Christian faith, who were "finders" rather than seekers. An evangelical, socially engaged, spirit-led, heart-centered spiritual expression with an emphasis on biblical authority, evangelism, conversion, and holiness largely characterized the Friends Church in the early twentieth century. However, in the 1920s and 1930s, a shift toward fundamentalism developed as a strong reactionary force against liberalism and, with some notable exceptions, became the more dominant form of evangelical Quaker identity and spirituality in the Midwest and on the West Coast of the United States until the 1940s. A spirit of separatism, antimodernism, declining interest in social action, and biblical inerrancy and premillennialism prevailed in this period, until the midcentury brought a return to a more broadly evangelical culture.[42]

The spirituality of the Friends Church became a fusion of Wesleyan Holiness, modern evangelicalism, and fundamentalism, with an added mix of Quaker testimonies (more or less emphasized depending on the church) of holy living, simplicity, peacemaking, gender equality, silent waiting, and social ministry. Evangelical corporate spirituality was largely expressed in what is termed "programmed" worship, with pastoral preaching, vocal prayer, and hymns, analogous to other evangelical worship services, though usually a period of silence was added. Private devotions of prayer and Bible reading were expected. As missions spread Quakerism globally in the early part of the twentieth century, especially in Africa and Latin and South America, evangelicalism eventually became the largest worldwide form of Quaker spirituality (see chapter 10).

CHAPTER 9

Quakers and the Social Order, 1830–1937

NICOLA SLEAPWOOD AND THOMAS D. HAMM

In March 1917, Philadelphia Yearly Meeting of Friends (Orthodox) took up a request from some members. As the clerk summarized it, they asked the yearly meeting "that we consider what course be pursued by our Yearly Meeting and its members, to more completely live out the ideals suggested in our Queries, and how to promote the establishment of the Kingdom of God on earth." The writers made clear that they had been inspired by the model of London Yearly Meeting, which had established a War and Social Order Committee two years earlier. The Philadelphia Yearly Meeting (Orthodox) united in forming a similar committee.[1]

A year later, the new Social Order Committee made its first report, offering some reflections on Quaker history. "By the time the Society had been gathered for a generation they had established among themselves a very distinct social order," one based on equality, education, individualism, and business integrity. But, the report continued, while "Friends ... in their relations with others ... were generally kindly and helpful, and in public benevolences they were often leaders," they had located "morals in personal relations rather than in the control of social situations." Now, the committee urged, the time had come for Friends to apply Quaker principles "to promote the Kingdom of God on earth, particularly as it relates to social, political, and industrial conditions." This put them in a somewhat more conservative position than their British counterparts. The War and Social Order Committee in London aimed boldly at "not merely bettering present conditions but at nothing short of the introduction of the Kingdom of God into this present world."[2]

These Friends, both British and American, never defined what they meant by "social order." Context, however, makes it clear that they had in mind the systems that governed society nationally and locally, particularly in matters of economic relationships, social classes, the treatment of the "less fortunate," philanthropy, and morality, both private and public.

Between 1830 and 1937, both British and American Friends largely followed the trajectory that Philadelphia Friends described in 1918. Before 1900, Friends advocated on behalf of those they perceived as oppressed, most notably enslaved Africans and Indigenous peoples, but only a handful of radicals challenged social and economic structures. In the twentieth century, however, influenced by socialist movements in Britain and progressivism in the United States, many Friends came to challenge basic social institutions.

Because the courses of British and American Quakerism increasingly diverged after 1830, this essay treats them separately. American Quakerism, because of the series of separations in the nineteenth century, became increasingly diverse. By 1900, over two dozen yearly meetings existed in North America. British Quakerism experienced only minor formal separations; its story is almost entirely that of London Yearly Meeting. As the history of British Friends was more linear, a chronological structure is appropriate. But because of the diversity of American Quakerism, with different groups of American Friends taking up different issues at different times, they are dealt with in a topical fashion. Friends in other parts of the world—Latin America, Asia, Africa—doubtless also had views on their own social orders, but we currently lack the materials to analyze these views with sufficient care.

BRITAIN

Between 1830 and 1937, the way in which Quakers in Britain interacted with and influenced the social order changed quite dramatically. The Society of Friends went from being withdrawn and reticent to pioneering and confident in its interactions with the social order. Much of this interaction and influence was mediated by Quaker businessmen, particularly in the nineteenth century. The term "businessmen" is used here as Quaker women were far more active in social causes such as philanthropy, and later in politics, than in business. Dorothy Cadbury is the main exception, as she was active in the Cadbury family chocolate firm as a managing director from 1919 onward, showing that by this point, the idea of a woman in an authoritative position was at least no longer inconceivable.

The liberal "renaissance" in Quakerism emerged in the later nineteenth century, and the "testimony against war," later the peace testimony, was tested and revitalized by the First World War. These factors, combined with the diminishing influence of some Quaker business stalwarts, led to greater Quaker engagement with their own role in relation to the social order. This engagement was dynamic and has not been without controversy, with some, such as Brian Phillips, viewing Quakers before the First World War as active endorsers of an imperialist monarchical state and others, such as Thomas Kennedy, painting their later pacifist resistance to the state in a more sympathetic light. The evidence supports both of these positions: between 1830 and 1937, Quakers went from not engaging with the social order to any great extent, to defying their antiestablishment roots to become closely aligned with the social order and state by the late nineteenth century, and then to resisting the state and trying to alter the social order upon the advent of the First World War (see chapters 1 and 11).[3]

1830–1858

In 1830, at least some Quakers were still largely separate from the rest of society, and therefore the social order, in many ways. For example, they still wore plain dress. And by the Society of Friends' regulations, they were still required to marry only other Quakers, or risk expulsion. However, evangelicalism was on the rise at this time, and some Quakers were coming to resemble other evangelicals more than their own spiritual ancestors. Here, then, were the seeds, particularly for some wealthy Quaker businessmen, of a move away from Quakerism and toward Anglicanism and wider Christianity, and therefore toward a closer affinity with the current social order.[4]

The effect of the 1832 Reform Act, combined with the Sacramental Test Act four years earlier in 1828, paved the way for Quakers to enter Parliament. Joseph Pease was the first Quaker to do so, in 1832. He was the only Quaker in Parliament until John Bright's election in 1843. Bright, like Pease, began his adult life as a businessman. Bright was concerned with humanitarian causes in principle. However, he believed that business should be free of legislative interference above all else. He therefore opposed the Factory Acts in the 1840s, which sought to limit daily labor for women to ten hours, on the grounds of its interfering with free trade (see chapter 12).[5]

As late as 1843, the Society of Friends was still formally expressing disquiet about political activity. Brian Phillips has argued convincingly that there was a clear division in the minds of these early Quaker public figures between their Quakerism and their parliamentarianism, with John Bright refusing eldership on the grounds of his position as a politician.[6]

The lack of legal framework in many areas of life, from health and safety and welfare at work to education, highlighted and enhanced the impact of Quaker philanthropy and Quakers' social work, particularly at a local level. Businesspeople were well represented in areas like the adult school movement that began in 1845, a Quaker-led initiative to educate adults in areas such as literacy and arithmetic with a biblical focus.[7]

This local work to improve the social order grew more consolidated as some Quakers embraced their expanded opportunities in the broader society and became members of city or town councils. These included Joseph Rowntree in York, who, as Edward Milligan has pointed out, worked particularly hard to improve housing and sanitation.[8]

Quakers in the years from 1830 to 1858 sometimes still had relatively little interaction with broader society, or left the Society to marry out. However, evangelicalism had begun to undermine their separate identity and sense of detachment from those of other faiths, particularly Anglicans. Friends largely interacted with the social order on a local, philanthropic level, though they had begun to make forays into parliamentary life.

1859–1889

This period was a key one for the reform and revival of the Society of Friends in Britain. It began with an essay contest in 1859 to comment on the decline in membership of the Society over the previous half-century. The winning essay was *Quakerism Past and Present*, by Quaker businessman John Stephenson Rowntree. This was, according to Thomas Kennedy, "a work of seminal influence in the transformation of British Friends." In order to return to Quaker theological roots, Rowntree argued that "Quakers needed 'more knowledge of the wider world,' and of the Bible in relation to this, coupled with 'liberty of thought and action.'" He recommended the relaxation of Quaker discipline and rejuvenation of ministry, as this would lead to greater engagement with the social order.[9]

Although a shift had begun in 1850 with reform on the possibility of gravestones by London Yearly Meeting, 1859 was the year that visible change began to occur, despite the ire of conservative Friends. John Bright, as a member of Parliament (MP), advised on the viability of legal changes to allow Quakers to marry non-Quakers in the meetinghouse that year, and the law was changed the following year. Plain dress and plain speech were also made optional in 1861, as part of the revision of the Quaker discipline. By 1861, then, Quakers could dress and speak as they wished and marry whom they wished without facing the possibility of disownment (see chapter 3).[10]

Quaker social change cannot be divorced from that of society more broadly. This period saw trade unions and socialism grow in size and vigor as movements, the establishment of the Trades Union Congress, and the legalization of union activities. The Christian Socialist F. D. Maurice was chosen to judge the 1859 Quaker essay competition, suggesting that some Quakers were beginning to hold socialist sympathies.[11]

Over the course of Queen Victoria's reign (1837–1901), thirty-three Quakers held office as MPs, and the number grew steadily from the 1850s onward. In terms of using their position to influence the social order, Brian Phillips argues that these politicians were "more concerned with the extension of newly acquired Quaker respectability into Westminster than with securing a place for Quaker principles in national government." There was no single Quaker line on issues in Parliament at the time; Philip Ashton has shown how Quakers were divided on the issue of Irish Home Rule.[12]

In the years between 1859 and 1889, Quakers consolidated their positions within the social order, enabled by the relaxation of the discipline of the Society of Friends. This was almost entirely led by businessmen with the wealth, time, and social standing to be influential. The Society was growing more accustomed to Quakers in politics. Through business interests and political positions, wealthy Quakers were continuing to influence society for better and worse, and some, such as Joseph Whitwell Pease (son of the aforementioned Joseph Pease) and his family, were forgoing Quaker values to become more closely aligned with the state by accepting titles and adopting luxurious lifestyles.[13]

1890–1913

The Manchester Conference of 1895 was, in some sense, the culmination of the revival within the Society of Friends. It was where the many small developments of the preceding forty-five years came to fruition. It also gave considerable momentum to the revival and led to its broadening in the twentieth century. The speech given by John Wilhelm Rowntree, businessman and pioneer of the Quaker renaissance, was a high point for many. In it, Rowntree called for a deepening of Quaker faith based in love and suggested that the challenges of the modern age could be a strength rather than a weakness. The vast majority of Friends at the conference were less radical, though, and plenty were still evangelical and conservative.[14]

What did come of the socialist tendency within Quakerism was the Socialist Quaker Society (SQS), founded in 1898. Its two principal founders, Mary O'Brien and J. Theodore Harris, were both educators. However, there was at least one businessman who was a member of the SQS: Arthur Priestman was both a town councillor in Bradford and a cloth manufacturer. The SQS was not given a platform by the Society of Friends at first, and its membership remained small. Its existence, however, demonstrates that there was a contingent of Quakers seeking to replace the capitalist social order.

Not convinced by socialism, the majority of Quakers were drawn to social reform based on science, of the kind that would be advocated by Seebohm Rowntree. The Friends Social Union (FSU) was consequently founded in 1903 by such prominent Quakers as Rowntree and George Cadbury. It organized lectures and reading circles on diverse topics, including child labor, housing, and unemployment. And while its committee and ranks were made up mostly of "heavyweight," respectable Friends, it also drew socialists. However, as Thomas Kennedy laments, for all the union's ideas, it was not particularly productive in terms of social consequences.[15]

Progressive businessmen such as the Cadburys and Rowntrees were prominent in influencing the social order in other ways, including building model villages for employees. Seebohm Rowntree's *Poverty: A Study of Town Life*, which had a considerable impact, was published in 1901. Yet he went still further, helping Lloyd George as president of the Board of Trade and as a leading member of the Land Enquiry Committee.[16]

Nine Quakers, at least six of whom were businessmen, were elected to Parliament in 1906 as part of what Brian Phillips calls "the great Nonconformist electoral triumph." Then, in 1910, another Quaker joined the ranks of the MPs: Arnold Rowntree, who also worked at Rowntree's confectionery firm. Ian Packer has shown how Arnold Rowntree used most of his time in Parliament to advocate for social reform, in terms of wages and conditions for railway, coal, and mine workers, for example.[17]

Another influential Quaker businessman was John William Wilson, a director of the chemical firm Albright & Wilson. In 1895, he became MP for Worcestershire North, initially as a Liberal Unionist and from 1903 on as a Liberal. Like John Bright, Wilson was thoroughly committed to free trade: when protectionism was introduced by Joseph Chamberlain as leader of the Liberal Unionists in 1903, Wilson felt strongly enough about maintaining this commitment to change parties. In 1901, he was also a justice of the peace (a local judge) and a local county councillor. He gained some influence in Parliament, being admitted to the privy council (of the monarch) in 1911.[18]

Phillips has argued that 1890 to 1910, specifically, was a period during which Quakers were reacting against their radical antiestablishment roots to prove their respectability by entering public life and even by embracing some forms of patriotism, suggesting that they were putting public Quaker representation before their broadness as a movement and their "autonomy." That Quakers around the turn of the twentieth century were even pro-empire as a means of Christian evangelism seems to risk undermining the Quaker concern for some humanitarian causes, though one can imagine that some Quakers saw Quakerism and empire as similarly "civilizing" influences that both worked toward better human relations in the long term (see chapter 1).[19]

Phillips's evidence of the diversity of views in Quakerism explains the presence of two Quaker businessmen who sat in Parliament as Conservatives: Frederick Leverton Harris from 1900 and Alfred Bigland from 1910. Bigland, at least, was certainly pro-empire. That the Society of Friends as a body did not pronounce in favor of suffrage, Pam Lunn has noted, tends to confirm Phillips's view of Friends. However, this allegiance to state and Crown did not undermine the work for social good that Quakers were doing between 1890 and 1913.[20]

There was an increasing diversity of views among businessmen on the emerging social order. Some, like the Cadburys and the Rowntrees, were inspired by the new thinking of the Quaker renaissance and other broader social trends to actively pursue social reform. But few besides Arthur Priestman and his family were socialists. Then there were those, like John William Wilson and the Pease family, who were at the more socially conservative end of the liberal spectrum, favoring free trade and the philanthropy of old as the best means of business and social reform. Further removed still from the Priestmans were Bigland and Harris as Conservative MPs.

1914–1937

To a much greater degree than any other time between 1830 and 1937, the First World War was a flashpoint for British Quakers and their engagement with the social order. It forced Friends, individually and corporately, to engage with their history of resistance to war. Further, in the context of the rise of socialism, it led many Quakers to question the socioeconomic system that they felt had given rise to the war. Capitalism was the problem to which some of these Friends sought a solution. Others, including both Quaker Conservative MPs, resigned from the Society of Friends and wholeheartedly joined in the war effort. Of course, many more Friends sat somewhere in between resistance to the war effort and strong support for it. The war also brought out tensions in the Society's relationship to the state and permanently altered it: conscription in 1916 forced Quakers of military serving age to choose whether to comply or resist, and this led to the Society of Friends as a formal body actively campaigning against the government's decision. Kennedy notes, however, that about a third of Friends were pro-war, and a similar proportion enlisted. This demonstrates that some Quakers were still content enough with the present social order in this regard (see chapter 11).[21]

One of the first actions of a large group of individual Quakers after the outbreak of war was to establish the Friends Ambulance Unit (FAU) to help wounded soldiers. The FAU contributed significantly to the war effort. Given that contribution, however, there was some disagreement among Friends as to whether the FAU's work conflicted with their peace testimony.[22]

A War and Social Order Committee (WSOC) was formed by London Yearly Meeting in 1915 at the Friends Social Union's proposal. Some of those involved were clearly conscious of the divisions among Friends on the issue, for they argued against the name "War and Social Order Committee" on the grounds that it was similar to "socialism." Again, the group featured many Quaker businessmen, including George Cadbury and Roger Clark. It also featured socialists. It was a larger body than the FSU itself, probably because of the interest that the outbreak of war had stimulated, and it was fairly broad in its base and appeal.[23]

Phillips identifies a certain sense of confidence and ambition among Friends between 1890 and 1910, and this ambition is evident in the WSOC's vision: the general conference committee declared, "Let the opening note be the need to realise that we do not aim at merely bettering present conditions but at nothing short of the introduction of the Kingdom of God into this present world." Kennedy's recognition that the aims of these and other radical Friends of the time had much in common with those of Friends in the 1650s, however, is more pertinent. Despite the breadth of its membership, this committee produced radical ideas and materials. The WSOC was so prolific and so successful that in 1917, the FSU merged with it.[24]

When conscription was introduced in 1916, Quakers, including those in Parliament such as Arnold Rowntree and T. Edmund Harvey, were significant among those who lobbied for a conscience clause within the act. This clause passed and allowed those who felt unable to serve in the military on grounds of conscience to perform alternative service, such as serving in the FAU.[25]

Two key events for Quakers in relation to their interactions with the social order took place just months before the end of the war. Both emerged as a consequence of the WSOC. The first of these, in April 1918, was a conference of Quaker employers held at Woodbrooke. The opening address was given by Arnold Rowntree, MP and businessman. In it, he condemned the laissez-faire, free-trade approach to business. Given this stance, perhaps unsurprisingly, John William Wilson did not attend on behalf of his firm. However, the conference attracted a good number of participants from a wide range of firms.[26]

As John Kimberley notes, the first section, on the claims of labor, heard directly from three representatives of the labor movement. This demonstrates recognition on the part of the conference's organizers of the importance of the rising labor and unionist movements, a recognition that seems unimaginable even for paternalistic Quaker employers thirty years before. The conference also acknowledged the rise in legislation that left less of a place for such paternalism. Rowntree explicitly called for industrial democracy in his address. The very fact that employers met in this way shows a collective desire to alter the social order for the better in the twentieth century and a transformation in their outlook.[27]

The second event, at and by London Yearly Meeting, 1918, was the issuing of eight "Foundations of a True Social Order." This was a high point for the WSOC. The hand of the committee's socialists is visible within the document. The second "foundation" envisioned "a social order which is directed, beyond all material ends, to the growth of personality truly related to God and man." Interrelation, then, was key. The seventh foundation—"Mutual service should be the principle upon which life is organised. Service, not private gain, should be the motive of all work"—was radical. It demonstrated great boldness both in its content and in its very nature; Friends as a body had moved from feeling that they should remain distant from public life in 1837 to feeling, by 1918, that it was imperative that they pronounce on and alter the social order.

The forces leading the Society of Friends to become involved in broader social action over the latter half of the nineteenth century and the early twentieth gained strength and complexity with the outbreak of war and its testing of the peace testimony. This largely carried over into the years that followed: the 1920s book of discipline guided Quakers to "work for the coming of the Kingdom of Heaven on earth." An Industrial and Social Order Council was established in 1928 to succeed the WSOC, and there was another employers' conference in 1928 to consider Quakers and industry, though its attendance was lower than that of the 1918 conference, suggesting that fewer employers were interested in transforming the social order through their work. Quakers also set up pioneering local projects for social reform. These included working with Welsh mining communities, as highlighted by Pamela Manasseh, which grew out of Quaker concern following the general strike of 1926.[28]

Between 1830 and 1937, then, British Quakerism went through several phases in its interactions with the social order. It had moved from being largely set apart to being led, mostly by influential businessmen, into a close allegiance with the state by the late nineteenth and early twentieth centuries, and from there to being provoked into active rebellion and called anew to broader social action by the First World War. The Society of Friends became known, after the war, as an organization that challenged the social order largely out of concern for peace in a way that it had not for the preceding centuries of its history.

NORTH AMERICA

Central to American Quakerism in this period was its diversity. Nevertheless, certain lines of development are clear. In 1830, most American Friends shared certain assumptions about the social order: its basis in private property, social classes, and a market economy. They denounced oppression of people of color. They were conspicuous philanthropists. William White, the first Episcopal bishop of Philadelphia, said: "I can organize any good work in Philadelphia if I can get three or four Quakers associated with me."[29]

Variations from these broad views reflected the increasing diversity of Quakerism. Before 1900, the most socially conservative Friends expected Friends to bear witness against evils like slavery but resisted efforts that joined them with "the world's people," which they saw as a threat to the distinctiveness of Friends. By 1900, the diversity of American Quakerism produced a more striking divergence. On one side of the divide were now Friends, in both the Orthodox and Hicksite traditions, who embraced the precepts of the larger Social Gospel movement in American Protestantism; increasingly they spoke of furthering the Kingdom of God through reform. Opposed to them were fervently evangelical Friends tied to the emerging fundamentalist movement, who despaired of making America Christian.

Quakers in the American Social Order
"Did you ever see a poor Quaker?" was the question a Black newspaper in New York City asked in 1842. Certainly, throughout the nineteenth century, Friends shared the perception that they were prosperous. "As a society we are rich, as the world counts riches," a New York Hicksite wrote in 1851. Analyses of Philadelphia Yearly Meeting in the 1820s concluded that Orthodox Friends were, as a group, more prosperous than Hicksites, but it is not clear whether that was true of other yearly meetings. Philip Benjamin's study of Philadelphia Friends after 1865 found that any differences had disappeared by that time. Articles in Philadelphia Quaker weeklies spoke of "the servant problem," revealing class assumptions. This perception continued into the twentieth century. Friends were mostly "the privileged, property holding class of society," one wrote in 1924.[30]

This analysis was probably skewed by the prominence of urban Friends in Philadelphia, New York, and Baltimore. There was more diversity in the rural areas, where most Friends lived during this period. Martha Paxson Grundy's analysis of the Quaker community of Middletown, Pennsylvania, found that in 1850, Friends there were mainly farmers, with a scattering of merchants, physicians, and teachers and, significantly, no laborers. A New Yorker remembered of his meeting: "Many a time have I seen an old man sitting at the 'head of the meeting' who earned his bread by daily labor of a severe kind, while next to him sat one worth his thousands yearly." As late as the 1930s, the assumption in North Carolina was that most Friends were in modest circumstances. As Friends moved into cities, pastoral Friends showed an interest in attracting the poor. Cleveland minister J. Walter Malone emphasized this. Membership records in small cities, such as New Castle, Indiana, or Des Moines, Iowa, or High Point, North Carolina, suggest that Friends included a cross section of the population. On the other hand, a member's description of the Orthodox Chicago Friends Meeting in 1920 described its members as "excellently educated men and women—physicians, teachers, engineers, social workers and the like."[31]

Friends credited their general prosperity to lives of prudence and moderation. "They attend to their business with care and are generally industrious and economical," was the judgment of an Indiana Hicksite. A non-Quaker historian of Rush County, Indiana, offered a measured judgment in 1888: "You never see a poor Friend. . . . By industry, economy and close attention to business they have succeeded in amassing large wealth and in this particular command, in proportion to numbers, greater wealth than all the other orders of the county combined. When you strike the hand of a Friend you strike the hand of an honest man, but one, too, that wants its own, even to a penny." But in 1877, James E. Rhoads, a leading Philadelphia Gurneyite, worried: "It does not seem to me that the fact of a man's being a Friend in good standing is as much of an evidence as it once was, that he will pay his debts, or that he will not take improper advantage of another in his dealings."[32]

Our information about American Quakers as employers is limited, and what we have suggests that few saw Quakerism as enjoining them to practices different from their non-Quaker competitors. In a study of Lynn, Massachusetts, Alan Dawley wrote that Ebenezer Breed was an "entrepreneur who epitomized the Yankee [New England] trader. Cupidity gushed like a geyser from his Quaker soul." He found no difference between the methods of the close-knit Quaker business community and those of their non-Quaker neighbors. Joseph Wharton used every tool at his disposal to keep unions from his works, not out of a commitment to free-market economics (he was a passionate protectionist) but because he resented any restraints on his rights as a manager. Nor do we have evidence that Quaker furniture manufacturers in North Carolina were especially enlightened. There were, to be sure, some exceptions. Joseph Bancroft, a textile operator in Delaware, made a point of not laying off hands during down times. And Jonathan W. Plummer, one of the leading members of Illinois Yearly Meeting, instituted a profit-sharing plan in his pharmaceutical firm.[33]

American Quaker Philanthropy

Early in 1861, Gideon Frost, a Long Island Hicksite, wrote to the *Friends' Intelligencer*. "There is no trait in the character of Friends more noted than their earnest efforts for the relief of human suffering," he asserted. "How much so ever other professors may question our evangelical orthodoxy, they appear not to doubt that we are right upon all subjects connected with human weal and human woe."[34]

Friends of all persuasions agreed on the desirability of aiding the less fortunate. In cities, Friends both formed Quaker organizations and joined with non-Friends in charity societies to aid the "deserving poor" with clothing, food, fuel, and work projects. Women Friends were especially active. And rural Friends sometimes participated. A good example is the case of the Irish Potato Famine of the 1840s: Friends in Britain and Ireland took the lead in furnishing relief, and American Friends enthusiastically raised money. An Orthodox Friend in Springfield, Pennsylvania, wrote at the time: "There seems to me a weighty obligation on us to remember the suffering poor, and to the extent of our means ... to send of our abundance to relieve the starving multitudes." Before 1830, many American Friends, both Hicksite and Orthodox, regarded ties with non-Friends even in good causes as threatening to Quaker distinctiveness, but such attitudes faded except among the most uncompromising Wilburites. When wealthy New York Hicksite Samuel Willets died in 1883, a biographer noted not only his service to Friends but also his work as president of charitable groups such as the Infant Asylum, the Working Women's Protective Union, the New York Society for the Relief of the Ruptured and Crippled, and the New York Infirmary for Women and Children.[35]

Friends had mixed views about poverty. Some shared general attitudes in American society that emphasized a need to distinguish between the "worthy" and the "unworthy" poor. The *Friends' Intelligencer* in 1861 argued that the "improvident and thriftless" should be "allowed, to some extent, at least, the consequences of their folly." But an Orthodox Friend writing in 1848 offered a different view: "That the poor do not make the best use of what they get, is in general, true. This calls for instruction, and sometimes for admonition, but it is no good excuse for withholding our aid. We all have our failings." Friends urged education as the best preventive.[36]

The Laws of Nations

Two years before his death in 1830, Elias Hicks preached at New York Yearly Meeting. "The laws of nations are no rule for Christians at all, in relation to what is justice; for the laws of men are suited to the condition of those that they were made for; and therefore they indulge in an abundance of injustice and oppression," he told his audience. Yet he qualified his remarks significantly. "I am not upbraiding our country's government," he continued. "We cannot expect a nation to be born at once, or to be converted at once to truth and righteousness." From 1830 to 1937, Friends had definite views on how government could further truth and righteousness in the United States.[37]

Before 1860, a number of Friends, both Hicksite and Orthodox, had reservations about "intercourse with the parties and policies of the world." In 1833, an Orthodox Friend argued: "The present political state of our country is greatly calculated to draw us off our guard, and under the specious appearance for the welfare of civil affairs, to introduce us into a state of insensibility to that which is imperishable and permanent in its nature." Many Hicksite Friends worried that even to vote for officials who exercised military power was to compromise Friends' testimony against war, and so they refrained. Nevertheless, whatever their view of voting, Friends had clear ideas about how government should shape public and private morality. From the 1830s to the 1930s, Friends generally urged government to act against slavery and racism. After the Civil War, they denounced lynching and disenfranchisement. Such official stances did not prevent eastern Friends from segregating their schools, however, or Indiana Quaker pastor Daisy Douglas Barr from becoming a Ku Klux Klan leader in the 1920s. Similarly, although they objected to forced removal of and called for justice toward Native Americans, Friends generally supported the dismantling of tribal life.[38]

If anything united American Friends from the 1830s to the 1930s, it was opposition to alcoholic beverages. "Of all the evils of our land, this transcends them all," was the judgment of the Hicksite Baltimore Yearly Meeting in 1878. By the late nineteenth century, almost all Friends embraced prohibition. In 1867, an Orthodox Friend from upstate New York, John J. Thomas, wrote: "Intemperance . . . has become all-sweeping and overwhelming, destroying its tens of thousands yearly, and sending tens of thousands of criminals to prison.... There is but one remedy, total abstinence; and a law, sustained by the people, treating rum selling ... as a crime." Another Friend in 1924 called the Eighteenth Amendment, which imposed a federal prohibition of alcohol in the United States, "the greatest act of humanitarian legislation ever put through by any government." Friends united in favoring enforcement in the 1920s and opposing repeal in the 1930s. Walter C. Woodward, the editor of the *American Friend*, was ferocious on the subject in 1932, writing of opponents of Prohibition: "To yield to their captious clamor would be to surrender cravenly to the enemies of civilized society and social progress."[39]

The Social Gospel
In the nineteenth century, American Friends generally accepted market-based capitalism, although there were some notable exceptions. By the late nineteenth century, a diversity of economic views was becoming apparent. After 1900, an articulate group of Friends embraced the ideals of the Social Gospel, which many of them saw as taking up long-standing Quaker concerns; some later became socialists.

In 1819, Elias Hicks had preached: "riches is a great hurt to society." But he drew the line at schemes for "a community of property." In the 1830s, some Hicksites in Wilmington, Philadelphia, and New York City threw themselves into the Workingmen's Party movement, which, inspired by Robert Dale Owen, urged unionism and political activism to protect the rights of working people in emerging industries. Significantly, at least one critic said that such agitation was "calculated to operate on the passions of the uninstructed class of hearers." He branded "*equality* by legislation" as "chimerical." Between 1842 and 1846, Hicksites in the Ohio Valley and New York were part of the Society for Universal Inquiry and Reform, which repudiated both government use of deadly force and competitive capitalism and founded a series of utopian communities. Neither movement had lasting impact.[40]

Between 1865 and 1900, Friends expressed few reservations about capitalism and a competitive market-based economy. Henry Hartshorne of the *Friends' Review* decried proposals like Free Silver and defended the use of strikebreakers. Given a choice between the tyranny of capital and the tyranny of labor, he concluded, the former was preferable as "more intelligent and orderly." That "great questions of supply and demand" could not be resolved "by legal enactment" was the conclusion of many Friends. Dissenters like Lucretia Mott, who "was often constrained to bear her testimony against those large monopolies which she believed had a tendency to make the rich richer and the poor poorer," were the exception.[41]

By 1900, a modernist strain had appeared among both Hicksite and Orthodox Friends. It dominated Hicksite Quakerism and, though it was a minority position among Orthodox bodies of Friends, was well articulated and influential. Its most prominent exponent was Rufus Jones, a philosophy professor at Haverford and active Friend who produced a steady stream of books and articles. Jones and supporters were central to making Friends part of the larger Protestant movement known as the Social Gospel. Proponents argued that through both philanthropy and legislation, the United States, and the world, could be remade along Christian lines. The goal was to advance the Kingdom of God through human efforts. Friends should be "a fellowship at work for the Kingdom of Jesus Christ."[42]

Such Friends argued what was needed was "social reconstruction" and "Christian democracy." Earlham College professor Elbert Russell listed what he believed was required: "employers' liability laws, workmen's compensation, old age pensions, child labor laws, compulsory education, laws regulating the hours of women's labor, laws providing for faculty inspection, minimum wages, proper housing, and pure food." Of particular significance was the decision at the end of the First World War to continue the American Friends Service Committee (AFSC), formed in 1917 for European relief work, and to include within its mission alleviating poverty and eliminating injustice in the United States. So, the organization went to work to aid striking textile workers in North Carolina in 1929 and destitute coal miners in Appalachia in the 1930s.[43]

With the onset of the Great Depression in 1929, some American Friends came to see socialism as the answer. One proclaimed in 1933: "What there is of significance in Quakerism expresses itself today in Socialism." He continued: "The soul cries out against the unfairness of capitalism, its sordidness, the essential ugliness and the manner in which it debauches politics, writing, art and the human being itself." A few Friends even spoke well of Soviet Russia, such as Clarence Pickett, who became head of the AFSC in 1929. "Whatever may be the result in Russia, they are putting intelligence, work and sacrifice into the heroic venture to make the venture succeed," he wrote in 1930.[44]

We do not know how many Friends such radicals spoke for. The editors of the *American Friend* and the *Friends' Intelligencer* commented in 1932 and 1933, respectively, that support among Friends for such a course was quite limited. Quaker defenders of capitalism urged that all that was necessary was acting according to the Golden Rule. In 1935, conservatives, led by Earlham College president William C. Dennis, derailed an attempt by socialist-minded Friends to commit the Five Years Meeting to a program of "economic justice."[45]

By the early twentieth century, moreover, many Orthodox Friends were moving closer to the emerging fundamentalist movement. Key to that movement was premillennialism, the belief that the world would inevitably decline until the return of Christ. Attempts at reform would be fruitless. As one Quaker evangelist summed it up: "We are not here in this world to reform it. We do not believe the world is going to be saved as a whole. Our duty is to get people to the lifeboats and be rescued." In the depths of the Depression, a like-minded Friend agreed: "The present world needs to recover from its financial woes," he granted, but human efforts would be unavailing. "Nothing but the atoning blood of the Son of God can wash it clean, and nothing but the oil of the Holy Spirit can heal its open wounds." These were the Friends who had embraced the pastoral system and would lay the foundations for the contemporary Evangelical Friends Church International.[46]

Thus, by the 1930s, American Friends' views of the social order reflected their theological diversity. Some were political and economic liberals. Others maintained devotion to capitalist orthodoxies. And the most evangelical were convinced that only the return of Christ would put the world to rights.

CONCLUSION

Between 1830 and 1937, Friends in the British Isles and North America solidified the popular perception of Quakers as humanitarians and philanthropists. Over the course of that century, however, as diversity among Friends grew, so did different attitudes toward the social order. As a smaller and more socially homogeneous group, the British Quakers moved from a humanitarianism combined with classical liberalism toward socialism, from the Liberal Party to the Labour Party. In North America, as Friends came to embrace every variety of Protestantism, from Unitarianism to fundamentalism, there was likewise an increased diversity in social attitudes. Some American Friends, inspired in part by British counterparts, challenged capitalism. Others embraced it but advocated reform. And still others saw the mission of Friends not as changing this world but as saving lost souls from it.

CHAPTER 10

Quakers and Missions, 1861–1937

STEPHEN W. ANGELL

In the mid-nineteenth century, very few of the world's 120,000 Quakers—less than 1 percent—lived outside the North Atlantic region of North America and the British Isles. Quaker missions can be said to have begun in the 1650s, but their reach escaped nearly all non-English-speaking cultures, and nearly all nationalities of people of color, before the mid-nineteenth century. Unlike in the earlier period, the long-term efforts in the late nineteenth and early twentieth centuries by Quakers who often devoted much of their adult lives to these missions sometimes had significant effects in terms of membership. By the mid-twentieth century, Quaker presence was expanding quickly in the Global South, while it was steady, and soon contracting, in the North Atlantic region. By midcentury, almost 20 percent of the 140,000 Quakers in the world lived in the Global South, including about 18,000 in Africa, 6,000 in Latin America, and 1,500 in Asia.[1]

This chapter seeks to explain the forces within Quakerism that brought these developments about. It looks at certain long-term Quaker mission projects within Latin America (Bolivia and Guatemala), Africa (Kenya, Pemba, and Madagascar), and Asia (Japan, India, and China). Earlier short missionary trips had led to a sense that a more concerted, collective, long-term missionary effort was needed, and this chapter focuses on those efforts.

The mission work featured a large degree of involvement by women, among both the senders and receivers. This chapter also therefore explores the ramifications of gender in mission work. It looks, too, at the theories and philosophies underpinning mission work, including the degree to which Quaker mission work emphasized Christian commonalities or, alternatively, Quaker distinctives. It then explores certain crises in Quaker mission work that arose during the period, notably the World War I crisis, and the growing divide between Christians and Quakers with liberal and conservative theologies.[2]

THE DIVERSE ORIGINS OF QUAKER MISSIONS

From its origins, the missionary Quakerism inspired by nineteenth- and twentieth-century Quakers has been exceptionally diverse in nationality, race, gender, and theology. An exhaustive illustration of this principle would be impossible, but brief examples from Bolivia, Japan, Kenya, and India are offered here.

The arrival and flourishing of Quakerism among the Aymara peoples of Bolivia owes much to a man named Juan Ayllón (ca. 1897–?), whose father was a Catholic priest from Spain and whose mother, Rosaura Herrera, was an Aymara woman. In his adult years, Ayllón was influenced by Methodists, Baptists, and the Salvation Army, before casting his lot with a group of four Quaker street preachers: William Abel (1870–1919), a Native American and converted Friend who was a graduate of the Wesleyan-Holiness-influenced Training School for Christian Workers in Whittier, California, and three North American Quaker women, Union Bible Seminary–educated Emma Morrow, Mattie Blount from Indiana, and Florence Smith from Kansas. Ayllón decided that he needed the same kind of Quaker missionary training that his companions had, so in 1920, he stoked the boilers of a steamship headed for Guatemala, where he studied for three years at the Berea Bible Institute, a school for Christian workers, headed by Ruth Esther Smith (1870–1947), another Quaker graduate of the Training School for Christian Workers and a classmate of Abel's. On Ayllón's return, he found that Abel had died from smallpox, but Ayllón set up the first Quaker church among the Aymara people and remained active in Quaker ministry until 1944. Ayllón informed the Aymara that he had been sent to provide the message of salvation to them as "victims of sin, superstition, and darkness, to the weary and heavy-laden ones, that they might find rest of soul." He traveled extensively around Lake Titicaca and mentored other young Aymara men to serve the Quaker church.³

The Women's Foreign Missionary Association of Philadelphia Yearly Meeting (Orthodox) had been involved in Quaker missions in Japan since the 1880s. They had been prompted to undertake this work by a Methodist businessman, William Cogswell Whitney. Whitney's sister-in-law, Mary Caroline Braithwaite Whitney, who also lived in Japan, was an evangelical Quaker from Britain. Also promoting the idea of Quakers undertaking missions in Japan were two young Japanese men, Inazo Nitobe (a rising Japanese diplomat who married a Philadelphia Quaker, Mary Elkinton, and became Quaker himself; see chapter 12) and Kanzo Uchimura, later a Christian evangelist and founder of the "non-church" movement within Japanese Christianity. During this Westernizing phase of the Meiji era, the Japanese elite were anxious that all forms of Christianity be represented in Japan, and by the early 1880s, the Quakers, seen by the Japanese as Christian lovers of peace and humanitarians, were not yet present. This perceived lack was remedied in 1885, when women from the Women's Foreign Missionary Association of Philadelphia Yearly Meeting recruited a Quaker couple from Kansas, Joseph (1851–1932) and Sarah Ann Cosand (1846–1915), to begin a mission centered in Tokyo and, quickly, a girls' school in Tokyo as well. The Cosands, who remained affiliated with the Quaker mission until 1901, converted a number of notable Japanese people to Quakerism. Their converts included Chuzo Kaifu (?–1942), who became the first Quaker graduate of Earlham College in 1897 and subsequently a noted schoolteacher and evangelist, and Bunji (fl. 1901–1940) and Toshi Kida, who undertook extensive evangelistic work with Japanese Americans under the auspices of California Friends from 1907 until 1919. The Americans and Japanese associated with the mission in Japan embodied a range of theological perspectives, including Holiness Christianity and the Social Gospel. The work of the Quaker mission in Japan nurtured ties with the Japanese elite, including, among others, Japanese royalty. It was hardly a surprise when Emperor Hirohito, after World War II, selected a Quaker woman, Elizabeth Gray Vining, as the tutor for his son, Akihito, his eventual successor as emperor.⁴

In 1902, graduates of the Cleveland Bible Institute, another Holiness-Christianity-oriented educational institution affiliated with the Society of Friends, established the first American Quaker mission in Africa, in Western

Kenya. The Friends mission was the first Christian mission in the area; by 1909, the Church of God, the Anglicans, and the Catholics had also established missions in that area. Three Quaker missionaries went to Kenya in 1902—Willis Hotchkiss (1873–1948), Edgar Hole (1870–1942), and Arthur Chilson (1872–1939). Hotchkiss stayed only six months with the Quaker mission, but Hole and Chilson eventually brought their wives (Adelaide Hole and Edna Chilson) to the Kenya Quaker mission, and other Quaker couples also joined them in Western Kenya. Hole and Chilson stayed at Kaimosi, while Emory and Deborah Rees, who arrived in 1904, established themselves nearby in Vihiga. In 1906, the Kenya mission reported five African converts, of the Maragoli tribe of the Luhya nation (notably, Daudi Lung'aho and his wife, Maraga). By 1914, the Friends church included about fifty members. In the early 1920s, there were more than one thousand Quakers in Kenya; by 1926, more than four thousand; by 1932, about seven thousand.[5]

The Maragoli converts played a role in shaping Quaker teachings for Africans. It had been taboo for Maragoli women to consume chicken or eggs; some believed the consequence would be the women's infertility. At the initiative of Maragoli Friends, it was decided, as a rite of passage, that women who wished to join the Quakers should be required to eat chicken or eggs. Since only men had previously been able to eat these foods, women's consumption of them was seen as a statement of African Friends' belief in the equality of women and men. As in Japan, Quaker missionaries championed the education of girls and women. Rasoa Mutua (ca. 1906–1996), a recently converted Christian who was then about fifteen years old, experienced a call to preach in 1921 while attending the Quaker Girls' Boarding School in Lugulu, Kenya, and persevered with her call despite severe opposition from her family. She vigorously pursued her ministry, preaching in the mission field and other venues, from 1924 until her death in 1996.[6]

British Friends also became intimately involved in mission work in the nineteenth century. In 1861, an Indo-Portuguese couple, Mariano and Cecilia D'Ortez, visited London Yearly Meeting. Their band of Friends in Calcutta, having read Quaker literature such as Robert Barclay's *Apology*, were already holding Quaker meetings for worship, and they requested that a missionary be sent to India to aid them. While the yearly meeting attenders expressed interest and sympathy, the event provided useful publicity for the cause of Quaker missions, and correspondence with the Calcutta group was maintained, it would be five years before the British Friends would undertake any formal action to reach out to those in India who might be interested in Quakerism.[7]

In 1866, British Quaker Rachel Metcalfe (1828–1889) was released by the Friends Foreign Mission Association (FFMA) for service in India. To the dismay of Calcutta Quakers, the FFMA did not notify them of Metcalfe's arrival, nor direct her to visit them, likely because, in Ormerod Greenwood's words, the organization was unwilling "to wrestle with the difficult social, cultural, and theological issues which would arise in finding a *modus vivendi* with an independent group who were working out their own way of being Quaker." So, Metcalfe established the British mission at Hoshangabad, in the interior of India. Metcalfe, and the missionaries who followed, became deeply involved in a variety of projects to assist Indians of low social standing, including schools for orphans and assistance for weavers to market their goods. The converts that resulted from such Quaker witness, however, were few.[8]

Later, in 1892, Quaker women from Ohio Yearly Meeting, beginning with Delia Fistler (1867–1916) and Esther Baird (1861–1950), discerned a missionary call and were sent to India by an all-female mission board. (The London Yearly Meeting mission board was composed of men.) They opened an orphanage and saved the lives of children during a severe famine. The missions from Britain and Ohio, both eventually located in the state of Madhya Pradesh, had some contact; the Ohio mission sent some orphans for care to the London mission. As the Indian independence movement connected with Mohandas Gandhi grew apace in the early twentieth century, Friends such as Marjorie Sykes (1905–1995) and Horace Alexander (1889–1989) associated with Gandhi and participated in interreligious dialogue instead of Christian missionary work.[9]

From the beginning of their mid-nineteenth-century engagement with the modern Protestant missionary movement through the 1930s and beyond, women played a crucial role in Quaker missionary work. While much of the Quaker missionary movement issued from Holiness Christianity and its affiliated institutions, such as Bible institutes and training schools for Christian workers, Quaker missions never came solely from this impulse. The theological convictions underlying missionary work could be quite varied. Indeed, by the 1930s, the importance of interreligious dialogue, as compared to proselytization, had been dramatically heightened by the Gandhians and their Quaker friends.

Quaker women involved in missions displayed a wide variety of ideological views on issues of gender. While some supported the "separate spheres" view that women's place was in the home and men should care for business concerns in the world, there were many Quaker women who were dedicated to establishing greater gender equality than had existed hitherto. Carole Spencer has described how "evangelical, revivalist women" who were Quaker "became outspoken advocates of an egalitarian vision." Female leaders in Quaker missions tended to model egalitarian Christian views to their intended converts, even when their rhetoric did not quite match their example.[10]

The most important evidence of this Quaker missionary tendency toward egalitarianism was the persistent championing of the education of girls. In 1869, Sybil (1808–1873) and Eli Jones (1807–1899), American Quakers who took extensive interest in Protestant missionaries' education of girls in the Middle East, were approached by Miriam, a fifteen-year-old living in Ramallah (now part of Palestine), who noted that boys were being educated in that city but not girls and wondered whether the Joneses would start a school for girls. Miriam had previously attended a school in Jerusalem sponsored by German missionaries, and she volunteered to begin teaching female students; other teachers were also found. Thus began Quaker educational efforts in Ramallah.[11]

Roxie Reeve, a Quaker from Kansas, twenty-six years old at the time of her arrival in Kenya in 1913, was a driving force in establishing a girls' school among the Maragoli people in North Nyanza. She would remain in Kenya for thirteen years, presenting a dissenting voice and a contrary example to the other American missionaries, both male and female, who were committed to teaching "domesticity" to their female Kenyan converts. According to Samuel Thomas, Reeve's feminism "was a complicated mix of the nineteenth-century emphasis on the domestic, and strikingly modern views on the equality of women."

American missionaries in East Africa were divided over the propriety of unmarried women in their mission field. One of the first American missionaries in Kenya, Arthur Chilson, strongly opposed the presence of unmarried women in the mission field, believing that gender imbalance in the mission staff would create an appearance of American tolerance of polygyny, and thus he objected to Reeve's presence altogether. Disregarding

African ideas of motherhood, Chilson articulated a philosophy of Western domesticity. In his view, the presence of married women and families in the mission field was "important because it enables the women missionaries to conduct a most blessed work with the native women, teaching them how to care for their children and homes and to be real wives and mothers." Emory Rees, another missionary in Kenya, did not oppose unmarried women serving as missionaries but differed with Reeve over her orphanage and other matters of educational policy.

By 1925, Reeve's physical and mental health had suffered, and her opponents, Chilson and Rees, were able to ensure that when she went to the United States for health reasons, the American Friends Board of Foreign Missions would not return her to the mission field in Kenya, despite her desire to resume her work there. The girls' boarding school remained an enduring part of Reeve's legacy in Kenya.[12]

Unmarried women also played a key role in establishing and maintaining American Friends' missions in Bundelkhand, India, and Nanjing, China, and elsewhere. These women, who had more freedom as missionaries than did married women, included Esther Baird and Delia Fistler in India; Esther Butler, Lenna Stanley, Lucy Gaynor, Effie Murray, and Margaret Holme in China; and Ruth Esther Smith in Guatemala.

Friends found a common cause with other Protestant missionary movements in the late nineteenth-century mission fields, seeing themselves as championing the interests of women by opposing foot-binding in China and polygyny in East Africa. Of course, the colonialist desire to remake societies of subject peoples in the Western image—which Quakers shared, at least in this respect—was far more complicated in both intention and outcome than the idealist vision that justified the actions of Quakers and others a century or more ago (see chapter 1). Kenyan Quaker scholar Esther Mombo has explained that polygyny was obviously much more advantageous to men than to women and the missionaries' instructions for men to put away their plural wives was "heartless," because it left the abandoned wives destitute, and that, in general, the missionaries' teachings on such matters as marriage did not improve the position of Luhya women. Still, Quakers were seen as distinctive even among other Protestants in the mission field in the extent to which they championed the interests of women, especially in their embrace of women's ministry, including that of Rasoa Mutua, and in their eagerness to establish girls' schools. This was a defining characteristic of Quaker missions.[13]

QUAKER DISTINCTIVES IN THE MISSION FIELD

For Quaker missionaries, simply communicating the basic Christian message of salvation through Christ as a remedy for sin seemed imperative and was often challenging enough, given the large numbers of non-Christians who surrounded them. In 1885, when the first Quaker missionaries to Japan, Joseph and Sarah Cosand, arrived, they instituted a "Confession of Faith" for their converts that asserted belief in the existence of "one true God," confession that one had "broken the laws of God," and affirmation that salvation was available only through Jesus Christ and that the Holy Spirit would guide the convert "to live a life in accordance with the teachings of Holy Scriptures," but this included nothing about the Quakers' distinctive teachings. Those who agreed signed a "Believers' Book." William Ellis, a longtime British supporter of Friends' missions, wondered in the 1860s if he had been right in this support, as "he feared the effect of introducing different views of Christian truth."[14]

However, Quaker missions were commonly born of two motivations: an attempt to share a basic Christianity common to all Christians and an aim to share the Quaker version of Christianity, with its distinctives that were objectionable to many other Christian groups as well as to non-Christians. There was sometimes considerable tension between these two motivations. Accordingly, an appropriate balance needed to be sought, and that was not always easy to achieve. In India, the existing Calcutta group was strongly attracted by the spiritualization of the Christian sacraments, objecting to the bitter disputes between Christian sects on the proper mode of administering sacraments and seeing Quakers' spiritual sacraments as a development anticipated by certain indigenous Indian religious sects, such as Ram Mohun Roy's Brahmo Samaj, which had rejected the sacredness of the Ganges River water. Meanwhile, other Indians feared being trapped in a small, insecure social grouping. Entrance into all other Christian groups required water baptism, and when Christians as a whole faced social ostracism, to be shunned by both non-Christians and other Christians (for lack of baptism) seemed too much to bear for some Indian Quakers. Both the British Friends Mission and the Ohio Friends Mission in India maintained traditional Friends' teachings on spiritual baptism and communion, but one of their most significant converts, Bal Mukand Naik (1857–1950), a former Brahmin who was the first convert of the British mission, eventually accepted water baptism to be of better service to the broader Christian community. Through the Church Missionary Society, Mukand became ordained as a minister.¹⁵

The Japan mission begun by the Cosands would face the problem of how to present Quaker distinctives within a few years of its founding in 1885. An 1887 conference of Orthodox Friends in Richmond, Indiana, produced a declaration enjoining Friends not to use physical sacraments and to avoid participation in wars. That precipitated tensions among Japanese who had been attracted to the Society of Friends. The brief "confession" that they had been asked to sign contained no mention of these matters. By 1888, the Richmond Declaration of Faith had been translated into Japanese, and Friends' converts were requested to make additional commitments, including the rejection of outward sacraments. Japanese Friend Inazo Nitobe wrote to Margaret Haines, head of the Women's Foreign Missionary Association of Philadelphia Yearly Meeting, urging that the Quaker mission in Japan accommodate its Japanese converts by relaxing its position against outward sacraments. He was especially concerned about the lack of water baptism. "If the Quaker missionary teaches the people that no outer ordinance is necessary, as a gateway of admission to Christ's church," he asked, "will not the *less spiritual* rush in with even more eagerness than the spiritual?"¹⁶

A more important consequence of the Richmond Declaration came six years later, in 1894. When the Sino-Japanese War broke out, some influential Japanese Friends wished to support the emperor in this war, noting that the emperor permitted loyal Christians to proselytize among the members of the armed forces and contending that the Richmond Declaration's opposition to all wars surely did not proscribe their support of the Japanese nation in an effort as worthy as this one. Quaker missionary Joseph Cosand took the extreme step of completely withdrawing the mission's support of the Friends' meeting in Tokyo and beginning a new Quaker meeting, with international missionaries as members, to forestall the Japanese Quakers from supporting their nation's war. The members of the previous meeting could join only when they were willing to commit themselves to a pacifist position; six of the eight Friends from the old meeting eventually did join the new meeting on those terms, while the others left Quakerism.¹⁷

Sometimes Friends' distinctives constituted a part of the reason for establishing Quaker missions in the first place. The British Quaker mission in the Sichuan province of China was largely begun by Robert (1861–1942), William, Warburton, and Alfred Davidson. Their father, Corporal Adam

Davidson, had participated in a British and French military campaign in China in 1860 that resulted in considerable looting and destruction, and Corporal Davidson had become a pacifist as a result. He became a convinced Friend and taught his pacifist values to his children, four of whom then, at their father's urging, were instrumental in initiating a mission to China, beginning with Robert's arrival in Sichuan in 1889. The Quaker mission to Pemba, part of Zanzibar, that began in 1896, arose out of London Yearly Meeting's strong commitment to antislavery. The island off the coast of Africa, then under control of the British government, had just decreed abolition of slavery, and British Friends wanted to assist the 250,000 formerly enslaved human beings on that island in their transition to freedom. The last British missionaries left Pemba in 1963, but a small group of Quakers carried on after their departure; it was reported that there were 140 Quakers in Pemba in 1976.[18]

In 1932, the Chaco War broke out between Bolivia and Paraguay, and the members of the fledgling Quaker mission in Bolivia, faced with decisions as to how to respond to their conscription into the Bolivian army, attempted to find ways to uphold the Friends' peace testimony. The Bolivian government did not permit the Aymara people who had become Friends to claim the status of conscientious objector. Some young Quaker men felt that they had no choice but to don the military uniform. One such convert framed his involvement this way: "I do not fear death nor do I want to take life. I am a soldier of Jesus Christ." Consequently, this convert refused to use his gun in battle. Others carried out their military duties like other soldiers, and still others hid rather than subject themselves to conscription. Several men in the latter category were killed.[19]

THE THEOLOGICAL BASIS OF FRIENDS' MISSION WORK

A historical narrative of Quakerism formed a core part of missionaries' and mission boards' understanding of their purpose, although it differed somewhat between individual Quaker missionaries. That narrative located the genesis of Quaker mission work in the mid-seventeenth-century beginnings of the Quaker movement, with the witness of fervent traveling evangelists such as George Fox and the "Valiant Sixty"—missionaries in the 1650s who carried the Quaker message, often in pairs, throughout the British Isles and overseas. According to Henry T. Hodgkin (1877–1933), an important participant in the Friends' missions of the late nineteenth century, early Friends imparted "their glorious gospel of life and power.... To every man, they believed was given a seed of God," and George Fox preached to Native Americans in order that they might "know the principles of Truth; so that they may know the way of salvation, and the nature of true Christianity, and how that Christ hath died for them, who 'tasted of death for every man.'" Walter R. Williams, who, like Hodgkin, was a participant in a Friends' mission in China, portrayed Fox as a soul winner for Christ and stated of the Valiant Sixty that they "had . . . the urge of the Holy Spirit, impelling those, who had come to enjoy the rest and victory which the gospel offers, to carry the good news to other neighborhoods and towns and cities. . . . Scores of Spirit-filled men and women . . . kept coming forward, eager for the task."[20] Reflecting in 1915 on the missionaries' recent efforts, Hodgkin wrote, "the experience of these fifty years of settled missionary work is of peculiar value and significance, [because] it is showing Quakerism as a working faith, universal in its efficacy and appeal."[21]

A statement issued by London Yearly Meeting in 1858 put forward the shared vision of British and American missionaries who departed for international missions in the late nineteenth century:

> It is a duty incumbent upon all, and especially upon those who bear the hallowed name of our one Lord and Redeemer, *to act towards man, everywhere, however uncivilized or unenlightened, with that respect, with that consideration and love, which are due to our common nature and to our common hopes.* To treat man with disdain because his colour differs from our own, is a reproach cast upon Him who made him. . . . Warmly do we desire that Christians everywhere may be more and more alive to their high vocation; and address themselves to the warfare against sin, ignorance and superstition, relying on the power of our Risen Redeemer, rather than on the protection of fleets and armies.[22]

In many Quaker mission fields, this meant close cooperation with other Christians. In Madagascar, for instance, Quakers worked closely with the London Missionary Society (LMS), an interdenominational mission agency with a heavy representation of Congregationalists and Anglicans, in setting up schools for Madagascar residents of all levels of age and skill. Quakers were most involved at the elementary level, but they supervised the curriculum at the secondary level in Tananarive and were even involved in teaching in the LMS theological seminary. As Madagascar moved toward independence between 1947 and 1961, Quakers felt they no longer could support missions there, and thus, in a process of "devolution," the Quaker meetings merged with the LMS and French Protestants to form a united Protestant church on the island.[23]

In West China, the British Friends Mission helped establish the West China Missionary Conferences, the first of which was held in 1899. According to historian Charles Tyzack, this "was a way of avoiding rivalry and duplication of effort, and it showed Anglicans, Methodists, Baptists, and Quakers agreeing that they preached the same gospel." In 1908, a second such conference led to a proposal for a united Protestant church in Sichuan, concluding with a joint worship service in which Friends were led by the Holy Spirit to abstain from the physical sacraments but, in the words of Henry Hodgkin, did not feel "in the least left out." This proposal did not produce an actual united church, but Friends did play an important role in the leadership of ecumenical Protestant endeavors in China, despite their small numbers. For example, Hodgkin was one of the secretaries of the National Christian Council of China from 1922 to 1929.[24]

FRIENDS' MISSIONS AND EMPIRE

The relationship between Quaker missions and the imperialist designs of Great Britain and the United States varied substantially. Quaker missionaries usually did not consciously desire to be the servants or accomplices of the nineteenth-century British Empire, nor any other empire.[25] However, many considerations made it difficult for them to disentangle themselves from the bonds of empire (see chapter 1). In Pemba, their stated aims to assist in the transition of enslaved peoples to a prosperous freedom motivated British Quaker missionaries such as Henry Stanley Newman (1837–1912) to closely tie the dissemination of the Christian gospel to economic schemes. As Newman saw it, the former slaves needed to be "civilized." Both Africans and the British people would thereby reap benefits: "While benevolently considering how much good we can do to the peoples we govern, in developing the magnificent natural resources these vast territories contain, we do not leave out of consideration the needs of our island home." Racial hierarchies would be preserved, even reinforced, in the process. "Everything points to the establishment of one leading axiom in all African affairs," declared Newman, "and that is, that *the future development of tropical Africa must be the work of the natives themselves under enlightened European supervision.*"[26]

Lorenzo Baker, a ship's captain who was president of the United Fruit Company, was instrumental in supporting nineteenth-century missions by American Quakers in Jamaica and Cuba through his contacts with Iowa Yearly Meeting superintendent Zenas Martin. There were other Quakers who inspired Cuban missions as well, ones without commercial entanglements, such as Episcopalian minister-turned-Quaker Francisco Cala from Mexico, whose short-lived missions were located in Havana, on the western end of the island. On the eastern end, the first missionaries to Cuba also included a young married couple who had just graduated from William Penn College in Iowa, Sylvester and May Mather Jones, and two Quakers from Mexico, Emma Phillips Martinez and Maria de los Santos Trevino. They arrived in 1900, just two years after the United States wrested Cuba away from Spain in the Spanish-American War. Their forthright evangelical aim was "to preach the Gospel, always preaching Christianity above denominationalism—Christ crucified, the Savior of men—and not beginning with the words or practices of the doctrines and concepts established by Friends." By 1905, they had established Friends' missions in four cities on the eastern end of the island: Banes, the headquarters of the United Fruit Company; Gibara, thirty miles to the east along the coast; Holguin, the provincial capital, located inland; and Puerto Padre, farther to the east. Zenas Martin and the five missionaries located the headquarters of the Friends' mission in Gibara as a gesture to show some independence from the United Fruit Company. Friends' schools were started in all four of these cities, and several of them flourished and became prestigious institutions, sometimes receiving substantial support from the United Fruit Company and the Cuban government.[27]

When armed conflicts arose within the mission fields, the European or North American missionaries often had to choose whether to accept protection by the imperialist powers. Ohio Friends in Nanjing were forced to evacuate in 1891 when insurrections seeking the expulsion of foreigners and Christians in the vicinity of Nanjing destroyed some Christian churches, resulting in the deaths of a few Christian missionaries who were not Quakers. Both the Ohio Quaker missionaries and the British Quaker missionaries in Sichuan were forced to evacuate during the 1900 uprising of Boxers, a militia of farmers and laborers seeking to get rid of the foreigners who they believed had brought humiliation and misery to China. This resulted in the death of 135 missionaries, none of them Quaker. In Madagascar, French armies invaded in 1895, displacing an indigenous monarchy nominally backed by the British Empire, and unleashed a furious resistance against all Europeans that resulted, among other sorrows, in the deaths of two British Quaker missionaries and their daughter in the interior of the island.[28]

When Warburton Davidson suffered a beating by a mob in Sichuan in 1899, the Friends' mission, burdened (as the mission saw it) with the privileges attached to being British, were induced to countenance the British consul's "exemplary punishment" for the attackers and accept compensation, while negotiating some slight amelioration of the terms. If this violence against Davidson had been allowed to go unpunished, all the British people resident in West China would have faced a heightened risk of violence. In the end, while the Friends' mission was compensated, the British consul had to be satisfied with less corporal punishment of the attackers than he had wanted, owing to "the well-known peculiar ideas of the Quakers prevent[ing] them ... from demanding redress adequate to the occasion."[29]

The crisis arising from conflicts between empires that became known as World War I had large consequences for Quaker missions everywhere (see chapter 11). Hu Ching-I, the governor of Sichuan, observed to one of the Quaker missionaries in his province, "Jesus said, 'Whosoever smite thee on thy right cheek, turn to him the other also.' How about the followers of Jesus in Europe now?" Former China missionary Henry Hodgkin, during that time residing in Britain, actively opposed the war and helped found the Fellowship of Reconciliation. Esther Baird, Ohio Yearly Meeting missionary in India, was "devastated" by her son Eugene's enlistment in the Canadian army (without discussing it with her first) and subsequently by his 1916 death on a battlefield in Flanders. In 1915, Ohio Yearly Meeting missionaries in Nanjing acknowledged that World War I subjected them and all Christian missionaries to "shame and humiliation," but that reality did not consequently lessen their evangelistic imperative: "'We dare not slack our hand' [Zeph. 3:16]."[30]

As colonial subjects, the Maragoli people in East Africa faced the prospect of British imperial conscription—they could be taken away without warning and without their consent. Maragoli Friend Mmboga wa Votega was forced into the King's African Rifles by the British during World War I, to serve as a porter or soldier, despite his pacifist principles. Whether the American Quaker missionaries protested against his conscription is not known. The King's African Rifles was created to defend British East Africa from German East Africa. Votega never came home, and his failure to return after the conflict was never dignified with any explanation or accounting for his loss. His wife, Dorika Bweyenda (d. 1983), had been pregnant when he was taken, and she named her son Ngeresa, meaning "English" in her native Luragoli language, signaling a surprising forgiveness of those responsible for her husband's death.[31]

MISSIONARY QUAKERISM AND NON-CHRISTIAN CULTURE

Quaker missionaries displayed a considerable range in degree of acceptance or rejection of the cultures of the peoples they sought to evangelize. In Christian missionary culture, it was often expected that converts would make a clean break with past religious practices, which the missionaries generally saw as idolatry. Thus, British missionaries in Sichuan and American missionaries in Nanjing both seemed to expect those Chinese who became Quakers to renounce their household gods, or "idols." The converts' burning of "idols" was an act of celebration that the foreign missionaries were usually invited to witness. In 1887, Mary Jane Davidson, an English Quaker in Sichuan, was invited to witness a poor woman named Chen burn her "idols": red paper with the characters for "heaven" and "earth" on them, and an incense stand. On another such occasion forty-five years later, in 1932, Freda Girsberger of the Ohio mission in Nanjing reported that while she "watched these things burn, we thanked God for his great victory. Scripture posters were placed on the walls." This model of conversion was built on an exclusivist binary, counterposing Christian salvation to a less fortunate fate for those who refused to accept Jesus as their savior. That was fairly standard thinking for British and American missionaries in the late nineteenth century, though some missionaries would change their position on this matter during the first third of the twentieth century.[32]

Some of their intended converts, to the missionaries' frustration, strongly resisted this exclusivist framework. In the 1880s and 1890s, Quaker missionaries in Japan translated biographies of Quaker humanitarians Elizabeth Fry and Stephen Grellet into the Japanese language and distributed them widely. Such publishing projects were successful in promoting admiration of Quakers among the Japanese but not in obtaining conversions. One Japanese princess, strongly committed to Buddhism and Shinto, stated, after reading the biography of Fry, that she admired Fry very much; this, however, did not make her want to convert to Quakerism. Japanese syncretism helped frustrate the missionaries' conversion efforts. A contributor to the *Friends Missionary Advocate* observed, "The Japanese might readily accept Christianity by adding the image of Jesus to their present collection and giving equal honor with Buddha and their ancestors, but they would find difficulty in the Christian belief of having 'no other gods besides' Jehovah." The exclusivism promoted by Christian missionaries, including Quakers, had little place in Japanese culture.[33]

Stanley Ngesa has documented a similar attitude toward Quakerism in Kenya. His great-grandmother Dorika Bweyenda converted to Quakerism, but she did so without giving up her ancestral shamanic traditions. The Luhya people followed the principles of peace (*mulembe* in Luragoli) even before the arrival of Quaker missionaries. After the disappearance and presumed death of her husband, Mmboga, in World War I, Dorika's father-in-law, Votega, initiated her as a shaman. She became a very active Christian Quaker as well as a Maragoli shaman. Ngesa writes that the Maragoli "were, on the whole, respectfully evangelized," and the American Quakers did not obstruct the preservation of the key aspects of Maragoli culture.[34]

Thus, while some evangelically oriented Quaker ministers continued to embrace an exclusivist binary, by the 1930s, there was considerable diversity, among both the missionaries and the peoples they were attempting to convert, on the matter of relationships with non-Christian cultures.

RISING NATIONALISM AND CONFLICTS AMONG QUAKER MISSIONARIES

In the 1920s, Quaker missions faced severe challenges from without and within. Quaker missions had often been isolated from each other, so there was little awareness of what Quaker missions administered by different Quaker mission agencies were doing. Even so, prior to about 1910, those approaches to mission work had been largely congruent. After World War I, however, they sometimes proved to be widely divergent.[35]

Quaker missions were affected by the growing conservative-liberal divide in the Society of Friends. The sponsor of many of the Quaker missions,

Five Years Meeting (FYM), was roiled by internal divisions as to whether it was proper for the Quaker organization to employ theological liberals. The presenting issue was whether certain Orthodox Christian faith statements previously adopted by FYM, most notably the 1887 Richmond Declaration of Faith, could be considered as "creeds." In 1912, the FYM minutes noted that the Richmond Declaration was "not to be regarded as constituting a creed"; a decade later, faced with a protest from Kansas Yearly Meeting on the subject, FYM rescinded the 1912 minute. The workers employed in the mission field, the majority of whom were employees of FYM, might have been greatly affected if the Richmond Declaration had been regarded as a binding statement of Quaker doctrine. In fact, however, the rescission of the 1912 minute had little or no discernible effect on FYM's mission or workforce. To the consternation of evangelically oriented Friends, the Richmond Declaration was no more utilized as a strict doctrinal standard after 1922 than it had been before.[36]

The Davidson brothers, long the mainstay of the British Friends mission in Sichuan, moved toward positing a strong commonality between Christianity and the Buddhist, Taoist, Confucian, and ancestral faiths of the Chinese whom they served as Christian missionaries. After World War I, they seem to have stopped urging the Chinese to destroy their household gods (in contrast to the more conservative Ohio mission of Friends in Nanjing, which continued its exclusivist condemnation of these gods). At a 1920 Buddhist worship service, Henry Davidson affirmed that he "could not doubt" that the Chinese Buddhists "were offering, according to their light, a true worship." His brother Robert found an admixture of truth and error in every religion, including Christianity, but affirmed a common foundation for each, in that they all worshipped "a good spirit greater than themselves upon whom they are dependent." Henry Hodgkin, who had worked alongside the Davidsons for years, found that he no longer assumed that his was "the better way." Now he recognized that "God needs all kinds of people and ways of living through which to manifest Himself in the world."[37]

Walter R. Williams (1884–1973), a missionary for Ohio Yearly Meeting in Nanjing between 1913 and 1927, believed that missionaries like the Davidsons (whom he did not name, and may not have known, given the approximately eight hundred miles of distance between their mission stations) were carrying "a mongrel message—a mixture of Biblical teaching and human philosophy." They had been "deceived by men with supposed 'superior scholarship,' [and thus] have put away 'the faith of the fathers.'" Williams championed a missionary approach of "teaching the Bible as the 'Good News' with its doctrines of human depravity, the vicarious blood-atonement and the bodily resurrection of Christ, the transforming power of the Spirit in regenerating and sanctifying the believer." While both Williams's and the Davidsons' missionary approach had roots in Quaker traditions going back to the seventeenth century, both approaches clearly were more strongly influenced by contemporary Christian theologies—in Williams's case, Holiness Christian theology and, in the case of the Davidsons, a modernist approach.³⁸

Rising Chinese and Indian nationalism complicated Christian missionary efforts in Asia, the Quakers' included. Mohandas Gandhi criticized the attempts to use medical care, education, and other means of "temporal liberation" to attract converts. In 1931, he was quoted by the press as saying that missionaries who "confine themselves to social and economic uplift" would be welcome in India, but if they were to use "hospitals and schools for the purpose of proselytizing then I should certainly ask them to withdraw." Gandhi implored Christians not to try to convert Hindus to Christianity but to make them better Hindus. Chinese nationalists advanced analogous arguments against Christian missions in China. Rufus Jones (1863–1948), whose aunt and uncle, Sybil and Eli Jones, had been instrumental in founding the girls' school in Ramallah but whose own efforts in international humanitarianism had been focused on service rather than missions, became interested in Christian and Quaker missionary work as these controversies became more heated. He sided largely with those, like Gandhi and the Davidsons, who were refocusing spiritual conversation as interfaith dialogue and seeking intercultural understanding.³⁹

In a paper read for him at an ecumenical missionary conference in Jerusalem in 1928, Rufus Jones lauded followers of non-Christian religions such as Hinduism as "witnesses of man's need of God and allies in our quest for perfection." As the only Quaker member of the fifteen-person Laymen's Foreign Missions Inquiry that issued an influential report on the subject in 1932, Jones reinforced this theme. Missionaries should actively care for others, preaching with their lives, more than with their words. They should recognize the strengths of other religions and be humble about the shortcomings of their own: "If God is truly *Father* we can well believe, with St. Paul at Lystra, that He has not left any of His people without some witness of himself [Acts 14:17]." The inquiry's report recommended that Christians allow truth, rather than tradition, to be their ultimate guide: "All fences and private properties in truth are futile: the final truth, whatever it may be, is the New Testament of every existing faith."[40]

That recommendation was roundly condemned by a wide assortment of moderate and conservative Christians, including many Quakers, for downplaying the role of Christ in human salvation. Consequently, these critics also saw it as undermining any fervor and passion that ordinary Christians might have for the mission endeavor. While acknowledging that he also had come to a place of emphasizing commonalities among religions rather than their differences, China missionary Robert Davidson criticized the Laymen's Inquiry report on similar grounds as insufficiently passionate about presenting the claims of Christianity upon all. The report lacked "the fire and passion of men who have found and possess a solution of and a remedy for world trouble and must make it known."[41]

In East Africa during the 1920s and 1930s, numerous divisions developed, including debates over the nature of the Holy Spirit and what it could do in the lives of individual believers and over proper missionary conduct toward peoples being evangelized. Arthur Chilson, one of the first three Quaker missionaries to Kenya, was instrumental in preaching a lively Holy Spirit revival in 1927. The revivals preached by Chilson had Pentecostal manifestations, with students at the Friends' school in Kaimosi shouting and speaking in tongues. Chilson, reading aloud the second chapter of Acts, encouraged these ecstatic expressions. Meanwhile, he had conflicts with other Quaker missionaries, whom Chilson accused of being unsound on the doctrine of scriptural inspiration.[42]

In 1928, Chilson left Kenya on furlough. After a short time in Kansas, he then sought to resume his ministry to Kenya, but the American Friends Board of Missions refused to permit his return, almost certainly because they objected to his intense revivalist philosophy and disapproved of his intolerance of other Friends missionaries' theologies. A decline in the board's finances was cited as the formal reason for not permitting Chilson's return to Kenya. When he did return to Africa in 1934, Chilson inaugurated a new mission under the sponsorship of Kansas Yearly Meeting in Urundi. In Kenya, some of the Africans most affected by the revival, holding fast to ecstatic forms of expression, had separated from Friends by 1932, and they established the Holy Spirit Church. Their loud worship practices were similar to those of the neighboring Pentecostalist churches, and the remaining Friends missionaries, some of whom were strongly evangelical, sought to discourage such practices.[43]

In the 1930s, Africans increasingly protested missionary paternalism, alienation from their lands, and forced labor, and they did so with the support of the younger American missionaries, who were more liberal and modernist than the fundamentalist old-timers. In 1934, Archibald Bond, a Quaker missionary and medical doctor in Kenya, supported by fellow missionary Margaret Parker, a nurse, condemned racism and paternalism in Friends' mission work, observing that this made impossible appropriate interaction between Friends missionaries and the Africans they intended to evangelize. The Luhya supported Bond and Parker's criticisms. Quaker elders from Kaimosi charged that Friends missionary Fred Hoyt, who taught carpentry and masonry, had beaten his students and had sought legal action to bar women from gathering firewood. According to Benson Amugamwa, Jonathan Mulobi later recalled that "Hoyt was hot-tempered and severely beat African students when they failed to perform perfectly. Sometimes, to avoid the disapproval of other missionaries who disliked corporal punishment, Hoyt took his African students to the interior of the forest next to the school and whipped them secretly before bringing them back to school. The beating was so severe that Africans thought Hoyt intended to kill them." The Kaimosi elders stole Hoyt's whip and, with Bond's assistance, sent it to the Friends' mission board in Richmond, Indiana. Amugamwa noted that Hoyt's actions were irreconcilable with the Quaker and Luhya principles of peace. In Urundi, Chilson was also accused of whipping Africans; whether he had done so in Kenya is not recorded.[44]

In Kenya, the conflict between theologically conservative and liberal missionaries had grown so sharp that, in 1937, the Friends' mission board had to send Merle Davis and Willard Trueblood to smooth out the working relationships between the Luhya and the missionaries of different theological orientations. According to Esther Mombo, "they managed to deal with the tensions between the missionaries by reprimanding the veteran missionaries over their attitudes and actions. . . . The visit of Davis and Trueblood to Kaimosi helped to restore an appearance of unity between the veteran and the young missionaries." Mombo has traced the beginnings of East Africa Yearly Meeting's organization to this visit, but the yearly meeting would not be established until 1946. Parker left Kenya in 1938 and did not return, but Hoyt remained until 1945, and Bond until 1948.[45]

CONCLUSION

Quaker missionary work from the 1860s to the 1930s was a complex phenomenon, one that emphasized both Christian commonalities and Quaker distinctives, although not always in equal measure. In the first half-century of Quaker missions up to the 1910s, Quakers, like other Christians, usually emphasized the exclusivist claims of a religion based on Christ. Still, often to the discomfort of English and American Quaker missionaries themselves, their intended converts sometimes perceived that the Quaker version of the Christian gospel, centered on attention to the "light of Christ within," implicitly allowed inclusivist or pluralist appropriations of the Quaker message, with its ethical and spiritual claims open to coexistence alongside other religious systems. Wars and imperialist designs of fellow Westerners brought multifaceted challenges to Quaker missionaries—and sometimes (in the case of the Davidsons) provided significant motivation to undertake Quaker missions in the first place. Among newly convinced Quakers, as was also the case among more seasoned Friends, the claims of individual conscience, on the one hand, and of collective testimonies such as the one against war, on the other hand, were not always easy to sort out, and in the case of the Japan missions in the 1890s, these issues were policed by American missionaries themselves. Quaker women took on a leading role in many Quaker missions, as members of Missions Committees, missionaries, and leaders among the missionary converts, and their tireless work gave new strength to Quaker testimonies relating to the education of women and girls and women's ministry.

The 1920s and 1930s saw further diversification in Friends' missions on theological matters such as the inspiration of the scriptures and the nature of relationships with other religions. One question was whether Quakers, with their differences and internal quarrels, could discover a center for their ministry worldwide that could hold together. In the mid-twentieth century, many Friends were hopeful in this regard. Christina Jones, a former Friends missionary to Palestine, emphasized the positive role that the Society of Friends could play in missions "when the need for its testimonies is very great." A 1966 book by Levinus Painter, a longtime member of the American Friends Board of Foreign Missions, would strike a hopeful tone in looking back on the first six decades of Quaker missions in Kenya, affirming that "the story of Friends in East Africa reads like a Twentieth Century supplement to the Acts of the Apostles."[46] While optimism concerning Quaker missions was a definite mid-twentieth-century theme, there was also a very strong sense of the limitations and drawbacks to mission work. Quaker churches did not grow as rapidly in an India on the verge of independence or in a China on the cusp of revolution. Troubling interactions along lines of race and gender showed how much further Friends had to progress in order to fully live into their testimonies of equality and peace. Friends in Britain and in the Philadelphia area tended to retreat from proselytization in the mid-twentieth century, investing more of their efforts in Quaker service, while evangelical Friends persisted strongly in their missionary calling, and a large body of Friends in East Africa, Bolivia, Guatemala, and other countries and regions would grow out of this continued work.

CHAPTER II

The Peace Testimony and the Crisis of World War I

ROBYNNE ROGERS HEALEY

Pacifism is strongly associated with Quakers today. Indeed, the refusal to use violence to resolve conflict may be the conviction that Friends themselves and non-Quakers most strongly identify with the Religious Society of Friends. The 1660 *Declaration from the Harmless and Innocent people of God, Called Quakers*, in which Friends assured King Charles II that they "[did] utterly deny ... all outward wars and strife and fightings with outward weapons, for any end or under any pretense whatsoever," is often cited as evidence of the Quaker commitment to peace. The Nobel Committee awarded the 1947 Nobel Peace Prize to the British Friends Service Council (FSC) and the American Friends Service Committee (AFSC) for their early twentieth-century peace work, particularly "the work done by the two recipient Quaker organizations during and after the two world wars to feed starving children and help Europe rebuild itself." Visitors to the AFSC's website can read that "the prize recognized 300 years of Quaker efforts to heal rifts and oppose war." Presented this way, it appears that the 1660 Declaration and the present-day commitment to peace are the same and that Quakers' position on war and peace has been both enduring and unchanging. Yet, as historians have demonstrated, though there were a handful of early individual conscientious objectors, including George Fox, Quakers had no collective testimony against war before 1660. Moreover, just as the 1660 Declaration had been shaped in war, ongoing Quaker views on pacifism have had a complex and complicated history formed and re-formed in response to the circumstances of specific wars. World War I, or the Great War, as it was known prior to World War II, was particularly influential in clarifying and shifting Quakers' interpretation and praxis of the peace testimony.[1]

Throughout the war, all yearly meetings in the Religious Society of Friends were officially pacifist. Individual Quakers were not. Quakers responded to the First World War in multiple ways, demonstrating that a commitment to unqualified pacifism was not essential for late nineteenth- and early twentieth-century Friends. Some Quakers were absolute pacifists—conscientious objectors who refused to participate in any war-related activities. Many of them suffered for their conscience and lost employment or were imprisoned. Some Quakers performed alternative service, most notably with the Friends War Victims Relief Committee, the Friends Ambulance Unit (FAU), or, after 1917, the AFSC. A significant number of Quakers enlisted for active service.

While accurate statistics on Quaker enlistment in World War I are not readily available, scholars generally accept that 30 percent of eligible British Quakers and 50 percent of eligible American Quakers enlisted for active military service. In some meetings, participation was even higher. Some who took up arms left the Society; others remained members and went on to assume important leadership positions in the postwar years. The reluctance of meetings to alienate Friends who, based on conscience, had enlisted is an indication of the ways Quakers negotiated the line between individual conscience and the peace testimony. While the yearly meetings remained pacifist, individual Quakers and the local meetings to which they belonged worked out the praxis of the peace testimony in the context of this war. That negotiation demanded sustained examination of the tradition of Quaker opposition to war, the conditions that caused and might prevent war, and the individual and corporate responsibility for the witness of peacemaking. In this way, World War I acted as a catalyst for a renewed commitment to peace and peacemaking and, for North American Friends, for reconciliation among Quakers who had been divided in nineteenth-century separations. The peace testimony, which historically had been a testimony against war, became a proactive testimony focused on opposition to war and commitment to facilitating the economic, social, and political conditions for a peaceful international world order.²

PRELUDE TO WORLD WAR I

Developments in nineteenth-century North American Quakerism created divisions over the historic peace testimony. Separations had divided the Society into multiple groups: Hicksite Friends, Gurneyite or evangelical Friends, and Wilburite or Conservative Friends. Holiness revivals in the 1870s and 1880s affected Quakers in Indiana, Kansas, Ohio, and Oregon and influenced the primacy of pacifism as a defining Quaker principle (see chapter 4). Some evangelical Friends, who absorbed converts from other denominations, even came to consider the testimony against war as superfluous. In 1900, yearly meetings with Hicksite origins formed the Friends General Conference (FGC), and in 1902, most Gurneyite meetings formed the Five Years Meeting of Friends. Despite the unifying appearance of these organizations, the impact of Holiness revivals and modernist theology divided Gurneyite Quakers in the years before World War I. The American Civil War (1861–65) was particularly disruptive. Quakers were torn between pacifism and their principled opposition to slavery. The American yearly meetings reiterated the importance of the testimony against war, but many individual Friends acted on the belief that the evils of slavery outweighed the evils of war and joined the Union cause, although this was not universal across meetings (see chapter 2). Significantly, both Hicksite and Gurneyite meetings were lenient in enforcing the discipline in these cases. The tradition of nonviolence remained strong, but its practice in the face of war and injustice had become unclear for American Friends by the second half of the nineteenth century.³

British Quakers had not experienced the nineteenth-century separations that divided the American yearly meetings. They had experienced the impact of Britain's imperial ambitions, part of the "Age of New Imperialism" (1870–1914) during which Britain and other Western powers, including the United States, aggressively expanded their colonial empires to take control of much of Africa, Asia, and the Middle East (see chapter 1). In an era of rapid industrialization, imperial expansion was fueled by the search for expanded markets, a need for sources of cheap labor and raw materials, the power and prestige of colonial holdings, the desire to control transport routes, and the impulse to spread what Europeans believed were the superiorities of Western civilization. These factors were buttressed by social Darwinism, an ideology articulated by Western powers that equated superior industrial military strength with the right to colonize and exploit land and resources. Britain gained control of many African colonies as part of the "Scramble for Africa" that followed the Berlin Conference (1884–85). It brought India under Crown rule in 1858 after crushing the Sepoy Mutiny. It gained preferential access to China's markets and goods after defeating China in the First (1839–42) and Second (1856–60) Opium Wars. And in the Middle East, Britain gained control of the Suez Canal and secured concessions throughout the region. Beyond imperial expansion, the second phase of the Concert of Europe, begun in the 1880s, was fragile. European nations' attempts to balance power on the Continent were eroded by the competition for colonial expansion and alliances that pitted the powers against one another. Antagonism between Britain and Germany became particularly strong from the late 1890s through the 1910s, fostered by a naval arms race in which both powers sought to outdo the other in the construction of warships.[4]

Within this context, Quakers participated in missions to Africa, Asia, and Latin America with a focus on evangelism, education, medicine, and vocational training (see chapter 10). They expressed concern about growing militarism and the arms race. Some Friends were active in the Society for the Promotion of Permanent and Universal Peace, formed in 1816. Known as the Peace Society, this group played an important role in the nineteenth-century peace movement by publishing tracts opposing war and condemning Britain's occupation of Egypt. While Quakers were significantly involved in the Peace Society, even those active in the peace movement questioned a commitment to complete nonviolence. Quakers provided relief to victims of both the Crimean War (1854–56) and the Franco-Prussian War (1870–75), establishing the Friends War Victims Relief Committee in direct response to the latter. Still, Friends were divided over what Martin Ceadel calls "pacifist" and "pacificist" approaches. By the 1880s, it was apparent that "Quakers seemed to be in some disarray as regards the extent and meaning of their witness for peace." Proponents of liberal or modern theology in British and American Quakerism addressed this disarray, advocating for education and deeper engagement with historical Quakerism as the means to inspire and equip young Friends to vanquish social ills like militarism.[5]

On both sides of the Atlantic, young Friends gathered to consider Quakerism and to transform the testimony against war into the peace testimony. Beginning in 1894, Albert Smiley began hosting an annual Conference on International Arbitration at his Lake Mohonk resort in New York State. North American Quakers united in an important initiative to renew the peace testimony. For three days at the end of 1901, Quakers representing all branches of the Society gathered in Philadelphia to discuss issues of war and peace. The conference invitation points to the desire for Quaker unity and the renewal of approaches to peace: "Do we not owe it to ourselves, to our history, to our profession before the church and the world, to the American public and to mankind everywhere, to declare ourselves anew today—and in a united way, as we have never done before—on the great and pressing question of the peace of the world, of the rescue of mankind from the awful iniquities and crushing burdens of modern militarism?" The schedule was grueling: forty-three papers in eight sessions over three twelve-hour days. Topics ranged from biblical exegesis on war and peace to historical analysis and theoretical papers on "internationalism" and "militarism." Peter Brock has observed that "the conference had little to say about the economic causation of war or about the clash of rival imperialisms and the search of finance capitalism for overseas markets" that socialist and labor movements of the day identified at the root of international conflict. Even so, the declaration that came out of the conference reaffirmed Friends' historic position on war, denouncing it as "the antithesis of Christianity and the negation, for the time being, of the moral order of the world." The declaration endorsed global efforts for arbitration, going as far as identifying the establishment of the international Permanent Court of Arbitration as "one of the greatest events in the history of human society." The conference marked a notable shift in North American Quaker approaches to war and activist peacemaking efforts. Isaac Sharpless's closing comments suggest this shift:

> Friends have not been very active propagandists. The very feeling of their own complete rightness has made many of them slow to take the stump and proclaim the arguments for the good cause. But this is changing.... Shall we lose this historic character as we part with the aloofness from the world which perhaps produced it...? Not so, I think, if he comes under the spirit of George Fox; if he is a peace man not because he believes war to be wasteful, and productive of suffering, or contrary to some pet theory of morals, but because down

in his heart he feels the warm spirit of divine love and power that takes away the occasion and the desire and the possibility of war and revenge and hatred.⁶

While North American Friends participated in arbitration and peace conferences, British Friends, including Quakers in the British Dominions and British colonies, faced the South African Boer War (1899–1902), which forced them to reconsider the principles at the heart of the peace testimony. Up to this point, individual Quakers had been active in antiwar, anti-imperialist movements, but the testimony against war itself had languished, despite London Yearly Meeting's commitment to arbitration and opposition to militarism. Quakers themselves were disappointed in their response to the Anglo-Boer War. A number of prominent Friends, including the most well-known convinced British Quaker, Caroline Stephen, supported Britain's imperial war, outraging "younger, spiritually and socially committed Friends." Stephen's outspoken support for the conflict was deeply disappointing to young liberal Friends working to stimulate a commitment to nonviolence. The context of the war itself and theological differences among British Friends complicated any straightforward response. Friends generally divided into two camps: evangelical Friends who were anti-Boer and supported British government policy and liberal Friends who were pro-Boer and opposed British government policy. Thomas Kennedy offers this assessment of the discord: "The conflict in South Africa so divided British Friends, old and young, male and female, that five months after it began *Reynolds Newspaper* could feel safe in declaring that the Society of Friends was 'no longer to be regarded as a strenuous and united peace organization.'"⁷

Imperial wars generated intense imperial pride. Both the Anglo-Boer War and the Spanish-American War celebrated colonial power and hinted at the future of warfare. While British Friends publicly denied any connection between their faith and warfare in their 1900 publication *Christianity and War*, the tract made no particular mention of the ongoing war in South Africa. It stated only that London Quakers did "believe it right, at the present time to give fresh expression to our testimony to the peaceable nature of Christ's Kingdom, and the lawfulness of war to the Christian." Friends called on Britons to abandon their dependence on armed force. Rather, "the energy, the self-sacrifice, and heroism which now sport their God-given strength in the service of death" should be harnessed to the "moral forces of righteousness and goodwill" that had "given our country her moral influence in the world, and are the true foundation on which her empire now rests." True Christians, Friends concluded, would "shrink with horror from the wholesale slaughter of the battlefield" and would turn themselves instead to a "higher service... the 'blessed ministry of reconciliation.'" Not evident in this statement are the public theological quarrels that had preceded its publication. These theological divisions, along with disagreements about whether Friends should address the government, manifested themselves in a deeply divided peace session at the 1900 London Yearly Meeting, where the South African War was the major topic of discussion.[8]

Women were at the center of these disagreements. Consider Ellen Robinson, an outspoken feminist and peace activist who had been particularly active in campaigning against the South African War. In 1885, Robinson had founded the Liverpool and Birkenhead Women's Peace and Arbitration Society. She was also active in the leadership of the Ladies' Peace Auxiliary and the Local Peace Association. Along with the efforts of another Friend, Priscilla Peckover, Robinson's peace work was local and directed at changing public opinion. Heloise Brown contends that this approach differed from that of men's peace movements, which aimed to change national policy. Robinson worked nationally through the Meeting for Sufferings Peace Committee (she was one of the first women members of the Meeting for Sufferings). As a dedicated feminist peace activist, she organized protest meetings against the war. When the 1900 London Yearly Meeting gathered without the guidance of a strong antiwar statement from the Meeting for Sufferings, Robinson presented her own antiwar message, which the yearly meeting watered down in *Christianity and War*. Kennedy maintains that socially prominent Quakers like Peckover had "an uncomfortably ambiguous attitude towards British imperialism... in the years before 1914." Robinson experienced no ambiguity; she believed that British imperialism was "motivated by militarism rather than any spirit of Christianity or civilisation." Her combination of feminism, Quakerism, and liberalism was different from Peckover's. Robinson's activism in both the Society of Friends and liberal women's associations pushed questions of peace, humanitarianism, and international arbitration to the fore and became a model for Quaker women during World War I.[9]

Throughout the Anglo-Boer War, peace advocates held meetings across Britain. In late 1899, the Meeting for Sufferings had appointed the Friends' South African War Victims' Fund committee to "receive funds for war victims in South Africa irrespective of nationality," although a royal proclamation later disallowed any support of Britain's enemies. Quakers' highly publicized relief work in South Africa exposed the conditions and mortality of children in concentration camps. As a result, the 1901 London Yearly Meeting was more unified about the war and approved "A Plea for a Peaceable Spirit." In this statement, Friends observed that "many who at first supported the war with honest conviction, recognise the moral deterioration that has marked its progress." They lamented "the reign of prejudice, the fever of passion, the riots, the orgies in our streets, the preaching of vengeance by the press and even from some pulpits" and declared that "in condoning militarism the Christian church destroys with one hand the edifice of love she seeks to build with the other." They concluded that "force" in South Africa had "complicated the racial and political problem."[10]

Inaccuracies about the response of Canadian Friends to the South African War show how Quakers' twentieth-century commitment to pacifism has shaped interpretations of Quakers and war. In his 1927 book *The Quakers in Canada*, Arthur Dorland asserted that "the Society passed strong resolutions condemning the war spirit in Canada, which were given as much publicity as possible." Over time, this claim has been repeated and altered so that resolutions against the war spirit have become resolutions against the war itself. The minutes of all three yearly meetings (Hicksite, Orthodox, and Conservative) do not support this interpretation. Despite Canadian Quakers' commitment to arbitration and opposition to militarism, their response to the South African War was not as resolute as they wished it had been when they reflected back on it decades later. Thomas P. Socknat contends that "the full impact of Quaker leadership [in the peace movement] was not felt in Canada until after the First World War when the three separate branches of the Society of Friends began to cooperate with one another."[11]

The Boer War ended on May 31, 1902. That year, London Yearly Meeting appointed a Peace Deputation to visit every monthly meeting in Britain to strengthen the testimony against war. Since British Quakers had been divided by the Boer War, this was an important milestone in revitalizing the peace testimony. The war changed corporate British Quaker attitudes toward imperialism. They began to see imperialism and war as problems that could be solved with education and social change. There were Friends who viewed the peace testimony as superfluous and left the Society, but among those who remained, a number became more firmly committed to renewing the peace testimony.[12]

Dedication to pacifism as integral to Quakerism motivated the Young Friends Movement, which expanded along with liberal Quakerism. The first national Young Friends Conference was held in 1911 at Swanwick in Derbyshire at the same time that the Second Moroccan Crisis brought the European powers perilously close to war. Over four hundred attendees gathered at Swanwick for lectures on "Quaker history, theology, spirituality, Quaker service, the peace testimony, and the ethical application of the Quaker message." An important outcome of this conference was the conviction that the peace testimony was not optional. As one conferee declared, it was "a necessary outcome of our root belief." The momentum generated by the Swanwick conference worked in tandem with the efforts of the Meeting for Sufferings' Peace Committee to encourage London Yearly Meeting to draft, in 1912, "Our Testimony of Peace"—British Quakers' first official statement that the peace testimony was fundamental to Quakerism. The statement made clear that armed conflict was unacceptable and Friends were to do everything in their power to prevent violence between nations or individuals. The hope inspired by "Our Testimony of Peace" was shattered, however, when war broke out in August 1914.[13]

WORLD WAR I

Although the renewed peace testimony implied a united front on pacifism, British Quakers became divided at the beginning of the war. A significant segment of the Society supported the war effort. As many as 33.6 percent of British men eligible for active service enlisted; as few as 44.5 percent became conscientious objectors. The latter figure included those willing to perform alternative service. The remainder may have tried their best to go unnoticed during the war. Some of them may have performed alternative service, itself a potentially contentious activity for Friends who debated whether alternative service supported the war (e.g., making munitions) or ameliorated suffering caused by war (e.g., relief work and tending to the wounded). Reflected in this debate were questions of patriotism and faithfulness. Could young Quakers be faithful Friends and patriotic citizens if patriotism required armed service? Personal conscience determined how Quakers responded to the war, whether as enlisted soldiers, as alternativists, or as absolute pacifists. Some held more than one of these positions throughout the war. Some equivocated and were relative instead of absolute pacifists. Those who were pacifists did not isolate themselves. Many Quakers functioned as "integrational pacifists," adapting their pacifism to exert influence on the liberal reform peace movement. This is evident in ecumenical initiatives like the Fellowship of Reconciliation, in which Quakers played a prominent founding role. Cooperating as they did with non-Quakers, Friends remained mindful that a deep commitment to peace was at the heart of their faith.[14]

Confusing for those both inside and outside the Society were Quakers who identified as pacifist but spoke as though they were war hawks. Consider statements made in 1916 by Herbert Sefton-Jones, chair of the London Peace Society's executive committee. In his pamphlet *German Crimes and Our Civil Remedy*, Sefton-Jones declared that "not only the Kaiser himself and his sons, but also the assassins through whom his will has been carried out, should answer with their lives for the misery they have caused." Similarly, Albert Wilson, a physician serving in the French Medical Corps, championed the war: "It is a Christian's war, a war against rape, massacre, cruelty, hate, injustice and every vice we can mention. May God bless our troops and our Allies." In these cases, London Yearly Meeting was able to do little else but remind Friends of its 1912 "Testimony of Peace" and express discontent with those who acted in opposition to it. The yearly meeting could not discipline those who enlisted or encouraged others to do so; that fell to the monthly meetings, and they seemed reluctant to discipline these cases. The mixed messages negatively affected the Society's position in the peace movement.[15]

The imposition of conscription with the Military Service Act (1916) sharpened the debate for the yearly meeting, dividing conscientious objectors into alternativists and absolutists. What was the limit for accommodation to the state? Was it the "middle course" of alternative service, the radical course of absolute pacifism and possible imprisonment, or something in between? Young Friends and women tended to adopt the radical position and insisted that Quakers not just oppose war but try to stop it.[16]

What of Friends in the British Dominions or colonies who were automatically part of Britain's war? In Australia, Margaret Thorp was instrumental in anticonscription work and in the peace movement. She spoke out against militarism and war and, in 1915, was elected secretary of the radical feminist Women's Peace Army, whose goal was to end all wars. The movement contended that capitalism was the source of armed conflict and social restructuring was necessary so that "the world's production can be carried on for the happiness of the people."[17]

Canadian Quakers also faced conscription under the Military Service Act of 1917. In Britain, exemption on the grounds of conscience was provided on an individual basis; in Canada, exemption was offered only to members of specific religious groups, including Quakers. Still, some Canadian Quakers voluntarily enlisted, and the meetings were curiously silent on the war until they faced conscription in 1917. At that point they became more vocal, declaring support for "those who, though not members of our Society, nevertheless hold genuine religious objections to war" and calling for expansion of the exemption clause to include those who objected to war regardless of religious identity. They also authorized monthly meetings to issue certificates of membership, should tribunals require them. But Friends were reminded that "while during the present crisis we should endeavor consistently to observe our traditional attitude as Friends against active participation in war, it is therefore our especial duty to exert ourselves as individuals and as a Society along these lines of work in which we can consistently engage so that we shall render to our country and to those who have suffered because of the war some equivalent service and even sacrifice." To this end, Pickering College was offered on loan as a convalescent hospital, evidence of Canadian Quakers' practical service to their country. Canadian Quaker opposition to conscription was tepid compared to that of British Friends. Amy Shaw suggests three reasons for this: there were far fewer Quakers in Canada than in the United Kingdom, there did not seem to be many Quaker males of service age, and Canadian Quakers, like Quakers everywhere, poured their energies into relief work instead of demonstrations.[18]

More work is needed to understand the full impact of the war on Quakers in Kenya and Palestine. Anecdotal evidence shows that Kenyan Quakers were conscripted into colonial forces. Stanley Ngesa speaks of a great-grandfather he never met: "Mmboga was conscripted by the occupying British into the King's African Rifles. Notwithstanding his Maragoli and Quaker pacifist principles, Mmboga, with many other young Maragoli men, was drafted to fight in a war about which he knew nothing. He and the other Maragoli never returned home, and to this day, nothing is known about their fate." Friends in Ramallah had their brand-new school appropriated first by the Turks, who used the ground-floor kitchen and dining room as a stable, and then by the British, who turned the school into a hospital in 1917 for the duration of the war.[19]

Alternative service, usually with the FAU or the Friends War Victims Relief Committee, was controversial for some British Friends. This is evident in the ambiguous relationship between the FAU and London Yearly Meeting. Formed largely by young Quakers in August 1914, the FAU was never officially affiliated with London Yearly Meeting, although many Quakers supported it financially. Regardless of their position, Quakers genuinely wanted to help those affected by war. The FAU's supporters believed it offered young Friends an opportunity to remain faithful to the peace testimony while demonstrating their loyalty and patriotism. Friends disagreed, however, on the FAU's support of the war effort. As Linda Palfreeman shows, the FAU's provision of emergency medical aid to fallen troops "represented a tremendous and sustained contribution to the military medical services of the allied nations throughout the war—a contribution that brought it into direct conflict with Quaker religious principles." That conflict lessened when the FAU began civilian relief in 1914 in Flemish war zones. Even those who criticized assistance to fallen soldiers agreed that support for refugees was an expression of Quaker love to those in need.[20]

The Friends Service Committee (FSC), created at yearly meeting in 1915 "to strengthen the Peace testimony among Friends of military age" and staunchly pacifist, took an especially dim view of the FAU. Rebecca Wynter contends that the FAU's middle course—between active service and prison—did not compromise Quaker belief. Rather, it created space for varying expressions of personal conscience. She notes that Quaker members of Parliament negotiated the inclusion of a conscience clause in the Military Service Act that permitted conscripts to enlist as noncombatants or to be exempted from active service if they were engaged in work "of national importance." This ensured that alternative service could be used to accommodate conscience. Moreover, the FAU identified appropriate service for those granted conditional exemptions but unwilling to engage in ambulance work.[21]

A minority of British Quakers of military age neither enlisted nor performed alternative service. Willing to accept only absolute exemption from any war-related service, these absolute pacifists resisted conscription and refused to cooperate with any war effort. They willingly accepted imprisonment to defend their conscientious objection. While a minority, this group had a profound influence on British Quakers' understanding and application of the peace testimony. Enlistment and alternative service removed a sizable number of military-age men from corporate decision-making in the Society. Those who remained, especially those active in the FSC, directed the discussion. The FSC was strongly committed to absolute pacifism. Its members, particularly women on the committee, rejected any compromise with the state. The FSC had been formed with separate women's and men's committees. After the men's committee was reduced by conscription, the separate committees were merged and Edith Ellis became treasurer and acting secretary. With fewer men on the committee, women assumed a significant leadership role in directing the Society's response to conscription and armed conflict in general. As Thomas Kennedy has concluded, "the radical thrust of Quaker pacifism, Quaker socialism, and Quaker feminism was to a considerable extent directed by radicalized female Friends whose views were significantly in advance not only of the larger wartime British society but of the consensus of their own religious society."[22]

The FSC's radical pacifists insisted on three forms of war resistance: refusing involvement in any war-related activity, producing antiwar propaganda, and willingly suffering in prison as witnesses against war. Leaders like Edith Ellis took an intolerant line on what constituted faithful conscientious objection. It was not enough to ask whether Friends should refrain from participation in war; they needed to show that they were attempting "by every possible means to stop the war." These Friends insisted that their interpretation of resistance was the only correct Quaker interpretation, despite their being only "145 absolutists who chose prison rather than compromise with the war-time State." The posture of Quaker absolutists echoed that of seventeenth-century Friends who had also suffered willingly for freedom of conscience. When London Yearly Meeting endorsed the FSC's stand in 1916, the FSC became the acknowledged leader in directing the meeting's war-related policies, replacing the Meeting for Sufferings' Peace Committee. In this way, "the war and the imposition of compulsory military service permitted a minority alliance of young radicals and middle-aged zealots to grasp the moment and lead their Society, kicking and screaming as may be, to support a radical interpretation of their historic, but previously amorphous, peace testimony."[23]

American Quakers remained on the periphery of the war for its first three years. Even so, they offered opinions on its causes and solutions for lasting peace. Shortly after the outbreak of war, FGC presented a peace memorial to President Woodrow Wilson on behalf of Hicksite Friends.

The memorial named group hatred, land hunger, and ambition for power as the causes of war and called for a "Parliament of Nations." According to these Friends, "a World Parliament with a World Court and a World Police to enforce its decisions can maintain peace." In 1915, the Winona Lake Peace Conference of Young Friends, known as the National Peace Conference, offered a similar, albeit much-expanded, solution that affirmed Quakers' commitment to peace and called for action from the federal government, American churches, and Friends themselves. Hicksite Friends returned to the idea of an international court and an international police force in 1916 at FGC, where William Hull delivered a paper titled "The Quaker Solution to the War Problem." Hull called for an international police force subject to "the control of a genuine international court of justice." Not all in attendance agreed. L. Hollingsworth Wood responded: "It is a good deal easier to give your pocket-book than it is your life. It is a good deal easier to stand up and talk than it is to go out and perform; it is a good deal easier to inherit a peace testimony, as we have in the Society of Friends, than it is to think one out for yourself." Wood directed those present to the work of the Fellowship of Reconciliation, which was sending an ambulance unit to Mexico to assist those affected by the Mexican Border War (1910–19). According to Wood, *that* was the real work of thinking out the peace testimony, "so that the Friend who can say to us 'I offer my life to my country,' shall be met not with platitudes nor theories, but with men and women willing to lay down their lives for their brethren."[24]

When the Five Years Meeting of Friends convened in 1917, six months after America's entrance into the war, it confirmed its "unaltered faith" in "religious principles which forbid engaging in war." It also admitted that "in every war-crisis, some of our members have gone along with the prevailing trend and method." Even so, "the body itself in its meeting capacity has remained through all the years unswervingly true to the spiritual ideal. We have always been and still are a loyal patriotic people, true to the ideals of citizenship, contributing in all possible ways to the promotion of stable and efficient government, and ready to take our full share in the labors, efforts, dangers and perils involved in the maintenance of a true democracy. But we cannot surrender the central faith by which we live." Five Years Meeting was clear that this was not a license to dodge responsibility. "It is our hope," they declared, "that our entire membership may now and in the future . . . exhibit in this desperate time a Christian faith colored with the red blood of virility and heroism. We must not do less than those who believe that war is necessary and who are ready to fight with carnal weapons, nor can we seek an easier way of life." A just and lasting peace required the hard work of peacemakers. The challenge remained that the praxis of peacemaking—beyond staying out of war—was still unclear.[25]

Like their British counterparts, many American Friends disagreed with the Society's position and made their views public. Albert G. Thatcher spoke out in a 1917 article in *The Advocate of Peace*. Identifying himself as a pacifist, but not "a non-resistant," Thatcher equated World War I with the Civil War, a war in which he fought. He reminded readers that many Quakers "had the anti-slavery cause so much at heart that it was a vital part of their religion," and they willingly took up arms to bring about its end. Thatcher was "convinced that no body of people would suffer more in spirit and probably in person than our Friends, should the barbaric German idea of Kultur win the ultimate victory and subdue the world." Toward those who enlisted, Thatcher insisted there could be no condemnation, "being convinced that all such decisions must be left to the court of the individual conscience."[26]

The appeal to personal conscience created immense tension for draft-aged men. Rufus Jones outlined the difficult choice "every serious young Friend" faced: "How far were they under obligation to serve their country in a mission which appeared to conflict with their ideals of right and wrong, and how far did the desperate world-situation which confronted them lay upon them a call to break with the settled teaching and attitude of their type of Christianity?" Undoubtedly, some of the Quakers who enlisted were not devout or were part of a meeting where pacifism was not considered a defining feature of the faith. Nonetheless, a number of committed Friends wrestled mightily with their choice between military duty and alternative service. Some of those who enlisted for active service remained faithful Quakers. Their cases are representative of the tension between conscience and testimony that characterized many Friends' experiences of the war.[27]

The Advocate of Peace noted the inconsistency between the Society's official position and that of some Friends. In May 1918, it juxtaposed the contents of the leaflet "Some Particular Advices for Friends and A Statement of Loyalty for Others" and the Philadelphia Yearly Meeting's official statement adopted at its March 29, 1918, session. The meeting's statement included the standard excerpt from the 1660 Declaration and affirmations of Friends' constancy to that position over the centuries; it also avowed the Society's "deep loyalty" to their country and fellow citizens. Contrast this to

"Some Particular Advices," placed immediately after the Philadelphia Yearly Meeting's statement. Signed by 120 prominent Quakers, including Albert G. Thatcher, from the Philadelphia and Baltimore Yearly Meetings, it railed:

> We do not agree with those who would utter sentimental platitudes while a mad dog is running amuck, biting women and children; with those who would stand idly by quoting some isolated passage of Scripture while an insane man murdered him, ravished his wife, bayoneted his babies, or crucified his friends; with any person who would discuss with some well and contented stranger the merits of various fire-extinguishers while his wife and children are calling to him from the flames of his burning house. We believe that wrong is relative and has degrees; that there are greater things than human life and worse things than war. There is a difference between peace as an end and peace as a means to an end. We do not want peace with dishonor or a temporary peace with evil. We will not equivocate with honor or compromise with wickedness. . . . Believing that it is not enough at this time to be neutral, and that the views of the Society of Friends have not been adequately represented by the official statements of its executives, nor by the utterances of many of its public speakers. . . . We therefore deem it consistent with our Quaker faith to act according to the dictates of our own consciences and proclaim a unity with the teachings of Jesus Christ and the messages of the President of our country.

The Advocate of Peace did not comment on the inconsistency between the two statements. It did not need to; their placement alone illuminated the factions. Quaker support for the war was strong enough that those who publicly opposed it could be censured. Haverford College professor Henry Cadbury experienced this censuring in October 1918 after he denounced the American media and public's "orgy of hate" against the Germans. Cadbury was condemned by faculty, alumni, and students and resigned his post.[28]

Under the National Defense Act (1916) and the Selective Service Act (1917), American Quakers opposed to the war could be exempted from combatant service on the basis of well-established religious beliefs. There was no exemption from noncombatant service. The American Friends Service Committee (AFSC) was founded in 1917 to provide alternative service opportunities for Quakers unable to accord with military demands. Organizers navigated the needs of multiple stakeholders. The government needed to respect religious freedom but could not be seen to be harboring shirkers. The War Department was especially challenging. It could not support absolute pacifism, but it might tolerate alternativist pacifism. The Society itself was divided, and the AFSC needed donors from across the Society; theological divisions were difficult to navigate, as organizers needed the support of all Friends. The yearly meetings' endorsement of pacifism as a central tenet of Quakerism did allow both pro- and antiwar Friends to support alternative service. The AFSC also needed the support of the entire peace community—other peace churches as well as secular pacifists. Finally, organizers had to appeal to the American public. As war fever swept across the country, there was little tolerance for anything that hinted of disloyalty.[29]

Public sentiment against pacifists was so strong in some areas that Quakers were subjected to violence, harassment, and general suspicion. Indeed, the confinement of conscientious objectors in military camps is indicative of how they were perceived by the War Department, if not society as a whole. Roughly two-thirds of American Friends who identified as conscientious objectors accepted alternative service. AFSC reconstruction work offered an outlet to some of these Quakers.[30]

Beyond providing an arena for Quaker wartime service, the AFSC worked across divisions within the Society. Young Friends had expressed concern about the separations among Quakers. At the final session of the 1915 Winona Lake Peace Conference, Samuel Howarth spoke on "The Society of Friends and the Problem." Howarth considered Quaker factions as representative of the problems of international politics, "for the same spirit that causes national and racial divisions acts in our own Society, and causes theological divisions ... and [Friends] must solve the lesser problem if [they] were to be worthy to help solve the greater." Despite the AFSC's early successes, its chair, Rufus Jones, recalled difficulties determining applicants' strength of conviction: "We endeavored as far as possible to have the group composed of men who were conscientiously opposed to war and for that reason unable to engage in it. The problem, however proved to be a very difficult one. Many of the applicants had never faced the question for themselves. They had not thought through the issues involved. They all hated war.... But here it was an existing fact.... The situation presented to them was an unescapable rivalry of loyalties." Measuring physical fitness was one thing; "the scrutiny of the inward process of the soul, was, on the other hand, a baffling undertaking."[31]

The Red Cross and the French government recognized the AFSC's work in France and requested that Friends take charge of postwar reconstruction work in the most heavily damaged areas around Verdun. Forty-four villages needed rebuilding. American and British Friends' acceptance of this responsibility changed the nature of the AFSC. Reconstruction work had little to do with pacifism, although it did have to do with healing the ravages of war. Friends translated religious convictions into humanitarian work. The numbers attest to its importance: there were more AFSC personnel in France in 1919 than during the war. Although it was not unchallenged, postwar work added to the AFSC's reputation as a nonpolitical, nonproselytizing relief organization; it became a permanent body in 1924. The AFSC helped American Quakers to see that they could work across their theological and political differences. Despite Jones's assessment that "nothing that our hands can do ever can atone for the agony, the losses and the suffering which have fallen upon the innocent during these years of world tragedy," the AFSC managed to combine patriotism and pacifism to provide space for alternative service of significant importance. The goodwill this generated at home and abroad went a long way toward healing differences among American Friends.[32]

AFTER THE WAR

World War I revealed the horrors of modern industrialized warfare. It also exposed Friends to challenging decisions over their peace witness. Quakers were not alone in their dismay about war, nor had the arguments of pacifists been entirely unheard. Those in the peace movement had been ridiculed, but the persistence of their arguments coupled with the destructiveness of the war resulted in this war being "the first in which people were widely capable of recognizing and being thoroughly repulsed by those horrors." War had become, as Winston Churchill observed in 1925, "the potential destroyer of the human race." Quakers, along with other peace advocates, became more determined to create a world in which a just and lasting peace was possible. To that end, Friends had agreed in 1917 to hold a global peace conference of all Quakers when the war ended. The All-Friends Conference of 1920 convened in London to discuss how to go "beyond the formal statement of our Peace testimony to the far-reaching issues of social and international behaviour that belongs to it." Over one thousand Quakers from around the world engaged in sustained discussion about the Quaker position on peace (see chapter 12). They were not united. In the years preceding the conference, Quakers had debated the peace settlement and the League of Nations in their publications. After the conference, they remained divided between those who opposed the League of Nations and those who believed it was necessary. These ongoing disagreements demonstrate the difficulties of translating the peace testimony in practical ways.[33]

The conference concluded with a "Message to Friends and Fellow-Seekers" that captured a clarified Quaker vision for peace and Friends' individual responsibility for peace: "The roots of war can be taken away from all our lives. . . . Day by day let us seek out and remove every seed of hatred and greed of resentment and of grudging in our own selves and in the social structure about us. . . . Fear and suspicion must give place to trust and the spirit of understanding. . . . Surely this is the way in which Christ calls us to overcome the barriers of race and class and thus to make all of humanity a society of friends." After World War I, Friends disagreed over the specifics of putting the peace testimony into practice. They united in their commitment to personal conscience and their obligation to transform the world in humanitarian ways. Sustained examination of the peace testimony resulted in a Society more acquainted with the history and trajectory of its own peace testimony and more conversant in the realities of global affairs. The pre-twentieth-century testimony against war, with its vague commitment to peace principles, was gone. In its place was a clearly defined, radical pacifist doctrine forged by young women and men who had been inspired by first-generation Quakers. These Friends did not retreat from World War I. Rather, they responded as "a body of moral pioneers," articulating a vision of a transformed world in which pacifism created flourishing peace.[34]

CHAPTER 12

Quakers in Politics

STEPHANIE MIDORI KOMASHIN AND RANDALL L. TAYLOR

In the seventeenth and eighteenth centuries, members of the Society of Friends had engaged in varied forms of political action, including lobbying through correspondence, print, electioneering, and envoys to policy makers; joining militia; and entering political office in Rhode Island, New Jersey, and Pennsylvania (where William Penn's "Holy Experiment" normalized Quaker men dominating civil office). In the nineteenth century, British Friends broke past England's 1673 Test Act (repealed in 1829) that required oath swearing to serve in Parliament, Quaker women achieved local public office, and non-Western Friends took up office outside the radius of Western culture. Significantly, in the United States, Noah Haynes Swayne (1804–1884), who worked in local and state offices before serving as the Supreme Court's first Republican and sole Quaker justice, focused on civil rights of African Americans. Across the Atlantic, Joseph Pease (1799–1872) ran on a pro-Dissenter and abolitionist platform, and the 1832 Reform Act's allowance for affirmation of loyalty instead of oath of office and without mandatory subscription to the Articles of Religion of the Church of England enabled him to take his seat in 1833 as the first Quaker member of Parliament (MP) in the House of Commons (the lower house). In this position, Pease introduced the Cruelty to Animals Act of 1835 and worked to abolish slavery (he was, simultaneously, clerk for Durham Quarterly Meeting and, later, minister). Though Friends had been functioning "without even a toehold in the country's ruling élite" at the beginning of the nineteenth century, enfranchisement of Dissenters and the economic power of Nonconformist industrialization centers chipped away at Anglican political dominion, and a "Quaker public culture" of taking office and appointments in order to achieve social reform emerged.[1]

This chapter focuses on three eminent Friends who pioneered the working out of Quaker testimonies as politicians: MP John Bright (1811–1889), the second Friend in the House of Commons; Japanese Imperial Diet parliamentarian Inazo Nitobe (1862–1933); and the first Quaker US president, Herbert Hoover (1874–1964). While representing constituents of differing nations and cultures, they all prioritized aid to the poor and domestic concerns while engaged in Quaker-informed international diplomacy and grappled with the challenges that peace principles posed to their political work. We also note in this chapter how Friends of this period concurred, cooperated, or clashed in their views of Quaker politicians and their undertakings.

John Bright represented Durham (1843–57) and Birmingham Central (1857–89), serving as president of the Board of Trade (1868–71) and chancellor of the Duchy of Lancaster (1873–74, 1880–82)—the first Nonconformist to hold cabinet office. Bright was a birthright Quaker, and his practice of family Bible reading and membership in Rochdale Preparative Meeting "did more to form his inner life than did any other influences." He was library committee member, auditor, assistant clerk, clerk, and doorkeeper in plain dress and made 1,175 visits among thirty-eight different meetinghouses. Personal health issues and family tragedies led Bright to consider leaving Parliament, but his inclination toward service kept him on until he died in office at age seventy-seven.[2]

Inazo Nitobe, member of Japan's House of Peers, the upper house of the Diet (1926–33), was baptized into the Sapporo Band, which practiced a plain, largely unprogrammed Christianity. In his college library, he became "absorbed in" a biography of John Bright, an account of the treaty between William Penn and the Lenape, and Thomas Carlyle's description of George Fox in *Sartor Resartus*, which, for him, "planted the idea that Quakers live up to the true nature of Christianity." Years later, he felt at home at a Friends meetinghouse through similarities in worship style, and, though initially a Just War theory proponent, he came around to the peace testimony through prayerful study of Quaker peace writings and joined Baltimore Monthly Meeting in 1886. Nitobe lectured at Central Philadelphia Monthly Meeting's (Orthodox) Philadelphia Friends Institute on religion, social reform, and treaty revision. In Japan, he and his wife, Mary P. Elkinton Nitobe, started meetings of silent prayer in their home, and he translated *The Life of George Fox* and *A Short Biography of William Penn* into Japanese.[3]

Herbert Clark Hoover was born in a West Branch, Iowa, Quaker settlement, where his uncle, John Y. Hoover (1834–1909), held Gurneyite revival meetings within Iowa Yearly Meeting (Conservative) (see chapter 4).[4] Hoover's Canadian mother, Huldah Minthorn Hoover, a popular temperance movement minister, had him study a Bible chapter each day. Orphaned at age nine by his mother's death, following the death of his father at age six, Hoover and his siblings were split up among Quaker relatives, including Laban J. Miles, who took Hoover along on his job with the Bureau of Indian Affairs—he spent eight months with the Osage Nation and attended Sunday school with the Native American children—and Henry John Minthorn, who had worked on the Underground Railroad. Later, without a Quaker meeting in Monterey, California, Hoover was married by a Catholic priest to Episcopalian Lou Henry Hoover and encouraged Lou, who called herself "only a Friend by adoption," to join the Salvation Army. Hoover did not regularly attend Friends' meetings while living abroad for two decades, was sworn into presidential office by oath, drank alcohol, and smoked. He participated in Washington Monthly Meeting (Orthodox), Washington Indulged Meeting (Hicksite), and an intended "cooperative" meeting but failed to convince the former two to merge into the latter independent pastoral Friends Meeting of Washington.[5]

Quaker perspectives in this period differed widely on the suitability of Friends pursuing public office and even of political action of any sort. Quakers "wrestled almost continually and inconclusively over the question of their Society's right relationship to the State," and World War I forced them to examine the peace testimony more robustly (see chapter 11). Pease's mother-in-law "bitterly opposed" his candidature, and his plain father rued MPs' wasting time drafting laws that failed to pass and never felt "easy in his mind" about his son "caring about earthly things," suffering recurring anxiety that "the spirit of this world [might] drink up the Spirit of the Lord which was in him" —yet his father appreciated when Pease dissuaded the government from military action, advocated for the Stockton and Darlington Railway Bill, or voted against an alternate route for the rail line. Bright's first wife, evangelical-leaning Elizabeth Priestman Bright, convinced her father that Bright's involvement in politics would not compromise his spiritual integrity, though his in-laws worried about his political agitation and considered Bright's attention to elections inappropriate while his wife lay on her deathbed. His second wife, Margaret Elizabeth Leatham Bright, overcame reservations about his political activities and took keen interest in them. When London Yearly Meeting's drafted 1843 epistle exhorted Friends to be "quiet in the land," Bright defended his work (the 1846 and 1848 epistles explicitly instructed Friends to avoid political involvement). While Japanese Quakers lacked a Quietist heritage that might question Nitobe's governmental service, his wife, in correspondence with her Orthodox American relatives, defended Japan's wartime actions and her husband's mitigation. Many Friends distanced themselves from involvement in government, with Philadelphia Yearly Meeting's 1806 Rules of Discipline instructing, "Decline the acceptance of any office or station in civil government" and stipulating disunity if any "shall persist in a conduct so reverse to our principles." Yet Quietist eschewing of politics was "never completely consistent or uniform." In stark contrast, *The Friend* urged its readers to write to their MPs in support of MP Joseph Allen Baker's resolution on naval armaments in 1909, and the degree to which Evangelicalism cultivated nineteenth-century Quaker societal reform "cannot be overestimated." Many Quakers conceptualized themselves as responsible for and integral to the health of their societies and global peace—some even engaging in self-congratulatory hubris. Friends' willingness to enter office reflected optimism toward structural change in markets and government. Other Friends, however, practiced a nonresistance of rejecting the coercive element in all governments.[6]

JOHN BRIGHT

John Bright, a key political figure in nineteenth-century Britain, was a highly respected reformer in an age of change, "a radical precisely because he was a Quaker," and a person who "put conscience, conviction, the working man and his country before party or any personal interest." Bright's Quaker beliefs directed his political positions and votes: "Much of my opinions and much of my course has been determined, or at least greatly influenced, by the training I received in that body." He stated that "the moral law was not written for men alone in their individual character, but that it was written as well for nations," and he declared, "Heaven will prosper those who are working in a cause that shall bless the world." His oratory, votes in Parliament, and actions as a cotton mill owner demonstrated his commitment to Quaker testimonies. Rufus Jones described Bright as among the most distinguished "since the days of George Fox and William Penn," noting that, in him, "Quakerism found a potent voice and attracted the attention of the world at large," and that "no member of Parliament in recent times, has drawn upon the Bible for point and illustration as frequently and effectively as John Bright did."[7]

Bright's first involvement with national issues was his opposition to the Corn Laws of 1815, which prohibited the importation of grains into Britain without a large duty—a great financial hardship for the lower class and a great benefit for the agricultural landowners. Richard Cobden and John Bright's long fight against the Corn Laws began with Bright standing on a platform with his father and brother, burgeoned into "the wealthiest, most intensive and most extensive political agitation ever seen up to this period," and resulted in repeal in 1846 after the Irish Potato Famine. Bright gave countless speeches on the subject that could, reportedly, "attract audiences of up to 200,000 people to open air meetings, even in bad weather." During this effort, Bright entered politics because of his Quaker convictions, becoming an MP in 1843.[8]

Bright and Cobden opposed the Borneo War (1849), the Kaffer War (1850), and the Burma War (1852), and they lost their seats in 1857 for opposing Britain's participation in the Crimean War—"The war cannot be justified," Bright stated—but he was quickly elected the same year to a different seat. Assessing that "peace principles could only be promulgated by slow degrees," Bright argued from areas of commonality, maintaining, "I have not opposed any war on the ground that all war is unlawful and immoral. . . . I shall be content when . . . all Christian men condemn war when it is unnecessary, unjust, and leading to no useful or good result," and appealing against "needless and guilty bloodshed." He declared, "I do not trouble myself whether my conduct in Parliament is popular or not," and he refused the post of secretary of state for India in 1868 because of the role of the military in governing.[9]

Bright helped keep Britain from joining the American Civil War on the side of the Confederate States of America (the South), which could have proven decisive, and Sandra Holton argues that this is "perhaps his most considerable achievement as a statesman." He campaigned against Britain's recognition of the Confederacy, fearing it would lead to war. Making use of the Emancipation Proclamation, he rallied public opinion in favor of the Union (the North). (President Abraham Lincoln carried Bright's reelection endorsement and owned a photograph of Bright, and President Rutherford B. Hayes invited Bright to the White House.) As a cotton mill owner, Bright acted against his personal financial interest by refusing to use any cotton imported from slaveholders.[10]

The 1849 Parliamentary Oaths Bill extended the precedent that affirmation sufficed in lieu of the prescribed oath. This precedent was set by Parliament in 1832 when seating the first Quaker MP, Joseph Pease, who had conscientious objections against swearing the oath. In the discussion preceding the bill, Bright stated that "no man could pretend that civil or religious equality in that House was complete so long as this system prevailed," in order to argue that elected Jewish alderman David Salomons take his seat by omitting the words "on the true faith of a Christian" in 1851. In the 1858 Jews Relief Act discussion over Jewish politician Lionel Nathan Freiherr de Rothschild's seat, Bright denounced the notion that "doctrinal differences in religion should be made the test of citizenship and political rights."[11]

Throughout his career, Bright furthered free trade, foreign affairs, and fair treatment. In 1849, Bright helped inaugurate the Commons League to enfranchise the middle class and workingmen, a particularly daring move in the aftermath of the 1848 revolutions in Europe that attacked monarchical structures to establish nation-states. Bright strongly supported the Reform Act of 1867 that enfranchised part of the urban working class, doubling the number of eligible voters. His continued push resulted in the Ballot Act of 1872, which created the secret ballot, and his 1859 proposal resulted in the Cobden-Chevalier Treaty of 1860, which reduced the pressures toward war between the longtime foes of England and France. During the 1860s cotton famine, Bright had to close his Bright Brothers mill but still paid his workers two-thirds wages "with no work in hand." In 1882, he again put principle over personal interest, resigning his chancellor post in disagreement over intervention in Egypt. Rufus Jones held that no Friend since Penn "put the Quaker peace-position to such a public test, and no other Friend has succeeded to the extent he did in carrying Quaker ideals into practice as the sound and stable basis of national policy." Bright consistently advocated for a decentralized government for Canada, India, Jamaica, and, especially, Ireland, speaking in favor of church disestablishment and land reform for Ireland. He opposed Home Rule for Ireland on the basis that it would not protect the rights of its Protestant minority.[12]

Bright always lived by his motto, "Be just and fear not." He was viewed as an inspirational and tireless national hero. As Bill Cash summarizes, Bright's "contributions to free trade and to Britain's relationship to the USA, to the eradication of slavery, to Irish and foreign affairs, the principles of self-government ... laid the foundations for the new politics of the twentieth century."[13]

INAZO NITOBE

Renowned in life, largely unnoticed following World War II, but reconsidered within Japan as an educator and internationally as a diplomat, Inazo Nitobe the parliamentarian remains obscured by his resistance to identifying as a politician. While Bright and Hoover were raised in Quaker families and entered politics as adults, Nitobe was born in 1862 into a politicized family and became a Quaker as an adult. After the Meiji Restoration ousted the last shogun in 1867, Nitobe's Nambu samurai clan, loyal to the shogun, fought to reestablish the military-run feudal system but lost. Attempting to restore his family's honor pushed Nitobe to utilize his education for the sake of the country. He deliberated between pursuing law, politics, economics, or pioneer work in Japan's undeveloped areas; little did he know that his career would encompass all of these. Nitobe came to view his own home region as a frontier to cultivate under the new government, and clan responsibility remained in play throughout his life.[14]

Nitobe held that Quakerism developed civil liberty through conviction in religion and politics, enabling him to live out "political maxims" of "Equality and Brotherhood"; by joining the Society, he reconciled "[his] ideas of nationality and of sects." Nitobe performed administrative service in Japan's colonization of Hokkaido, Chosen (Korea), and Formosa (Taiwan) and advised the Ministry of Agriculture and Commerce before being recommended for the lay position of League of Nations undersecretary general (1920–26). Nitobe directed the League's International Bureaux Section, which facilitated correspondence between member nations, prepared a *Handbook of International Organization*, and assisted in mediating the Baltic Sea's 1921 Åland Islands Question, resolving that Åland would preserve its Swedish language and culture under home rule within Finland.

Bringing together scholars such as Albert Einstein and Marie Curie, Nitobe founded the League's International Committee on Intellectual Cooperation for effectively organizing academic exchanges.[15]

Nitobe's League of Nations affiliation dwarfs his tenure as a legislator in the House of Peers of Japan's National Diet, beginning in 1926. Nitobe worried that Prime Minister Giichi Tanaka, who worked at partitioning Manchuria and Mongolia from China, would bankrupt Japan. After Tanaka coerced Rentarou Mizuno to remain in the office of minister of education after Mizuno's interference in the 1928 election, Nitobe appealed to the House in 1929 that Tanaka's cabinet bought counterfeit votes. His four-hour speech delineated terrorism, bribery, and false reports of the Huanggutun Incident (whereby the Japanese Kwantung Army assassinated Fengtian Clique warlord Zhang Zuolin). Nitobe received a standing ovation, and the resolution of reproof was approved, precipitating resignations from Tanaka and his entire cabinet.[16]

According to Nitobe, the Japanese accepted the nonaggression Kellogg-Briand Pact in good faith when it came before the Diet in 1929 by interpreting it as exempting cases of self-defense. Nitobe seemed not to grasp that Japan was the aggressor when the Kwantung Army framed the Chinese for destroying its own South Manchuria Railway track as pretense for conquering Manchuria in 1931. Nitobe called the League of Nations' 1932 Lytton Report that censured this invasion "a grave mistake." When Japan's Foreign Ministry requested that Nitobe respond to negative perceptions of Japan, he answered to "a Voice within [him that] said—Go on, depending on the light that is within you!" In the United States, Nitobe presented his interpretation of Japan's position, defining self-defense, quoting US secretaries of state, and making arguments by analogy.[17]

However, Nitobe found disturbing Japan's justifications for the Shanghai War of 1932, in which the Japanese Navy violated the International Settlement of Shanghai's neutrality, despite Mayor Te-chen Wu's written concession to Japan's demands. Following reports in a newspaper of Nitobe's comment—"Our country is being destroyed by the Communists and the military clique. And if we ask which is more dangerous, surely the answer must be the military"—in response, the Imperial Reserves dispatched a committee to censure him. Nitobe deftly defused this Matsuyama Incident without apologizing for his views: "The fact that my words were not reported as I said them is my own fault," and "I have caused much trouble to society. I sincerely regret this. I apologize before you all."[18]

In the production-cooperative movement, Nitobe chaired Iwate Production Cooperative Central Committee and initiated its vocational school "for the spiritual development of our countrymen and the economic development of our country," expecting this initiative to end a farming depression and generate world peace. He petitioned the Ministry of Finance regarding the Bill to Reform Banks as the only person of high international standing deigning to head a Japanese farmers' union, and he was the first president of Tokyo Medical Services Users' Cooperative "to do something useful ... for God and for the people." John F. Howes describes Nitobe as "choos[ing] to remain a moderate close to those in power rather than a prophet in the wilderness." Nitobe's contemporaneous disciples and adversaries alike overlooked the nuances of his tempered pacifism that acknowledged evil and sorrow as regrettable present realities while "insist[ing] upon the ultimate conquest of good and justice."[19]

HERBERT HOOVER

Though commonly remembered domestically for his failed presidency and as a foil for President Franklin D. Roosevelt, Herbert Hoover was arguably the leading humanitarian of his age. He was responsible for distributing nearly thirty-four million metric tons of food to Europeans during and following World War I—a "pioneering effort in global altruism" —and historians have reevaluated Hoover's international humanitarian relief efforts and Depression-era policies. After studying at Friends Pacific Academy and graduating in Stanford University's inaugural class, Hoover became a preeminent mining engineer, manager, and consultant around the world, finding new mines and making existing ones profitable in Australia, China, and other locations. He maintained that "the more men of engineering background who become public officials, the better for representative government."[20]

When World War I broke out in Europe in 1914, Hoover's life was forever changed: "When war came my professional career was ended. We had built up a great business." The US embassy called him to a meeting on the Belgian food crisis, and he organized the Committee of American Residents in London for Assistance of American Travellers to exchange currency and find ships home for over one hundred thousand Americans stranded in Europe.[21]

That role was just the beginning. Hoover chaired the Commission for Relief in Belgium, having to "find a billion dollars, to transport five million tons of concentrated food, to administer rationing, price controls, agricultural production, to contend with combatant governments and with world shortages of foods and ships." The commission fed nine million Belgians and French per day, which Belgian museums have described as "a Herculean undertaking of immense complexity" by "the Great Humanitarian" and which George Nash contextualizes as an enterprise "unprecedented in world history: an organized rescue of an entire nation from starvation."[22]

The challenge broadened in 1917, when President Woodrow Wilson asked Hoover to head the US Food Administration, responsible for feeding over eighty-three million starving people (likely a conservative estimate) in Europe during the war, recovery, and reconstruction. Total food exports tripled prewar figures. Hoover dealt with ports, railways, coal, typhus, and dueling countries. American charities paid to feed fourteen to sixteen million children in Europe. Hoover sought Quakers to fundraise and to manage the feeding of German children based on "implicit confidence" in "the right-mindedness of the people with whom I have been born and raised." The American Friends Service Committee (AFSC) chair Rufus Jones answered Hoover's "call to take entire charge" of this relief work, which expanded to feeding seventy-five thousand Russians a day as "the expression of a definite religious faith and sprang naturally out of an inner spirit and attitude to life." Hoover reported, "My organizations directed 19,346,821 tons of food, seed, clothing, medical and miscellaneous supplies from overseas to 22 nations," and Nash identifies Hoover ("the vanguard of the whole approach") as the person behind the fact that "the world [had] grown accustomed to determined efforts to save civilian lives. . . . In the aftermath—or even the midst of—such disasters, humanitarian experts and assistance [would] be there. One reason for this expectation, one reason for its acceptance, is the precedent created in World War I by Hoover and his fellow volunteers. Amid the horrors of 1914–18, there emerged a profound and enduring impulse (cultivated by Hoover and others) to mitigate suffering and heal the wounds of war."[23]

After being appointed by President Warren G. Harding, Hoover became the most active secretary of commerce (1921–28) to date. He held over three thousand domestic conferences for elimination of waste; added aeronautics, radio, and housing bureaus; convinced seven states to dam the Colorado River to develop hydroelectric power, irrigate lands, and reclaim land (the Hoover Dam scheme); and promoted fisheries conservation. In parallel, he provided Mississippi River flood relief in 1927, combating "the worst natural disaster in the nation's history," and obtained reductions in interest on the war debts of Belgium, France, and Italy.[24]

This catapulted Hoover to the Republican nomination for president and a landslide victory in the 1928 election. In the primary, he ran against Charles Curtis, his subsequent running mate—the first vice president of non-European ancestry and sole Native American vice president to date (of Kaw, Osage, and Potawatomi descent, raised in the Kaw Nation, and for whom English was a third language). Saying, "I come of Quaker stock," Hoover promised, "I stand for religious tolerance both in act and in spirit." Hoover, who had anonymously given a good part of his monthly engineering salary to friends and relatives and rejected compensation for any of his relief work, rejected a salary for his federal service as well, becoming the first president to do so.[25]

Hoover's presidency got off to a promising start. He made a goodwill visit to ten Central and South American countries and withdrew all American troops from the region. Treaties of arbitration and conciliation, including mandatory arbitration for disputes with Latin American countries, were a cornerstone of Hoover's foreign policy. He advanced flood control, irrigation, navigation, and hydroelectric power, choosing "eminent" Philadelphia Quakers to administer the Bureau of Indian Affairs. He promoted demilitarization with the 1930 London Naval Treaty, provided loans to farmer-owned cooperatives, established the National Institute of Health and Veterans Administration, undertook penal reform, and stopped oil leases on public lands.[26]

However, his administration began to be perceived as a failure following the stock market crash of October 1929, exacerbated by Hoover's signing of the Hawley-Smoot Tariff Act, which reduced imports (by raising tariffs) and exports (because the other countries had less money with which to buy American exports); America was soon mired in the Great Depression. Hoover tried countermeasures such as having manufacturers maintain wage rates, keeping unions from striking or asking for wage increases, keeping interest rates low, and urging a public works bill and tax cuts. To combat the Depression in Europe, which affected the United States, he postponed "all payments on intergovernmental debts, reparations and relief debts" from Europe to America for one year while not collecting war reparations from Germany.[27]

A severe drought made matters worse. Four million people were unemployed, twenty-five thousand businesses failed, six hundred banks failed, many people resorted to living in scrap shelters known as "Hoovervilles," a quarter of the nation's farms were lost, and Hoover called out the military to evict the Bonus Army of suffering war veterans. Keen to avoid direct government assistance, he signed a law approving the distribution of $45 million worth of wheat by the Red Cross and asked the AFSC in 1931 to feed children of coal miners and to provide matching funds, feeding forty thousand children. He set up the Reconstruction Finance Corporation authorizing over half the entire federal budget for loans and signed the Emergency Relief and Construction Act for $300 million in loans to states and $1.5 billion in loans for construction.[28]

Blamed for the Depression (which, in fact, continued until 1940), Hoover was soundly defeated for reelection in 1932. Though he came to be viewed negatively for his inability to meet Depression-era challenges and his unparalleled wartime humanitarian relief effort faded from American memory, the US Embassy Brussels Office of Public Diplomacy and numerous historians point out that feeding eighty-three million people is "a staggering figure. But whether this estimate is high or low, the bottom line is irrefutable": Hoover "averted a widespread breakdown of the European system" and directly "fed more people and saved more lives than any other man in history." Notwithstanding the far-reaching impacts of medical and scientific innovators, Hoover remains responsible for this prototype of relief "on a scale previously unknown and unimagined."[29]

QUAKER POLITICIANS IN CONCERT

Thirty-three different Quaker MPs served under Queen Victoria and often worked in tandem. Joseph Pease's family formed nearly one-third of the thirty-three, including Henry Pease (brother); Joseph Whitwell Pease and Arthur Pease (sons); Henry Fell Pease (nephew); and Alfred Edward Pease, Joseph Albert Pease, and Herbert Pike Pease (grandsons). Bright's Quaker MP relatives include Jacob Bright (brother), John Albert Bright and William Leatham Bright (sons), and William Henry Leatham and Edward Aldam Leatham (brothers-in-law), and he served alongside John and, in the post-Victorian period, Edward Ellis, who persuaded Joshua Rowntree (Ellis's brother-in-law) to run for office. Arnold Stephenson Rowntree (Rowntree's cousin), Thomas Edmund Harvey (Stephenson Rowntree's brother-in-law), and John Emmott Barlow drafted the "conscience clause" that legalized conscientious objection in the 1916 Military Service Act. Harvey also co-led the Friends Ambulance Unit (FAU) with Joseph Albert Pease, Joseph Allen Baker, Philip John Noel-Baker, and John William Wilson. Baker instilled his concern for the criticality of international peace in his son, Noel-Baker, who assisted the League of Nations covenant-drafting committee (1918–19) before becoming principal assistant to Inazo Nitobe's superior. Noel-Baker pressed the League to handle repatriation, famine, and a refugee crisis based on a Quaker Emergency and War Victims Committee report on four hundred thousand prisoners of war in Russia, and Nitobe coauthored the League report on their conditions; this coordination led to the League's prisoners-of-war commission. Noel-Baker made the transition into League representative to the Assembly (1922–32) and, concurrently, won MP seats; he also represented Britain at the United Nations.[30]

Bright's granddaughter, Esther Clark Clothier, served on her School Board (after Gladstone's 1870 Elementary Education Act permitted election of women as local councillors; Committee, Trade Board, and School Board members; and poor law guardians), chaired a subcommittee of Somerset Education Committee, and served on Somerset City Council, as well as catalyzed women's inclusion in Friends Service Committee and advocated "among the strongest" in the Bright-Priestman circle of the suffragist movement. After the 1902 Education Act disqualified women from election to Education Committees that replaced School Boards, the government conceded that each council should include at least two women, who filled these unelected policy-making positions until eligible for election per the Qualification of Women (County and Borough Councils) Act of 1907. Elizabeth Taylor Cadbury participated in the Worcestershire County Council Education Committee from 1903, as chair of Bournville Village Schools Management Committee, on the City of Birmingham Education Committee, as president of the Birmingham and Midland Home and School Council, won election as Birmingham City councillor for King's Norton, and became a justice of the peace in 1926. She also ministered at Warwickshire North Monthly Meeting, was highly involved in Bournville Meeting, collaborated in establishing Woodbrooke Quaker Settlement and its summer school at her former home with Joshua Rowntree and relatives, and represented Friends at the World Council of Churches.[31]

Despite kinship and religious connections, MP Friends did not vote as a bloc, and the *British Friend* balked at ten Quaker MPs for not allying to prevent financing of the Anglo-Egyptian War in 1882. Joseph Pease opposed Bright's stance on the Corn Laws, which the latter sharply criticized ("Half a million of his fellowmen declare a certain Law ... an atrocious violation of every principle of justice and a direct wrong and robbery inflicted on them, and yet a member of the Society of Friends above all men, is found in the ranks of those who insultingly ... scornfully resist every, even the slightest most moderate attempt to remedy it") and lamented ("I ... wish heartily no 'friend' were in parliament so to act").[32]

Friends dealt with plain dress at work in different ways. Joseph Pease attended in simple dress; Bright did not practice plain dress in Parliament but wore Court Dress without a sword to approach Queen Victoria, where a staff member removed his hat on approach and returned it to his head on departure; and, rather than grant Joseph Allen Baker an exception, the queen released the entire London City Council from the requirement of Court Dress.[33]

Nitobe and Hoover's shared faith did not outweigh their conflicting national interests. Nitobe wrote expectantly in 1930, "The Quaker Hoover ... of unquestioned probity—must inaugurate the age ... for real disarmament." However, after inheriting President Calvin Coolidge's Immigration Act of 1924, which capped immigration from "quota countries" and singled out Japanese as "ineligible for citizenship," and because of which Nitobe had resolved not to enter America again until its repeal, Hoover stated, "I have opposed the national origins basis ... but the President of the United States must be the first to obey the law," and he went further by "tightening up" immigration to exclude "aliens who may prove to become public charges," beyond the prior stipulation of being only "liable to" become so, reducing visa issuances by an additional 70 percent.[34]

Hoover supported the United States joining the League of Nations and proposed joining the Permanent International Court of Justice in 1929, but the Senate rejected both. He used executive action to cooperate with the League in "nonpolitical functions" but did not meet Nitobe's expectation that America would join the League. After Japan withdrew from the League following the Lytton Report, Nitobe confessed to being "inconsistent and self-contradictory" in deeming Japan's withdrawal justified, writing, "It has taken me years of thought and prayer to be contrary and inconsistent." Hoover, meanwhile, collaborated with Secretary of State Henry Stimson on the Stimson Doctrine, a policy determining that the United States would not recognize any "treaty or agreement" of territorial gains made by a country through aggression. Nitobe countered that the disqualification of Manchuria's case as self-defense was open to interpretation, and he framed possible economic sanctions as "war measures," arguing that boycotts and tariffs were "practically, and not rhetorically, warfare."[35]

Hoover met with Nitobe for seven minutes on June 2, 1932. Nitobe reported that Hoover told him, "We do not want another war," and "that I would be as good a man as any to promote the amity between the two countries." He later doubted Hoover's mettle, however: "I spoke of Mr. Hoover as a peace man, but he may find himself unequal to the task when the war-spirit is on." Nitobe cautiously assessed, "He has been emitting light from time to time.... More than once did he disappoint.... If Mr. Hoover sees a light, that light will radiate all over the world."[36]

This strained relationship differs markedly from Nitobe's unwavering praise of John Bright, "the only living Friend of whom I heard, and for whom I felt and still feel the highest admiration."[37] Nitobe lauded Bright's resignation from the position of chancellor of the Duchy of Lancaster over Britain's war in Egypt and unequivocally presented Bright as a model to emulate, "a passionate believer" who "did not simply speak. First, he would sit in a chair silently and think," and he "would never join any political party.... He could not act by following partisan principles, policies, etc. that differed from his own heart." Nevertheless, Bright is conspicuously absent from Nitobe's *Ijin Gunzou (Dynamic Portraits of Eminent Figures)*, where he only drops Bright's name in passing (in one sentence that lists the names of six men) within a three-hundred-page tome.[38]

Bright, the nineteenth century's "greatest" orator and concurrent businessman and career politician, was a devout, active Friend who conscientiously and intentionally acted out the beliefs of his Quaker identity and community; eloquent Nitobe, without a career outside of government service, was an adult convert who endeavored, with varying degrees of success, to amalgamate his culture and prior thinking with the Quaker views that he adopted; and Hoover, a poor orator but a businessman turned world hero, boldly believed in the Society's principles and sense of duty to humankind, though he eschewed some of its prevalent customs. These factors mark differences between these notable early Quaker politicians, but all three focused on domestic concerns of the lower classes during their simultaneous involvement in international affairs. While these three did not share one political approach, they and their fellow Quakers in office shared a concern for the poor and hungry, whose aid they fought for via prolonged legislative procedures as well as through more direct organizational efforts.[39]

Frederick B. Tolles summarizes that many Friends "avoid direct participation in politics, at least in the sense of seeking elective office," but that Quakers took "every possible position from full participation to complete withdrawal and abstention." While diverse contemporaneous Friends viewed their governmental work through admiring or disdainful lenses, each Quaker politician experienced "a real tension" in working from a dedication to pacifism in a world at war. A remark of Bright's illustrates the mixed feelings about political leadership and the state of their world: "Peace on earth has not come, and the goodwill among men is only partially and occasionally exhibited.... It lies within the power of the churches to do far more than statesmen can do.... Bring to the minds of statesmen that they ... ought to be, the Christian rulers of a Christian people." Reflecting on his own involvement in the political sphere, Bright expressed "hope that [he was] sowing some good seed in men's hearts and minds on great public questions and that fruit may one day not be wanting." By applying their Quaker commitments to domestic policy making and international cooperation as they navigated elected service, Bright, Nitobe, Hoover, and others pioneered the Society of Friends' official representation in politics.[40]

CHAPTER 13

The All-Friends Conferences and Their Effects

DOUGLAS GWYN

Major wars reframe the world in unforeseen ways. The First World War was a watershed moment for Anglo-American Friends. The British-led regime of capitalist expansion had presided over a century of relative peace through free-trade prosperity and sufficient military capability to quell most conflicts. Similar conditions on the American side since the Civil War had lulled the transatlantic Quaker community into a confidence that human progress was nearly inevitable, through the advances of science and technology, humanitarian concern, and mutual self-interest in peace and prosperity.[1]

Even such visionary Friends as Rufus Jones (1863–1948), who had studied and traveled extensively in Germany, experienced the outbreak of the war in 1914 as "a terrific jolt." A conference of British Friends at Llandudno, Wales, during the war's first weeks reaffirmed the absolute pacifist position. But a general unpreparedness for war resistance was revealed when large numbers of British and American Friends either enlisted or were willingly conscripted into the war effort. Nevertheless, the rapid development of the British Quaker Council for International Service (CIS) and the American Friends Service Committee (AFSC) evinced a resolve among many Friends to witness their conscientious objection to war through active relief work and other humanitarian service (see chapter 11).²

In 1915, New York Yearly Meeting (Hicksite) wrote to London Yearly Meeting offering help "in any joint enterprise for peace." That same year, London Yearly Meeting appointed a special committee under the leadership of John William Graham and Henry Hodgkin to explore the possibilities. Graham had been a catalyst for liberal Quaker renewal on both sides of the Atlantic. Hodgkin, an evangelical Friend, was central in founding the interdenominational Fellowship of Reconciliation in Britain in 1914 and in America in 1915. The 1916 sessions of London Yearly Meeting proposed a conference to be held "for all those who bear the name of Friend" concerning a "permanent universal peace." The 1917 sessions resolved to hold the conference in London as soon as possible after the war, in order to "clarify and deepen the historical Friends peace testimony, and to bind together the scattered branches of the Society of Friends in common work for the kingdom of God."³

In 1919, transatlantic travel was still difficult, so the conference was postponed until 1920. Some feared that the intensity of concern might wane after another year, but extensive planning and promotion produced a watershed event. British and American commissions were appointed to prepare advance study materials on the historic Quaker peace testimony, its implications for civil and international relations, personal and social relations, and the life of the Society of Friends, methods for its wider propagation, and how it would serve as the basis for continuing the international service begun during the war. Peace conferences had brought together a variety of American Friends before the war. Now Friends would unite worldwide to make the peace testimony the defining feature of a theologically scattered Society of Friends and the major focus of their witness to the world.⁴

THE ALL-FRIENDS CONFERENCE IN LONDON, AUGUST 12 TO 20, 1920

A total of 936 delegates attended, with more than 450 from London Yearly Meeting, over 350 from the United States and Canada, and 60 from Ireland, north and south. Fewer than ten each arrived from Australia, New Zealand, China, Denmark, France, India, Japan, Jamaica, Madagascar, Norway, and Syria. In all, sixteen nations were represented. Devonshire House, an organizational center for British Friends for 250 years, hosted the sessions. Friends around London provided hospitality in their homes.[5]

The conference began on the evening of August 12 with the 1920 Swarthmore Lecture, given by Rufus Jones in Westminster's Central Hall. Jones, professor of philosophy at Haverford College near Philadelphia, had given the first Swarthmore Lecture at the 1908 London Yearly Meeting sessions. Since the death in 1905 of his close friend and ally John Wilhelm Rowntree, Jones was the leading voice of liberal Quaker renewal on both sides of the Atlantic. His lecture, "The Nature and Authority of Conscience," was advertised to the general public as a major statement on behalf of Friends. Walter C. Woodward, editor of the Five Years Meeting (FYM) weekly *The American Friend*, reflected on the event in light of the persecution experienced by Early Friends: "Here was perhaps the largest Friends gathering ever held under one roof, meeting under the very eyes of the visible representations of Church and State."[6]

Jones told his listeners that human conscience is more than the natural accumulation of social custom and habit; it is evidence of human origins in a deeper spiritual universe. "The Beyond is within; we are embedded in a larger consciousness than that bounded by the margins of our finite self," he said. "We are at least at one inner point conjunct with that Person who is the life of our lives." Of course, the human conscience struggles with apparently conflicting ideals: love of family, country, truth, and God. But these, Jones argued, are fused together in the Spirit of Christ, "dying to selfish and utilitarian aims through inner assurance of fellowship with Him and the whole human family, in love, in faith, in life and in service."[7]

Jones's concept of human persons participating in the personhood of God articulated the Christian personalist philosophy he had earlier popularized in *Social Law in the Spiritual World* (1904). Other Friends made personalist statements at this conference. Personalism was popular among a variety of liberal Christians in the early twentieth century. Friends took hold of it as a modern expression of their traditional conviction of "that of God in every one" and as a bridge toward people of other faiths, for concerted social witness.[8]

Each subsequent morning at Devonshire House began with devotional meetings held in three rooms. Each morning's plenary session focused on one of the topics addressed by the preconference materials. Two speakers, usually one American and one British, addressed the topic, followed by general discussion. John Barlow, clerk of London Yearly Meeting throughout the war years, "maintained firm and courteous hold on the speakers, but also succeeded in a masterly way in summarizing the outcome of each discussion in a series of valuable minutes, which usually won the ready acceptance of the Conference." This characterization in the *Official Report* is generally accurate, but individual reports suggest more frustration with the process. Walter Woodward observed that British Friends were more articulate and had studied the issues more deeply in many cases but were too quick and repetitious in speaking: "The 'concerned Friend' par excellence is the English Friend, when concerned, as he generally is." Others despaired of finding opportunity to speak. On the other hand, Woodward "came to realize, for example, that liberalism, even socialism, is not *prima facie* evidence of mendacity or of diseased mentality. However much we may have differed with them, some of the finest and most representative spirits of the Conference were avowed socialists and from a deep sense of following thereby the way of life as found in Christ. May we accustom ourselves to liberal thinking—on the part of others at least."[9]

Among the appointed speakers, Joan Mary Fry described the peace testimony as "an integral part of our reading of Christianity," which she supplemented with modern scientific perspectives on war. Rufus Jones observed that "at last the glamour and glory have been stripped away from war and we see it, or at least may see it, in all its naked horror, in its unmitigated awfulness . . . and we know now that war is the occasion for more wars and not, as fondly hoped, a way to 'end all war.'" He hoped that international courts might help adjudicate international conflicts. But the task of Friends was "to make faith in moral and spiritual forces somewhat more real." In the ensuing discussion, Elizabeth Cadbury commented, "I would emphasise the spiritual side of our protest against war. Our strength is surely in our definite Christian testimony. I have felt that during the past years of war we have lost to a certain extent by associating ourselves too much as a Society with the political side of the question." Conference participants voiced various responses to the new League of Nations. Some viewed it as a "League of Victors," since Germany and Russia were initially excluded. Friends were also critical of the League's provision for military and economic coercion against international aggression.[10]

Appointed speakers were predominantly men. The one speaker who was not English or Anglo-American was J. N. C. Ganguly of India Yearly Meeting, who spoke on "The Race Problem." He noted the intimate relation between racism and war: as the world became more interconnected, race would need more attention. He defined racism as a creation of the West, an immoral and inhuman apostasy from Christian faith; continued missions to the East, he maintained, must be balanced with a reconversion of the West. In the ensuing discussions, White American, South African, and Australian Friends bemoaned the racial problems in their own countries. Rachel Knight of Philadelphia Yearly Meeting (Hicksite) said, "There is race prejudice in America, and it is because there has not been justness and fairness to the negro race. The negroes were brought to America under circumstances that were against the honour of the white race; and it is the white race that has suffered far more from slavery than has the coloured race. I know of no Friends' college which has as students members of another race." (Presumably, she meant damage to the White American conscience resulting from the enslavement of Africans. But it is hard to imagine that as greater than the suffering experienced by those who were enslaved.) A White Friend from Jamaica Yearly Meeting claimed that there was almost no racial problem there. British Friends were unusually quiet. The session proved more prophetic of the next war's horrors than anyone could have known at the time.[11]

British Friend Edward Hodgkin observed that the war had provided Friends with the greatest opportunity in their whole history to demonstrate their peace testimony to the world. But, he said, "We failed. That is to say, we did not present that united front against the forces of militarism which some of us had fondly assumed we should do as a matter of course." Notwithstanding inspired statements (such as the ones made at Llandudno) and the hardships of some for the sake of conscience (those imprisoned and abused as resisters to conscription), Hodgkin argued that Friends who had hoped for unity against militarism were in fact "divided in our views and attitude, and thus have our share of responsibility for the horrors of Armageddon." Some older and younger Friends admitted that this failure followed from the lack of a consistent life before the war. "The question we now have to ask ourselves is, How far the same unfitness which spoiled our chance of service in 1914 stands in the way of our work for God and humanity today," said Hodgkin. Similarly, Henry Cadbury of Philadelphia Yearly Meeting (Orthodox) admitted that American Friends had not held the testimony with sufficient conviction. A renewed peace witness "must not be mere sentiment or argument from expedience. It must not be intermittent or partial. . . . It must insist that the method should be as pure as the aim, and it must express itself in continuous active service."[12]

Edward Evans of Philadelphia Yearly Meeting (Orthodox) followed, addressing such economic issues as industrial relations and living conditions in the United States. But the conference found no resolution between those who wished to address economic conditions at the root of war and those who viewed criticism of capitalism to be a red herring. Henry Hodgkin made the only recorded contribution to the discussion that directly addressed personal integrity; he observed that John Woolman's simplicity was his greatest power in influencing others to renounce all forms of oppression. (Discouraged by the situation of postwar Europe, Hodgkin was about to return to the mission field in China, where he had already spent five years before the war.)[13]

Other sessions addressed spiritual and educational foundations. Rufus Jones warned, "We shall be weak in our work and message for the present hour unless we greatly deepen our manner and power of worship." He found worship at the conference especially weak and chatty. Anna Shipley Cox, a California Friend who had done Quaker relief work in Poland during the war, emphasized the role of education "because it builds highways of thought for the future." She married Howard Brinton the next year, and from 1936 to 1952 they served as directors of the Pendle Hill study center outside Philadelphia, a pioneering educational community for Friends and other pacifists.[14]

In a session on international service, Carolena Wood of New York Yearly Meeting (Hicksite) spoke to the motivations of service: "Let us bring what we have to the altar and the altar will sanctify the gift. The giving of a tin of condensed milk may become a sacrament because of the way it is given and received. This is a service of understanding hearts."[15]

The conference produced a public statement, titled "To Friends and Fellow-Seekers," that summarized the tenor of its proceedings: "The world to-day is in sore need. Does it not rest in part with us whether its pains are to be the agonizing of a dying civilization or the birth-pangs of a new and fairer life, in which justice shall dwell?" The statement continued:

> The one thing that matters in all our social structure is human personality, yet often we lose this essential fact in abstractions. We speak of a nation as the "enemy," we talk of a group as "labour" or "capital," and we forget the men and women who make up the group and who are the only realities there, each of them different, each bearing the impress of the Divine and capable of a new birth into a new social

order.... Progress is not inevitable. It depends upon men and women; upon what kind of men and women we are.[16]

The conference also adopted and published a restatement of the peace testimony drafted by Rufus Jones as part of the American commissions' preconference materials. *Friends and War: A New Statement of the Friends Position* served as the standard text for Quaker peace witness during the interwar years. The pamphlet cited the recent Quaker experience of relief and service work during the war, which had added new urgency and focus to peace work. The challenges would be great, but just as the abolition of slavery began with "a few pioneer spirits," so the abolition of war must draw together people of conscience: "The Christian way of life revealed in the New Testament, the voice of conscience revealed in the soul, the preciousness of personality revealed by the transforming force of love, and the irrationality revealed in modern warfare, either together or singly, present grounds which for those who feel them make participation in war under any conditions impossible."[17]

Both conference statements demonstrate the personalist philosophy Friends hoped would bridge their traditional testimony toward others in work for peace and justice.

REFLECTIONS

The 1920 All-Friends Conference enabled Friends to view themselves as a world body. Clarence Pickett later reflected that it inaugurated an "International Society of Friends," something beyond an "Anglo-Saxon sect." A continuation committee was appointed to organize another such conference in due course. Even a permanent council was envisaged, with representatives from yearly meetings around the world. But these larger designs lapsed. Still, Walter Woodward returned to Richmond, Indiana, proclaiming, "The day for world-wide Quaker co-operation is at hand.... This by no means implies uniformity either in thought or practice. But we *must* know each other, and knowing, sympathize and appreciate."[18]

Various minutes and addresses mentioned the need for "sympathy" across human differences. This usage is significant. Leigh Eric Schmidt notes "religious sympathy" as a motif of American liberal piety that began with the Quaker-raised poet Walt Whitman in the mid-nineteenth century.

Since then, European empires had integrated not only peoples but their cultures and religions into the world economy. While some responded with missionary endeavors, others were more concerned with learning from other religions and encountering the suffering of subject peoples and of the victims of war. "Cosmopolitan" (from the ancient Greek usage *kosmopolites*, "citizen of the world") describes this growing sensibility.[19]

The war and the 1920 conference helped advance a trend already growing among Friends. It drew evangelicals from the liberal end of FYM such as Walter Woodward, who could now countenance socialist Quakers. It also engaged those liberal and traditional Friends who were not overly scandalized by the innovations of pastoral Friends. Cosmopolitan Quakers, buoyed by the affective registers of religious sympathy and further emboldened by the philosophies of personalism and progressivism, retained individual affinities and affiliations within one Quaker branch or another but related in new ways across the branches and toward the wider world.

Woodward also noted that this was "the most representative meeting of American Friends ever held. It is appropriate and significant that it was held under the auspices of the mother yearly meeting, which has so warmly welcomed us home." Friends General Conference (FGC) Friend Thomas Jenkins noted that rapprochement began even aboard the steamer crossing the Atlantic, as different Friends got acquainted and studied and worshipped together.[20]

But the nascent cosmopolitanism that American Friends experienced in London met with resistance back home. Evangelicals had long objected to Rufus Jones's modernist editorship of *The American Friend*, leading him to withdraw in 1912. They found little improvement in Walter Woodward's editorship. His reporting on the 1920 conference increased their suspicions that he was betraying the evangelical movement. In step with the wider modernist-fundamentalist conflict among American churches, tensions within FYM reached a boiling point in the 1920s. Oregon Yearly Meeting seceded in 1926, with smaller withdrawals from within Indiana, Western, and Iowa Yearly Meetings the same decade. Kansas Yearly Meeting left in 1937. These separations were instigated by Friends most strongly affected by the Holiness movement of the 1880s and 1890s and by the neoevangelical resurgence of that historical moment (see chapter 4). By contrast, among Eastern yearly meetings, pervasive liberal renewal augured a gradual reunion of Orthodox and Hicksite Friends, which would reach formal completion in the 1950s.[21]

Certainly, evangelical and fundamentalist reactions to modernist developments in the wider Quaker family were often xenophobic, provincial, and creedal in motivation. But liberal Friends often did not countenance the deeper existential commitment at stake. The Christian experience of answering a call, or the more specifically evangelical moment of a "decision for Christ," had a galvanizing intensity often lacking in liberal religion. Existential "dread" or "fear and trembling," as Kierkegaard defined Christian spirituality, had strong resonances with the prophetic power of Early Friends. The cultured refinement of cosmopolitan "sympathy" among more laterally focused liberals could rarely attain that intensity. To "stand at the cross" of (and with) Jesus could produce a commitment to nonviolence that a well-articulated "peace position" did not always muster. The higher levels of conscientious objection and resistance to conscription among Conservative Friends and in some evangelical yearly meetings during the next war attested to that absoluteness. These reflections are relevant as we consider the next all-Friends gathering.

THE AMERICAN ALL-FRIENDS CONFERENCE, OSKALOOSA, SEPTEMBER 3 TO 9, 1929

Passmore Elkinton was a Philadelphia Quaker (Orthodox) whose business travels around the United States had inspired in him a concern for Quaker unity. He had not attended the 1920 conference but was spurred by reports of it to advocate a fuller encounter among American Friends. Notwithstanding the conflicts and divisions within FYM over the following decade, he persisted. Elkinton raised his concern at an AFSC meeting in Richmond in December 1925, just months before the withdrawal of Oregon Yearly Meeting from FYM over issues of theological purity. A committee was appointed to see if an American all-Friends conference might promote "more understanding and sympathy" among all groups of American Friends. The AFSC had drawn participation and leadership from across the American Quaker spectrum during and after the war and was thus in the best position to call such a conference. Wilbur Thomas was appointed to organize it for the summer of 1929. Thomas had served since 1922 as the general secretary for AFSC. But at the instigation of Rufus Jones, he resigned from that position early in 1929, owing to his public criticisms of fellow Quaker Herbert Hoover, the newly elected president of the United States.[22]

Thomas himself had served as a Friends pastor before working for AFSC and was a potential bridge-builder. His published announcement of the conference began with some historical background on American Friends. It noted that "in newer countries the absence of educational facilities, the lack of good roads and the poverty of the people had much to do with shaping their thoughts. The souls of the pioneers readily responded to the aggressive, conquering type of evangelism which has always characterized such periods." Differences grew, he explained, leading to formal divisions.

Thomas's account sounds rather pejorative toward evangelical Quaker developments, if the aim was bridge-building. He also appears unaware of the similar social and religious conditions that had attended Quaker beginnings in northern England. He continued, "Christianity is being challenged as never before." Professing Christians departed from the spirit and teachings of Jesus, he said, leading thoughtful people to depart from churches. Meanwhile, those who instigated the historic divisions among Friends a century before were now gone. Friends could unite in winning souls to Christ through their shared social concerns regarding war, alcohol, narcotics, gambling, and the treatment of prisoners. The announcement made clear that the conference aimed at no new organization or alignment of yearly meetings but that it hoped to renew fellowship in Christ through mutual acquaintance and sympathetic understanding.[23]

Thomas and former FGC chair Edward Janney traveled to Kansas Yearly Meeting sessions in Wichita in 1928 to ask if the conference could be held at the evangelical Friends University. Kansas Friends declined. In particular, they were concerned that young Friends from the East might influence their own young people. But soon after, William Penn College in Oskaloosa, Iowa, welcomed the conference, and plans moved forward.[24]

The conference brochure featured a photo of the William Penn campus and described the event as "an opportunity for all Friends in America to come together for a time of Worship and Fellowship." The sessions would open with greetings from Isabel Grubb of Ireland Yearly Meeting and John William Graham of London Yearly Meeting. Plenary addresses were scheduled for evening sessions, to attract local attenders. Discussion groups on each evening's topic ensued the next morning and afternoon. Conference topics were listed: outreach at home and abroad, education, application of Christian principles to social conditions, peace, and worship and ministry. Rufus Jones did not attend this gathering, perhaps anticipating that he would serve mainly as a lightning rod for evangelical animus. In her greetings on behalf of Irish Friends, Grubb set a conciliatory tone by noting that the call to service united Friends across their differences, and whatever language they used to describe it, they shared "the same fact" of Christian experience.[25]

The conference drew more than seven hundred registered attenders. In all, about a thousand attended at least one session. The total included eighty-five FGC Friends and forty-seven Conservative Friends, so attendance was overwhelmingly from the pastoral-evangelical wing. It was believed that all but two American yearly meetings were represented. Cars from twenty-six US states and Ontario, Canada, were counted.[26]

The first topic session, "Outreach of Quakerism—Home Fields," featured Edward Mott, superintendent of Oregon Yearly Meeting, and Frank Dell, superintendent of California Yearly Meeting. Mott had been instrumental in Oregon's 1926 departure from FYM and was determined to draw a line against the doctrinal impurity of liberal Friends. His address was largely a compilation of doctrinal affirmations drawn from the New Testament. He summarized: "May we unite with the Apostle in exclaiming, 'I am determined to know nothing among you save Jesus Christ and Him crucified.' We can in the very nature of the case have no sympathy with any effort to substitute for the Gospel a so-called gospel which is no gospel.... We keep the lines of demarcation between those who love Him and those who love Him not." Mott later recalled the address as "a strong presentation of reasons for withdrawal from association with those who are denying the Faith.... I have never regretted the stand I then took." He also noted: "I well knew that my message was not received by all Friends. Not only by words was their disapproval manifested: they looked it."[27]

Dell had attended the 1920 London conference, where he strongly affirmed the peace testimony: "Christ died for all, not for one nation. If any take up the absolute pacifist position, they must show that their spirit of sacrifice goes deeper than that of those who take up arms." He also participated in drafting the conference statement "To Friends and Other Seekers." But the conflicts under way in FYM and the wider range of topics addressed by this conference elicited a more critical tone. Dell suggested that Quaker traditions had slowly eclipsed the authority of the Bible and Christ, leading to division. Quaker traditions had fostered among many Friends a low estimation of Christ, an adherence to mere peculiarities, and irresponsible individualism. Dell reminded listeners, "George Fox's message began only when he got an experience of the person and power of Christ." He may not have considered that his evangelical faith had become a tradition in its own right, with peculiarities of its own.[28]

Raymond Binford, president of Guilford College in North Carolina, and Archibald Smith, principal of the Friends Academy on Long Island, spoke on education for service. Binford praised John Wilhelm Rowntree and Rufus Jones for their efforts in renewing Quaker education. Smith reflected that Quaker schools could not compete with larger colleges and universities in terms of resources, but they excelled in the spiritual interpretation of life. The war had made clear the need for such education.[29]

Thomas Jones, president of Fisk University, spoke regarding "Friends and the Negro in American Life." Observing Friends' creative response to war in recent years, he suggested that they now exert the same power on race. *The American Friend* later summarized: "The race problem as produced by the Negro in American life was presented in its delicacy and complexity: the lack of equality of opportunity; the barrier of prejudice and injustice; economic distress; lack of adequate educational facilities, etc.... Some practical suggestions were offered for acquainting ourselves with the situation and helping us to meet it." (The race problem as "produced by the Negro" may not have been Jones's wording but that of the unnamed reporter. But this was not an unusual perspective even among progressive White people in the early twentieth century.) In the ensuing forum, Anna Branson of Philadelphia Yearly Meeting (Hicksite) urged all Friends to "do everything we can to stop lynching" and "insist on the same justice in the courts for white and black."[30]

Wilbur Thomas reminded Friends that their lives were the only Bible many people would ever read and advocated that Friends seek out various service opportunities with the AFSC. William Hull of Philadelphia Yearly Meeting (Hicksite), a professor of international relations at Swarthmore College, saw the next war coming: "We must not be caught unprepared again as we were in 1914." He thought outreach to other churches to oppose war could unite Friends in renewed mission. Along similar lines, Levi Pennington, president of Pacific College (later George Fox College) in Oregon, emphasized that war must be confronted intellectually, emotionally, and with a living example of peace.[31]

Agnes Tierney of Philadelphia Yearly Meeting (Orthodox) and Willard Trueblood of FYM gave perspectives on worship and ministry. Tierney spoke of strengths she found in all types of Quaker worship. Trueblood added: "What makes a Friends meeting? It is not found in silence nor in a program, but in a Person and in persons—in a living communion with Christ." Regarding international outreach, Henry Cadbury suggested that Friends' distinctive interpretation of Christianity was their only excuse for continued existence. If other churches had caught up with Friends, it was because Friends were not moving on to new fields of service and witness. The greatest danger was not diversity among Friends but conformity with other groups.[32]

John William Graham had spoken at several Friends General Conferences in the East, but Oskaloosa was no doubt *terra incognita* for him. He had feared that some would be talked down by others, but he noted that "Eastern Friends have not been very quiet nor pastors aggressive. . . . I had thought that all hope of mutual approach was gone, when Edward Mott . . . gave a theological explanation of his fundamentalist faith. . . . Those who did not accept this scheme were to be cut out from Christian fellowship. . . . It was clear that this address . . . was not acceptable to most people. It was generally spoken of as having to be got through, and so better put first. . . . Relief was felt that it was over. It was well replied to the next morning." Some fifty-eight pastors were present, and the pastorate was vigorously defended. But Graham concluded, "Let us humbly acknowledge that the best defense against official preachers is to maintain a living voluntary ministry . . . in our own meeting. Is that always the case?" He had expressed concern over the decline of ministry in unprogrammed meetings as early as 1896.[33]

Walter Woodward's reporting on this conference in *The American Friend* was much less expansive than his reflections on the 1920 London conference. "While favorable in principle toward efforts to draw Friends more closely together in the bonds of friendship," he said, "we have doubted whether the plans for this Conference were altogether wise and practicable." He had expected some differences to dissolve upon better acquaintance, but "this was not evident." Still, Friends did become "more friendly and sympathetic," even if the "aggressive individualism of Friends" didn't always lead to forbearance. Given his own battered position as general secretary of FYM, Woodward concluded rather tepidly, "The holy experiment made at Oskaloosa should bestir Friends generally to similar ventures in conference and friendliness."[34]

FGC Friends reflected positively on the experience. Arthur Jackson, FGC's chair, found the gathering "epoch-making" for the spirit of mutual tolerance with which such wide-ranging expressions of ideals and beliefs were received. He cautioned, however, that any attempt at organic union would prove "worse than futile." Agnes Tierney witnessed love prevailing over all diversities of doctrine and method. Likewise, Passmore Elkinton savored "the tenderness which enveloped us together" and asked, "What of the future? Shall we not dream of another great Friendly gathering ten years from now?" *The Friend* (Philadelphia, Orthodox) noted contrasts not only in theology but in outward appearance—some attenders wore traditional plain dress, others were very modern—as well as professional differences: there was the dirt farmer from Oklahoma and the highly cultured professor from a metropolitan university. Still, almost every face suggested to the writer an independence of character that both diversified and unified the group.[35]

In reflecting on the 1920 conference, we noted the rise of a cosmopolitan Quakerism. In considering this conference, it becomes more evident that such a development was facilitated and perpetuated in part by the growing influence of the academic paradigm among Friends. Several of the speakers were teachers or administrators at Quaker colleges and schools. The "objective" study of various religious and social phenomena produced a growing number of "citizens of the world" among Friends.

Paradoxically, perhaps, everyone apparently avoided the fact that the first Quaker president was now in the White House. But then, Friends would be understandably ambivalent on that subject, especially since the president is also commander in chief of the armed forces. And, of course, only a month after the conference, the stock market crash began to reframe everything. Over the next two decades, Clarence Pickett, AFSC's newly appointed general secretary (who attended this conference), led the organization through an extraordinary period of service and wider influence.[36]

THE FRIENDS WORLD CONFERENCE, PHILADELPHIA, SEPTEMBER 1 TO 7, 1937

In Britain, the Friends Council for International Service (CIS), reorganized and renamed the Friends Service Council (FSC) under the leadership of Carl Heath, had established Quaker "consulates" to several major cities in Europe after the war. Drawing on the reputation Friends earned for relief work during and after the war, these centers generated new Friends meetings and yearly meetings. German Friends, now the largest European group outside Britain and Ireland, called for an "International Society of Friends" in 1929.

Meanwhile, in America, Quaker activism and service had inspired the rapid growth of independent Friends meetings that were unwilling to align with either side of the Great Separation split. The AFSC concluded, "the time has come to attempt boldly some form of a permanent link-up of Friends in different parts of the world who desire fellowship." Clarence Pickett and Passmore Elkinton canvassed two hundred leading Friends from forty yearly meetings with the idea. The largely positive response launched plans for a second world conference of Friends, to be held in 1937 at Swarthmore College and Haverford College. A committee of Friends from twelve nations published a paper in 1936, "Next Steps in the International Cooperation of Friends," as preparation for the conference. AFSC staff member Anna Griscom Elkinton chaired an organizing committee that eventually amassed 389 Friends and met in London and various locations in the United States. Leading the work to promote the gathering, Walter Woodward observed that "a great menace to the Society of Friends is that of localism," and the conference would "lift the horizons of local meetings to the wider field and purpose of a world-wide Quakerism."[37]

Earlier in the summer of 1937, the nascent World Council of Churches held preliminary gatherings at Oxford and Edinburgh (Woodward attended the latter, representing FYM). Evidently, a range of Christian groups, including Friends, were drawing together and organizing in part as the culmination of decades of desire for greater accord and cooperation and in part to prepare for the next global conflagration.[38]

A preconference gathering for Friends from abroad was held at Swarthmore from August 29 to September 1. These visitors met with Friends from three Orthodox quarterly meetings and three quarterly meetings from "the other branch [i.e., Hicksite]." In all, about 450 attended, offering visitors a helpful foretaste of (some) American Quakerism.[39]

A total of 986 official delegates attended the Friends World Conference in Philadelphia in 1937, with 754 from America and 231 from abroad (118 of whom were British Friends). Attendance by women and men was fairly even (though men spoke during plenary discussions five times more than women). At least twenty-three of the twenty-five US yearly meetings sent delegates. Twenty-four nations were represented, compared with sixteen at the 1920 conference. The new countries reflected both Quaker evangelical missions and FSC outreach in Europe: Cuba, Mexico, Austria, Czechoslovakia, Germany, the Netherlands, Sweden, and Switzerland. The only two

African delegates came from South Africa. The burgeoning mission field in Kenya was unrepresented.[40]

Rufus Jones reluctantly agreed to chair the conference. He confided in a July 1937 letter to British Friend Violet Holdsworth, "In regard to the World Conference, I sincerely hope for good results, but I have become a good deal disillusioned over 'big' conferences and large gatherings. I pin my hopes to quiet processes and small circles, in which vital and transforming events take place. But others see differently, and I respect their judgment." Perhaps Jones was influential in the design of the twenty-three Worship-Fellowship groups that met daily during the conference. Even these were not particularly small, with forty delegates assigned to each, premixed according to nationality and religious affinities. The conference report reflected, "Many of us felt that this was the most valuable feature of the Conference, demonstrating the way in which a small group of persons consciously sharing responsibility can experience true religious fellowship." There were major differences, but groups experienced a strong bond of common task and goodwill, notwithstanding "the professional talker with his set piece."[41]

Friends were free to self-select for the daily meetings that focused on various social and religious concerns. The large plenary sessions were held in Swarthmore's Clothier Hall, and three still larger evening meetings were held in the fieldhouse. Open to the public, these attracted as many as 3,500 local Friends and others.

Apart from the conference proceedings, Rufus Jones gave a broadcast message, "The Basis of Quaker Optimism," which aired in Europe courtesy of the BBC (and presumably on some American stations). Like his 1920 Swarthmore Lecture at Westminster, this address was intended for a wider audience, but more as a general introduction to Friends. Jones spoke of "the Quaker philosophy of life," which "has usually been implicit, embedded in the current of life, inarticulate, like the mathematics of the honey bee, rather than a clearly rationalized and explicitly expounded doctrine." He emphasized Quaker pacifism as an active life of service and reconciliation in times of both war and peace. Clearly anticipating the coming conflict, he concluded, "In the stress and strain of actual war, the Quaker has no alternative to continuing, as best he can, the practice of this way of life, this experiment of faith." In areas of conflict, he said, the Quaker shares in the suffering and pours life and means into channels of love. "But what opportunities there are in this present world for sharing in suffering and how little at best this small and humble group can pour of balm into the channels of love!"[42]

In his role as conference chair, Jones also spoke at the opening session. He compared the gathering's international scope to the scene at Pentecost: "May we once more hear in our own tongue the wonderful works of God, and once more may the spirit of the living God fall upon us and endue us with power for the tasks of today." That power would be needed as "we meet under a covering of shadow, which stretches over the earth." The neoorthodox Christian realism of Reinhold Niebuhr and others, ascendant at the World Council of Churches meetings that summer, had emphasized the intractable problem of evil, as evidenced by fascism in Germany, Italy, and Japan. By contrast, Jones emphasized Quaker idealism and optimism: "There is a powerful return to-day to a dark and pessimistic view of man as a seriously damaged being.... But it is safer to level up than to level down, to see divine possibilities in men than to make a census of sins and failures, as though *they* told the whole story of human life. And whatever the dark prophets may say to the contrary, we shall line up in this Conference on the side of the angels and proclaim the gospel of light and hope."

Assessing the present Society of Friends, Jones asserted that "we are in better condition to take our part in the spiritual tasks of the world than we were in 1920 when we met in London. We are slightly feebler in numbers, but we are more compactly united in spirit. We have somewhat enlarged our experience. We have deepened our lives. We have learned to face realities a little better, and, I think, we are more *sacrificially minded*." He went further: "The easiest way to be good, in fact the only way to be good, is to be *heroically good*." Once again, while he could not speak for the full spectrum of Friends, Jones articulated a growing cosmopolitan consensus of Quaker faith and practice, set in its historic moment. The sacrificial, indeed heroic, work of Friends during and after World War II, largely under the auspices of the Friends Service Council and American Friends Service Committee, would be commemorated with the Nobel Peace Prize ten years later.[43]

Racial justice continued to receive attention here, as in the preceding conferences. Isabel Ross of London Yearly Meeting noted that "whereas the problem of the Negro in America rose from his people having been stolen from their land, today the trouble in Africa is that the land has been stolen from the Negro." Rachel Davis DuBois of New York Yearly Meeting (Hicksite) presented her educational approach to work for racial justice. (She was a regular presenter of workshops on racial issues at Friends

General Conferences in these years.) Meanwhile, the conference received a message of greeting from five thousand Friends gathered in Kenya (noted as the largest single gathering of Friends anywhere to date), as if to say, "Hey, we're here!"[44]

After the conference, Rufus Jones reflected that his "grave apprehension" beforehand had been dispelled. The worldwide character of the gathering was evident in color, speech, and dress, he noted, and furthermore, "I have never seen a large gathering handle difficult questions in better manner." On the other hand, while Friends wrote beautifully about their worship, he lamented, "*to do the thing itself* in actual practice and experience is a rare achievement in any part of the Quaker heritage." On that count, he saw this conference as no exception, though no worse than large conferences generally. He also expressed concern that central Quaker principles were not as well articulated as the many "world alarms." But with tea, ices, food, and friendly talkers everywhere, he said, it had amounted to "a happy type of Quakerism."[45]

There was a strong desire to issue a conference message, given the state of the world. A drafting committee labored for two days to produce one, "but the right word, kindled with fire, did not quite emerge; and failing that, it was thought wise not to issue 'just another' statement, with which church gatherings are characteristically prolific," *The American Friend* reported. Friends were instead encouraged to return to their meetings and homelands as "living epistles." Kati Lotz, a young delegate from Germany, found in that decision "the appreciation and value of human personality . . . not the individual in its selfishness or isolation but of the inspired human being trying to work out his inspiration toward his fellowmen in the world as a whole, . . . a co-worker with God to create the higher society of human brotherhood."[46]

A symposium on "Quakerism in My Country" featured speakers from Sweden, Cuba, Japan, Madagascar, Syria, and India. Elbert Russell of Baltimore Yearly Meeting found in the variety of races, tongues, and costumes "the passing of the first stage of the modern expansion of Quakerism." The vision was that missionary efforts from home bases would be displaced by a sense of all being on an equal basis. New and weaker Friends groups would still need help from stronger ones, but no longer on the basis of domination or patronage. L. Hollingsworth Wood of New York Yearly Meeting (Hicksite) reported how he "took pains to sit in a side seat near the front of the plenary meetings so that I could look into the faces of these Friends gathered from all over the world, and I seemed to see as a sort of background to their faces a suggestion of something held in common which gave even somber faces a glowing look as if they were wrapt in some lovely contemplation.... The poise, calm and serenity of our Friends from Continental Europe made one think of Whittier's lovely line, 'The beauty of thy peace.'" He and other participants in the section on racial justice determined to remain in correspondence: "Surely some such spiritual hand-hold is needed in a world torn such as ours seems to be in the Ninth month 1937."[47] Hollingsworth Wood's description of the affective registers of the conference complements Jones's more penetrating analyses.

A statement near the end of the conference by Herbert George Wood, director of studies at Woodbrooke, posed a challenge to Friends. Noting a gap at the gathering between those drawn by the spiritual message of Friends and those more concerned with wider social issues, he located in the neglected middle between the two the notion of simplicity. Trust in God and true friendship, he argued, were being "limited and imperiled by our reliance on comfort and our differences in standard of living—by our class differences.... We are too comfortable." He questioned "whether we can, so to speak, maintain the heroic in the midst of the rather high standard of comfort that belongs to us as a Society.... Our middle-class point of view is a limitation that we have to overcome."[48]

The lasting outcome of the conference was the decision to establish a "Consultative Committee to promote better knowledge and understanding among Friends the world over." The Friends World Committee for Consultation (FWCC) was founded to sustain dialogue among Friends worldwide. Carl Heath, who had retired from the Friends Service Council in 1935, was appointed as its first chair. By 1939, all but six yearly meetings had appointed representatives. War interrupted further progress until a conference was held in Richmond, Indiana, in 1947. The FWCC also received "nongovernmental organization" status with the United Nations, a culmination of the cosmopolitanism that had grown from these three major Quaker gatherings. The establishment of the FWCC could be viewed as a microcosmic Quaker anticipation of the Bretton Woods agreements among the Allies in 1943, mapping out the way for the United Nations and other institutions to coordinate but not compel a postwar world order.[49]

Clarence Pickett wrote in appreciation of Walter Woodward at the time of the latter's death in 1942: "Early in Walter Woodward's editorship of *The American Friend* came the World Conference of Friends in London in 1920.

From that time to the end of his editorial career he conceived of the Society of Friends in its world relationships. He had no illusions about the size, weight or power of this little religious body, but he did understand that its vitality and its contribution to the structure of society at any given point depended upon the recognition of the Society as a spiritual organism which had its constituency in most of the countries of the world."[50]

Framed by two world wars, the three all-Friends conferences under our consideration were indeed "epoch-making" in Quaker history. Neoevangelical Friends continued to stand apart from this new cosmopolitan Quaker identity. But as many families know, that too can be a way of belonging.

Afterword
Rufus Jones and Quaker History

DAVID HARRINGTON WATT

As Pink Dandelion points out in this book's introduction, Rufus Jones profoundly influenced the historiography of the Society of Friends. Jones played, for instance, a crucial role in planning, researching, writing, and editing what may well be the most influential account of Quaker history ever produced: the famous Rowntree History Series that appeared in the early decades of the twentieth century.

The final installment of that series—a mammoth two-volume book written by Jones himself, called *The Later Periods of Quakerism*—was published in 1921. The book, most of which focused on the years between 1725 and 1900, presented Jones's influential—and controversial—interpretations of eighteenth- and nineteenth-century Quaker history.

This afterword highlights some of the differences between the interpretations of Quaker history in *The Later Periods* and those found in this volume, *The Creation of Modern Quaker Diversity, 1830–1937*, in an effort to shed light on the ways in which the practice of writing Quaker history has changed over the past one hundred years. This essay is divided into three sections. The first presents a brief overview of Rufus Jones's life and thought. The second looks at *The Later Periods*. The third considers how the stories told in that volume compare to the ones told here.

Jones was born in the rural village of South China, Maine, on January 25, 1863. Many of his ancestors were members of the Society of Friends, and many came from what Jones called "good English stock." He grew up in a devout family of Orthodox Quakers who had been deeply influenced by evangelical Christianity. When he was ten years old, Jones suffered a life-threatening illness. On a day when he feared he was going to die, his beloved aunt, Peace Jones, assured him that God would let him live. "In her faith," Jones later recalled, "I found my own."[1]

He attended schools in Maine and Rhode Island and graduated from Haverford College in 1885. In 1897, after teaching at Oakwood Seminary, Providence Friends School, and Oak Grove Seminary, Jones joined the faculty of Haverford. He taught there until his retirement in 1934. During the 1900–1901 academic year, Jones took a leave from Haverford and attended courses at Harvard University. Harvard, like a good many other schools, eventually awarded Jones an honorary degree. Some of those degrees were listed in the frontmatter of the books that Jones published. People often addressed him as "Dr. Jones," though he never earned a PhD.[2]

Jones married Sarah Coutant in 1888. She died in 1899. Three years later, Jones married a member of a highly respected family of Philadelphia Quakers: Elizabeth Bartram Cadbury. She had studied at Friends Select School and Bryn Mawr College, and she had a better command of German than her husband did. Elizabeth, under her married name of Elizabeth Cadbury Jones, performed some of the research for the books that Rufus Jones published. In 1904, she gave birth to a girl, Mary Hoxie Jones, who grew up to become a fine writer and scholar. After her father's death, Mary Hoxie Jones worked diligently to assemble and organize his vast personal correspondence; his papers now take up nearly ninety linear feet in the archives of Haverford College's library.[3]

Rufus Jones was a prolific writer. During his lifetime, he published thousands of essays and more than fifty books. Some of Jones's writings include passages that now seem somewhat opaque or stilted, but such passages are rare: he was a gifted prose stylist, and many readers were fascinated by what he had to say. (The Jones papers at Haverford include a letter that an English Friend sent him in 1940 that begins, "Just about midnight, with German planes zooming overhead, by the light of my candle, I finished reading 'The Later Periods.'"[4])

Twelve of the thirteen chapters in this volume have something to say about Jones. (The one chapter that doesn't mention him, Julie Holcomb's "Quakers and Reform in Nineteenth-Century America," discusses three of his relatives: Sybil, Eli, and James Parnell Jones.) That is only natural. Few individuals affected the modern history of the Society of Friends as much as Jones did.

Jones's work for the American Friends Service Committee—an organization that he helped create—is highlighted in this volume in Robynne Rogers Healey's "The Peace Testimony and the Crisis of World War I" and in the chapter on "Quakers and the Social Order, 1830–1937" written by Nicola Sleapwood and Thomas Hamm. The role Jones played in creating two important Quaker centers for study, Pendle Hill and Woodbrooke, is discussed in Carole Spencer's "The Delineation of Quaker Spiritualities" and Joanna Dales's "Quakers of the Liberal Renaissance, 1870–1930." Stephen Angell's "Quakers and Missions, 1861–1937" notes that Jones was the only Quaker who was part of the famous Laymen's Foreign Missions Inquiry, an investigation that received generous support from John D. Rockefeller Jr. and that profoundly influenced the way many Protestant Christians thought about the things that missionaries ought—and ought not—to do. (In "Quakers and the Growth of the Pastoral System," Isaac May notes that Rockefeller was Jones's "friend and patron.")

As Dales points out, Jones hated "quarrels and divisions." And as Emma Jones Lapsansky explains in "The Loss of Peculiarity and the New Quaker Identity," Jones was deeply interested in building bridges between groups of Quakers who did not trust one another. But Jones himself was viewed with deep suspicion—and even antipathy—by some Friends. In "The All-Friends Conferences and Their Effects," Douglas Gwyn suggests that Jones sometimes functioned "as a lightning rod for evangelical animus." Lapsansky adds that controversies swirled around Jones. (And that is certainly true. A Friend who lived in California wrote Jones in September 1935 to tell him that he was a "weak-kneed" coward who had done "incalculable and irreplaceable harm . . . to the Society of Friends."[5])

Some of the controversies that surrounded Jones had to do with his ideas about mystics and mysticism. Those ideas are explored by Dales, Spencer, and Richard Evans. In "Quakers and 'Religious Madness'" Evans draws readers' attention to Jones's efforts to distinguish between those forms of mysticism that he associated with mental health and those he associated with madness. Spencer notes that Jones wrote about mysticism in a way that made it more "attractive to twentieth-century spiritual seekers." Dales suggests that Jones believed early Friends such as George Fox, who had been deeply influenced in his formative years by mystical Christians who lived in continental Europe, were mystics. Jones, she says, thought that Quakerism ought to be classified as a "mystical religion" and believed that Quaker mysticism and Quaker attempts to improve human society should be "inseparable."

Dales and Spencer both provide careful analyses of the books that Jones wrote about the history of the Society of Friends. And both of them suggest that Jones's historical writings should be read with a certain amount of caution. Dales's analysis of Jones's ideas about the relationship between mysticism and Quakerism recognizes that some writers (Hugh Rock, for instance) have concluded that Jones "never did establish that Quakerism is a mystical religion." Spencer likewise acknowledges that Jones's claims about the role that mysticism played in Quaker history have not been universally accepted. She says that Jones's "historical theory of Quaker mysticism was largely rejected by a new generation of Quaker scholars who claimed Early Friends were not mystics, at least not in the way Jones described."

Spencer goes on to say that although the Rowntree History Series that Jones and his colleagues produced is often regarded as "the standard history" of the Society of Friends, it also has been seen as a reinterpretation of the Quaker religion. Jones and the other Friends who created the series, Spencer notes, all looked at Quakerism from a distinctly liberal perspective. Spencer makes another important point about Jones's approach to Quaker history: "All the books that Jones produced, including his historical studies, had a *devotional* aspect," she observes. "They were meant to both inform and *inspire*." Jones's determination to write books about Quaker history that were both inspirational and informative helps to explain some of the controversies that surround them. Overall, the books seem a complicated mixture of straightforward history narratives, homiletical exhortations, and theological pronouncements.[6]

THE LATER PERIODS OF QUAKERISM

Jones's *The Later Periods* was published in 1921. In the book's preface, Jones told his readers that for the six years he was working on the book, his life "had been crowded with many practical tasks." (Given the work he was doing with the American Friends Service Committee during the First World War, this was, of course, a considerable understatement.) He went on to say that writing *The Later Periods* had nourished his soul. He had "often found solace and relief from the strain and agony of the world tragedy" when he read the texts that previous generations of Friends had produced. Contemplating "the patient, constructive spiritual labours of... holy men and women" had deepened his awareness of the power of the "silent spiritual forces" that shaped human history.[7]

As he was writing *The Later Periods*, Jones received a great deal of assistance. In all likelihood, one of the people who contributed the most to the project was a woman named Ada Smith. From 1903 to 1948, Smith—who was the daughter of enslaved persons—devoted her life to meeting the needs of Mary Hoxie, Elizabeth, and Rufus Jones. Smith lived with the Jones family in a house on Haverford's campus. The domestic work that she performed was the foundation on which their achievements rested. Given the attitudes of Jones's day, it is not at all surprising that he did not acknowledge Smith's work in the preface to *The Later Periods*. It would in fact have been shocking if he did. Jones did refer to Elizabeth's contribution to the book, but he did not mention her by name. (He simply said: "My wife has been a true fellow-labourer in the entire undertaking.") Jones did, on the other hand, tell his readers the names of three men who had assisted him as he was writing the book.[8]

At the conclusion of his labors, Jones had written a book of over a thousand pages about a group of Christians that many outsiders thought of as a tiny sect. Reviewers commented on the anomaly. One of them noted, for example, that Quakerism was "a small world" and implied that he had his doubts about the wisdom of writing such a long book about a group that had never attracted all that many adherents. Jones was not beset by such doubts. As he understood it, the history of the Society of Friends was, in large part, the story of Friends' halting but ultimately successful attempts to respond faithfully to the revelations that had continually been given to them. Over the centuries, God had, in a number of ways, sent messages to Quakers—and the Friends had heard those messages, and heard them more fully, Jones seems to have suspected, than had many other Christian groups. As Jones presented them, Quakers were, in fact, unique. They had much in common with other groups of Christians, but they were also quite special: Jones asserted that "no other large, organized, historically continuous body of Christians" had been as "fundamentally mystical, both in theory and practice, as the Society of Friends."[9]

Scholars who reviewed *The Later Periods* did find much to praise. Writing in the *American Historical Review*, W. W. Fenn expressed admiration for the care with which Jones explored Quakers' approach to mysticism and the skill with which he differentiated between various groups of Friends, such as the Gurneyites and the Wilburites. An English Quaker who reviewed the book said it demonstrated that Jones had a "full and accurate" grasp of the details of the history of the Society of Friends in Great Britain and a profound understanding of the way the rise of evangelical Christianity had affected the Society of Friends. W. H. Frere reported, in the pages of the *English Historical Review*, that he had spent a profitable and enjoyable week perusing Jones's book and had been struck by its "balanced" presentation of the recent history of Quakerism.[10]

Jones was very likely delighted to see his book referred to as "balanced." "Impartiality" was, he said, what he was aiming for as he narrated modern Quaker history. Referring to himself in the plural, Jones affirmed: "We have not been writing an apology or defending a favoured position. We have been presenting the historical unfolding of a religious movement as it moved and not as we wished it to have moved." Perhaps Jones really had tried to do that. But if he had, then he certainly failed to accomplish what he set out to do. *The Later Periods* displays a number of clear biases.[11]

Consider, for example, the way that Jones wrote about people whose ancestors did not come from Europe. He often emphasized what he saw as their weaknesses. He suggested that Native Americans were "a lowly people" who needed to be civilized. He described "aboriginal tribes" all over the world as "morally immature." He presented Black people who had previously been enslaved as "utterly helpless." Jones never used such condescending language when speaking about White Hicksites. However, something akin to an anti-Hicksite bias—or at least an assumption that the history of Hicksite Friends was less important than the history of Orthodox Friends—is evident throughout the final 546 pages of *The Later Periods*. Jones had surprisingly little to say about the history of the Hicksites after the Great Separation, and he was aware of, and apparently not bothered by, the lack of proportionality. The first footnote in the chapter on "American Quakerism in the Latest Period" simply reads: "This chapter deals only with the orthodox bodies."[12]

While that chapter does contain a wealth of information about Orthodox Friends, it includes a total of only about thirty footnotes. Indeed, relatively few chapters in *The Later Periods of Quakerism* contain extensive notes, and few of those notes refer to secondary works on the history of the Society of Friends. This is not surprising. When Jones was researching and writing his book, the secondary scholarly literature was quite meager. There is a real sense in which Quaker history as we understand it today was invented in the early twentieth century by Jones and a handful of other writers.[13]

As Jones told it, Quaker history was largely the story of impressive women (such as Elizabeth Fry, Sybil Jones, Hannah Whitall Smith, and Caroline Stephen) and influential men (such as Levi Coffin, Joseph John Gurney, John Wilhelm Rowntree, and John Wilbur). Jones did not try to hide how much he admired great Friends. He devoted an entire chapter of *The Later Periods* to singing the praises of John Bright and John Greenleaf Whittier. Jones did not pretend that Friends were infallible. Far from it: he devoted a good deal of his book to pointing out the errors of previous generations of Friends. But he did imply that Friends had a knack for recognizing and correcting the errors they made. *The Later Periods* was an extremely optimistic book.[14]

Jones's firm belief in progressive revelation and human progress influenced the way he presented Quaker history in *The Later Periods*. Indeed, a progress narrative structures much of the book. According to Jones, the Quietist era was one of the low points in the history of the Society of Friends. That period was followed by catastrophe: the Great Separation of the 1820s, which split Hicksite and Orthodox Quakers into two warring camps. And Jones flatly declared that the twenty years during which Gurneyites quarreled with Wilburites, from 1835 to 1855, were "the darkest and saddest in the history of Quakerism." He maintained, however, that in the years between 1855 and 1900, the health of Quakerism improved dramatically. Quakers began to realize that mysticism lay at the heart of their faith. They began to develop a fuller understanding of what it meant to stand for peace. And by 1900, Jones said, the Society of Friends was far more unified than it had been for many decades. The separations and divisions that had bedeviled previous generations were gradually being overcome. (Considering how many controversies Jones—who was often a polarizing figure—was involved in throughout his life, his insistence that Friends were becoming more unified was quite remarkable.)

Jones suggested, in the pages of *The Later Periods*, that the progress toward reuniting Quakerism was bound up with a wide variety of Friends achieving a fuller understanding about which elements of Quakerism were essential to the faith and which were not. As Jones presented it, the essence of Quakerism did not involve seeing the Bible as the final authority. Nor did it involve a commitment to a particular set of doctrines. At its heart, Quakerism was, Jones asserted, an "essentially mystical" religion. A principled opposition to war and violence was also, he suggested, a part of its essence, as were a deep passion for "relieving human suffering" and a keen interest in solving social problems.[15]

Jones's understanding of the fundamental nature of Quakerism shaped his presentation of evangelicalism. In *The Later Periods*, Jones did not suggest that evangelical Quakerism was completely wrongheaded. Indeed, he made a point of singling out some aspects of it for praise. But most of the things that Jones had to say about evangelical Quakerism were quite negative. When describing the spread of some practices associated with it, as Hamm notes, Jones spoke of "contagion." He called the Richmond Declaration of Faith—a text that was dear to the hearts of many evangelicals—"a poor, thin, mediocre expression" of Quakerism that should be regarded as "a relic" of outmoded ideas. Jones generally presented evangelical versions of the Quaker religion as expressions of excess that had to be tempered or as problems that needed to be solved. He cast evangelical forms of Quakerism as inferior to—and ultimately superseded by—the liberal form that he had helped develop. But perhaps that isn't putting the matter strongly enough. For there are some passages in *The Later Periods* in which Jones seems to suggest that "evangelical Quakerism" is a contradiction in terms. Whenever Friends tried to make Quakerism more evangelical, he said, they tended to create a religion that was radically at odds with "the mystical movement inaugurated by George Fox." When readers finished *The Later Periods*, some of them must have concluded that Jones's form of Quakerism—the one that we now call liberal Quakerism—was the *only* authentic form of modern Quakerism, the one on the right side of history. Evangelical Quakerism, they may have assumed, was destined to end up consigned to the ash heap of history.[16]

THE CREATION OF MODERN QUAKER DIVERSITY, 1830–1937

The Later Periods has had a profound influence on the way that scholars—including the ones who wrote the body of this book—understand the history of the Society of Friends. For that reason and others, there are a number of important similarities between *The Later Periods* and *Modern Quaker Diversity*. Although the time periods examined in the two books are somewhat different, many of the people and events that figure prominently in Jones's volume also receive close attention in this one. And the authors of this book analyze some of the topics that Jones treated in ways that are congruent with his analyses. For example, Healey's discussion of Quakers' attitudes toward peace, like Jones's, indicates that many modern Friends were more actively committed to promoting the cause of peace than were some of their predecessors. Like Jones, Hamm and May see nineteenth-century evangelical Quakerism as a remarkably innovative version of Quakerism—one that differed in several fundamental respects from earlier expressions of the faith.

In the present context, however, the similarities between the two books are less important than the differences. Those differences, which have to do with things such as point of view, use of secondary works, consideration of new questions, and understanding of the overall trajectory of Quaker history, will be the focus of the remainder of this essay. One of the most important differences between the two books is that *Modern Quaker Diversity*, unlike *The Later Periods*, is a multiauthored book. The points of view from which it narrates Quaker history are more various and complex than the point of view from which that history is told in *The Later Periods*. Without overstating the disparities among the various viewpoints presented in this volume—they are not vast—one can discern clear differences between (to give but two examples) the ways in which Holcomb and Evans talk about antebellum reform movements and between the ways that Spencer and Dales understand the nature of liberal Quakerism. The differing perspectives on Quaker history are a strength of the book, not a weakness. They remind us that there are many different stories that can be told about the history of the Society of Friends. To tell one version of Quaker history is, of course, to *not* tell others. One could make the case that, as a general rule, more stories are better than fewer when it comes to the telling of a history.[17]

And in recent decades, the range of stories that scholars have told about the Society of Friends has expanded exponentially. Unlike Jones, the authors of *Modern Quaker Diversity* were able to draw on a wide range of perceptive secondary works as they wrote their own narratives. The references to such works in this book dwarf in quantity those to be found in *The Later Periods*. Jones's book did not include a bibliography; a complete bibliography for *Modern Quaker Diversity* would include over five hundred citations. That is a stark illustration of how much the historiography of Quakerism has changed since the publication of *The Later Periods*. In the past century, scholars have given us convincing accounts of many developments in Quaker history that had received little scholarly attention when Jones wrote. Those scholars' labors have illuminated aspects of the Quaker past that were far murkier when Jones tried to summarize the modern history of the Society of Friends. Empirically speaking, scholars know more about Quaker history now than they did one hundred years ago.

The authors of this book do not put mysticism at the heart of the history of the Society of Friends. Nor do they try to show that Quakerism has a stable essence. These authors repeatedly emphasize the transformations that the Society of Friends underwent in the years between 1830 and 1937. Some of those transformations could be described, as Dandelion suggests, as revolutionary. And some of them occurred quite rapidly. Healey shows how quickly Friends' understanding of the peace testimony changed during the First World War. Dales demonstrates how swiftly British Friends moved away from evangelicalism and toward liberalism. Hamm, noting the dizzying speed with which Gurneyite Friends embraced revivalism in the 1860s and 1870s, goes so far as to suggest that "few religious groups have ever been transformed so dramatically in so short a period of time." When the authors of this book try to explain why Quakerism changed in the ways that it did, they don't suggest that the changes ought to be seen as the unfolding of God's plan. Instead, they consider a range of explanations that could be applied to a great many other cultural, social, and political movements.

As they narrate the history of the Society of Friends, the authors of this book highlight several issues that received scant attention in *The Later Periods*. They do so, moreover, in ways that reframe the general contours of modern Quaker history. One of those issues has to do with the way that Quakers figure in international debates about the relationship between reason and religion. According to Evans, "Until around the 1830s, European and American theorists of the mind—including medical practitioners, natural scientists, theologians, and philosophers—believed that Quakerism was an inherently dangerous religion that frequently drove Quakers insane." But within just a few decades, he argues, Friends had managed to convince non-Friends that Quakerism was an especially "safe" religion—one that did a better job than others of "protect[ing] its adherents from insanity." (Quakers' successful efforts to persuade outsiders that Friends were an unusually sane and exceptionally rational collection of human beings were part of a broader public relations campaign. The campaign aimed to persuade the world that Quakers were adherents of a perfectly respectable branch of Christianity—not members of an idiosyncratic religious sect. Jones's *The Later Periods* was—among many other things—a literary expression of that campaign. Jones wanted to demonstrate the respectability of the Society of Friends. Accordingly, he downplayed those aspects of Quaker history that modern liberal Protestants might find disreputable or embarrassing.)

In *The Later Periods*, Jones paid scant attention to the connections between the history of empire and the history of the Society of Friends. Those connections are highlighted by some of the authors of this book. In "Quakers and Empire," Johnson and Angell note that "Quakers put their stamp on the contours of Western empire." They go on to say that "from the heart of the British metropole and American Empire to the various peripheries of colonized regions, Quaker religion was both conditioned by the exigencies of colonial regimes and engaged in determining the direction and destiny of imperial power." Johnson and Angell argue that "slavery and racism" were not accidental features of Western imperialism but instead should be seen as "pillars" on which the imperial project was built. Friends lived their lives within the context of Western imperialism, whether or not they fully realized it, Johnson and Angell observe. The lives Quakers lived "were far messier than [the] ideals" they espoused.

A third issue highlighted in *Modern Quaker Diversity* is the relationship between Quakerism and the Global South. This is most evident in the chapter on missions, in which Angell notes that during the early decades of the period covered by this book, over 99 percent of the world's Quakers lived in "the North Atlantic region of North America [or] the British Isles." By the middle decades of the twentieth century, writes Angell, nearly "20 percent of the 140,000 Quakers in the world lived in the Global South." To put this a different way, in the middle decades of the twentieth century, the Society of Friends was well on its way to becoming what it is today: a denomination that has far fewer members in the United States and Europe than it has members in Africa, Central America, and South America. Unsurprisingly, members of the Society of Friends who live in Kenya (the nation in which most of world's Friends currently reside) practice their religion in ways that are, in many respects, quite different from the ways Quakers who live in the United Kingdom practice theirs.[18]

This brings us to what may well be the most important differences between *The Later Periods* and *Modern Quaker Diversity*: the treatment of unity and diversity. Jones's book concentrates on the historical processes that had, in his opinion, produced greater unity within the Society of Friends. Although those historical processes do receive attention in several chapters of *Modern Quaker Diversity* (including those written by Healey, Gwyn, and Stephanie Midori Komashin and Randall L. Taylor), obtaining greater unity is not a central theme of this book. Instead, it focuses on those historical processes that made the Society of Friends less homogeneous and more fractured.

Spencer's chapter, for example, describes a movement toward "two divergent forms of worship that created two distinct traditions of corporate spirituality." She argues that the increasing diversity within the Society of Friends should be regarded as a strength rather than a weakness, though she acknowledges that differing expressions of the faith sometimes sparked controversies that were both "painful" and "bitter." May draws attention to long-term effects of differences of opinion concerning the movement to accept paid pastors within the Society of Friends. He argues that many Orthodox Quakers in the United States avidly embraced the movement, while American Hicksite Quakers and British Quakers generally resisted it. That resulted in a split, May says, "between a large number of 'programmed' or pastoral Friends, who have paid ministers and whose worship resembles that of other Protestants, and a much smaller community of 'unprogrammed' Friends, who have largely eschewed paid ministry and who worship in silence except when individuals feel moved to speak." Unprogrammed Friends were generally attracted, May observes, to liberal theology; programmed Friends, on the other hand, generally embraced more evangelical beliefs.

May's observation is connected to another important difference between Jones's book and this one: the degree to which they suggest that the future of Quakerism lies with liberal versions of Quakerism. *The Later Periods* was based on the assumption that it did. *Modern Quaker Diversity* is not built on that assumption. It is clear now, in a way that it was not in 1921, that evangelical versions of Quakerism are flourishing. The authors of this book are fully cognizant of that fact. They do not suggest that evangelicalism's presence in the Society of Friends is waning. Nor do these authors portray liberalism as the form of Quakerism that is best suited to modern society. Between 1921 and 2021, the percentage of the world's Friends that are liberal has steadily declined. Liberals now make up a relatively small proportion—perhaps about one-tenth—of the world's Friends. The authors of this book, knowing that, realize that liberal Quakerism—the form Jones regarded as the most authentic—now appears to be facing a quite challenging future. That realization affects the way that they narrate the general contours of Quaker history.[19]

CONCLUSION

As the introduction to *Modern Quaker Diversity* observes, the New History of Quakerism series of which this book is a part is intended to give readers "an updated version of the Rowntree History Series"—a version that gives them "a fuller and more nuanced picture of the complexities of the Quaker past." But the differences between the way Quaker history is presented in *Modern Quaker Diversity* and the way it was presented in *The Later Periods* are quite substantial. They are so substantial, in fact, that some readers might conclude that it is not quite accurate to say this book is an "updated version" of *The Later Periods*. Those readers might prefer to say that this book ends up presenting a startlingly different interpretation of Quaker history than what is to be found in Jones's book.

The influence that *The Later Periods* has exercised on Friends' understanding of Quakerism has been immense. Together with a host of other works published by Quakers like Jones, *The Later Periods* helped convince a large portion of the world's Quakers that liberal Quakerism was a more authentic form of Quakerism than its rivals. Today, many liberal Quakers still assume, as Spencer notes, that Quakerism is a mystical religion. Many still talk about the relationship between human beings and God in ways that echo Jones. Many still give messages in meetings for worship in which they quote things that Jones said. Judged as a work of devotion, *The Later Periods* succeeded in a way that *Modern Quaker Diversity* will not. And the authors of this book will not, of course, have the last word on this period of Quaker history. At present, Quaker Studies is a remarkably vibrant field. If that vibrancy continues, the way that scholars write about Quaker history in 2044 will, by necessity, differ greatly from the way scholars are writing about it now. That is a good thing. Fluid historiographies are far more interesting than frozen ones.

NOTES

INTRODUCTION

1. Rosemary Moore, *The Light in Their Consciences: The Early Quakers in Britain, 1646–1666*, 2nd ed. (University Park: Penn State University Press, 2020); Richard C. Allen and Rosemary Moore, eds., *The Quakers, 1656–1723: The Evolution of an Alternative Community* (University Park: Penn State University Press, 2018); Robynne R. Healey, *Quakerism in the Atlantic World, 1690–1830* (University Park: Penn State University Press, 2021).

2. The series consisted of the following: Rufus Jones, *Studies in Mystical Religion* (London: Macmillan, 1909); Rufus Jones, Isaac Sharpless, and Amelia Gummere, *The Quakers in the American Colonies* (London: Macmillan, 1911); William C. Braithwaite, *The Beginnings of Quakerism* (London: Macmillan, 1912); Rufus Jones, *Spiritual Reformers in the Sixteenth and Seventeenth Centuries* (London: Macmillan, 1914); William C. Braithwaite, *The Second Period of Quakerism* (London: Macmillan, 1919); Rufus Jones, *The Later Periods of Quakerism* (London: Macmillan, 1921).

3. Pink Dandelion, *An Introduction to Quakerism* (Cambridge: Cambridge University Press, 2007), 85–92. "Yearly meeting" is the name given to an autonomous, geographically based body of Quakers. At their annual gatherings, an epistle, or message, to all other Quakers is drafted, and epistles from other yearly meetings are received. Disownment involved terminating the membership of an individual, although worship remained a public event.

4. Dandelion, *Introduction to Quakerism*, 106; Chuck Fager, *Remaking Friends: How Progressive Friends Changed Quakerism and Helped Save America, 1822–1940* (Durham, NC: Kimo Press, 2014).

5. Dandelion, *Introduction to Quakerism*, 99–102; Rosemary Mingins, *The Beacon Controversy and Challenges to British Quaker Tradition in the Early Nineteenth Century: Some Responses to the Evangelical Revival by Friends in Manchester and Kendal* (Lampeter, UK: Edwin Mellen Press, 2004).

6. Thomas D. Hamm, *The Transformation of American Quakerism: Orthodox Friends, 1800–1907* (Bloomington: Indiana University Press, 1988), 21, 60–61, 74. "Release" is a term used to denote payment while allowing the Quaker witness against being paid for ministry to remain intact. The ministry is free, but the minister is "released" (from the need to earn a living)

to focus on that ministry. See Dandelion, *Introduction to Quakerism*, 110–11; Hamm, *Transformation of American Quakerism*, 127.

7. Dandelion, *Introduction to Quakerism*, 104–10, 114–17; Hamm, *Transformation of American Quakerism*, 48–49. "First Day" is the traditional Quaker nomenclature for Sunday; Quakers have historically preferred to number days rather than use the pagan-derived names.

8. Timothy J. Burdick and Pink Dandelion, "Global Quakerism, 1920–2015," in *The Cambridge Companion to Quakerism*, ed. Stephen W. Angell and Pink Dandelion (Cambridge: Cambridge University Press, 2018), 49–65; Gregory P. Hinshaw, "Five Years Meeting and Friends United Meeting, 1887–2010," in *The Oxford Handbook of Quaker Studies*, ed. Stephen W. Angell and Pink Dandelion (Oxford: Oxford University Press, 2013), 97–99.

9. Dandelion, *Introduction to Quakerism*, 124; Timothy J. Burdick, "Neo-Evangelical Identity Within American Religious Society of Friends (Quakers): Oregon Yearly Meeting, 1919–1947" (PhD diss., University of Birmingham, 2013); Thomas D. Hamm, "Friends United Meeting and Its Identity: An Interpretative History," *Quaker Life* (January/February 2009): 4.

10. Thomas D. Hamm, "The Hicksite Quaker World, 1875–1900," *Quaker History* 89 (2000); Hamm, *Transformation of American Quakerism*, 150–66.

11. Thomas D. Hamm and Isaac B. May, "Conflict and Transformation, 1808–1920," in Angell and Dandelion, *Cambridge Companion to Quakerism*, 31–48; Thomas C. Kennedy, *British Quakerism, 1860–1920: The Transformation of a Religious Community* (Oxford: Oxford University Press, 2001); J. William Frost, "Modernist and Liberal Quakers, 1887–2010," in Angell and Dandelion, *Oxford Handbook of Quaker Studies*, 85–86; Stephen W. Angell, "The Dog That Did Not Bark: Yearly Meeting Reunifications in North America, the Case of Canada's Yearly Meetings," in *An Early Assessment: U.S. Quakerism in the 20th Century*, ed. Chuck Fager (Durham, NC: Kimo Press, 2017), 59–81.

12. Hamm and May, "Conflict and Transformation," 44.

13. Hans Eirik Aarek and Julia Ryberg, "Quakers in Europe and the Middle East," in Angell and Dandelion, *Cambridge Companion to Quakerism*, 218; Stephanie Midori Komashin, "Quakers in Asia-Pacific," in Angell and Dandelion, *Cambridge Companion to Quakerism*, 237–56; Hamm and May, "Conflict and Transformation," 44; Dandelion, *Introduction to Quakerism*, 155.

14. American and British Quakers were also involved in social service to unemployed miners in the 1920s. Pamela Manasseh, "Quaker Relief and the Brynmawr Experiment," *Woodbrooke Journal* 7 (2000): 1–28; Burdick, "Neo-Evangelical Identity"; Allan W. Austin, *Quaker Brotherhood: Interracial Activism and the American Friends Service Committee, 1917–1950* (Urbana: University of Illinois Press, 2012).

15. Wolf Mendl, *Prophets and Reconcilers: Reflections on the Quaker Peace Testimony* (London: Friends Home Service Committee, 1974); Pink Dandelion, *The Cultivation of Conformity: A General Theory of Internal Secularisation* (London: Routledge, 2019), 75–76.

16. Pink Dandelion, "Guarded Domesticity and Engagement with 'the World': The Separate Spheres of Quaker Quietism," *Common Knowledge* 16, no. 1 (2010): 95–109; Dandelion, *Cultivation of Conformity*, 68–71.

17. Dandelion, *Cultivation of Conformity*, 88.

18. Mike Nellis and Maureen Waugh, "Quakers and Penal Reform," in Angell and Dandelion, *Oxford Handbook of Quaker Studies*, 377–91; Charles L. Cherry, "Quakers and Asylum Reform," in Angell and Dandelion, *Oxford Handbook of Quaker Studies*, 392–404; Dandelion, *Cultivation of*

Conformity, 69. "Peculiarity" had a positive connotation and is a reference to 1 Titus 2:15 and how a peculiar people are to be purified unto God. See Dandelion, *Introduction to Quakerism*, 113; Hannah F. Rumball, "The Relinquishment of Plain Dress: British Quaker Women's Abandonment of Plain Quaker Attire, 1860–1914" (PhD diss., University of Brighton, 2016).

19. Dandelion, *Introduction to Quakerism*, 131; Hamm and May, "Conflict and Transformation," 45; Brian Phillips, "Friendly Patriotism: British Quakerism and the Imperial Nation, 1890–1910" (PhD diss., University of Cambridge, 1989); Brian Phillips, "Apocalypse Without Tears: Hubris and Folly Among Late Victorian and Edwardian British Friends," in *Towards Tragedy / Reclaiming Hope: Literature, Theology, and Sociology in Conversation*, ed. Pink Dandelion et al. (Aldershot, UK: Ashgate, 2004), 57–76. See Jennifer Graber's work for the earlier history of relations between Quakers and Native Americans: Jennifer Graber, *The Gods of Indian Country: Religion and the Struggle for the American West* (New York: Oxford University Press, 2018).

20. Elizabeth A. O'Donnell, "Quakers and Education," in Angell and Dandelion, *Oxford Handbook of Quaker Studies*, 405–19; Stephen W. Angell and Clare Brown, "Quakers and Education," in Angell and Dandelion, *Cambridge Companion to Quakerism*, 128–46; John W. Oliver Jr., Charles L. Cherry, and Caroline L. Cherry, eds., *Founded by Friends: The Quaker Heritage of Fifteen American Colleges and Universities* (Lanham, MD: Scarecrow Press, 2007).

21. Elaine Bishop and Jiseok Jung, "Seeking Peace: Quakers Respond to War," in Angell and Dandelion, *Cambridge Companion to Quakerism*, 106–27; Dandelion, *Introduction to Quakerism*, 112.

22. Roger Homan, "Quakers and Visual Culture," in Angell and Dandelion, *Oxford Handbook of Quaker Studies*, 492–506.

23. Dandelion, *Cultivation of Conformity*, 89; Robynne R. Healey, *From Quaker to Upper Canadian: Faith and Community Among Yonge Street Friends, 1801–1850* (Montreal: McGill-Queen's University Press, 2006), chap. 7; Thomas C. Kennedy, "Why Did Friends Resist? The War, the Peace Testimony and the All-Friends Conference of 1920," *Peace and Change* 14 (1989): 355–71.

24. Jones, *Later Periods of Quakerism*; Hamm, *Transformation of American Quakerism*, 172; Alice Southern, "The Rowntree History Series and the Growth of Liberal Quakerism," *Quaker Studies* 16 (2011): 7–73.

25. Mingins, *Beacon Controversy*; Elizabeth Isichei, *Victorian Quakers* (Oxford: Oxford University Press, 1970); Kennedy, *British Quakerism*; Phillips, "Friendly Patriotism"; Martin Davie, *British Quaker Theology Since 1895* (Lampeter, UK: Edwin Mellen Press, 1997); Anna V. Kett, "'Without the Consumers of Slave Products, There Would Be No Slaves': Quaker Women, Antislavery Activism, and Free-Labor Cotton Dress in the 1850s," in *Quakers and Abolition*, ed. Brycchan Carey and Geoffrey Plank (Urbana: University of Illinois Press, 2014), 56–72; Elizabeth A. O'Donnell, "Woman's Rights and Woman's Duties: Quaker Women in the Nineteenth Century, with Special Reference to Newcastle Monthly Meeting of Women Friends" (PhD diss., University of Sunderland, 1999); Sandra S. Holton, "Family Memory, Religion and Radicalism: The Priestman, Bright and Clark Kinship Circle of Women Friends and Quaker History," *Quaker Studies* 9, no. 2 (2014): 156–75; Mijin Cho, "British Quaker Women and Peace, 1880s to 1920s" (PhD diss., University of Birmingham, 2010); Pam Lunn, "'You Have Lost Your Opportunity': British Quakers and the Militant Phase of the Women's Suffrage Campaign, 1906–1914," *Quaker Studies* 2,

no. 1 (1997): 30–55; Julia Bush, "Caroline Stephen and the Opposition to British Women's Suffrage," *Quaker Studies* 15, no. 1 (2010): 32–52.

26. A. Glenn Crothers, *Quakers Living in the Lion's Mouth: The Society of Friends in Northern Virginia, 1730–1865* (Gainesville: University Press of Florida, 2012); Hugh Barbour et al., *Quaker Crosscurrents: Three Hundred Years of Friends in the New York Yearly Meeting* (Syracuse, NY: Syracuse University Press, 1995); John M. Moore, ed., *Friends in the Delaware Valley* (Haverford, PA: Friends Historical Association, 1981); Ralph K. Beebe, *A Garden of the Lord: A History of Oregon Yearly Meeting of Friends Church* (Newberg, OR: Barclay Press, 1968); George Selleck, *Quakers in Boston, 1646–1964: Three Centuries of Friends in Boston and Cambridge* (Cambridge, MA: Cambridge Friends Meeting, 1976); Hiram H. Hilty, *Toward Freedom for All: North Carolina Quakers and Slavery* (Richmond, IN: Friends United Press, 1984); David C. Le Shana, *Quakers in California: The Effects of 19th Century Revivalism on Western Quakerism* (Newberg, OR: Barclay Press, 1969); Arthur O. Roberts, *Tomorrow Is Growing Old: Stories of the Quakers in Alaska* (Newberg, OR: Barclay Press, 1978); Arthur G. Dorland, *The Quakers in Canada: A History* (Toronto: Ryerson Press, 1968 [1927]).

27. Clare R. Brown, "To Faithfully Do Our Part: The Contribution of Joseph Sturge to the Anti-Slavery Movement in Britain and America, with Special Reference to the Principles Which Motivated His Work" (PhD diss., University of Bristol, 2015); Helen V. Smith, "Elizabeth Taylor Cadbury (1858–1951): Religion, Maternalism, and Social Reform in Birmingham, 1888–1914" (PhD diss., University of Birmingham, 2012); Sian L. Phillips, "Place, Life Histories, and the Politics of Relief: Episodes in the Life of Francesca Wilson, Humanitarian, Educator, Activist" (PhD diss., University of Birmingham, 2010); Joanne C. Dales, "John William Graham (1859–1932): Quaker Apostle of Progress" (PhD diss., University of Birmingham, 2016); Alessandro Falcetta, *The Daily Discoveries of a Bible Scholar and Manuscript Hunter: A Biography of James Rendel Harris (1852–1941)* (London: T&T Clark, 2018); Carole D. Spencer, *Holiness, the Soul of Quakerism* (Milton Keynes, UK: Paternoster, 2007), 207–24.

28. Carol Faulkner, *Lucretia Mott's Heresy: Abolition and Women's Rights in Nineteenth-Century America* (Philadelphia: University of Pennsylvania Press, 2011); Christopher Densmore et al., eds., *Lucretia Mott Speaks: The Essential Speeches and Sermons* (Urbana: University of Illinois Press, 2017); Beverly Wilson Palmer, ed., *Selected Letters of Lucretia Coffin Mott* (Urbana: University of Illinois Press, 2002). The broader context of this women's rights witness is illuminated in Judith Wellman, *The Road to Seneca Falls: Elizabeth Cady Stanton and the First Woman's Rights Convention* (Urbana: University of Illinois Press, 2004); see also Carole D. Spencer, "Hannah Whitall Smith's Highway of Holiness," in *Quakers and Mysticism: Comparative and Syncretic Approaches to Spirituality*, ed. Jon Kershner (New York: Palgrave, 2019), 141–60.

29. Nancy A. Hewitt, *Radical Friend: Amy Kirby Post and Her Activist Worlds* (Chapel Hill: University of North Carolina Press, 2018).

30. Aarek and Ryberg, "Quakers in Europe and the Middle East," 218; Sheila Spielhofer, *Stemming the Dark Tide* (York, UK: William Sessions, 2001); Farah Mendlesohn, *Quaker Relief Work in the Spanish Civil War* (Lampeter, UK: Edwin Mellen Press, 2002).

31. Thomas D. Hamm, *The Quakers in America* (New York: Columbia University Press, 2003); Hamm, *Transformation of American Quakerism*; H. Larry Ingle,

Quakers in Conflict: The Hicksite Reformation (Knoxville: University of Tennessee Press, 1986); Robert W. Doherty, *The Hicksite Separation: A Sociological Analysis of Religious Schism in Early Nineteenth Century America* (New Brunswick, NJ: Rutgers University Press, 1967); Guy Aiken, "Social Christianity and the American Friends Service Committee's Pacifist Humanitarianism in Germany and Appalachia, 1919–1941" (PhD diss., University of Virginia, 2017); Arthur O. Roberts, "Evangelical Quakers, 1887–2010," in Angell and Dandelion, *Oxford Handbook of Quaker Studies*, 108–25; Frost, "Modernist and Liberal Quakers," 78–92; Douglas Gwyn, *A Gathering of Spirits: The Friends General Conferences, 1896–1950* (Philadelphia: Friends General Conference, 2018).

32. Christy Randazzo and David Russell, "The Unifying Light of Allah: Ibn Tufayl and Rufus Jones in Dialogue," in Kershner, *Quakers and Mysticism*, 161–80; Matthew S. Hedstrom, "Rufus Jones and Mysticism for the Masses," *Cross Currents* 54, no. 2 (2004): 31–44; Matthew S. Hedstrom, *The Rise of Liberal Religion: Book Culture and American Spirituality in the Twentieth Century* (New York: Oxford University Press, 2012); Stephen W. Angell, "Howard Thurman (1899–1981): Universalist Approaches to Buddhism and Quakerism," in Kershner, *Quakers and Mysticism*, 181–200.

33. Fager, *Remaking Friends*; Thomas D. Hamm, *God's Government Begun: The Society for Universal Inquiry and Reform, 1842–1846* (Bloomington: Indiana University Press, 1995).

34. Lloyd Lee Wilson, "Conservative Quakers, 1845–2010," in Angell and Dandelion, *Oxford Handbook of Quaker Studies*, 126–37; Wilmer Cooper, *Growing Up Plain Among Conservative Wilburite Quakers: The Journey of a Public Friend* (Richmond, IN: Friends United Press, 1999).

35. Healey, *From Quaker to Upper Canadian*; Albert Schrauwers, *Awaiting the Millennium: The Children of Peace and the Village of Hope, 1812–1889* (Toronto: University of Toronto Press, 1993).

36. Esther M. Mombo, "A Historical and Cultural Analysis of the Position of Abaluyia Women in Quaker Christianity: 1902–1979" (PhD diss., University of Edinburgh, 1998); Esther Mombo, "Haramisi and Jumaa: The Story of the Women's Meetings in East Africa Yearly Meeting 1902–1979," *Woodbrooke Journal* 5 (1999): 1–28; Ramon G. Longoria and Nancy Thomas, "Latin American Quakerism," in Angell and Dandelion, *Cambridge Companion to Quakerism*, 179–96; Nancy J. Thomas, *A Long Walk, a Gradual Ascent: The Story of the Bolivian Friends Church in Its Context of Conflict* (Eugene, OR: Wipf and Stock, 2019).

37. A major exception is Edward H. Milligan, *Biographical Dictionary of British Quakers in Commerce and Industry 1775–1920* (York, UK: William Sessions, 2007).

CHAPTER 1

1. Thomas Benjamin, *Encyclopedia of Western Colonialism Since 1450: A–E* (New York: Macmillan Reference USA, 2007); Richard H. Immerman, *Empire for Liberty: A History of American Imperialism from Benjamin Franklin to Paul Wolfowitz* (Princeton, NJ: Princeton University Press, 2010); Linda Gregerson and Susan Juster, *Empires of God: Religious Encounters in the Early Modern Atlantic* (Philadelphia: University of Pennsylvania Press, 2010); David Chidester, *Empire of Religion: Imperialism and Comparative Religion* (Chicago: University of Chicago Press, 2014); Sylvester A. Johnson, *African American Religions, 1500–2000: Colonialism, Democracy, and Freedom* (New York: Cambridge University Press, 2015); Gerald Horne, *The Dawning of the Apocalypse: The Roots of Slavery, White Supremacy, Settler*

Colonialism, and Capitalism in the Long Sixteenth Century (New York: Monthly Review Press / NYU Press, 2020); Daniel Immerwahr, *How to Hide an Empire: A Short History of the Greater United States* (London: The Bodley Head, an imprint of Vintage, 2019).

2. Michael Hechter, *Internal Colonialism: The Celtic Fringe in British National Development* (Berkeley: University of California Press, 1975); Michael Hardt and Antonio Negri, *Empire* (Cambridge, MA: Harvard University Press, 2000); Philip J. Stern, *The Company-State: Corporate Sovereignty and the Early Modern Foundation of the British Empire in India* (New York: Oxford University Press, 2011); Giovanni Arrighi, *The Long Twentieth Century: Money, Power, and the Origins of Our Times* (New York: Verso, 1994); Robert Blauner, "Internal Colonialism and Ghetto Revolt," *Social Problems* 16, no. 4 (1969): 393–408, https://doi.org/10.2307/799949.

3. Richard C. Allen and Rosemary Moore, *The Quakers, 1656–1723* (University Park: Penn State University Press, 2018), 35–38; Meredith Baldwin Wallace, *Walking in the Way of Peace* (Oxford: Oxford University Press, 2001), 143–233.

4. Richard S. Dunn and Mary Maples Dunn, eds., *The Papers of William Penn* (Philadelphia: University of Pennsylvania Press, 1982), 2:127–28; Lewis Hanke, "The 'Requerimiento' and Its Interpreters," *Revista de Historia de America*, March 1938, 25–34; Jack D. Marietta, *The Reformation of American Quakerism, 1748–1783* (Philadelphia: University of Pennsylvania Press, 2007).

5. Marietta, *Reformation of American Quakerism*; Jon R. Kershner, *John Woolman and the Government of Christ* (Oxford: Oxford University Press, 2018), 23–25; Hugh Barbour and J. William Frost, *The Quakers*, 2nd ed. (Richmond, IN: Friends United Press, 1994), 147–49.

6. Donna McDaniel and Vanessa Julye, *Fit for Freedom, Not for Friendship: Quakers, African Americans, and the Myth of Racial Justice* (Philadelphia: Quaker Press of Friends General Conference, 2009), 75–76, 195–97; Harold D. Weaver Jr., Paul Kriese, and Stephen W. Angell, eds., *Black Fire: African American Quakers on Spirituality and Human Rights* (Philadelphia: Quaker Press of Friends General Conference, 2011), 27–29.

7. Weaver et al., *Black Fire*, 15–19; Johnson, *African American Religions*, 177–87.

8. From 1820 to 1847, the ACS acted like a sovereign power in what would become Liberia, pursuing a mixture of paternalistic commercial, evangelistic, and ostensibly humanitarian (i.e., antislavery) goals. From the 1820s to the early 1840s, the White ACS board members had limited success in dictating governance through their White governor thousands of miles away in Liberia. See James Ciment, *Another America: The Story of Liberia and the Former Slaves Who Ruled It* (New York: Hill and Wang, 2013), 77–89.

9. Johnson, *African American Religions*, 187–208; Hiram H. Hilty, *Toward Freedom for All: North Carolina Quakers and Slavery* (Richmond, IN: Friends United Press, 1984), 50–60; Ciment, *Another America*, 27–35, 166–68; Rufus M. Jones, *Eli and Sybil Jones: Their Life and Work* (Philadelphia: Porter and Coates, 1889), 91–103; Emma J. Lapsansky-Werner and Margaret Hope Bacon, *Back to Africa: Benjamin Coates and the Colonization Movement in America, 1848–1880* (University Park: Penn State University Press, 2005), 58–59.

10. Judith Wellman, *The Road to Seneca Falls: Elizabeth Cady Stanton and the First Woman's Rights Convention* (Urbana: University of Illinois Press, 2004), 35–40; Beverly Wilson Palmer, ed., *Selected Letters of Lucretia Coffin Mott* (Urbana: University of Illinois Press, 2002), 165–67, 170.

11. Wellman, *Road to Seneca Falls*, 42; Anna Davis Hallowell, *James and Lucretia Mott: Life and Letters* (Boston: Houghton Mifflin, 1884), 86–87; Christopher Densmore, "The Dilemma of Quaker Anti-Slavery: The Case of Farmington Quarterly Meeting, 1836–1860," *Quaker History* 82 (Fall 1993): 83–84.

12. Wellman, *Road to Seneca Falls*, 74–75.

13. Nicola Sleapwood, "The Birmingham Quaker Community, 1800–1900," in *Quakers, Business, and Industry*, ed. Stephen W. Angell and Pink Dandelion (Longmeadow, MA: Full Media Services and Friends Association for Higher Education, 2017), 216; Priya Satia, *Empire of Guns: The Violent Making of the Industrial Revolution* (New York: Penguin, 2018), 183–90, 316–20; W. Ross Yates, *Joseph Wharton: Quaker Industrial Pioneer* (Bethlehem, PA: Lehigh University Press, 1987), 110.

14. Clayton Sumner Ellsworth, "The American Churches and the Mexican War," *American Historical Review* 45 (January 1940): 317; Peter Brock, *The Quaker Peace Testimony, 1783–1861* (Princeton, NJ: Princeton University Press, 1968), 252; Peter Brock, *Pacifism in Europe to 1914* (Princeton, NJ: Princeton University Press, 1972), 357–58; Barbour and Frost, *The Quakers*, 197–200.

15. President Grant referenced this history in his December 1869 message to the US Congress: "The Society of Friends is well known as having succeeded in living in peace with the Indians in the early settlement of Pennsylvania, while their white neighbors of other sects in other sections were constantly embroiled. They are also known for their opposition to all strife, violence, and war, and are generally known for their strict integrity and fair dealings. These considerations induced me to give the management of a few reservations of Indians to them and to throw the burden of the selection of agents upon the society itself. The result has proven most satisfactory." Quoted in Joseph E. Illick, "'Some of Our Best Indians Are Friends': Quaker Attitudes and Actions Regarding the Western Indians During the Grant Administration," *Western Historical Quarterly* 2 (July 1971): 283–94, quotation on 284.

16. Jennifer Graber, *The Gods of Indian Country: Religion and the Struggle for the American West* (New York: Oxford University Press, 2018), 54, 77–81, 86–97, 103–4; Lee Cutler, "Lawrie Tatum and the Kiowa Agency, 1869–1873," *Arizona and the West* 13 (Autumn 1971): 227–44; Samuel Janney, *Memoirs of Samuel M. Janney, Late of Lincoln, Loudoun County, Virginia* (Philadelphia: Friends' Book Association, 1881), 250–87.

17. Graber, *Gods of Indian Country*, 142; Carlos Figueroa, "Quakerism and Racialism in Early Twentieth-Century U.S. Politics," in *Faith and Race in American Political Life*, ed. Robin Dale Jacobson and Nancy D. Wadsworth (Charlottesville: University of Virginia Press, 2012), 56–79; Anon., "In Honor of Albert K. Smiley," *Advocate of Peace* 75 (January 1913): 9.

18. Thomas C. Kennedy, *British Quakerism, 1860–1920: The Transformation of a Religious Community* (Oxford: Oxford University Press, 2001), 247, 252, 268–69. See also chapter 10 in this volume: Stephen W. Angell, "Quakers and Missions, 1861–1937."

19. Philip S. Benjamin, *The Philadelphia Quakers in the Industrial Age, 1865–1920* (Philadelphia: Temple University Press, 1976), 194; Figueroa, "Quakerism and Racialism," 62.

20. Kennedy, *British Quakerism*, 259–60.

21. Deborah Cadbury, *Chocolate Wars: The 150-Year Rivalry Between the World's Greatest Chocolate Makers* (New York: Public Affairs, 2010), 173–203.

22. Mark Freeman, "Quakers, Business, and Philanthropy," in *The Oxford Handbook of Quaker Studies*, ed. Stephen W.

Angell and Pink Dandelion (Oxford: Oxford University Press, 2013), 425; Cadbury, *Chocolate Wars*, 132–34; Paul Chrystal, "The Rowntrees: Tales from a Chocolate Family," in Angell and Dandelion, *Quakers, Business, and Industry*, 180–83.

23. Robert Kanigel, *The One Best Way: Frederick Winslow Taylor and the Enigma of Efficiency* (New York: Viking, 1997), 525–26.

24. William C. Kashatus, *Conflict of Conviction: A Reappraisal of Quaker Involvement in the American Revolution* (Lanham, MD: University Press of America, 1990), 123–25; Jennifer Connerley, "Fighting Quakers: A Jet Black Whiteness," *Pennsylvania History* 73 (Autumn 2006): 373–411.

25. Smedley D. Butler, "America's Armed Forces," *Common Sense* 4 (November 1935): 8–12; Hans Schmidt, *Maverick Marine: General Smedley D. Butler and the Contradictions of American Military History* (Lexington: University Press of Kentucky, 1987), 6, 112, 215–46. The relevant portion of Butler's article in *Common Sense* is quoted on page 231 of Schmidt, *Maverick Marine*.

26. Robert K. Murray, "The Outer World and the Inner Light: A Case Study," *Pennsylvania History* 36 (July 1969): 265–89; Julie M. Powell, "Making 'the Case Against the Reds': Racializing Communism, 1919–1920," in *Historicizing Fear: Ignorance, Vilification, and Othering*, ed. Travis D. Boyce and Winsome M. Chunnu (Boulder: University Press of Colorado, 2019), 108.

27. Stephen W. Angell, "Colonizer William Penn and Engineer Herbert Hoover: How Their Businesses Affected Their Philanthropy and Statesmanship," in Angell and Dandelion, *Quakers, Business, and Industry*, 199–201.

28. Ibid., 201–4; Charles Rappleye, *Herbert Hoover in the White House: The Ordeal of the Presidency* (New York: Simon and Schuster, 2016), 12.

29. Hugh Barbour et al., *Quaker Crosscurrents: Three Hundred Years of Friends in New York Yearly Meeting* (Syracuse, NY: Syracuse University Press and New York Yearly Meeting, 1995), 248–49, 299–300; David Levering Lewis, *W. E. B. Du Bois: The Fight for American Equality and the American Century, 1919–1963* (New York: Henry Holt, 2000), 270–72; Eugene Kinckle Jones, "L. Hollingsworth Wood," *Phylon* 6 (1945): 17–21; Christina Szi, "Throughout the Years: Race at Haverford College" (2015), accessed August 30, 2018, http://wrpr christinaszi.weebly.com/early-years.html; Howard Thurman, *With Head and Heart: The Autobiography of Howard Thurman* (San Diego, CA: Harcourt Brace Jovanovich, 1979), 74–77; Stephen W. Angell, "Howard Thurman and Quakers," *Quaker Theology* 16, no. 9 (2009): 31–38; John D'Emilio, *Lost Prophet: The Life and Times of Bayard Rustin* (New York: Free Press, 2003), 7–14; Dwight W. Hoover, "Daisy Douglass Barr: From Quaker to Klan Kluckeress," *Indiana Magazine of History* 87 (June 1991): 171–95.

30. Rappleye, *Herbert Hoover in the White House*, 25, 131–45; Robert E. Weems Jr. and Lewis A. Randolph, "'The Right Man': James A. Jackson and the Origins of U.S. Government Interest in Black Business," *Enterprise and Society* 6 (June 2005): 257, 264; Henry Lewis Suggs, "The Response of the African American Press to the United States Occupation of Haiti," *Journal of Negro History* 73 (1988): 33–45; Lee Nash, ed., *Herbert Hoover and World Peace* (Lanham, MD: University Press of America, 2010).

CHAPTER 2

1. *Centennial Anniversary of the Pennsylvania Society for Promoting the*

Abolition of Slavery, the Relief of Negroes Unlawfully Held in Bondage, and for Improving the Condition of the African Race (Philadelphia: Grant, Faires & Rodgers Printers, 1876), 6, 13. Unable to attend, Garrison and Whittier each sent a letter that was read at the event.

2. J. William Frost, "Why Quakers and Slavery? Why Not More Quakers?," in *Quakers and Abolition*, ed. Brycchan Carey and Geoffrey Plank (Urbana: University of Illinois Press, 2014), 29–42; Thomas D. Hamm, "George F. White and Hicksite Opposition to the Abolitionist Movement," in Carey and Plank, *Quakers and Abolition*, 43–55; Thomas D. Hamm, *The Transformation of American Quakerism: Orthodox Friends, 1800–1907* (Bloomington: Indiana University Press, 1988); Carol Faulkner, *Lucretia Mott's Heresy: Abolition and Women's Rights in Nineteenth-Century America* (Philadelphia: University of Pennsylvania Press, 2011); Nancy A. Hewitt, *Radical Friend: Amy Kirby Post and Her Activist Worlds* (Chapel Hill: University of North Carolina Press, 2018); Julie L. Holcomb, *Moral Commerce: Quakers and the Transatlantic Boycott of the Slave Labor Economy* (Ithaca, NY: Cornell University Press, 2016); Ryan P. Jordan, *Slavery and the Meetinghouse: The Quakers and the Abolitionist Dilemma, 1820–1865* (Bloomington: Indiana University Press, 2007); Donna McDaniel and Vanessa Julye, *Fit for Freedom, Not for Friendship: Quakers, African Americans, and the Myth of Racial Justice* (Philadelphia: Quaker Press of Friends General Conference, 2009).

3. In addition to the works cited earlier, see also Judith Wellman, *The Road to Seneca Falls: Elizabeth Cady Stanton and the First Woman's Rights Convention* (Urbana: University of Illinois Press, 2004); William C. Kashatus, *Abraham Lincoln, the Quakers, and the Civil War* (Santa Barbara, CA: Praeger, 2014).

4. James Brewer Stewart, *Holy Warriors: The Abolitionists and American Slavery* (New York: Hill and Wang, 1976), 35–74; Faulkner, *Lucretia Mott's Heresy*, 62–63; Manisha Sinha, *The Slave's Cause: A History of Abolition* (New Haven, CT: Yale University Press, 2016), 214–21; Thomas E. Drake, *Quakers and Slavery in America* (New Haven, CT: Yale University Press, 1950), 131–32. For Heyrick and Chandler, see Holcomb, *Moral Commerce*, 89–122.

5. J. William Frost, "Years of Crisis and Separation: Philadelphia Yearly Meeting, 1790–1860," in *Friends in the Delaware Valley: Philadelphia Yearly Meeting, 1681–1981*, ed. John M. Moore (Haverford, PA: Friends Historical Association, 1981), 95; Jordan, *Slavery and the Meetinghouse*, 26–27; Faulkner, *Lucretia Mott's Heresy*, 64–66; Sinha, *Slave's Cause*, 225–27.

6. Leonard L. Richards, *Gentlemen of Property and Standing: Anti-Abolition Mobs in Jacksonian America* (New York: Oxford University Press, 1970); Beth Salerno, *Sister Societies: Women's Antislavery Organizations in Antebellum America* (DeKalb: Northern Illinois University Press, 2005), 49–78, 85–92.

7. *Register of Debates*, 24th Congress, 1st Session, 100; Drake, *Quakers and Slavery in America*, 146; Jordan, *Slavery and the Meetinghouse*, 30.

8. *Speech of Mr. Wall, of New Jersey, on the Memorial of the Caln Quarterly Meeting of the Society of Friends, of Lancaster County, Pennsylvania, Praying for the Abolition of Slavery and the Slave Trade in the District of Columbia, in Senate, February 29, 1836* (Washington, DC: Blair & Rives, 1836), 3–4 (emphasis in original). See also *Congressional Globe*, 24th Congress, 1st Session, 95–99, 100; *Liberator*, January 30, 1836; *Christian Reporter and Boston Observer*, January 30, 1836; Jordan, *Slavery and the Meetinghouse*, 30; Drake, *Quakers and Slavery*, 146–47; *The Friend*, May 16, 1835, and November 5, 1836. For the Senate "gag

rule,'" see Daniel Wirls, "'The Only Mode of Avoiding Everlasting Debate': The Overlooked Senate Gag Rule for Antislavery Petitions," *Journal of the Early Republic* 27 (Spring 2007): 115–38.

9. *An Address from the Farmington Quarterly Meeting of Friends, to Its Members on Slavery* (Rochester, NY: Hoyt & Parker, 1836), 5, 7; *Address to the Citizens of the United States of America on the Subject of Slavery* (New York: New York Yearly Meeting of Friends, 1837); *Address of the Yearly Meeting of the Religious Society of Friends . . . to the Professors of Christianity in the United States on the Subject of Slavery* (New York: James Egbert, 1852); Christopher Densmore, "The Dilemma of Quaker Anti-Slavery: The Case of Farmington Quarterly Meeting, 1836–1860," *Quaker History* 82 (Fall 1993): 82–84; *Address of Farmington Quarterly Meeting (New York) to the Monthly Meetings Constituting It, and to the Members of the Same Generally* (Mount Pleasant, OH: Managers of the Free Produce Association of Friends of Ohio Yearly Meeting, 1850).

10. Frost, "Why Quakers and Slavery," 37–38. See also Alicia J. Rivera, "Fear of Miscegenation in the Antebellum Riots of New York 1834, Boston 1835, and Philadelphia 1838" (PhD diss., University of California, Santa Barbara, 2014).

11. Minutes, September 20, 1839, Meeting for Sufferings, Philadelphia Yearly Meeting (Orthodox), Friends Historical Library, Swarthmore College; Frost, "Years of Crisis and Separation," 95; *A Brief Statement on the Rise and Progress of the Testimony of the Religious Society of Friends, Against Slavery and the Slave Trade* (Philadelphia: Joseph and William Kite, 1843); Samuel Rhoads, *Considerations on the Use of the Productions of Slavery, Addressed to the Religious Society of Friends*, 2nd ed. (Philadelphia: Merrihew and Thompson, 1845).

12. Jordan, *Slavery and the Meetinghouse*, 32–33; Christopher Clark, *The Communitarian Moment: The Radical Challenge of the Northampton Association* (Ithaca, NY: Cornell University Press, 1995), 195. Bassett as quoted in Jordan.

13. Holcomb, *Moral Commerce*, 137–38.

14. *The Friend*, May 23, 1835; Minutes, Philadelphia Yearly Meeting (Hicksite), April 14, 1837, 24, Friends Historical Library, Swarthmore College; Jordan, *Slavery and the Meetinghouse*, 37; Densmore, "Dilemma of Quaker Anti-Slavery," 82–84.

15. *Minutes of the Proceedings of the Requited Labor Convention held in Philadelphia, on the 17th and 18th of the Fifth month, and by adjournment on the 5th and 6th of Ninth month, 1838* (Philadelphia: Merrihew and Gunn, 1838), 9–14. For Gunn's address, see Lewis C. Gunn, *Address to the Abolitionists* (Philadelphia: Merrihew and Gunn, 1838).

16. Holcomb, *Moral Commerce*, 170–74; Rhoads, *Considerations on the Use of the Productions of Slavery*, 27 (emphasis in original).

17. Holcomb, *Moral Commerce*, 127–31; Minutes of the Philadelphia Female Anti-Slavery Society Papers, August 10, 1837, Historical Society of Pennsylvania, Philadelphia; Buckingham Female Anti-Slavery Society to Mary Grew, August 4, 1837, PFASS Incoming Correspondence, PFASS, Historical Society of Pennsylvania, Philadelphia; *Genius of Universal Emancipation*, October 1837; *Pennsylvania Freeman*, August 30, 1838.

18. Holcomb, *Moral Commerce*, 131; David Walker, *David Walker's Appeal to the Coloured Citizens of the World*, ed. Peter P. Hinks (University Park: Penn State University Press, 2000), 67.

19. Sinha, *Slave's Cause*, 383–88; Eric Foner, *Gateway to Freedom: The Hidden History of the Underground Railroad* (New York: W. W. Norton, 2015), 19–22; Joseph A. Barome, "The Vigilant Committee of Philadelphia," *Pennsylvania Magazine of*

History and Biography 92 (January 1968): 320–51; Nat Brandt and Yanna Kroyt Brandt, *In the Shadow of the Civil War: Passmore Williamson and the Rescue of Jane Johnson* (Columbia: University of South Carolina Press, 2007).

20. McDaniel and Julye, *Fit for Freedom*, 96–106; Levi Coffin, *Reminiscences of Levi Coffin, the Reputed President of the Underground Railroad* (Cincinnati: Robert Clarke, 1880), 112; Sinha, *Slave's Cause*, 400–401, 438.

21. Keith E. Melder, *Beginnings of Sisterhood: The American Woman's Rights Movement, 1800–1850* (New York: Schocken, 1977), 77–112; Kathryn Kish Sklar, *Women's Rights Emerges Within the Antislavery Movement, 1830–1870: A Brief History with Documents* (Boston: Bedford / St. Martin's, 2000), 36–37; Salerno, *Sister Societies*, 49–118; Faulkner, *Lucretia Mott's Heresy*, 69. See also Gerda Lerner, *The Grimké Sisters from South Carolina: Pioneers for Women's Rights and Abolition* (New York: Schocken, 1967).

22. Salerno, *Sister Societies*, 79–118; Faulkner, *Lucretia Mott's Heresy*, 87–108.

23. Wellman, *Road to Seneca Falls*, 135–54; Nancy Isenberg, *Sex and Citizenship in Antebellum America* (Chapel Hill: University of North Carolina Press, 1998), 172–74.

24. Wellman, *Road to Seneca Falls*, 165, 172; Margaret Hope Bacon, *Valiant Friend: The Life of Lucretia Mott* (New York: Walker, 1980), 126. Stanton as quoted in Bacon, 126.

25. Bacon, *Valiant Friend*, 126–30; Wellman, *Road to Seneca Falls*, 189–208; Faulkner, *Lucretia Mott's Heresy*, 139–40; Hewitt, *Radical Friend*, 127–28.

26. Hamm, *Transformation of American Quakerism*, 20–35.

27. Ibid., 20–35. Edgerton as quoted ibid., 31.

28. Ibid., 20–35; Charles Osborn, *Journal of That Faithful Servant of Christ: Charles Osborn* (Cincinnati: Achilles Pugh, 1854), 344.

29. Densmore, "Dilemma of Quaker Anti-Slavery," 86–87; Christopher Densmore, "'Be Ye Therefore Perfect': Anti-Slavery and the Origins of the Yearly Meeting of Progressive Friends in Chester County, Pennsylvania," *Quaker History* 93 (Fall 2000): 28–46; *The Non-Slaveholder*, May 1, 1850, 103; Minutes of New England Yearly Meeting, 1836–1847, June 1837, as quoted in Drake, *Quakers and Slavery*, 147.

30. *National Anti-Slavery Standard*, February 6, 1845.

31. Densmore, "Be Ye Therefore Perfect," 34–35; Margaret S. Young, *The Memories and History of Ercildoun, 1976* (n.p., 1976), 16.

32. Hamm, "George F. White," 43.

33. Ibid.; *Correspondence between Oliver Johnson and George F. White, a Minister of the Society of Friends* (New York: Oliver Johnson, 1841); *Narrative of the Proceedings of the Monthly Meeting of New York, and Their Subsequent Confirmation by the Quarterly and Yearly Meetings, in the Case of Isaac T. Hopper* (New York, 1843); *National Anti-Slavery Standard*, March 25, 1841; Hamm, "George F. White"; Faulkner, *Lucretia Mott's Heresy*, 83–85, 120–21; Jordan, *Slavery and the Meetinghouse*, 99.

34. Densmore, "Be Ye Therefore Perfect," 35–43; Densmore, "Dilemma of Quaker Anti-Slavery," 86–87. Mott as quoted in Wellman, *Road to Seneca Falls*, 181.

35. Holcomb, *Moral Commerce*, 165.

36. Ibid.

37. Coffin, *Reminiscences*, 223–34; Walter Edgerton, *A History of the Separation in Indiana Yearly Meeting of Friends; Which Took Place in the Winter of 1842 and 1843, on the Anti-Slavery Question* (Cincinnati: Achilles Pugh, 1856); Drake, *Quakers and Slavery in America*, 164–65; Ruth Ketring Nuermberger, *The Free Produce Movement: A Quaker Protest Against Slavery* (Durham, NC: Duke University Press, 1942), 48–49; Jordan, *Slavery and the Meetinghouse*,

46–58; Stacey Robertson, *Hearts Beating for Liberty: Women Abolitionists in the Old Northwest* (Chapel Hill: University of North Carolina Press, 2010), 81–82; Thomas D. Hamm et al., "Moral Choices: Two Quaker Communities and the Abolitionist Movement," *Indiana Magazine of History* 87 (June 1991): 117–54.

38. Nuermberger, *Free Produce Movement*, 33–34; Jordan, *Slavery and the Meetinghouse*, 61.

39. Kashatus, *Abraham Lincoln*, 24.

40. Ibid., 25–26; Peter H. Curtis, "A Quaker and the Civil War: The Life of James Parnell Jones," *Quaker History* 67 (Spring 1978): 35–41; Jacquelyn S. Nelson, "Civil War Letters of Daniel Wooton: The Metamorphosis of a Quaker Soldier," *Indiana Magazine of History* 85 (March 1989): 50–57. Jones as quoted in Curtis. Wooton as quoted in Nelson.

41. Coffin, *Reminiscences*, 658–59, 666–67; Kashatus, *Abraham Lincoln*, 104–5; McDaniel and Julye, *Fit for Freedom*, 141–67.

42. Kashatus, *Abraham Lincoln*, 105–7.

43. Amy Murrell Taylor, *Embattled Freedom: Journeys Through the Civil War's Refugee Camps* (Chapel Hill: University of North Carolina Press, 2018), 164–67.

44. Kashatus, *Abraham Lincoln*, 54–96; Max L. Carter, "Elizabeth Kirkbride Gurney's Correspondence with Abraham Lincoln: The Quaker Dilemma," *Pennsylvania Magazine of History and Biography* 133 (October 2009): 389–96; Thomas C. Kennedy, *A History of Southland College: The Society of Friends and Black Education in Arkansas* (Fayetteville: University of Arkansas Press, 2009).

CHAPTER 3

1. Edward Balleisen, *Navigating Failure: Bankruptcy and Commercial Society in Antebellum America* (Chapel Hill: University of North Carolina Press, 2001); Paul A. Gilje, "The Rise of Capitalism in the Early Republic," *Journal of the Early Republic* 16, no. 2 (1996); Jessica M. Lepler, *The Many Panics of 1837: People, Politics, and the Creation of a Transatlantic Financial Crisis* (Cambridge: Cambridge University Press, 2013).

2. Bliss Forbush, *Elias Hicks, Quaker Liberal* (New York: Columbia University Press, 1956), 193.

3. David W. Maxey, "New Light on Hannah Barnard, a Quaker 'Heretic,'" *Quaker History* 78, no. 2 (1989): 61–86. Though Friends have traditionally avoided establishing a central authority or hierarchy that designated "leaders," it was not uncommon for an individual monthly meeting to recognize the dedication and wisdom of a given member by identifying and honoring them as a "recorded minister."

4. Robert Doherty, "Religion and Society: The Hicksite Separation of 1827," *American Quarterly* 17, no. 1 (1965): 63–80; Robert Doherty, "Non-Urban Friends and the Hicksite Separation," *Pennsylvania History* 33, no. 4 (1966); Norris Hansell, *Josiah White, Quaker Entrepreneur* (Easton, PA: Canal History and Technology Press, 1992); Thomas D. Hamm, *The Transformation of American Quakerism* (Bloomington: University of Indiana Press, 1988), chap. 2; Forbush, *Elias Hicks*, 281; Mitchell Santine Gould, "Friends of the New York Seaport: Antebellum Quaker Commerce, Culture, and Concerns," *Quaker History* 108, no. 1 (2019): 34. Historian Theodore Paullin has aptly described Josiah White: "He took part in philanthropic activities, and used religious terminology in his journal; but he was first of all a man of enterprise rather than of religion. There was little in his business dealings which would distinguish them from those of hundreds of other visionary businessmen of his day." See Paullin, "Josiah White, Prince of Pioneers," *Bulletin of Friends Historical Association* 36, no. 1 (1947): 39–40. For a discussion of Quaker involvement in the railroads of Hicks's era, see Robert J. Kapsch, *Over the*

Alleghenies: Early Canals and Railroads of Pennsylvania (Morgantown: West Virginia University Press, 2013).

5. The mid-nineteenth-century ascendancy of American Unitarianism and its sociophilosophical underpinnings is illuminated in Philip F. Gura, *American Transcendentalism: A History* (New York: Hill and Wang, 2007). See also Forbush, *Elias Hicks*, 280–81; Hamm, *Transformation of American Quakerism*, 18, 28–30.

6. Chuck Fager, *Remaking Friends: How Progressive Friends Changed Quakerism and Helped Save America* (Durham, NC: Kimo Press, 2014); Hamm, *Transformation of American Quakerism*; Elizabeth Heyrick, *Immediate, Not Gradual Abolition; or an Inquiry into the Shortest, Safest, and Most Effectual Means of Getting Rid of West Indian Slavery* (London: R. Clay, 1823); Elias Hicks, *Observations on the Slavery of Africans and Their Descendants* (New York: Samuel Wood, 1811); Julie L. Holcomb, *Moral Commerce: Quakers and the Transatlantic Boycott of the Slave Labor Economy* (Ithaca, NY: Cornell University Press, 2016), 151; Forbush, *Elias Hicks*, 241–52; Ruth Ketring Nuermberger, *The Free Produce Movement: A Quaker Protest Against Slavery* (Durham, NC: Duke University Press, 1942), 9; *The Genius of Universal Emancipation*, September 2, 1829, x, 4; Merton Lynn Dillon, *Benjamin Lundy and the Struggle for Negro Freedom* (Urbana: University of Illinois Press, 1966); Richard J. M. Blackett, *Building an Antislavery Wall: Black Americans in the Atlantic Abolitionist Movement, 1830–1860* (Ithaca, NY: Cornell University Press, 1983), 119; Fager, *Remaking Friends*, 124; Chuck Fager, *Angels of Progress: A Documentary History of the Progressive Friends, 1822–1940* (Durham, NC: Kimo Press, 2014).

7. This and the next paragraph are based on Julie Holcomb's discussion of Quakers' concerns about global capitalism in Holcomb, *Moral Commerce*, 13–89;

Carolyn J. Weekley, "Edward Hicks: Quaker Artist and Minister," in *Quaker Aesthetics: Reflections on a Quaker Ethic in American Design and Consumption, 1720–1920*, ed. Emma Jones Lapsansky and Anne A. Verplanck (Philadelphia: University of Pennsylvania Press, 2003), 212–34.

8. See, for example, Nancy Jiwon Cho, "Literature," in *The Cambridge Companion to Quakerism*, ed. Stephen Angell and Pink Dandelion (Cambridge: Cambridge University Press, 2018), 77–82; Lapsansky and Verplanck, *Quaker Aesthetics*; Wolfgang Keller, Ben Li, and Carol H. Shiue, "China's Foreign Trade: Perspectives from the Past 150 Years" (CEPR Discussion Paper no. DP8118, November 2010); Elizabeth A. Clark, *Founding the Fathers: Early Church History and Protestant Professors in Nineteenth-Century America* (Philadelphia: University of Pennsylvania Press, 2011). See also Jeffrey Munger, "East and West: Chinese Export Porcelain," Metropolitan Museum of Art website, October 2003, https://www.metmuseum.org/toah/hd/ewpor/hd_ewpor.htm; Sara J. Oshinsky, "Exoticism in the Decorative Arts," Metropolitan Museum of Art website, October 2004, https://www.metmuseum.org/toah/hd/exot/hd_exot.htm.

9. Forbush, *Elias Hicks*, 290–92; William Penn, *No Cross, No Crown: A Discourse Shewing the Nature and Discipline of the Holy Cross of Christ, and that the Denyal of Self, And Daily Bearing of Christ's Cross is the Alone Way to the Rest and Kingdom of God. To Which Are Added the Living and Dying Testimonies of Divers Persons of Fame and Learning, in Favour of This Treatise* (London: Andrew Sowle, 1682), 82.

10. Thomas D. Hamm and Isaac Barnes May, "Conflict and Transformation, 1808–1920," in Angell and Dandelion, *Cambridge Companion to Quakerism*, 31–48.

11. For further discussion of Gurney and the arts, see Cho, "Literature," 80.

12. Hansell, *Josiah White, Quaker Entrepreneur*; Hamm, *Transformation of American Quakerism*, 114–35. Also see, for example, Dickson D. Bruce, *And They All Sang Hallelujah: Plain-Folk Camp-Meeting Religion, 1800–1845* (Knoxville: University of Tennessee Press, 1974); Frank Hickenlooper, *An Illustrated History of Monroe County, Iowa: A Complete Civil, Political, and Military History of the County, From Its Earliest Period of Organization Down to 1896* (Albia, IA, 1896), accessed August 1, 2020, 237–79, http://iagenweb.org/monroe/history/chapt15_hickenlooper_1896.html; Hamm, *Transformation of American Quakerism*, 20–50, 117.

13. Though Brown was disowned by his Quaker meeting for marrying a Presbyterian woman, his novels were republished and widely read during the 1820s and 1830s. See Richard P. Moses, "The Quakerism of Charles Brockden Brown," *Quaker History* 75, no. 1 (1986): 22–23; Edward Wagenknecht, *John Greenleaf Whittier: A Portrait in Paradox* (New York: Oxford University Press, 1967); Ann Farrant, *Amelia Opie, The Quaker Celebrity* (Hindringham, UK: JJG Publishing, 2014).

14. Sarah Stickney Ellis, *Friends at Their Own Fireside* (London: Richard Bentley, 1858), 3 (emphasis added); Ashley Lynn Carlson, "Influence, Agency and the Women of England: Victorian Ideology and the Works of Sarah Stickney Ellis" (PhD diss., University of New Mexico, 2011), 4–5.

15. Cho, "Literature," 80; Michael Stuart Freeman, "Innocent Scandals: The Secret Library of the Everett Society," lecture manuscript, 1993, Special Collections, Haverford College. In Freeman's intriguing short essay, he recounts the adventures of mid-nineteenth-century Haverford students who would sneak into the woods at night to indulge in the scandalous activity of reading fiction.

16. J. William Frost, "From Plainness to Simplicity: Changing Quaker Ideals for Material Culture," in Lapsansky and Verplanck, *Quaker Aesthetics*, 17–30; Mary Anne Caton, "The Aesthetics of Absence: Quaker Women's Plain Dress in the Delaware Valley, 1790–1800," in Lapsansky and Verplanck, *Quaker Aesthetics*, 266–69.

17. Thomas D. Hamm, *God's Government Begun: The Society for Universal Inquiry and Reform, 1842–1846* (Bloomington: University of Indiana Press, 1995), 236. Contextualized biographies of the Nicholson and Wattles families are interwoven throughout Hamm, *God's Government Begun*; Rufus M. Jones, *Eli and Sybil Jones: Their Life and Work* (Philadelphia: Porter and Coates, 1889); John W. Oliver Jr., *Stone Man Preacher: J. Walter Malone* (Canton, OH: Oliver House, 2016), 119–29.

18. Roger C. Wilson, "The Work of the Friends War Victims Relief Committee," *Social Work* [1939–70] 2, no. 3 (January 1942): 114–22; Paul Huddie, "The Society of Friends in Ireland and the Crimean War, 1854–1856," *Quaker History* 102, no. 2 (2013): 1–9; Stephen W. Angell and John Connell, "Quakers in North America," in Angell and Dandelion, *Cambridge Companion to Quakerism*, 164–68; Hamm and May, "Conflict and Transformation," 42.

19. Fager, *Remaking Friends*; Fager, *Angels of Progress*. Chuck Fager has presented provocative analysis of the Richmond Conference, available at Quaker.org, accessed January 13, 2020, http://quaker.org/legacy/against-richmond.html. See also Hamm and May, "Conflict and Transformation," 40–44; Karen I. Halbersleben, "Elizabeth Pease: One Woman's Vision of Peace, Justice, and Human Rights in Nineteenth-Century Britain," *Quaker History* 84, no. 1 (1995): 26–36; Nancy F. Cott, *The Grounding of Modern Feminism* (New Haven, CT: Yale University Press, 1987); Claus Bernet and Douglas Gwyn, *Life and Bibliography of an American Scholar* (New York: Oxford University Press, 2009); Gregory Allen

Barnes, *A Centennial History of the American Friends Service Committee* (Philadelphia: Friends Press, 2016).

20. Ane Marie Bak Rasmussen, *A History of the Quaker Movement in Africa* (New York: I. B. Tauris, 1995); John F. Howes, ed., *Nitobe Inazo: Japan's Bridge Across the Pacific* (Boulder, CO: Westview Press, 1995); Emma Condori Mamani, *Quakers in Bolivia: The Early History of Bolivian Friends* (La Paz, Bolivia: Publicaciones CALA, 2017); Horace Alexander, *Quakerism and India*, Pendle Hill Pamphlet 31 (Wallingford, PA: Pendle Hill, 1945); Friends Foreign Mission Association, *Eighteenth Annual Report* (London, 1885), accessed August 11, 2020, http://findit.library.yale.edu/bookreader/BookReaderDemo/index.html?oid=11352673; Sally Rickerman, "The Breadth, Depth and Stretch of Quakerism in North America," map (Philadelphia, 1993); Sally Rickerman, "Geographic Areas, North America, of Its 20 Unprogrammed Yearly Meetings," map, Swarthmore Friends Historical Library (Landenberg, PA: Troll Press, 2010).

21. Robert Barclay, *An Apology for the True Christian Divinity, Being an Explanation and Vindication of the Principles and Doctrines of the People Called Quakers*, 8th ed. (Birmingham, UK: John Baskerville, 1765), Proposition XI, VIII, 309.

22. Margaret Fraser, *A Short History of Friends World Committee for Consultation* (Philadelphia: Friends World Committee for Consultation, 2007), available at Swarthmore Friends Historical Library; Herbert M. Hadley, *Quakers Worldwide: A History of Friends World Committee for Consultation* (London: Friends World Committee for Consultation, in association with William Sessions, 1991).

CHAPTER 4

1. "Address by Dr. Dougan Clark" (n.p., 1858).

2. "Dr. Dougan Clark on Temperance," *Christian Worker*, 7th Mo. 24, 1879, 354; Thomas D. Hamm, *Earlham College: A History, 1847–1997* (Bloomington: Indiana University Press, 1997), 36–41.

3. *In the Court of Appeal. Appeal from the Chancery Division of the High Court of Justice, Between John T. Dorland and Others Plaintiffs (Appellants) and Gilbert Jones and Others, Defendants (Respondents)* (Belleville: Ontario Steam Printing, 1884), 426; Joseph John Gurney, *Observations on the Distinguishing Views and Practices of the Society of Friends* (London: John and Arthur Arch, 1834), 65; Thomas D. Hamm, *The Transformation of American Quakerism: Orthodox Friends, 1800–1907* (Bloomington: Indiana University Press, 1988), 2–7, 20–28.

4. Hamm, *Transformation of American Quakerism*, 28.

5. Ibid., 28–31; John Wilbur, *A Narrative and Exposition of the Late Proceedings of New England Yearly Meeting, with Some of Its Subordinate Meetings & Their Committees, in Relation to the Doctrinal Controversy Now Existing in the Society of Friends: Prefaced by a Concise View of the Church, Showing the Occasion of Its Apostacy, Both under the Former and Present Dispensations* (New York: Piercy & Reed, 1845), 14–15, 30.

6. Hamm, *Transformation of American Quakerism*, 42–48.

7. Ibid., 51–58; Z., "The Question Stated," *Herald of Peace*, 8th Mo. 15, 1869, 21; L. Tatum, "Marriage," *American Friend* 1 (2nd Mo. 1867): 38–39.

8. Hamm, *Transformation of American Quakerism*, 59–60; "Cant Words and Scripture Quotations," *Herald of Peace*, 5th Mo. 1, 1869, 78; "Tones and Gestures in Preaching," *Friends' Review*, 6th Mo. 7, 1856, 616–17; Francis W. Thomas, *An Address to the Society of Friends* (Richmond, IN: Central Book and Tract Committee, 1863), 10–11; J. M., "The Heart and Lip," *American Friend* 1 (12th Mo.

1867): 301; Clarkson Butterworth Diary, May 4, 1861 (Friends Collection, Earlham College Archives).

9. Hamm, *Transformation of American Quakerism*, 47–48, 60; Hamm, *Earlham College*, 32–33; Z., "Preparation," *American Friend* 2 (2nd Mo. 1868): 38–39; "Cant Words," 78; "To the Editors," *The Friend*, 12th Mo. 3, 1870, 117 (emphasis in original). "Hireling minister" was a pejorative term that Friends used for anyone who took pay for preaching.

10. Hamm, *Transformation of American Quakerism*, 50–51; William Tallack, *Friendly Sketches in America* (London: A. W. Bennett, 1861), 15–16.

11. Josiah Forster to M. C. Cope, 11th Mo. 6, 1860, Box 1, Marmaduke C. Cope Papers (Quaker Collection, Haverford College, Haverford, PA); Robert Howard to John Hodgkin, 3rd Mo. 27, 1861, Hodgkin Family Papers (Library of the Religious Society of Friends, London, UK).

12. Rufus M. Jones, *The Later Periods of Quakerism* (London: Macmillan, 1921), 2:897; "Indiana Yearly Meeting," *Friends' Review*, 10th Mo. 20, 1860, 104–5; Mary Coffin Johnson, ed., *Rhoda M. Coffin: Her Reminiscences, Addresses, Papers, and Ancestry* (New York: Grafton, 1910), 80–81; Mary C. Johnson, ed., *The Life of Elijah Coffin, with a Reminiscence by His Son Charles F. Coffin* ([Cincinnati]: E. Morgan & Sons, 1863), 217; Mary Coffin Johnson and Percival Brooks Coffin, comps., *Charles F. Coffin: A Quaker Pioneer* (Richmond, IN: Nicholson, 1923), 116; E[lijah]. C[offin]., "Foreign Correspondence," *The Friend* (London), n.s., 1 (1st Mo. 1, 1861): 20–21.

13. Hamm, *Transformation of American Quakerism*, 60; "Indiana," *Herald of Peace*, 4th Mo. 15, 1868, 86; Johnson, *Rhoda M. Coffin*, 81–84. For the records of such a group, see Minutes of Mill Creek Social Circle, 1865 (Indiana Division, Indiana State Library, Indianapolis).

14. W[illiam] B[ell], "Late Meeting at Richmond, Indiana," *British Friend* 19 (5th Mo. 1 and 10th Mo. 1, 1861): 115–16 and 250–52; W[illiam] B[ell], "A Voice from the West. no. V," *British Friend* 20 (2nd Mo. 1, 1862): 45; W[illiam] B[ell], "A Voice from the West—No. IX," *British Friend* 21 (12th Mo. 1, 1863): 303–4; Editorial, *British Friend*, 5th Mo. 31, 1862, 311; Editorial, *British Friend*, 1st Mo. 2, 1864, 143. "W. B." is identified as William Bell in "William Bell of Richmond, Indiana," *British Friend* 20 (5th Mo. 1, 1862): 116.

15. Hamm, *Transformation of American Quakerism*, 69.

16. Ibid., 69–70; J. H. Douglas, "Thoughts and Suggestions about the Freed-People," *Friends' Review*, 3rd Mo. 3, 1866, 425–26 (emphasis in original); Thomas C. Kennedy, *A History of Southland College: The Society of Friends and Black Education in Arkansas* (Fayetteville: University of Arkansas Press, 2009).

17. Hamm, *Transformation of American Quakerism*, 58; Jacalynn Stuckey Welling, "Mission," in *The Oxford Handbook of Quaker Studies*, ed. Stephen W. Angell and Pink Dandelion (Oxford: Oxford University Press, 2013), 311–16.

18. Johnson, *Rhoda M. Coffin*, 81.

19. E. B. Mendenhall, "When and Where the Revival Flame Was First Kindled," *Christian Worker*, 12th Mo. 15, 1887, 591; Howard H. Brinton, ed., "The Revival Movement in Iowa: A Letter from Joel Bean to Rufus M. Jones," *Bulletin of Friends Historical Association* 50 (Fall 1961): 106; W. Y. Brown to Newton D. Woody (ca. February–March 1866), Box 4, Woody Family Papers (Manuscripts Department, Duke University Library, Durham, NC); "Correspondence," *Herald of Peace*, 8th Mo. 15, 1868, 23.

20. Hamm, *Transformation of American Quakerism*, 75; Darius B. Cook, *History of Quaker Divide* (Dexter, IA: Dexter Sentinel, 1914), 67–68.

21. The sympathetic account is by D[aniel] Clark, "From Walnut Ridge," *American Friend* 1 (12th Mo. 1867): 302–4. The more sensational is from "The Little Band," *Rushville Republican*, November 18, 1880, 2. For the farm family, see Gurney Binford, *As I Remember It: 43 Years in Japan* (n.p., 1950), 6–8. For second thoughts, see J[ohn] B[ell], "Letter from Indiana, U.S.," *British Friend* 27 (6th Mo. 1, 1869): 218. I am indebted to Gregory P. Hinshaw for the "Little Band" reference.

22. Jones, *Later Periods*, 900; Hamm, *Transformation of American Quakerism*, 76; Joel Bean letter, *Friends' Review*, 7th Mo. 9, 1870, 731.

23. Hamm, *Transformation of American Quakerism*, 71–72. In 1892, these quarterly meetings became Wilmington Yearly Meeting.

24. Ibid., 76–77; "A Practical Ministry the Need of the Society of Friends," *Herald of Peace*, 7th Mo. 1, 1869, 144. For examples of early general meetings, see "General Meeting of Friends in Chicago," *Herald of Peace*, 1st Mo. 31, 1868, 6–7; Henry Charles, "General Meeting of Friends," *Herald of Peace*, 9th Mo. 1, 1868, 38–39; and "General Meeting in Kansas," *Herald of Peace*, 7th Mo. 15, 1869, 155–56.

25. Timothy L. Smith, *Revivalism and Social Reform: American Protestantism on the Eve of the Civil War* (New York: Harper and Row, 1965), 103–47; Melvin Easterday Dieter, *The Holiness Revival of the Nineteenth Century* (Metuchen, NJ: Scarecrow, 1980), 96–156.

26. Hamm, *Transformation of American Quakerism*, 78–84. For a somewhat different account of the Holiness revival among Friends, see Carole Dale Spencer, *Holiness: The Soul of Quakerism* (Milton Keynes, UK: Paternoster, 2007), 161–93.

27. Hamm, *Transformation of American Quakerism*, 78; Dougan Clark and Joseph H. Smith, *David B. Updegraff and His Work* (Cincinnati: M. W. Knapp, 1895), 28–29.

28. "Field Notes," *Friends' Expositor* 2 (October 1888): 208; *Friends' Expositor* 6 (October 1892): 718.

29. Hamm, *Transformation of American Quakerism*, 74, 77–85; Editorial, *Christian Standard*, reprinted in Editorial, *Western Friend* 2 (4th Mo. 1881): 32; David B. Updegraff, *Open Letters for Interested Readers* (Philadelphia: n.p., 1880), 22; John Henry Douglas, "What Hath God Wrought?," *Friends Minister*, June 12, 1919, 2–3; *Richmond Telegram*, April 4, 1873, quoted in Editorial, *Friend*, 4th Mo. 19, 1873, 272.

30. Hamm, *Transformation of American Quakerism*, 87–88; H[annah] W[hitall] S[mith], "Diversities of Gifts and the Unity of the Spirit," *Christian Worker*, 6th Mo. 10, 1880, 283; Spencer, *Holiness*, 183–92.

31. See, for example, the letter from Updegraff and Thomas W. Ladd in *Friends' Review*, 12th Mo. 1, 1877, 250.

32. *In the Court of Appeal*, 48, 60, 94, 251.

33. Hamm, *Transformation of American Quakerism*, 90–91.

34. Ibid., 90; Cyrus W. Harvey to Herman Newman, 11th Mo. 2, 1906, Herman Newman Collection (Friends Collection, Earlham College Archives).

35. Hamm, *Transformation of American Quakerism*, 124–25.

36. Thomas D. Hamm, *The Quakers in America* (New York: Columbia University Press, 2003), 53–54.

37. Elbert Russell, "Present Tendencies in the Society of Friends," *The Quaker*, 5th Mo. 13, 1921, 22; Seth Beeson Hinshaw, "The Evolution of Quaker Meeting Houses in North America, 1670–2000" (MA thesis, University of Pennsylvania, 2001), 90–98.

38. Hamm, *Transformation of American Quakerism*, 79–80; "True Womanhood," *Herald of Peace*, 6th Mo. 15, 1868, 146; Isaac May, "Opening the Shutters: Gurneyite Quakerism and the Struggle for Women's Equality in the Meeting for Business, 1859

to 1930," *Quaker Studies* 18, no. 2 (2013): 170–90; Emma F. Coffin, "Women as Preachers and Pastors," *American Friend*, 7th Mo. 29, 1920, 679–83. For examples of the interest of non-Friends in women ministers, see the clippings from 1879 to 1885 in the Mary Moon Meredith scrapbook in the Nellie Moon Taylor Papers (Quaker Archives, Guilford College, Greensboro, NC).

39. Hamm, *Transformation of American Quakerism*, 92–95, 99–102; "An Action of a Conference of Friends," *The Friend*, 6th Mo. 30, 1877, 365; Editorial, *The Friend*, 12th Mo. 19, 1885, 159; A., letter, *The Friend*, 9th Mo. 30, 1876, 54; *In the Court of Appeal*, 459.

40. Hamm, *Transformation of American Quakerism*, 90–91; *Autobiography of Allen Jay: Born 1831, Died 1910* (Philadelphia: John C. Winston, 1910), 205–14; Allen Jay to Martha Jay, 1st Mo. 28, 1875, G–L Box, Allen Jay Papers (Friends Collection, Earlham College Archives).

41. Hamm, *Transformation of American Quakerism*, 94–97, 111–16.

42. Thomas D. Hamm, "Joel Bean and the Revival in Iowa," *Quaker History* 76 (Spring 1987): 33–49; J[oel] B[ean], "The Issue," *British Friend* 39 (3rd Mo. 1, 1881), 49–51.

43. "Some Observations on the Decline of the Society of Friends in Connexion with the Recent Prize Essays," *The Friend* (London), o.s., 18 (4th Mo. 1, 1860): 70; "Robert Barclay's Lectures," *British Friend* 26 (7th Mo. 1, 1868): 172; "London Yearly Meeting," *British Friend* 28 (6th Mo. 2, 1870), 142–43.

44. Thomas C. Kennedy, *British Quakerism, 1860–1920: The Transformation of a Religious Community* (Oxford: Oxford University Press, 2001), 120–22; Thomas D. Hamm, "'Chipping at the Landmarks of Our Fathers': The Decline of the Testimony Against Hireling Ministry in the Nineteenth Century," *Quaker Studies* 13 (March 2009): 149–51; "General Meetings," *The Friend* (London), n.s., 16 (12th Mo. 1, 1876): 320.

45. "A Letter to a Friend on the Past and Present Condition of the Society of Friends," *British Friend* 23 (4th Mo. 1, 1865): 93. I discuss this question at greater length in Hamm, "Chipping at the Landmarks of Our Fathers," 151–55.

46. Hamm, *Transformation of American Quakerism*, 144–72.

47. For a good overview of these developments in one yearly meeting, see Timothy John Burdick, "Neo-Evangelical Identity Within American Religious Society of Friends (Quakers): Oregon Yearly Meeting, 1919–1947" (PhD diss., University of Birmingham, 2013).

CHAPTER 5

1. Thomas D. Hamm, *The Quakers in America* (New York: Columbia University Press, 2003), 65–85. The "programmed" versus "unprogrammed" distinction refers to the planning of the content of the worship service in advance. In addition to these binaries, there are also a few "semi-programmed meetings," which combine fixed liturgies with periods of silent worship.

2. The one notable exception would be Conservative Friends, who are classified as unprogrammed but whose practices show a strong continuity with earlier Quaker practices toward ministry.

3. George Fox, *Journal of George Fox*, ed. John L. Nickalls (London: Religious Society of Friends, 1975), 7.

4. Robert Barclay, *Apology for the True Christian Divinity* (Farmington, ME: Quaker Heritage Press, 2002 [1678]), 15–16.

5. Douglas Gwyn, *Apocalypse of the Word: The Life and Message of George Fox* (Richmond, IN: Friends United Meeting, 1986), 149–50; George Fox, *The Woman Learning in Silence: Or, The Mysterie of the Womans Subjection to Her Husband* (London: Thomas Simonds, 1656), https://

quod.lib.umich.edu/e/eebo2/A84840.0001.001/1:2?rgn=div1;view=fulltext; Margaret Fell, "Women's Ministry Justified," in *Quaker Writings: An Anthology*, ed. Thomas D. Hamm (New York: Penguin, 2010), 95–105; Rebecca Larson, *Daughters of Light: Quaker Women Preaching and Prophesying in the Colonies and Abroad, 1700–1775* (Chapel Hill: University of North Carolina Press, 2000); Barbara K. Wittman, "Mary Borden Rodman's Register of Publick Friends, 1656–1804," *Quaker History* 104, no. 1 (2015): 20–49, https://doi.org/10.1353/qkh.2015.0003; Catherine A. Brekus, *Strangers & Pilgrims: Female Preaching in America, 1740–1845* (Chapel Hill: University of North Carolina Press, 1998), 29–30.

6. John Punshon, *Portrait in Grey*, rev. ed. (London: Quaker Home Service, 1984), 91, 141.

7. Thomas D. Hamm, "'Chipping at the Landmarks of Our Fathers': The Decline of the Testimony Against Hireling Ministry in the Nineteenth Century," *Quaker Studies* 13 (March 2009): 136–59.

8. John Joseph Gurney, *Observations on the Distinguishing Views and Practices of the Society of Friends* (New York: Mahlon Day, 1840), 167.

9. Thomas D. Hamm, *The Transformation of American Quakerism: Orthodox Friends, 1800–1907* (Bloomington: Indiana University Press, 1988), 125.

10. R. G. Robins, *A. J. Tomlinson: Plainfolk Modernist* (New York: Oxford University Press, 2004), 98; Hamm, *Transformation of American Quakerism*, 124–25.

11. Robins, *A. J. Tomlinson*, 94–95.

12. Hamm, *Transformation of American Quakerism*, 125; Luke Woodward, quoted in Hamm, *Transformation of American Quakerism*, 125.

13. Dougan Clark Jr. and Joseph H. Smith, *David B. Updegraff and His Work* (Cincinnati, OH: M. W. Knapp, 1895), 60.

14. J. H. Douglas, quoted in Darius B. Cook, *History of Quaker Divide* (Dexter, IA: Dexter Sentinel, 1914), 112.

15. E. Brooks Holifield, *God's Ambassadors: A History of the Christian Clergy in America* (Grand Rapids, MI: Wm. B. Eerdmans, 2007), 150; Thomas D. Hamm, "The Divergent Paths of Iowa Quakers in the Nineteenth Century," *Annals of Iowa* 61, no. 2 (2002): 145.

16. Isaac May, "Opening the Shutters: Gurneyite Quakerism and the Struggle for Women's Equality in the Meeting for Business, 1859 to 1930," *Quaker Studies* 18, no. 2 (2013): 184–85.

17. T. Vail Palmer, *A Long Road: How Quakers Made Sense of God and the Bible* (Newberg, OR: Barclay Press, 2017), 110–11, 105.

18. D. Elton Trueblood, "The Paradox of the Quaker Ministry," *Quaker Religious Thought* 8, no. 1 (1962): 8 (emphasis in original). This article was originally the 1960 Quaker lecture delivered at Indiana Yearly Meeting.

19. Thomas D. Hamm, *Earlham College: A History, 1847–1997* (Bloomington: Indiana University Press, 1997), 65–66.

20. Palmer, *Long Road*, 216, 191.

21. John D. Rockefeller Jr. to Rufus M. Jones, August 14, 1939, Rufus M. Jones Papers, Haverford College, Box 40; John D. Rockefeller Jr. to Rufus M. Jones, August 13, 1943, Rufus M. Jones Papers, Haverford College, Box 43.

22. Ane Marie Bak Rasmussen, *A History of the Quaker Movement in Africa* (New York: I. B. Tauris, 1995), 45–45, 69.

23. Jacalynn Stuckey Welling, "Mission," in *The Oxford Handbook of Quaker Studies*, ed. Stephen W. Angell and Pink Dandelion (Oxford: Oxford University Press, 2013), 316–17; Isaac Barnes May, "The Blessed Channel of Work: Gender, Power and the Union of the Women's Foreign Missionary Societies in the Religious Society of Friends," *Quaker History* 107, no. 1 (2018): 27–53.

24. Hamm, "Chipping at the Landmarks of Our Fathers," 140.

25. *Lucretia Mott, 1793–1880* (Philadelphia: Friends' Intelligencer, 1880), 7–8; Carol Faulkner, *Lucretia Mott's Heresy: Abolition and Women's Rights in Nineteenth-Century America* (Philadelphia: University of Pennsylvania Press, 2011), 124.

26. Allen C. Thomas, "Congregational or Progressive Friends: A Forgotten Episode in Quaker History," *Bulletin of Friends' Historical Society of Philadelphia* 10, no. 1 (1920): 21–32; Chuck Fager, *Remaking Friends: How Progressive Friends Challenged Quakerism and Helped Save America* (Durham, NC: Kimo Press, 2014), 149, 175.

27. Thomas D. Hamm's forthcoming book on nineteenth-century Hicksite Quakerism covers this crisis.

28. Fager, *Remaking Friends*, 156–57; Douglas Gwyn, *A Gathering of Spirits: The Friends General Conferences, 1896–1950* (Philadelphia: Friends General Conference, 2018), 70–71; Emily Cooper Johnson, *Under Quaker Appointment: The Life of Jane P. Rushmore* (Philadelphia: University of Pennsylvania Press, 1953), 107–9.

29. Thomas Kelly, *A History of Adult Education in Great Britain* (Liverpool: Liverpool University Press, 1992), 204; Stephen W. Angell and Clare Brown, "Quakers and Education," in *The Cambridge Companion to Quakerism*, ed. Stephen W. Angell and Pink Dandelion (Cambridge: Cambridge University Press, 2018), 140; Stuckey Welling, "Mission," 310; Elizabeth Isichei, *Victorian Quakers* (Oxford: Oxford University Press, 1970), 261–74.

30. Isichei, *Victorian Quakers*, 276.

31. "Dublin and London Yearly Meetings," *Friends' Intelligencer United with The Friends' Journal* 43, no. 28 (1886): 445–47; J. B. Hodgkin, "Worship and Ministry," *Friends' Intelligencer* 56, no. 34 (1899): 657–58. Letter originally issued by London Yearly Meeting.

32. Thomas C. Kennedy, *British Quakerism, 1860–1920: The Transformation of a Religious Community* (Oxford: Oxford University Press, 2001), 171–77.

33. Kennedy, *British Quakerism*, 177–96; Hamm, *Earlham College: A History*, 281–84.

34. Sylvia Stevens, "Travelling Ministry," in Angell and Dandelion, *Oxford Handbook of Quaker Studies*, 292–305.

35. James Freeman Clarke, *Steps of Belief; or, Rational Christianity Maintained Against Atheism, Free Religion, and Romanism* (Boston: American Unitarian Association, 1870), 244.

36. Wilmer A. Cooper, *A Living Faith: An Historical and Comparative Study of Quaker Beliefs*, 2nd ed. (Richmond, IN: Friends United Press, 2006), 7–12; Hamm, *Quakers in America*, 147–51.

37. Kennedy, *British Quakerism*, 154–55.

38. James Luther Adams, *Not Without Dust and Heat* (Chicago: Exploration Press, 1995), 63.

39. D. Elton Trueblood quoted in George A. Selleck, *Quakers in Boston, 1646–1964: Three Centuries of Friends in Boston and Cambridge* (Cambridge, MA: Friends Meeting Cambridge, 1976), 190.

CHAPTER 6

1. William James, *The Varieties of Religious Experience: A Study in Human Nature* (New York: Modern Library, 1994). The author gratefully acknowledges the Thomas Scattergood Behavioral Health Foundation and the staff of the Quaker & Special Collections at Haverford College for making this project possible.

2. Anne Digby, *Madness, Morality, and Medicine: A Study of the York Retreat, 1796–1914*, Cambridge History of Medicine (Cambridge: Cambridge University Press, 1985); Jonathan Paul Mitchell, "Religious Melancholia and the York Retreat, 1730–1830" (PhD diss., University of Leeds, 2018). Pinel used the phrase "*traitement moral*" to distinguish his approach from the two prevailing approaches to interacting

with the mentally ill, incarceration and heroic medical treatment—both of which sought to act on the body rather than the mind. Pinel did not mean to suggest that his approach was moral and the others were immoral, though he believed that. Later, in 1808, a German doctor named Johann Christian Reil invented a new word, *psychiatrie*, to describe the distinction Pinel was making. See D. B. Weiner, "Philippe Pinel's 'Memoir on Madness' of December 11, 1794: A Fundamental Text of Modern Psychiatry," *American Journal of Psychiatry* 149, no. 6 (1992): 725–32; Andrew Scull, *Madness in Civilization: A Cultural History of Insanity, from the Bible to Freud, from the Madhouse to Modern Medicine* (Princeton, NJ: Princeton University Press, 2016), 221.

3. Andrew Scull, *The Most Solitary of Afflictions: Madness and Society in Britain, 1700–1900* (New Haven, CT: Yale University Press, 1993); Benjamin Reiss, *Theaters of Madness: Insane Asylums and Nineteenth-Century American Culture* (Chicago: University of Chicago Press, 2008).

4. The standard work on Quaker approaches to mental illness is Charles L. Cherry, *A Quiet Haven: Quakers, Moral Treatment, and Asylum Reform* (Rutherford, NJ: Fairleigh Dickinson University Press, 1989); see also Charles L. Cherry, "Quakers and Asylum Reform," in *The Oxford Handbook of Quaker Studies*, ed. Stephen W. Angell and Pink Dandelion (Oxford: Oxford University Press, 2013), 392–404; on the prevalence of Quakers and Quaker ideas in psychiatry, see Robert A. Clark and J. Russell Elkinton, *The Quaker Heritage in Medicine* (Pacific Grove, CA: Boxwood Press, 1978).

5. Philippe Pinel, *A Treatise on Insanity: In Which Are Contained the Principles of a New and More Practical Nosology of Maniacal Disorders than Has Yet Been Offered to the Public*, trans. D. D. Davis (Sheffield, UK: Printed by W. Todd for Cadell and Davies, 1806), 74.

6. Benjamin Rush and George Washington Corner, *The Autobiography of Benjamin Rush: His Travels Through Life Together with His Commonplace Book for 1789–1813* (Westport, CT: Greenwood Press, 1970), 287; Juan José López Ibor et al., *Anthology of Spanish Language Psychiatric Texts* (Thônex, Switzerland: World Psychiatric Association, 2001), 31; Benjamin Rush, *Medical Inquiries and Observations, upon the Diseases of the Mind* (Philadelphia: Kimber & Richardson, 1812), 115–16, 47; Johann Christian August Heinroth, *Textbook of Disturbances of Mental Life: Or, Disturbances of the Soul and Their Treatment* (Baltimore: Johns Hopkins University Press, 1818), originally published as Johann Christian August Heinroth, *Lehrbuch der Störungen des Seelenlebens oder der Seelenstörungen und ihrer Behandlung: zwey Theile. Erster oder theoretischer Theil* (Leipzig: Vogel, 1818).

7. Cherry, *Quiet Haven*, 27–29; J. William Frost, *The Quaker Family in Colonial America: A Portrait of the Society of Friends* (New York: St. Martin's Press, 1973), 161.

8. George Man Burrows, *Commentaries on the Causes, Forms, Symptoms, and Treatment, Moral and Medical, of Insanity* (London: T. and G. Underwood, 1828), 28–29; Cherry, *Quiet Haven*, 49.

9. Jacobi's study was translated into English by James Cowles Prichard in *A Treatise on Insanity and Other Disorders Affecting the Mind* (London: Sherwood, Gilbert and Piper, 1835), 187–98.

10. Technically speaking, Falret succeeded Pinel's protégé Jean-Étienne Dominique Esquirol, who ran Salpêtrière from Pinel's death in 1826 until 1831; Jean Pierre Falret, *De l'hypochondrie et du suicide: Considérations sur les causes, sur le siège et le traitement de ces maladies, sur les moyens d'en arrêter les progrès et d'en prévenir le développement* (Paris: Croullebois, 1822); William Saunders Hallaran, *Practical Observations on the Causes and Cure of Insanity* (Cork: Edwards and

Savage, 1818), 32; B. D. Kelly, "Dr William Saunders Hallaran and Psychiatric Practice in Nineteenth-Century Ireland," *Irish Journal of Medical Science* 177, no. 1 (2008): 79–84; Joseph Guislain, *Traité sur les phrénopathies, ou doctrine nouvelle des maladies mentales: Basée sur des observations pratiques et statistiques, et l'étude des causes, de la nature, des symptômes, du pronostic, du diagnostic et du traitement de ces affections* (Brussels: Établissement Encyclographique, 1835); Vincenzio Chiarugi, *Della pazzia in genere, e in specie. Trattato medico-analitico / T. II et III* (Florence: Luigi Carlieri, 1794).

11. Samuel Tuke, *Description of the Retreat, an Institution near York for Insane Persons of the Society of Friends Containing an Account of Its Origins and Progress, the Modes of Treatment and a Statement of Cases* (Philadelphia: Isaac Pierce, 1813); Prichard, *Treatise on Insanity*, 199.

12. John Thurnam, Samuel Tuke, and Royal College of Physicians of London, *The Statistics of the Retreat, Consisting of a Report and Tables Exhibiting the Experience of That Institution for the Insane from Its Establishment in 1796 to 1840* (York, UK: John L. Linney, 1841), 1–12.

13. Prichard, *Treatise on Insanity*, 142. Prichard also introduced to psychiatry the concepts of the "psychopathic personality" and "psychopathic inferior" and the idea that someone can momentarily lose their moral conscience and thus be legally not guilty for crimes committed during spells of "moral insanity."

14. *Biographical Sketch of Amariah Brigham, M.D. Late Superintendent of the New York State Lunatic Asylum, Utica, N.Y.* (Utica, NY: W. O. McClure, 1858); Lawrence B. Goodheart, *Mad Yankees: The Hartford Retreat for the Insane and Nineteenth-Century Psychiatry* (Amherst: University of Massachusetts Press, 2003).

15. Amariah Brigham, *Observations on the Influence of Religion upon the Health and Physical Welfare of Mankind* (Boston: Marsh, Capen & Lyon, 1835), 127–29.

16. Ibid., 135, 292.

17. Ibid., 127, 269, xxi.

18. Jacobi made these remarks in his German translation of Samuel Tuke's 1813 *Description of the Retreat*; Prichard translated those remarks into English. See Prichard, *Treatise on Insanity*, 198; *First Report: Minutes of Evidence Taken Before the Select Committee Appointed to Consider of Provision Being Made for the Better Regulation of Madhouses, in England. Ordered, by the House of Commons, to Be Printed, 25 May 1815*, Parl. H.C. Reports and Papers (London, 1815).

19. "Memoir of Mrs. Elizabeth Fry—Her Care and Labors for the Insane," *American Journal of Insanity* V, no. 3 (1849): 234; Edward Ryder, *Elizabeth Fry: Life and Labors of the Eminent Philanthropist, Preacher, and Prison Reformer, Compiled from Her Journal and Other Sources*, 3rd ed. (New York: E. Walker's Son, 1884), 158–61.

20. J. H. Worthington, "Friends' Asylum, Near Frankford," *Friends' Review* (Philadelphia), May 6, 1854; Andrew Scull, *The Asylum as Utopia: W. A. F. Browne and the Mid-Nineteenth Century Consolidation of Psychiatry* (London: Routledge, 2014); Ann Goldberg, *Sex, Religion, and the Making of Modern Madness: The Eberbach Asylum and German Society, 1815–1849* (New York: Oxford University Press, 1999); Kyla Schuller, *The Biopolitics of Feeling: Race, Sex, and Science in the Nineteenth Century*, ANIMA Series (Durham, NC: Duke University Press, 2018); Patricia D'Antonio, *Founding Friends: Families, Staff, and Patients at the Friends Asylum in Early Nineteenth-Century Philadelphia* (Bethlehem, PA: Lehigh University Press, 2006).

21. "Insanity Among Quakers," *Globe* (London), November 22, 1844; Samuel Tuke, untitled, *Globe* (London), December 6, 1844. Quakers on both sides of the Atlantic paid attention to this controversy.

See "Insanity in the Society of Friends," *The Friend*, March 8, 1845; "Insanity Among Quakers," *Workingman's Advocate*, January 25, 1845; "The Quakers," *Friends' Review*, April 2, 1870.

22. Brigham, *Observations on the Influence of Religion*, 156; Pliny Earle, "On the Causes of Insanity," *American Journal of Insanity* 4, no. 3 (1847); "Increase of Insanity," *Friends' Intelligencer* (Philadelphia), May 14, 1853; Friends Hospital Records, 1812–1968 (HC.MC.1261), Admission Record Books, vol. 1, 1817–1885 (item 31), Haverford College Quaker & Special Collections, Haverford, PA.

23. John Charles Bucknill and Daniel Hack Tuke, *A Manual of Psychological Medicine* (Philadelphia: Blanchard and Lea, 1858).

24. James, *Varieties of Religious Experience*, 9.

25. Ibid., 453.

26. Ibid., 111.

27. Stephen A. Kent, "Psychological and Mystical Interpretations of Early Quakerism: William James and Rufus Jones," *Religion* 17 (1987): 251–74. See also Alice Southern, "The Rowntree History Series and the Growth of Liberal Quakerism," *Quaker Studies* 16, no. 1 (2011): 7–73; J. William Frost, "Modernist and Liberal Quakers, 1887–2010," in Angell and Dandelion, *Oxford Handbook of Quaker Studies*, 78–91.

28. Elizabeth Gray Vining, *Friend of Life: The Biography of Rufus M. Jones* (Philadelphia: J. B. Lippincott, 1958), 85–86.

29. Rufus M. Jones, *Studies in Mystical Religion* (London: Macmillan, 1923), xxviii.

30. Bucknill and Tuke, *Manual of Psychological Medicine*, 171–73, 318–19.

CHAPTER 7

1. *A Reasonable Faith: Short Religious Essays for the Times*, by Three "Friends" [William Pollard, Francis Frith, William E. Turner] (London: Macmillan, 1885). See Thomas C. Kennedy, *British Quakerism 1860–1920: The Transformation of a Religious Community* (Oxford: Oxford University Press, 2001), 101–6; for Emerson and Fuller, see Leigh Eric Schmidt, *Restless Souls: The Making of American Spirituality*, 2nd ed. (Berkeley: University of California Press, 2012), chap. 1.

2. Owen Chadwick, *The Secularization of the European Mind*, Gifford Lectures (Cambridge: Cambridge University Press, 1973), 186; *Reasonable Faith*, 23.

3. For Coleridge and Emerson, see Gary Dorrien, *The Making of American Liberal Theology: 1805–1900* (Louisville, KY: Westminster John Knox Press, 2002), 60, 61; Schmidt, *Restless Souls*, 13. Schmidt describes the "Emersonian turn—the sense that religion was fundamentally about the sacredness of the individual, not the institution of the church."

4. Hugh Rock, "Rufus Jones Never Did Establish That Quakerism Is a Mystical Religion," *Quaker Studies* 21, no. 1 (2016): 49–66; see also Helen Holt's rejoinder, "The Enigma of Humanism in the Transformational Mysticism of Rufus Jones," *Quaker Studies* 24, no. 2 (December 2019): 49–68; Rufus M. Jones, *Social Law in the Spiritual World: Studies in Human and Divine Inter-relationship*, new ed. (London: Headley Brothers, [1904]), 11, 15–17; Edward Grubb, *Authority and the Light Within* (London: James Clarke, 1908), 93.

5. For a classic statement of the necessary connection between mysticism and conduct, see Howard H. Brinton, *Ethical Mysticism in the Society of Friends*, Pendle Hill Pamphlets 156 (Wallingford, PA: Pendle Hill, 1967).

6. For Quaker "peculiarities," see Thomas Clarkson, *A Portraiture of Quakerism: Taken from a View of the Moral Education, Discipline, Peculiar Customs, Religious Principles, Political and Civil Economy, and Character, of the Society of Friends*, 2nd ed., 3 vols. (London: Longman, Hurst, Rees, and Orme, 1807); Pink Dandelion, *An*

Introduction to Quakerism (Cambridge: Cambridge University Press, 2007), 62, 83; Jack D. Marietta, *The Reformation of American Quakerism, 1748–1783* (Philadelphia: University of Pennsylvania Press, 1984). Marietta writes of attempts in America to revive and enforce the peculiar Quaker discipline.

7. Rosemary Moore, *The Light in Their Consciences: Early Quakers in Britain, 1646–1666* (University Park: Penn State University Press, 2000), 196; Jones, *Social Law*, 161–81; Edward Grubb, "Past and Present: The Yearly Meeting of 1836," *Friends' Quarterly Examiner* (1896): 99–120, 118.

8. For the Beaconites, see Roger C. Wilson, *Manchester, Manchester and Manchester Again: From "Sound Doctrine" to "a Free Ministry"—the Theological Travail of London Yearly Meeting Throughout the Nineteenth Century* (London: Friends Historical Society, 1990), 11–17; Elizabeth Isichei, *Victorian Quakers* (Oxford: Oxford University Press, 1970), 8–9.

9. Susan Budd, *Varieties of Unbelief* (London: Heinemann, 1977); Frank M. Turner, "The Victorian Crisis of Faith and the Faith That Was Lost," in *Victorian Faith in Crisis: Essays on Continuity and Change in Nineteenth-Century Religious Belief*, ed. Richard J. Helmstadter and Bernard Lightman (Stanford, CA: Stanford University Press, 1990), 9–38; and other chapters in this volume. On atonement, see J. A. Froude, *The Nemesis of Faith* (London: John Chapman, 1849), 9, 15, 61–62. For Froude, see Robert Lee Wolff, *Gains and Losses: Novels of Faith and Doubt in Victorian England* (New York: Garland, 1977), 389–402.

10. For Martineau, see Adrian Desmond and James Moore, *Darwin* (London: Michael Joseph, 1991), 486.

11. Victor Shea and William Whitla, eds., *Essays and Reviews: The 1860 Text and Its Reading* (Charlottesville: University Press of Virginia, 2000), 197; Josef L. Altholz, *Anatomy of a Controversy: The Debate over Essays and Reviews, 1860–1864* (Aldershot, UK: Ashgate, 1994), 32; for the internal witness, see 1 John 5:10; George Fox, *The Journal of George Fox*, ed. John L. Nickalls (Philadelphia: Religious Society of Friends, 1997), 32; Thomas Hodgkin, "The Message of Quakerism to the Twentieth Century," *British Friend*, April 4, 1892, 76.

12. See Martin Davie, *British Quaker Theology Since 1895* (Lewiston, NY: Edwin Mellen, 1997), for the influence on liberal Quakers of figures like the Anglican leader Charles Gore and the Congregationalist R. W. Dale; Bernard M. G. Reardon, "Maurice, (John) Frederick Denison (1805–1872)," in *Oxford Dictionary of National Biography*, https://doi.org/10.1093/ref:odnb/18384; H. G. Wood, *Frederick Denison Maurice* (Cambridge: Cambridge University Press, 1950); "The Manchester Conference," editorial, *Friends' Quarterly Examiner* (January 1896): 1–18, 2.

13. For American religious diversity, see William R. Hutchison, *Religious Pluralism in America: The Contentious History of a Founding Ideal* (New Haven, CT: Yale University Press, 2003). For stirrings of liberalism among Quakers of the early nineteenth century in the United States, see Thomas D. Hamm, *Liberal Quakerism in America in the Long Nineteenth Century, 1790–1920* (Leiden: Brill, 2020), 6–14.

14. Dorrien, *American Liberal Theology*, 34, 48, 49 (quoting Channing, *Works*, 292–93).

15. Ralph Waldo Emerson, "An Address Delivered Before the Senior Class in Divinity College, Cambridge," in *Selected Essays of Ralph Walso Emerson* ([s.l.]: T. Nelson & Sons, [1909]), 291–311, 296. For the furor caused by Emerson's address, see Dorrien, *American Liberal Theology*, 70–74; Schmidt, *Restless Souls*, 13, 14.

There is an article by F. B. Tolles on "Emerson and Quakerism" in *American Literature* 10 (1938), but Tolles is interested in the influence of Quakers on Emerson rather than the other way around.

16. Rufus M. Jones, *The Trail of Life in College* (London: Macmillan, 1929), 89–90; Schmidt, *Restless Souls*, 50. For Calvin, see articles on "Reformation Theology," "Predestination," and "Redemption" in *The Oxford Companion to Christian Thought*, ed. Adrian Hastings, Alastair Mason, Hugh Pyper (Oxford: Oxford University Press, 2000); for Jones on Whittier, see Rufus M. Jones, *The Later Periods of Quakerism* (London: Macmillan, 1921), 2:660.

17. For Hicks and his insistence on the absolute primacy of the Light, see Jones, *Later Periods*, 1:444–46; compare Carole Dale Spencer, *Holiness: The Soul of Quakerism: An Historical Analysis of the Theology of Holiness in the Quaker Tradition* (Milton Keynes, UK: Paternoster, 2007), 121–23; Hamm, *Liberal Quakerism*, 20.

18. Jones, *Later Periods*, 1:517–37; Thomas D. Hamm, *The Transformation of American Quakerism: Orthodox Friends, 1800–1907* (Bloomington: Indiana University Press, 1988), 20–22, 28–35, 99–102; Thomas D. Hamm, "The Problem of the Inner Light in Nineteenth-Century Quakerism," in *The Lamb's War: Quaker Essays to Honor Hugh Barbour*, ed. Michael Birkel and John W. Newman (Richmond, IN: Earlham College Press, 1992), 101–17; Edward H. Milligan, "'The Ancient Way': The Conservative Tradition in Nineteenth Century British Quakerism," *Journal of the Friends Historical Society* 57 (1994): 74–97; Hamm, "Problem of the Inner Light," 115.

19. H. Larry Ingle, *Quakers in Conflict: The Hicksite Reformation* (Knoxville: University of Tennessee Press, 1986), 41; Chuck Fager, *Remaking Friends: How Progressive Friends Changed Quakerism and Helped Save America* (Durham, NC: Kimo Press, 2014). The latter monograph is accompanied by a selection of texts, *Angels of Progress: A Documentary History of the Progressive Friends, 1822–1940*, compiled and edited and with introductions by Chuck Fager (Durham, NC: Kimo Press, 2014). See also Hamm, *Liberal Quakerism*, 35–43, 46–48.

20. Hugh Barbour and J. William Frost, *The Quakers* (Richmond, IN: Friends United Press, 1988), 355.

21. Edwin B. Bronner, "*The Other Branch*": *London Yearly Meeting and the Hicksites, 1827–1912* (London: Friends Historical Society, 1975), 39–60; Joanna Clare Dales, "John William Graham: Quaker Apostle of Progress" (PhD diss., University of Birmingham, 2016), 196–98.

22. For Finney, see David W. Bebbington, *Evangelicalism in Modern Britain: A History from the 1730s to the 1980s* (London: Unwin Hyman, 1989), 116. For the American revival, see Carole Dale Spencer, "Quakers in Theological Context," in *The Oxford Handbook of Quaker Studies*, ed. Stephen W. Angell and Pink Dandelion (Oxford: Oxford University Press, 2013), 141–57, 150–51. For the Richmond Conference and Declaration, see Mark Minear, *Richmond 1887: A Quaker Drama Unfolds* (Richmond, IN: Friends United Press, 1987); Hamm, *Transformation of American Quakerism*, 137–39; Kennedy, *British Quakerism*, 111–18; Isichei, *Victorian Quakers*, 52–53; Anna Braithwaite Thomas et al., *J. Bevan Braithwaite: A Friend of the Nineteenth Century, by His Children* (London: Hodder & Stoughton, 1909), 71–72, 84, 319–21; Wilson, *Manchester*, 32.

23. Rufus M. Jones, *A Dynamic Faith*, 3rd ed. (London: Headley, 1906); Jones, *Later Periods*, 2:930–32; letter from John William Graham to his sister, May 31, 1888, in the John William Graham Papers (JWGP) held in the University Library archives of Manchester University, Box 7; Kennedy, *British Quakerism*, 115; Minear, *Richmond 1887*, 138; Bronner, "Other Branch," 37, 38.

24. Hamm, *Liberal Quakerism*, 54; Spencer, *Holiness: The Soul of Quakerism*,

59–74; Hamm, *Transformation of American Quakerism*, 115–16; Hamm, *Liberal Quakerism*, 62.

25. Jones, *Trail of Life*, 114–15; Jones, *Social Law*, 61–76; Jones, *Finding the Trail*, 142–43; Joanna Dales, *The Quaker Renaissance and Liberal Quakerism in Britain, 1895–1930: Seeking a Real Religion* (Leiden: Brill, 2020), 13–15; Jones, *Later Periods*, I:xix–xxii, xxiii; Rex Ambler, *Mind the Oneness: The Mystic Way of the Quakers*, 2nd ed. (Wallingford, PA: Pendle Hill, 2017), 17.

26. See Wilson, *Manchester*, 20–26; Kennedy, *British Quakerism*, 50–85; Milligan, "Ancient Way," 89–92. For Graham's comment, see Milligan, "Ancient Way," 92; for Hodgson, see Kennedy, *British Quakerism*, 81.

27. Hamm, *Transformation of American Quakerism*, 83–84, 124–30. See *British Friend*, January 1894, 7–8. London Yearly Meeting, which retained a kind of parental role toward Friends in America, sent its epistles to Orthodox meetings but not to the Hicksites, or "Other Branch." See "Our Correspondence with American Yearly Meetings" (editorial), *The Friend*, June 3, 1892, 365–66; Thomas Hodgkin, "Some Notes on the Yearly Meeting of 1892," *Friends' Quarterly Examiner* (1892): 424–31, 427. For the adult schools, see Kennedy, *British Quakerism*, 44; and Jones, *Later Periods*, 2:955–60. For mission meetings, see Kennedy, *British Quakerism*, 121–22; and Isichei, *Victorian Quakers*, 258–79. For early Friends' views on ministry and payment, see W. C. Braithwaite, *The Beginnings of Quakerism* (London: Macmillan, 1912), 138; Moore, *Light*, 129–30. See also Thomas D. Hamm, "'Chipping at the Landmarks of Our Fathers': The Decline of the Testimony Against Hireling Ministry in the Nineteenth Century," *Quaker Studies* 13, no. 2 (2009): 136–59; Joseph Bevan Braithwaite Jr., Letter to the Editor, *British Friend*, April 1892, 93; and *The Friend* 11 (November 1892): 746; for the "property qualification," see George Gillett, *The Friend*, May 27, 1892, 354; John Stephenson Rowntree, "Gospel Ministry in the Society of Friends," *Friends' Quarterly Examiner* (1893): 85–103; J. W. Graham, "The Maintenance of Ministers," *British Friend*, April 1893, 93–94.

28. For the Home Mission Committee, its evangelical bent, and the conference of 1892, see Kennedy, *British Quakerism*, 119–31; for the conference, see also Dales, "John William Graham," 199–202. For Graham's attitude toward typical home mission preaching, see *The Friend*, November 11, 1892, 747; *British Friend*, February 1894, 31, 33; Edward Grubb, "On the Ministry in our Meetings," *Friends' Quarterly Examiner* (1888): 366–69.

29. J. W. Rowntree, Letter to Graham, August 16, 1899, quoted from a copy sent by Thomas Kennedy; John William Graham, *The Faith of a Quaker* (Cambridge: Cambridge University Press, 1920), 195.

30. Letter from Graham to James Clark, a teacher at Bootham School, May 19, 1881, JWGP, Box 8; letter from Graham to his parents, February 27, 1881, JWGP, Box 5.

31. Michael R. Watts, *The Dissenters*, vol. 3, *The Crisis and Conscience of Nonconformity* (Oxford: Clarendon, 2015), 67.

32. "A Declaration of Some of the Fundamental Principles of Christian Truth as Held by the Religious Society of Friends, Made by the General Conference of Friends Held in Richmond, Indiana USA 1887," from proceedings published by Nicholson and Bro. (1887), 11; for Joseph Rowntree, see Kennedy, *British Quakerism*, 116; George MacDonald, *Robert Falconer* [1868] (New York: Garland, 1975); see Jones, *Trail of Life*, 85; Jones, *Reasonable Faith*, 12, 17–19.

33. Edward Worsdell, *The Gospel of Divine Help* [1886], 2nd ed., with prefatory note by J. G. Whittier (London: Samuel Harris, 1888), 71, 176; 74; 79.

34. Letter from John W. Graham, September 27, 1886, JWGP, Box 6.

35. A. B., "The Late Yearly Meeting," *British Friend*, July 1893, 193 (emphasis in original); Silvanus P. Thompson, *British Friend*, 1893, 150A.

36. The Society of Friends, *Report of the Proceedings of the Conference of Members of the Society of Friends, held, by Direction of the Yearly Meeting, in Manchester—from Eleventh to Fifteenth of Eleventh Month, 1895* (London: Headley, 1896), 203–47; 207, 222, 232, 241, 245.

37. Thomas et al., *J. Bevan Braithwaite*, 88. Anna Braithwaite Thomas credits her father with passing through "fires of discussion" before reaching this settled assurance. See *Report of the Proceedings*, 216. For Driver, see "Driver, Samuel Rolles," *Oxford Dictionary of National Biography*, https://doi.org/10.1093/ref:odnb/32897. The Revised Version of the New Testament was published in 1881, and the Old and New Testaments together in 1885.

38. J. W. Rowntree, in *Report of the Proceedings*, 79, 76.

39. Obituary notice in *The Friend*, March 17, 1905, 164; Roger C. Wilson, "'We Shall Never Thrive upon Ignorance': The Service of John Wilhelm Rowntree, 1893–1905," in *A Quaker Miscellany for Edward H. Milligan*, ed. David Blamires, Jeremy Greenwood, and Alex Kerr (Manchester: Friends Book Centre, 1985), 153–60.

40. Matilda Sturge, "Early Quakerism—Its Spirit and Power," in *Report of the Proceedings*, 27–34. For Sturge, see Margaret Allen, "Matilda Sturge, Renaissance Woman," *Women's History Review* 7, no. 2 (1998): 209–26.

41. For Penney, see Kennedy, *British Quakerism*, 199–200; for the histories, see T. C. Kennedy, "History and the Quaker Renaissance: The Vision of John Wilhelm Rowntree," *Journal of the Friends' Historical Society* 55, nos. 1–2 (1986): 35–56, 49, 51; Alice Southern, "The Rowntree History Series and the Growth of Liberal Quakerism," *Quaker Studies* 16, no. 1 (2011): 1–73, 21.

42. Southern, "Rowntree History Series," 21. For Jones's helpers, see Southern, "Rowntree History Series," 23. The series comprises seven volumes, the first two volumes by William Charles Braithwaite and last five volumes by Rufus Jones: (1) *The Beginnings of Quakerism* (first published in 1912), with an introduction by Rufus M. Jones; (2) *The Second Period of Quakerism* (1919); (3) *Studies in Mystical Religion* (1909); (4) *Spiritual Reformers in the 16th and 17th Centuries* (1914); (5) *The Quakers in the American Colonies* (1911), with the acknowledged collaboration of Isaac Sharpless and Amelia Gummere; (6) and (7) *The Later Periods of Quakerism*, 2 vols. (1921). For Jones's views on Puritanism, see Southern, "Rowntree History Series," 25–26. For his view of Quaker mysticism, see his introduction to Braithwaite's *Beginnings of Quakerism*, which Braithwaite found "quite admirable" but which was omitted from the 1955 edition on the grounds that it had been discredited (Kennedy, *British Quakerism*, 209); Geoffrey F. Nuttall, *The Holy Spirit in Puritan Faith and Experience* [1946] (Chicago: University of Chicago Press, 1992); see J. William Frost, "Modernist and Liberal Quakers, 1887–2010," in Angell and Dandelion, *Oxford Handbook of Quaker Studies*, 87; Melvin B. Endy Jr., "The Interpretation of Quakerism: Rufus Jones and His Critics," *Quaker History* 70 (1981), 3–21.

43. Kennedy, "History," 44. For J. W. Rowntree and the beginnings of Woodbrooke, see Kennedy, *British Quakerism*, 177–96; and Robert Davis, ed., *Woodbrooke, 1903–1953: A Brief History of a Quaker Experiment in Religious Education* (London: Bannisdale, 1953). For the summer schools, see Davie, *British Quaker Theology*, 84; for a detailed account of the first, see Thomas Hodgkin, "Remembrances of Scarborough Summer School," *Friends' Quarterly Examiner* (1897): 461–77.

44. *British Friend*, October 1899, quoted in Michael Birkel, *Quakers Reading Mystics* (Leiden: Brill, 2018), 52. The quotation occurs in the chapter on Caroline Stephen and her reading of Tauler. See also Frances E. Cooke, "The Story of Tauler, the German Mystic," *British Friend*, 1893, 88–89.

45. Graham, *Faith of a Quaker*, 250; see Fox, *Journal of George Fox*, 7, for Fox's realization that "being bred at Oxford or Cambridge was not enough to fit and qualify men to be ministers of Christ"; Kennedy, *British Quakerism*, 194; John W. Graham, "The Intellect in Religion," *British Friend*, September 1894, 253–57; *British Friend*, November 1894, 306–7; "Paul on Theology and Religion," *British Friend*, January 1895, 3–5.

46. Kennedy, *British Quakerism*, 179, 181–82; Alessandro Falcetta, *The Daily Discoveries of a Bible Scholar and Manuscript Hunter: A Biography of James Rendel Harris (1852–1941)* (London: T&T Clark, 2018), 222–27; Kennedy, *British Quakerism*, 190; Geoffrey Carnall, *Gandhi's Interpreter: A Life of Horace Alexander* (Edinburgh: Edinburgh University Press, 2010), 56.

47. Pink Dandelion, *An Introduction to Quakerism* (Cambridge: Cambridge University Press, 2007), 133; Moore, *Light*, 80–81; Braithwaite, *Beginnings*, 277; Southern, "Rowntree History Series," 26; Braithwaite, *Beginnings*, 36–37; Jones, *Trail of Life*, 123.

48. Caroline Emelia Stephen, *Quaker Strongholds* [1890], 3rd ed. (London: Edward Hicks, 1891), 26, 27, 29, 49.

49. Robert Barclay, *Apology for the True Christian Divinity*, first published in 1678 (Farmington, ME: Quaker Heritage Press, 2002) (see Proposition 5 for fallen human nature); Edward Grubb, *Authority and the Light Within* (London: James Clarke, 1908), 83.

50. Edward Grubb, *The Historic and Inward Christ*, Swarthmore Lecture, 1914 (Bishopsgate: Headley, 1914), 49.

51. Edward Grubb, *The Religion of Experience: An Examination of Some of the Difficulties of Christian Faith* (London: Headley, [1918]), 18; John William Graham, *The Divinity in Man* (London: George Allen & Unwin, 1927), 99; Dales, "John William Graham," 128–58.

52. H. G. Wood, "What Do We Mean by the Inner Light?," *Friends' Quarterly Examiner* (1930): 197–211, 208; for More, see Nuttall, *Holy Spirit*, 18; F. J. Powicke, "Henry More, Cambridge Platonist; and Lady Conway, of Ragley, Platonist and Quakeress," *Friends' Quarterly Examiner* (1921): 199–220. For Conway and her circle, see also Marjorie Hope Nicolson, ed., *The Conway Letters* [1930], rev. ed. (Oxford: Clarendon Press, 1992); Wood, "Inner Light," 211.

53. J. Rendel Harris, *The Guiding Hand of God* (London: Thomas Law, 1905); William E. Wilson, "Quaker and Evangelical," Rendel Harris Lecture, *Friends Quarterly* (1948): 205–17; L. Violet Hodgkin Holdsworth, "The Cardinal Tenets of Quakerism," *Friends' Quarterly Examiner* (1914): 273–85, 275; Douglas Gwyn, *Apocalypse of the Word: The Life and Message of George Fox* (Richmond, IN: Friends United Press, 1986), 113–18; John W. Graham, *The Quaker Ministry*, Swarthmore Lecture, 1925 (London: Swarthmore Press, 1925), 71.

CHAPTER 8

1. Elizabeth Gray Vining, preface to *Quaker Spirituality: Selected Writings*, ed. Douglas Steere, Classics of Western Spirituality (New York: Paulist Press, 1984), ix.

2. The most thorough study of this period of American Quaker history is Thomas Hamm's *The Transformation of American Quakerism: Orthodox Friends 1800–1907* (Bloomington: Indiana University Press, 1988).

3. Elias Hicks, *Journal of the Life and Religious Labours of Elias Hicks* (New York: Isaac T. Hopper, 1832), 278.

4. For example, Hicksite Friends did not support suffrage until 1918. For a reassessment of Mott's contributions to contemporary feminism and her understanding of systemic oppression, see Carol Faulkner, *Lucretia Mott's Heresy: Abolition and Women's Rights in Nineteenth-Century America* (Philadelphia: University of Pennsylvania Press, 2011). Collections of her sermons can be found in Dana Greene, ed., *Lucretia Mott: Her Complete Speeches and Sermons* (New York: Edwin Mellen, 1980); and Margaret Hope Bacon, ed., *Lucretia Mott Speaking: Excerpts from the Sermons and Speeches of a Famous Nineteenth Century Quaker Minister and Reformer* (Wallingford, PA: Pendle Hill, 1980).

5. Benjamin Seebohm, ed., *Memoirs of the Life and Labours of Stephen Grellet* (London: A. W. Bennett, 1862), 1:142–43.

6. Frances Anne Budge, *A Missionary Life: Stephen Grellet* (London: James Nisbet, 1888).

7. Quoted in Fred R. Shapiro, ed., *The Yale Book of Quotations* (New Haven, CT: Yale University Press, 2006), 325.

8. Quakers, as nonconformists, were not admitted to British universities. But Gurney was from a wealthy banking family and was privileged to study at Oxford with private tutors. Gurney came from a family of "gay" Quakers, a term that meant they did not adopt plain dress and other symbols of strict Quaker practice, such as renouncing sports and music. He struggled to sacrifice the dress that symbolized his privileged place as an upper-class Englishman, but by doing so he publicly identified as a devout, "plain" Quaker. See Joseph Bevan Braithwaite, ed., *Memoirs of Joseph John Gurney*, 2 vols. (Norwich: Fletcher and Alexander, 1854); Joseph John Gurney, *Observations on the Distinguishing Views and Practices of the Society of Friends* (London: Gilpin, 1824); Gurney, *Essays on the Evidences, Doctrines, and Practical Operations of Christianity* (London: J. and A. Arch, Cornhill, and Hamilton, Adams, 1825); Gurney, *Essays on the Habitual Exercise of Love to God, Considered as a Preparation for Heaven* (Norwich: Joseph Fletcher, 1834).

9. Robert Barclay, *Apology for the True Christian Divinity* (Farmington, ME: Quaker Heritage Press, 2002 [1678]); John Wilbur, *Journal of the Life of John Wilbur* (Providence, RI: G. H. Whitney, 1859); Colossians 1:27, King James Version. Published theological and spiritual writing from Quaker conservatives read beyond the bounds of the conservative meetings rarely appeared until the mid-twentieth century. Since then, Quakers seeking spiritual depth and guidance have found inspiration in many significant publications that have attracted wide readership across the branches. See, for example, Wilmer Cooper, William Taber, and Lloyd Lee Wilson.

10. "The Issue," *British Friend* 39 (March 1881): 49–51; and *British Friend*, November 1, 1883, 282–84; David C. Le Shana, *Quakers in California: The Effects of 19th Century Revivalism on Western Quakerism* (Newberg, OR: Barclay Press, 1969), 141; "Why I Am a Friend," *American Friend*, 12th mo. 20, 1894, 534–36.

11. Dougan Clark, *The Theology of Holiness* (Chicago: Christian Witness Publishing, 1893).

12. *A Guide to True Peace or the Excellency of Inward and Spiritual Prayer* (Wallingford, PA: Pendle Hill, 1946), vii (published anonymously, this was compiled and edited by two Quakers, William Backhouse and James Janson, in 1813); Michael Birkel, *Quakers Reading Mystics* (Leiden: Brill, 2018), 4; quotation in Birkel, 81.

13. John Greenleaf Whittier, *The Poetical Works in Four Volumes* (Boston: Houghton Mifflin, 1892).

14. The Gurneyite abolitionist Levi Coffin (1798–1877) was disowned for his abolitionist activities. But after his *Reminiscences* was published a year before his death, he became celebrated for his leadership in the African American resistance movement known as the Underground Railroad.

15. The single comparable figure to Whittier as public theologian would be Lucretia Mott, an eloquent public speaker whose reputation extended well beyond the Society of Friends, but she left almost no publications. See Ian High, "In War Time: Whittier's Civil War Address and the Quaker Periodical Press," *Quaker Studies* 19, no. 2 (2015): 231.

16. John Greenleaf Whittier, ed., *The Journal of John Woolman* (Boston: James R. Osgood, 1871); Philips P. Moulton, ed., *The Journal and Major Essays of John Woolman* (Richmond, IN: Friends United Press, 1989); Leigh Eric Schmidt, *Restless Souls: The Making of American Spirituality* (San Francisco: HarperCollins, 2005), 81, 168.

17. Frederick B. Tolles, "Emerson and Quakerism," *American Literature* 10 no. 2 (1938): 142, 146, 165.

18. Ibid., 144, 157.

19. Ann Braude, *Radical Spirits: Spiritualism and Women's Rights in Nineteenth-Century America*, 2nd ed. (Bloomington: Indiana University Press, 2001), 10–13. Braude claims that Spiritualism was one of the primary vehicles for the spread of women's rights and thus drew many radical Quakers.

20. Hannah Whitall Smith, *The Christian's Secret of a Happy Life* (London: Willard Tract Repository, 1875).

21. Letter from James to Smith, May 11, 1886, Smith Collection, Asbury Seminary, Wilmore, KY; see William James, "The Gospel of Relaxation," in *Talks to Teachers on Psychology and to Students on Some of Life's Ideals* (New York: Henry Holt, 1899).

22. Hannah Whitall Smith, *My Spiritual Autobiography: Or, How I Discovered the Unselfishness of God* (New York: Fleming H. Revell, 1903).

23. David Bebbington, *Evangelicalism in Modern Britain: A History from the 1730s to the 1980s* (Grand Rapids, MI: Baker, 1989), 157.

24. Ray Strachey, ed., *Religious Fanaticism* (London: Faber & Gwyer, 1928), 206, 241.

25. Caroline Stephen, *Quaker Strongholds*, 3rd ed. (Philadelphia: H. Longstreth, 1891), 20.

26. Caroline Stephen, *Light Arising* (Cambridge: W. Heffer & Sons, 1908), 1, 12.

27. William James, *The Varieties of Religious Experience: A Study in Human Nature* (London: Longmans, Green, 1902). See also Friedrich von Hügel, *The Mystical Element in Religion* (London: J. M. Dent, 1908); Evelyn Underhill, *Mysticism: A Study in the Nature and Development of Man's Spiritual Consciousness* (London: Methuen, 1911); and Matthew S. Hedstrom, "Rufus Jones and Mysticism for the Masses," *Cross Currents* 54, no. 2 (2004), 32.

28. For his memoirs, see Rufus M. Jones, *A Boy's Religion from Memory* (Philadelphia: Ferris, 1902); Jones, *Finding the Trail of Life* (New York: Macmillan, 1926); Jones, *The Trail of Life in College* (New York: Macmillan, 1929); Jones, *The Trail of Life in the Middle Years* (New York: Macmillan, 1934); Jones, *A Small-Town Boy* (New York: Macmillan, 1941). See also Rufus M. Jones, *Social Law in the Spiritual World: Studies in Human and Divine Relationship* (Philadelphia: John Winston, 1904). For a detailed analysis of Jones's major role in the making of modern mysticism, see Hedstrom, "Rufus Jones and Mysticism for the Masses."

29. Rufus M. Jones, *The Later Periods of Quakerism*, 2 vols. (London: Macmillan, 1921), xiii; Elizabeth Gray Vining, *Friend of Life: The Biography of Rufus M. Jones* (New York: J. B. Lippincott, 1958).

30. Birkel, *Quakers Reading Mystics*, 6.

31. John W. Oliver edited and published "Lifestories" in 1993 as *J. Walter Malone:*

The Autobiography of an Evangelical Quaker (Lanham, MD: University Press of America).

32. John W. Oliver, "J. Walter Malone: 'The American Friend' and an Evangelical Quaker's Social Agenda," *Quaker History* 80 (Fall 1991): 67–69; Hamm, *Transformation of American Quakerism*, 166; Vining, *Friend of Life*, 77–78; Betty Hagglund, "Quakers and Print Culture," in *The Oxford Handbook of Quaker Studies*, ed. Stephen W. Angell and Pink Dandelion (Oxford: Oxford University Press, 2013), 490.

33. Alice Southern, "The Rowntree History Series and the Growth of Liberal Quakerism," *Quaker Studies* 16, no. 1 (2011); John Wilhelm Rowntree, "The Rise of Quakerism in Yorkshire," in *Essays and Addresses*, ed. Joshua Rowntree (London: Healey Brothers, 1905).

34. Edward Grubb, a staunch peace activist, was a prolific author of theological and devotional books expressing the new liberal outlook and editor of the *British Friend*. He was a leading British voice in opposing the adoption of the 1887 Richmond Declaration of Faith by London Yearly Meeting.

35. For further study of this colorful figure, see Alessandro Falcetta, *The Daily Discoveries of a Bible Scholar and Manuscript Hunter: A Biography of James Rendel Harris (1852–1941)* (London: T&T Clark, 2018).

36. William Littleboy, *The Appeal of Quakerism to the Non-mystic* (London: Friends' Book Centre, 1916), 4–5.

37. Howard Brinton, *Creative Worship* (London: G. Allen & Unwin, 1931).

38. Howard Brinton, *The Nature of Quakerism* (Wallingford, PA: Pendle Hill, 1940); Howard Brinton, *Friends for 300 Years* (Wallingford, PA: Pendle Hill, 1952).

39. Henry Hodgkin and William C. Braithwaite, *The Message and Mission of Quakerism* (Philadelphia: John C. Winston, 1912).

40. Dave D'Albert, *A Lexicon of Spiritual Leaders in the IFOR Peace Movement*, Part I (2010), 18.

41. Schmidt, *Restless Souls*, 18–19.

42. The most detailed study of this period in American evangelical Quakerism can be found in Timothy J. Burdick's "Neo-Evangelical Identity Within American Religious Society of Friends (Quakers): Oregon Yearly Meeting, 1919–1947" (PhD diss., University of Birmingham, 2013).

CHAPTER 9

1. Philadelphia Yearly Meeting (Orthodox) Minutes, 1917, 9–10, 1–15, Earlham College Quaker Archives; Thomas C. Kennedy, *British Quakerism, 1860–1920: The Transformation of a Religious Community* (Oxford: Oxford University Press, 2001), 371.

2. Philadelphia Yearly Meeting (Orthodox) Minutes, 1918, 78, 80–81; Minutes of the War and Social Order Committee, Library of the Society of Friends (LSF), London, 39 (hereafter cited as Minutes, War and Social Order Committee).

3. Brian D. Phillips, "Friendly Patriotism: British Quakerism and the Imperial Nation, 1890–1910" (PhD diss., University of Cambridge, 1989); Kennedy, *British Quakerism*.

4. Elizabeth Isichei, *Victorian Quakers* (Oxford: Oxford University Press, 1970), 144–47, 3–4.

5. Edwin B. Bronner, "John Bright and the Factory Acts," *Bulletin of Friends Historical Association* 38, no. 2 (1949): 96.

6. Maurice H. Bailey, "The Contribution of Quakers to Some Aspects of Local Government in Birmingham, 1828 to 1902" (MA thesis, University of Birmingham, 1952); Isichei, *Victorian Quakers*, 197; Phillips, "Friendly Patriotism," 20–21.

7. Richard Turnbull, "Quakers, Free Trade and Social Responsibility," in

Quakers, Business and Corporate Responsibility, ed. Nicholas Burton and Richard Turnbull (Cham, Switzerland: Springer, 2019), 105; Isichei, *Victorian Quakers*, 213; Andy Vail, "Protestant Nonconformists: Providers of Educational and Social Services," in *Alternatives to State-Socialism in Britain*, ed. Peter Ackers and Alastair J. Reid (Cham, Switzerland: Palgrave Macmillan, 2016), 133–34.

8. Edward H. Milligan, *Biographical Dictionary of British Quakers in Commerce and Industry, 1775–1920* (York, UK: William Sessions, 2007), 378.

9. Kennedy, *British Quakerism*, 40.

10. Pink Dandelion, *An Introduction to Quakerism* (Cambridge: Cambridge University Press, 2007), 11; Kennedy, *British Quakerism*, 42, 43.

11. F. D. Maurice, J. P. Nichol, and E. S. Pryce, "Preface," in John Stephenson Rowntree, *Quakerism Past and Present* (London: Smith, Elder, 1859), vi.

12. Phillips, "Friendly Patriotism," 21; Philip Ashton, "Divided Ideals: The Religious Society of Friends and the Irish Home Rule Controversy, 1885 to 1886," *Woodbrooke Journal* 6 (Summer 2000).

13. M. W. Kirby, "The Failure of a Quaker Business Dynasty: The Peases of Darlington, 1830–1902," in *Business and Religion in Britain*, ed. D. Jeremy (Aldershot, UK: Gower, 1988), 142. See also M. W. Kirby, *Men of Business and Politics: The Rise and Fall of the Quaker Pease Dynasty of North-East England, 1700–1943* (London: George Allen & Unwin, 1984).

14. Kennedy, *British Quakerism*, 153, 156.

15. Ibid., 280; Friends Social Union Annual Reports, Library of the Society of Friends (LSF); Friends Social Union Annual Reports, Members of Committee for 1909, LSF; Kennedy, *British Quakerism*, 281.

16. Ian Packer, "Religion and the New Liberalism: The Rowntree Family, Quakerism, and Social Reform," *Journal of British Studies* 42, no. 2 (2003): 247–48.

17. Phillips, "Friendly Patriotism," 35; Packer, "Religion and the New Liberalism," 250.

18. Richard E. Threlfall, *100 Years of Phosphorus Making: 1851–1951* (Oldbury, UK: Albright and Wilson, 1951), 84; *Debretts House of Commons and Judicial Bench* (London: Dean, 1901), 161; *London Gazette*, July 7, 1911, 5025.

19. Phillips, "Friendly Patriotism," 48, 69–70.

20. Kennedy, *British Quakerism*, 312; Nigel Keohane, *The Party of Patriotism: The Conservative Party and the First World War* (Farnham, UK: Ashgate, 2010), 202; Pam Lunn, "'You Have Lost Your Opportunity': British Quakers and the Militant Phase of the Women's Suffrage Campaign, 1906–1914," *Quaker Studies* 2, no. 1 (1997): Article 2.

21. See, for example, letters in *The Friend* of August 14, 1914 (William E. Wilson) and September 4, 1914 (John Moyle), as well as the activities of the SQS; Kennedy, *British Quakerism*, 4, 314.

22. Henry Mennell, letter in *The Friend*, August 28, 1914, 640.

23. Kennedy, *British Quakerism*, 371; Minutes, War and Social Order Committee, meeting of June 16, 1915.

24. Phillips, "Friendly Patriotism"; Minutes, War and Social Order Committee, 39; Kennedy, *British Quakerism*, 360; Minutes, War and Social Order Committee, 62–63.

25. Kennedy, *British Quakerism*, 329.

26. John Kimberley, "Employee Relations and the Quaker Employers Conference of 1918: The Cadbury Company," *Quaker Studies* 24, no. 2 (2019): 231–32; Reimagining a True Social Order research project, accessed January 24, 2020, https://quakersocialorder.org.uk/home/basics; *Quakerism and Industry: Being the Full Record of a Conference of Employers, Chiefly Members of the Society of Friends* (Birmingham, UK, 1918), 15.

27. Kimberley, "Employee Relations," 235–40; *Quakerism and Industry*, 18.

28. Reimagining a True Social Order project; Pamela Manasseh, "Quaker Relief Work and the Brynmawr Experiment," *Woodbrooke Journal* 7 (Winter 2000).

29. Quoted in J. Henry Bartlett, "Our Institutional Absorptions," Philadelphia *Friend*, 11th Mo. 27, 1930, 253.

30. Quoted in "How Shall We Organize?," reprinted in *Liberator*, May 15, 1842, 73; T. T., "Grave Stones," *Friends' Intelligencer*, 3rd Mo. 22, 1851, 409; "House Servants' Wages," *Friends' Intelligencer*, 11th Mo. 6, 1886, 717–18; Robert W. Doherty, *The Hicksite Separation: A Sociological Analysis of Religious Schism in Early Nineteenth Century America* (New Brunswick, NJ: Rutgers University Press, 1967), 43–44, 56–59; Philip S. Benjamin, *The Philadelphia Quakers in the Industrial Age, 1865–1920* (Philadelphia: Temple University Press, 1976), 49–72, 10; Robert H. Maris, letter, Philadelphia *Friend*, 8th Mo. 21, 1924, 91.

31. Martha Paxson Grundy, *The Evolution of a Quaker Community: Middletown Meeting, Bucks County, Pennsylvania, 1750–1850* (Lewiston, NY: Edwin Mellen, 2006), 209–16; James M. DeGarmo, *The Hicksite Quakers and Their Doctrines* (New York: Christian Literature, 1897), 28; "Hens to the Rescue in North Carolina," *American Friend*, March 3, 1932, 164; Marjorie Hill Allee, "An Orthodox-Hicksite Contact," *The Quaker*, 5th Mo. 28, 1920, 30; John Oliver, "J. Walter Malone: *The American Friend* and an Evangelical Quaker's Social Agenda," *Quaker History* 80 (Fall 1991): 70–71. New Castle records are in the Friends Collection, Earlham College, Richmond, IN. Des Moines Monthly Meeting records are on microfilm there. High Point Monthly Meeting records are in the Quaker Archives, Guilford College, Greensboro, NC.

32. Frederick Hoover Reminiscences, typescript (Friends Collection), 8–9; *History of Rush County, Indiana* (Chicago: Brant and Fuller, 1888), 535; J. E. R., "Is It So?," *Friends' Review*, 9th Mo. 8, 1877, 49–50.

33. Alan Dawley, *Class and Community: The Industrial Revolution in Lynn* (Cambridge, MA: Harvard University Press, 1976), 21, 27–28; W. Ross Yates, *Joseph Wharton: Quaker Industrial Pioneer* (Bethlehem, PA: Lehigh University Press, 1987), 271; Damon D. Hickey, *Sojourners No More: The Quakers in the New South* (Greensboro: North Carolina Friends Historical Society, 1997); "Death of a Noted Manufacturer" (n.d.), clipping, Box 3, Bird-Bancroft Collection (Delaware Historical Society, Wilmington, DE); Elizabeth Warren, *Jonathan Wright Plummer: Quaker Philanthropy* (Bloomington, IN: AuthorHouse, 2006), 30–31.

34. Gideon Frost, "The Kansas Famine," *Friends' Intelligencer*, 1st Mo. 26, 1861, 729.

35. Editorial, Philadelphia *Friend*, 1st Mo. 9, 1847, 128; W. L. K., *A Memoir of Samuel Willets, 1795–1883* (n.p., n.d.), 10. For philanthropy generally, see Mark Freeman, "Quakers, Business, and Philanthropy," in *The Oxford Handbook of Quaker Studies*, ed. Stephen W. Angell and Pink Dandelion (Oxford: Oxford University Press, 2013), 420–33; and Benjamin, *Philadelphia Quakers*, 100–125.

36. "Winter Charities," *Friends' Intelligencer*, 1st Mo. 18, 1861, 712; A. B. C., "Ye Have the Poor Always with You," Philadelphia *Friend*, 3rd Mo. 11, 1848, 197; "The Shelter," Philadelphia *Friend*, 2nd Mo. 29, 1848, 174. See also Bruce Dorsey, *Reforming Men and Women: Gender in the Antebellum City* (Ithaca, NY: Cornell University Press, 2002), 50–89.

37. "Sermon by Elias Hicks," *Quaker* 3 (July 1828): 148–50.

38. "For 'The Friend,'" Philadelphia *Friend*, 3rd Mo. 15, 1834, 184; O. D., "For 'The Friend,'" Philadelphia *Friend*, 12th Mo. 14, 1833, 75; John Jackson, *Considerations on the Impropriety of Friends Participating in the Administration of Political Governments* (Philadelphia: J. Richards, 1840). For examples of Quaker calls for racial justice, see "Black Laws in Ohio," Philadelphia

Friend, 3rd Mo. 18, 1848, 203; "The White Peril," Philadelphia *Friend*, 1st Mo. 19, 1901, 209; and Lloyd Balderston, "Thoughts on Fair Play," Philadelphia *Friend*, 12th Mo. 6, 1928, 165–66. For Native Americans, see Editorial, Philadelphia *Friend*, 5th Mo. 3, 1834, 236; and Gideon Frost, "The Indians," *Friends' Intelligencer*, 8th Mo. 12, 1876, 388–89. For qualifications of these commitments, see Donna McDaniel and Vanessa Julye, *Fit for Freedom, Not for Friendship: Quakers, African Americans, and the Myth of Racial Justice* (Philadelphia: Quaker Press of Friends General Conference, 2009), 216–19, 319–59; and Jennifer Graber, *The Gods of Indian Country: Religion and the Struggle for the American West* (New York: Oxford University Press, 2018), 103–9.

39. "Intemperance," *Journal*, 11th Mo. 13, 1878, 339; Editorial, Philadelphia *Friend*, 8th Mo. 10, 1833, 351–52; "Temperance," Philadelphia *Friend*, 8th Mo. 7, 1924, 66; "Passages from Correspondence," *Friends' Review*, 3rd Mo. 30, 1867, 491; Walter C. Woodward, "The Ballyhoo for Booze," *American Friend*, March 31, 1932, 228.

40. Thomas White Pryor Journal, 10th Mo. 31, 1819, 82 (Friends Historical Library, Swarthmore College); Thomas D. Hamm, "The Radical Hicksite Critique of the Emerging Capitalist Order: Cornelius C. Blatchly, Benjamin Webb, and Friends, 1827–1833," in *Quakers, Politics, and Economics*, ed. David R. Ross and Michael T. Snarr (Philadelphia: Friends Association for Higher Education, 2018), 214–34; Thomas D. Hamm, *God's Government Begun: The Society for Universal Inquiry and Reform, 1842–1846* (Bloomington: Indiana University Press, 1995).

41. Editorial, *Friends' Review*, 7th Mo. 21, 1892, 825; *Friends' Review*, 2nd Mo. 2, 1888, 424; *Friends' Review*, 10th Mo. 6, 1883, 136–37; "Before Election," *Journal*, 10th Mo. 31, 1877, 324; *Philadelphia Yearly Meeting Minutes (Hicksite)*, 1882, 51–52.

42. "Friendly News Notes," Philadelphia *Friend*, 9th Mo. 4, 1924, 118.

43. Elbert Russell, "The Burden of the Child," *American Friend*, 8th Mo. 29, 1912, 554–55; Paul Moke, "Quakers in the Coalfields: Economic Justice and the American Friends Service Committee, 1920–Present," in Ross and Snarr, *Quakers, Politics, and Economics*, 120–43.

44. "The Open Forum," *Friends' Intelligencer*, 3rd Mo. 4, 1933, 176; Clarence E. Pickett, "Symbol in Religion," Philadelphia *Friend*, 7th Mo. 24, 1930, 38–39.

45. "Our Open Forum," *Friends' Intelligencer*, 1st Mo. 7, 1933, 4; "Are We Still Pioneers?," *American Friend*, August 18, 1932, 592; Alvin T. Coate, "Some Reflections," *American Friend*, January 21, 1932, 51; "Consideration of Report Brings Varied Opinions," *Richmond Palladium*, October 25, 1935, 1, 10.

46. Thomas D. Hamm, *The Transformation of American Quakerism: Orthodox Friends, 1800–1907* (Bloomington: Indiana University Press, 1988), 163; Claude A. Roane, "Challenge of the Present World," *Evangelical Friend* 5 (January 1933): 5; Timothy John Burdick, "Neo-Evangelical Identity Within American Religious Society of Friends (Quakers): Oregon Yearly Meeting, 1919–1947" (PhD diss., University of Birmingham, 2013).

CHAPTER 10

1. Margery Post Abbott, "Global Quakerism and the Future of Friends," in *The Oxford Handbook of Quaker Studies*, ed. Stephen W. Angell and Pink Dandelion (Oxford, UK: Oxford University Press, 2013), 550; Hugh Barbour and J. William Frost, *The Quakers*, 2nd ed. (Richmond, IN: Friends United Press, 1994), 234–35.

2. Ane Marie Bak Rasmussen, *A History of the Quaker Movement in Africa* (New York: I. B. Tauris, 1995), 19; Henry T. Hodgkin, *Friends Beyond Seas* (London: Headley Brothers, 1916), 31–32.

3. Ron Stansell, *Missions by the Spirit: Learning from Quaker Exemplars* (Newberg,

OR: Barclay Press, 2009), 109–12, 209; Nancy J. Thomas, *A Long Walk, a Gradual Ascent: The Story of the Bolivian Friends Church in Its Context of Conflict* (Eugene, OR: Wipf and Stock, 2019), 23–33; Ramon Longoria and Nancy Thomas, "Latin American Quakerism," in *The Cambridge Companion to Quakerism*, ed. Stephen W. Angell and Pink Dandelion (Cambridge: Cambridge University Press, 2018), 185, 188.

4. Stephen W. Angell, "Joseph and Sarah Cosand and the Formation of the Friends' Mission in Japan, 1885–1901" (Earlham School of Religion Dean's Lecture: unpublished paper, 2002); Stephen W. Angell, "Bunji and Toshi Kida and Friends' Missions to the Japanese in California," *Quaker History* 95, no. 1 (2006): 1–25; John Ormerod Greenwood, *Quaker Encounters*, vol. 2, *Vines on the Mountains* (York, UK: William Sessions, 1977), 222; Elizabeth Gray Vining, *Windows for the Crown Prince* (Tokyo: Kenkyusha, 1955).

5. Rasmussen, *History of the Quaker Movement in Africa*, 64, 159; Esther Moraa Mombo, "A Historical and Cultural Analysis of the Position of Abaluyia Women in Kenyan Quaker Christianity: 1902–1979" (PhD diss., University of Edinburgh, 1998), 179–81; Stansell, *Missions by the Spirit*, 17–41.

6. Rasmussen, *History of the Quaker Movement in Africa*, 44–45, 55; Levinus Painter, *The Hill of Vision* (Nairobi, Kenya: East Africa Yearly Meeting, 1966), 21–32, 142–45; Esther Mombo, "Haramisi and Jumaa: The Story of Women's Meetings in East Africa Yearly Meeting, 1902–1979," *Woodbrooke Journal* 5 (1999): 5–6; Mombo, "Abaluyia Women in Kenyan Quaker Christianity," 270–71; Stephen W. Angell, "Quaker Women in Kenya and Human Rights Issues," in *Freedom's Distant Shores: American Protestants and Post-Colonial Alliances with Africa*, ed. R. Drew Smith (Waco, TX: Baylor University Press, 2006), 119–20; Elisabeth McMahon, "A 'Spiritual Pilgrim': The Life of Rasoah Mutuha, an East African Quaker," *Quaker History* 95, no. 1 (2006): 44–56; Samuel S. Thomas, "Gender and Religion on the Mission Station: Roxie Reeve and the Friends' African Mission," *Quaker History* 88, no. 2 (1999): 24–46.

7. Hodgkin, *Friends Beyond Seas*, 47–50; Marjorie Sykes, *An Indian Tapestry: Quaker Threads in the History of India, Pakistan, and Bangladesh* (York, UK: William Sessions, 1997), 42–45; John Ormerod Greenwood, *Quaker Encounters*, vol. 3, *Whispers of Truth* (York, UK: William Sessions, 1978), 10–14.

8. Sykes, *Indian Tapestry*, 108–10, 150–51; Greenwood, *Whispers of Truth*, 12 (quotation, 14); Hodgkin, *Friends Beyond Seas*, 57–59, 67–72; Sykes, *Indian Tapestry*, 55–73; Stephanie Midori Komashin, "Quakers in Asia-Pacific," in Angell and Dandelion, *Cambridge Companion to Quakerism*, 244–45; Jacalynn Stuckey Welling, "Mission," in Angell and Dandelion, *Oxford Handbook of Quaker Studies*, 312. The Calcutta Meeting developed a distinctive type of Hindu Quakerism. Contact with British missionaries would be rare.

9. Sykes, *Indian Tapestry*, 112–14; Margery Post Abbott et al., *Historical Dictionary of the Friends (Quakers)* (Lanham, MD: Scarecrow Press, 2003), 269–70; Komashin, "Quakers in Asia-Pacific," 246; E. Anna Nixon, *A Century of Planting: A History of the American Friends Mission in India* (Canton, OH: Evangelical Friends Church Eastern Region, 1985), 7–52.

10. Carole D. Spencer, "Evangelism, Feminism, and Social Reform: The Quaker Woman Minister and the Holiness Revival," *Quaker History* 80, no. 1 (1991): 25.

11. Hodgkin, *Friends Beyond Seas*, 80–83, 107; Christina H. Jones, *American Friends in World Missions* (Elgin, IL: Brethren Publishing House, 1946), 72, 125, 192–93; Rufus M. Jones, *Eli and Sybil Jones: Their*

Life and Work (Philadelphia: Porter and Coates, 1889), 193–95.

12. Thomas, "Gender and Religion," 24–40 (quotation, 26); Stansell, *Missions by the Spirit*, 85–133; Mombo, "Abaluyia Women in Kenyan Quaker Christianity," 153, 167–68; Charles E. DeVol, *Fruit That Remains: The Story of the Friends Mission in China and Taiwan* (Canton, OH: Evangelical Friends Church Eastern Region, 1988), 5–9; Nixon, *Century of Planting*, 9–21, 86–88; Jones, *American Friends in World Missions*, 50, 173; Thomas, "Gender and Religion," 37.

13. Hodgkin, *Friends Beyond Seas*, 230; Mombo, "Abaluyia Women in Kenyan Quaker Christianity," 39, 133–34, 142.

14. Hodgkin, *Friends Beyond Seas*, 60; Angell, "Joseph and Sarah Ann Cosand."

15. Sykes, *Indian Tapestry*, 40–42, 81–82, 87–88, 107, 123; Komashin, "Quakers in Asia-Pacific," 244.

16. Letter from Inazo Nitobe to Margaret Haines, February 8, 1886, Women's Foreign Missionary Association Papers, Haverford College Quaker Archives, Haverford, PA; Angell, "Joseph and Sarah Ann Cosand."

17. Gurney Binford, *As I Remember It: 43 Years in Japan* (n.p., 1950), 42–47; Otis Cary, *A History of Christianity in Japan: Protestant Missions* (New York: Fleming H. Revell, 1909), 249–52; *Friends Missionary Advocate*, November 1894; *Friends Missionary Advocate*, August 1895.

18. Hodgkin, *Friends Beyond Seas*, 113, 120, 142; Charles Tyzack, *Friends to China: The Davidson Brothers and the Friends' Mission to China, 1886–1939* (York, UK: William Sessions, 1988), 1–3; Charlotte Dando, "Pemba, Plantations, Power: A Critical Evaluation of Britain Yearly Meeting's First African Mission," *Quaker Studies* 19, no. 1 (2014): 159–60; Greenwood, *Whispers of Truth*, 180.

19. Longoria and Thomas, "Latin American Quakerism," 189.

20. Welling, "Mission," 306–8; Hodgkin, *Friends Beyond Seas*, 14–19 (quotation, 15); Jones, *American Friends in World Missions*, 11–20; DeVol, *Fruit That Remains*, 2; Walter R. Williams, *These Fifty Years with Ohio Friends in China* (Damascus, OH: Friends Foreign Missionary Society of Ohio Yearly Meeting, 1940), 32.

21. Hodgkin, *Friends Beyond Seas*, 216, 224.

22. *Extracts from the Minutes and Proceedings of the Yearly Meeting of Friends held in London* (1858), 16–18, quoted in Hodgkin, *Friends Beyond Seas*, 38 (emphasis in original).

23. Bonar A. Gow, "The Quaker Contribution to Education in Madagascar, 1867–1895," *Quaker History* 66, no. 2 (1977): 87–97; Edward H. Milligan, *The Past Is Prologue: 100 Years of Quaker Overseas Work, 1868–1968* (London: Friends Service Council, 1968), 54.

24. Tyzack, *Friends to China*, 47–48, 93; H. G. Wood, *Henry T. Hodgkin: A Memoir* (London: Student Christian Movement Press, 1937).

25. Stansell, *Missions by the Spirit*, 5; Welling, "Mission," 311–12; Hodgkin, *Friends Beyond Seas*, 118.

26. H. S. Newman (1898), quoted in Dando, "Pemba, Plantations, Power," 160–61, 165 (emphasis in original).

27. Jones, *American Friends in World Missions*, 162–65; Longoria and Thomas, "Latin American Quakerism," 179–80; Hiram H. Hilty, *Friends in Cuba* (Richmond, IN: Friends United Press, 1977), 1–38, 47–69.

28. Stephen W. Angell, "Interaction of Mission-Oriented Quakers with Buddhists," *Quaker History* 93, no. 2 (2004): 16; Gow, "Quaker Contribution to Education," 96.

29. Hodgkin, *Friends Beyond Seas*, 166; Walter R. Williams, *Ohio Friends in the Land of Sinim* (Mt. Gilead, OH: Friends Foreign Missionary Board of Ohio Yearly Meeting, 1925), 33, 71–72; Tyzack, *Friends to China*, 41–46, 50–51 (quotation, 45); Gow, "Quaker Contribution to Education," 96.

30. Tyzack, *Friends to China*, 115; Sykes, *Indian Tapestry*, 63; Nixon, *Century of Planting*, 62–63; Angell, "Interactions of Mission-Oriented Quakers," 17.

31. Stanley Chagala Ngesa, "Maragoli Tradition Absorbs Quaker Christianity" (MA thesis, Earlham School of Religion, 2020), 4–6.

32. Angell, "Interactions of Mission-Oriented Quakers," 4–5; Tyzack, *Friends to China*, 19.

33. *Friends Missionary Advocate*, January 1924, 23, quoted in Angell, "Interactions of Mission-Oriented Quakers," 12–13.

34. Ngesa, "Maragoli Tradition Absorbs Quaker Christianity," 1, 7–8, 37. On the importance of *mulembe* for the Luhya, see also Benson Khamasi Amugamwa, "Quakerism and the Isukha Culture: The Impact of Quakerism on the Culture of the Isukha People of Western Kenya" (MA thesis, Earlham School of Religion, 2008), 10–11.

35. Milligan, *Past Is Prologue*, 21.

36. Barbour and Frost, *Quakers*, 224, 239–40; Gregory P. Hinshaw, "Five Years Meeting and Friends United Meeting, 1887–2010," in Angell and Dandelion, *Oxford Handbook of Quaker Studies*, 95, 98–99.

37. Angell, "Interactions of Mission-Oriented Quakers," 19–20.

38. Williams, *Ohio Friends*, 181; William R. Hutchison, *Errand to the World: American Protestant Thought and Foreign Missions* (Chicago: University of Chicago Press, 1987), 148–58.

39. Lalsangkima Pachuau, "A Clash of Mass Movements? Christian Missions and the Gandhian Nationalist Movement in India," *Transformation* 31, no. 3 (2014): 161, 163, 168.

40. The Commission of Appraisal, *Re-thinking Missions: A Laymen's Inquiry After One Hundred Years* (New York: Harper, 1932), 37, quoted in Stephen W. Angell, "Rufus Jones and the Laymen's Foreign Mission Inquiry: How a Quaker Helped to Shape Modern Ecumenism," *Quaker Theology* 2, no. 2 (2000): 170, 183–85.

41. Angell, "Rufus Jones and the Laymen's Foreign Missions Inquiry," 186–91; Robert J. Davidson, *The Christian Approach to Other Religions* (London: Friends Service Council, 1933), 5.

42. Stansell, *Missions by the Spirit*, 60–62; Rasmussen, *History of the Quaker Movement in Africa*, 58–61.

43. Stansell, *Missions by the Spirit*, 63, 65–67; Rasmussen, *History of the Quaker Movement in Africa*, 62–66.

44. Jonathan Mulobi's testimony collected by Benson Khamasi Amugamwa, "Quakerism and the Isukha Culture," 14–15; Mombo, "Abaluyia Women in Kenyan Quaker Christianity," 112. On Chilson, see Stansell, *Missions by the Spirit*, 76. On Quaker missionary attitudes in Pemba toward corporal punishment, see Greenwood, *Vines on the Mountains*, 279.

45. Rasmussen, *History of the Quaker Movement in Africa*, 67; Mombo, "Abaluyia Women in Kenyan Quaker Christianity," 113–14; Jones, *American Friends in World Missions*, 273, 277, 282; Painter, *Hill of Vision*, 75, 77, 91, 94, 143.

46. Jones, *American Friends in World Missions*, 259; Painter, *Hill of Vision*, 136.

CHAPTER II

1. "A Declaration from the Harmless and Innocent people of God, called Quakers . . . ," in *Quaker Writings: An Anthology, 1650–1920*, ed. Thomas D. Hamm (New York: Penguin, 2010), 322; "AFSC and the Nobel Peace Prize," American Friends Service Committee website, accessed September 15, 2019, https://www.afsc.org/nobel-peace-prize. For a sense of the historiography of Quakers, pacifism, and what is now called the peace testimony, see James F. Maclear, "Quakerism and the End of the Interregnum," *Church History* 19, no. 4 (1950):

240–70; Peter Brock, *Pacifism in Europe to 1914* (Princeton, NJ: Princeton University Press, 1972), 255–303; Hugh Barbour, "The Lamb's War and the Origins of the Quaker Peace Testimony," in *The Pacifist Impulse in Historical Perspective*, ed. Harvey L. Dyck and Peter Brock (Toronto: University of Toronto Press, 1996), 145–58; and Lonnie Valentine, "Quakers, War, and Peacemaking," in *The Oxford Handbook of Quaker Studies*, ed. Stephen W. Angell and Pink Dandelion (Oxford: Oxford University Press, 2013), 363–76.

2. For enlistment numbers, see Margaret E. Hirst, *Quakers in Peace and War: An Account of Their Peace Principles and Practice* (London: Swarthmore Press, 1923), 372; Thomas D. Hamm et al., "The Decline of Quaker Pacifism in the Twentieth Century: Indiana Yearly Meeting of Friends as a Case Study," *Indiana Magazine of History* 96, no. 3 (2000): 54; Andrew Thompson Miller, "A Quaker Community in Times of War: Friends in Salem, New Jersey," *New Jersey Folklife* 15 (1990): 37–49; Peter Brock, *Pioneers of a Peaceable Kingdom: The Quaker Peace Testimony from the Colonial Era to the First World War* (Princeton, NJ: Princeton University Press, 1968), 354; Elaine Bishop and Jiseok Jung, "Seeking Peace: Quakers Respond to War," in *The Cambridge Companion to Quakerism*, ed. Stephen W. Angell and Pink Dandelion (Cambridge: Cambridge University Press, 2018), 106–27.

3. Brock, *Pioneers of a Peaceable Kingdom*, 350; Cecil B. Currey, "The Devolution of Quaker Pacifism: A Kansas Case Study, 1860–1955," *Kansas History* 6 (1983): 120–33; Hamm et al., "Decline"; J. William Frost, "Modernist and Liberal Quakers, 1887–2010," in Angell and Dandelion, *Oxford Handbook of Quaker Studies*, 78–83; Gregory P. Hinshaw, "Five Years Meeting and Friends United Meeting, 1887–2010," in Angell and Dandelion, *Oxford Handbook of Quaker Studies*, 96–98; Thomas D. Hamm, *Liberal Quakerism in America in the Long Nineteenth Century, 1790–1920* (Leiden: Brill, 2020); Christopher Densmore and Thomas Bassett, "Quakers, Slavery, and the Civil War," in *Quaker Crosscurrents: Three Hundred Years of Friends in the New York Yearly Meetings*, ed. Hugh Barbour et al. (Syracuse, NY: Syracuse University Press, 1995), 190–94; Thomas D. Hamm, "Hicksite, Orthodox, and Evangelical Quakerism, 1805–1887," in Angell and Dandelion, *Oxford Handbook of Quaker Studies*, 71–73; Miller, "A Quaker Community," 41; Thomas C. Kennedy, "Quaker Women and the Pacifist Impulse in Britain, 1900–1920," in Dyck and Brock, *Pacifist Impulse in Historical Perspective*, 182–206; Cyrus G. Pringle, *The Record of a Quaker Conscience* (New York: Macmillan, 1918); Peter Brock, ed., *Liberty and Conscience: A Documentary History of the Experiences of Conscientious Objectors in America Through the Civil War* (Oxford: Oxford University Press, 2002). Cecil Currey, in "Devolution," shows that in the relatively small Kansas Preparative Meeting, there was almost no participation in the Civil War (120). Andrew Miller, in "A Quaker Community," notes a similar response in Salem Monthly Meeting, although a number of members did pay for military substitutes, which itself was at odds with the peace testimony (41).

4. Jonathan A. Grant, *Rulers, Guns, and Money: The Global Arms Trade in the Age of Imperialism* (Cambridge, MA: Harvard University Press, 2007); Carl Cavanagh Hodge, *Encyclopedia of the Age of Imperialism, 1800–1914* (Westport, CT: Greenwood Press, 2008); Harry Magdoff, *The Age of Imperialism: The Economics of U.S. Foreign Policy* (New York: Monthly Review Press, 1969); Karen R. Jones, Giacomo Macola, and David Welch, eds., *A Cultural History of Firearms in the Age of Empire* (New York: Routledge, 2016).

5. Jacalynn Stuckey Welling, "Mission," in Angell and Dandelion, *Oxford Handbook of Quaker Studies*, 312; Martin Ceadal, "The Quaker Peace Testimony and Its Contribution to the British Peace Movement: An Overview," *Quaker Studies* 7, no. 1 (2002): 16–18; Margaret McKechnie Glover, "Aspects of Publishing by the Peace Committee of the Religious Society of Friends (London Yearly Meeting), 1888–1905," *Quaker Studies* 3, no. 1 (1998): 27–51; Ceadal, "Quaker Peace Testimony," 11, 19–21. In Ceadal's usage, "pacifists" are those who reject all armed conflict. Those who are "pacificist" are willing to use military force to bring about the reforms necessary to abolish war. Thomas C. Kennedy, *British Quakerism, 1860–1920: The Transformation of a Religious Community* (Oxford: Oxford University Press, 2001), 247; Thomas C. Kennedy, "History and the Quaker Renaissance: The Vision of John Wilhelm Rowntree," *Journal of the Friends Historical Society* 55, nos. 1–2 (1986): 35–56.

6. Hugh Barbour et al., "Quaker Service and Peacemaking, 1900–1948," in Barbour et al., *Quaker Crosscurrents*, 241–44; *The American Friends' Peace Conference Held at Philadelphia, Twelfth Month 12th, 13th, and 14th, 1901* (Philadelphia: Published by the Conference, 1902), 4; Brock, *Pioneers of a Peaceable Kingdom*, 358; "Declaration of the American Friends' Peace Conference," in *American Friends' Peace Conference*, 208, 209; *American Friends' Peace Conference*, 232. Sharpless was president of Haverford College from 1887 to 1916.

7. Ceadal, "Quaker Peace Testimony," 14–17; Thomas C. Kennedy, "Early Friends and the Renewal of British Quakerism," *Quaker History* 93, no. 1 (2004): 88–89; Thomas C. Kennedy, "A Body Divided: British Quakers, Patriotism and War, 1899–1919," *Quaker Studies* 21, no. 2 (2016): 160; Richard A. Rempel, "British Quakers and the South African War," *Quaker History* 64, no. 2 (1975): 78, 93; first quote from Kennedy, "Body Divided," 160; Hope Hay Hewison, *Hedge of Wild Almonds: South Africa, the "Pro-Boers" and the Quaker Conscience, 1890–1910* (Portsmouth, NH: Heinemann, 1989), 129; Kennedy, "Quaker Women," 186–87.

8. Valentine, "Quakers, War, and Peacemaking," 372; *Christianity and War: An Address by the Religious Society of Friends* (London: West, Newman, 1900), 3, 9, 12. Two hundred thousand copies of the tract were printed and distributed globally. Rempel, "British Quakers and the South African War," 87–88; Brian D. Phillips, "Friendly Patriotism: British Quakerism and the Imperial Nation, 1890–1910" (PhD diss., University of Cambridge, 1989), https://www.repository.cam.ac.uk/handle/1810/272201; Hewison, *Hedge of Wild Almonds*, 139–43.

9. Kennedy, "Quaker Women," 188–90; Heloise Brown, *"The Truest Form of Patriotism": Pacifist Feminism in Britain, 1870–1902* (Manchester, UK: Manchester University Press, 2003), 99–111.

10. Hewison, *Hedge of Wild Almonds*, 145–46; Rempel, "British Quakers and the South African War," 90; London Yearly Meeting, "A Plea for a Peaceable Spirit: Addressed by the Yearly Meeting of the Religious Society of Friends, Held in London, Fifth Month 1901, to Its Members and to the Christian Churches," in *The Diaries of Edward Pease: The Father of English Railways*, ed. Alfred Edward Pease (1907; repr., Cambridge: Cambridge University Press, 2013), 351–53.

11. For an examination of the historiography of Canadian Quakers and the South African War, see Robynne Rogers Healey, "Canadian Quakers and the South African War," in *Empire from the Margins: Religious Minorities in Canada and the South African War, 1899–1902*, ed. Gordon L. Heath (Eugene, OR: Pickwick, 2017), 120–34. Quote from Arthur G. Dorland, *The Quakers in Canada: A History* (1927; repr., Toronto: Ryerson, 1968), 327. Thomas P.

Socknat, *Witness Against War: Pacifism in Canada, 1900–1945* (Toronto: University of Toronto Press, 1987), 21.

12. Kennedy, "Early Friends," 89; Rempel, "British Quakers and the South African War," 92–93; David Saunders, "Challenge, Decline and Revival: The Fortunes of Pacifism in Nineteenth- and Early Twentieth-Century Newcastle," *Northern History* 54, no. 2 (2017): 238–39; Joanna Dales, *The Quaker Renaissance and Liberal Quakerism in Britain, 1895–1930: Seeking a Real Religion* (Leiden: Brill, 2020).

13. Kennedy, *British Quakerism*, 285–311; Max L. Carter and Simon Best, "Quakers, Youth, and Young Adults," in Angell and Dandelion, *Oxford Handbook of Quaker Studies*, 464; *Swanwick 1911, Being a Report on a Conference of Young Friends . . .* [1911], quoted in Kennedy, "Early Friends," 89. The speaker was Geoffrey Hoyland.

14. Ceadal, "Quaker Peace Testimony," 23; Rebecca Wynter, "Conscription, Conscience, and Controversy: The Friends' Ambulance Unit and the 'Middle Course' in the First World War," *Quaker Studies* 21, no. 2 (2016): 221–31; Joanna Dales, "John William Graham and the Evolution of Peace: A Quaker View of Conflict Before and During the First World War," *Quaker Studies* 21, no. 2 (2016): 169–92; Brock, *Pacifism in Europe to 1914*, 475; Gijsbert Gerrit Jacob den Boggende, "The Fellowship of Reconciliation, 1914–1945" (PhD diss., McMaster University, 1986); Paul R. Dekar, *Creating the Beloved Community: A Journey with the Fellowship of Reconciliation* (Telford, PA: Cascadia, 2005).

15. Sefton-Jones quoted in Martin Ceadal, *Semi-detached Idealists: The Peace Movement and International Relations, 1854–1945* (Oxford: Oxford University Press, 2000), 193; Albert Wilson, *The Friend*, February 5, 1915, 109; Owain Gethin Evans, "Quakers in Wales and the First World War," *Quaker Studies* 21, no. 2 (2016): 205; Ceadal, "Quaker Peace Testimony," 23.

16. Thomas C. Kennedy, "Fighting About Peace: The No-Conscription Fellowship and the British Friends' Service Committee, 1915–1919," *Quaker History* 69, no. 1 (1980): 7; Wynter, "Conscription, Conscience, and Controversy," 212–33; Bert den Boggende, "Reluctant Absolutist: Malcolm Sparkes' Conscientious Objections to World War One," *Quaker Studies* 10, no. 1 (2005): 67–86; Dales, "John William Graham," 191; Thomas C. Kennedy, "What Hath Manchester Wrought? Change in the Religious Society of Friends, 1895–1920," *Journal of the Friends Historical Society* 57, no. 3 (1996): 289–92; Kennedy, "Body Divided," 163–64.

17. Hilary Summy, *Peace Angel of World War I: Dissent of Margaret Thorp* (Brisbane: Australian Centre for Peace and Conflict Studies, 2006); "Margaret Thorp," School of Historical and Philosophical Inquiry, accessed August 19, 2020, https://hpi.uq.edu.au/margaret-thorp.

18. Amy J. Shaw, *Crisis of Conscience: Conscientious Objection in Canada During the First World War* (Vancouver: University of British Columbia Press, 2014), 43–54; Brian John Fell, "A Question of Conscience: British and Canadian Quakers and Their Socialist and Parliamentary Allies Face the Great War" (MA thesis, University of Manitoba, 1969); *Minutes of Canada Yearly Meeting, 1917* (Orthodox), 23–24, Canadian Yearly Meeting Archives.

19. Stanley Chagala Ngesa, "Quaker Christianity in Kenya," *Friends Journal*, October 1, 2019, https://www.friendsjournal.org/quaker-christianity-in-kenya; Christian Koller, "The Recruitment of Colonial Troops in Africa and Asia and Their Deployment in Europe During the First World War," *Immigrants and Minorities* 26, no. 1/2 (2008): 111–33; Joy Totah Hilden, *A Passion for Learning: The Life Journey of Khalil Totah, a Palestinian Quaker Educator and Activist* (Bloomington, IN: Xlibris, 2016), chapter 2, https://

books.google.ca/books/about/A_Passion_for_Learning.html.

20. Throughout the war, the FAU received £138,000 in voluntary donations, largely from Friends. Linda Palfreeman, "The Friends' Ambulance Unit in the First World War," *Religions* 9, no. 5 (2018): 171, 175, 177, http://dx.doi.org/10.3390/rel9050165.

21. Friends' Service Committee, "Minutes, Records of Work and Documents Issues," 1:7–8, Library of the Society of Friends; Wynter, "Conscription, Conscience, and Controversy," 217, 232, 219, 220–21.

22. Kennedy, "What Hath Manchester Wrought?," 291–94; Kennedy, "Quaker Women," 194–97.

23. Kennedy, "Fighting About Peace," 9; Kennedy, "Quaker Women," 196; Kennedy, "Body Divided," 163; Kennedy, "Early Friends"; Kennedy, *British Quakerism*, 322.

24. *Proceedings of Friends' General Conference, 1914* (Philadelphia: Supplement to the *Friends' Intelligencer*, 1914), 130; "The Peace Conference," *Friends' Intelligencer*, 8th Mo. 14, 1915, 522–23; *Proceedings of Friends' General Conference, 1916* (Philadelphia: Supplement to the *Friends' Intelligencer*, 1916), 80, 81.

25. *Minutes of the Five Years Meeting of the Friends in America, Held in Richmond, Indiana, Tenth Month 16th to Tenth Month 22nd (Inclusive), 1917* (Richmond, IN: Balinger, 1922), 188, 189.

26. Albert G. Thatcher, "The Quakers' Attitude Toward War," *Advocate of Peace* 79, no. 8 (1917): 238, 239.

27. Rufus M. Jones, *A Service of Love in Wartime: American Friends Relief Work in Europe, 1917–1919* (New York: Macmillan, 1920), 14; Currey, "Devolution," 123–26; Hamm et al., "Decline," 48–49; Andrew Thompson Miller, "A Quaker Community in Times of War: Friends in Salem, New Jersey," *New Jersey Folklife* 15 (1990): 37–49.

28. "The Society of Friends and the War," *Advocate of Peace* 80, no. 5 (1918): 145–46;

"Some Particular Advices for Friends and A Statement of Loyalty for Others," *Advocate of Peace* 80, no. 5 (1918): 146; Allan Kohrman, "Respectable Pacifists: Quaker Response to World War I," *Quaker History* 75, no. 1 (1986): 50–52; James Krippner and David Harrington Watt, "Henry Cadbury, the Peace Testimony, and the First World War," *Quaker Religious Thought* 133 (2019): 5–13.

29. Kohrman, "Respectable Pacifists," 41; J. William Frost, "'Our Deeds Carry Our Message': The Early History of the American Friends Service Committee," *Quaker History* 81, no. 1 (1992): 3–6; Selective Service Act of 1917, accessed January 22, 2021, https://www.govinfo.gov/app/details/USCODE-2011-title50/USCODE-2011-title50-app-selective/context.

30. Not all conscientious objectors were Quakers, and a reliable statistical compilation of conscripted Friends is not available. Hirst (*Quakers in Peace and War*, 519) reports that the United States government offered the AFSC two hundred conscientious objectors for reconstruction work in France. Ninety-nine of those were released from military camps; fifty-four of them were Quaker. Others were furloughed to farms. Of the 527 sentenced to prison, only thirteen were Quaker. Anne M. Yoder, in "World War I Conscientious Objection" (accessed December 15, 2019, https://www.swarthmore.edu/Library/peace/conscientiousobjection/WWI.COs.coverpage.htm), cites the following statistics: "One unofficial source states that 3,989 men declared themselves to be conscientious objectors when they had reached the camps: of these, 1,300 chose noncombatant service; 1,200 were given farm furloughs; 99 went to Europe to do reconstruction work for the American Friends Service Committee (AFSC); 450 were court-martialed and sent to prison; and 940 remained in camps until the Armistice was discharged."

31. "The Peace Conference," 521; Jones, *Service of Love in Wartime*, 13–14.

32. Sian Roberts, "A 'Position of Particular Responsibility': Quaker Women and Transnational Humanitarian Relief, 1914–1924," *Quaker Studies* 21, no. 2 (2016): 235–55; Frost, "Our Deeds," 27–29, 35–40, 47; Lyndon S. Back, "The Quaker Mission in Poland," *Quaker History* 101, no. 2 (2012): 1–23; Jones, *Service of Love*, 265.

33. John Mueller, "Changing Attitudes Towards War: The Impact of the First World War," *British Journal of Political Science* 21, no. 1 (1991): 12; Churchill's quote in Mueller, "Changing Attitudes Towards War," 17; Kennedy, *British Quakerism*, 405; *Conference of All Friends Held in London, August 12 to 20, 1920: Official Report* (London: Friends' Bookshop, 1920), 31. Hirst, who attended the conference and presented a paper on the historic peace testimony, cites over one thousand attendees (*Quakers in Peace and War*, 521). Kennedy cites 936 official delegates, of which 53 percent represented London Yearly Meeting and 36 percent represented North American meetings (*British Quakerism*, 406); William D. Witte, "American Quaker Pacifism and the Peace Settlement of World War I," *Bulletin of Friends Historical Association* 46, no. 2 (1957): 87–95; Maureen Waugh, "Quakers, Peace and the League of Nations: The Role of Bertram Pickard," *Quaker Studies* 6, no. 1 (2001): 62–64.

34. *Conference of All Friends*, 201; London Yearly Meeting, *Peace Testimony of the Society of Friends* (London: Peace Committee of the Society of Friends, 1920); Kennedy, "Quaker Women," 197–98; Roberts, "Position of Particular Responsibility."

CHAPTER 12

1. George Southcombe, "The Quakers and Politics, 1660–1689," in *The Quakers, 1656–1723: The Evolution of an Alternative Community*, ed. Richard C. Allen and Rosemary Moore (University Park: Penn State University Press, 2018), 112–14, 117–20; Robynne Rogers Healey, "Into the Eighteenth Century," in Allen and Moore, *Quakers, 1656–1723*, 184–85, 191–93; Richard C. Allen, "Beyond Britain: The Quakers in the European Continent and the Americas, 1666–1682," in Allen and Moore, *Quakers, 1656–1723*, 75–77; Richard C. Allen, "Quakers," in *The Oxford History of Protestant Dissenting Traditions*, vol. 2, *The Long Eighteenth Century c. 1689–c. 1828* (Oxford: Oxford University Press, 2018), 95–96; Melvin I. Urofsky, *Biographical Encyclopedia of the Supreme Court: The Lives and Legal Philosophies of the Justices* (Washington, DC: CQ Press, 2006), 520–21; Jonathan Lurie, "Noah Haynes Swayne," in *American National Biographies* (Oxford University Press, February 2000), http://www.anb.org/view/10.1093/anb/9780198606697.001.0001/anb-9780198606697-e-1100830; M. W. Kirby, *Men of Business and Politics: The Rise and Fall of the Quaker Pease Dynasty of North-East England, 1700–1943* (London: George Allen & Unwin, 1984), 6, 49, 57–58; Jordan Curnutt, *Animals and the Law: A Sourcebook* (Santa Barbara, CA: ABC-CLIO, 2001), 71; Keith Wilson, "Political Radicalism in the North East of England, 1830–1860: Issues in Historical Sociology" (PhD diss., University of Durham, 1987), 213–14; Eugenio Biagini, "Politics and Social Reform in Britain and Ireland," in *The Oxford History of Protestant Dissenting Traditions*, vol. 3, *The Nineteenth Century* (Oxford: Oxford University Press, 2017), 408–12, 417–18; Brian David Phillips, "Friendly Patriotism: British Quakerism and the Imperial Nation, 1890–1910" (PhD diss., University of Cambridge, 1989), 19–20.

2. George Barnett Smith, *The Life and Speeches of the Right Hon. John Bright, M.P.* (London: Hodder and Stoughton, 1881), 1:7; Bill Cash, *John Bright: Statesman, Orator, Agitator* (New York: I. B. Tauris, 2012), 2,

222–27, 246, 282; J. Travis Mills, *John Bright and the Quakers* (London: Methuen, 1935), 2:41; Howard F. Gregg, "John Bright: Called to the Lord's Service," *Quaker Religious Thought* 73, no. 4 (1990): 11.

3. Stephanie Midori Komashin, "How Ecology and Economics Brought Winstanley and Nitobe to Quakerism," in *Quakers and Mysticism: Comparative and Syncretic Approaches to Spirituality*, Interdisciplinary Approaches to the Study of Mysticism, ed. Jon R. Kershner (Cham, Switzerland: Palgrave Macmillan, 2019), 65; Kei Sasaki, "Nitobe Inazo No Shuukyou [Inazo Nitobe's Religion]," in *Nitobe Inazo Ni Manabu—Bushidou, Kokusaijin, Guroobaruka [Studying Inazo Nitobe—Bushidou, Internationalist, Globalized]*, ed. Kazuyori Yuhazu and Kei Sasaki, HokuDai Bungaku Kenkyuuka Raiburari [Hokkaido University Faculty of Letters Library] 11 (Sapporo: Hokkaido Daigaku Shuppansha, 2015), 74; Inazo Nitobe, *Nitobe Inazo Zenshuu [The Complete Works of Inazo Nitobe]* (Tokyo: Kyobunkwan, 1987), 23:221, 230, 232–33, 244–45; Stephanie Midori Komashin, "Quakers in Asia-Pacific," in *The Cambridge Companion to Quaker Studies*, ed. Stephen W. Angell and Pink Dandelion (Cambridge: Cambridge University Press, 2018), 248.

4. William E. Leuchtenburg, *Herbert Hoover*, ed. Arthur M. Schlesinger Jr. and Sean Wilentz, The American Presidents Series (New York: Times Books, 2009), 1, 3; Thomas D. Hamm, "The Divergent Paths of Iowa Quakers in the Nineteenth Century," *Annals of Iowa* 61, no. 2 (2002): 140–41. See also Thomas D. Hamm, "The Revival, 1860–1880," chapter 4 in this volume.

5. Herbert Hoover, *The Memoirs of Herbert Hoover, 1874–1920: Years of Adventure*, 5th ed. (New York: Macmillan, 1951), 1–2, 4–10; Gary Scott Smith, *Religion in the Oval Office: The Religious Lives of American Presidents* (New York: Oxford University Press, 2015), 197–98; Nancy Beck Young, "Lou Henry Hoover (1874–1944) First Lady: 1929–1933," in *American First Ladies: Their Lives and Their Legacy*, ed. Lewis L. Gould, 2nd ed. (New York: Routledge, 2014), 276; Marjorie G. Jones, "The Joy of Sympathetic Companionship: The Correspondence of Mary Vaux Walcott and Lou Henry Hoover," *Quaker History* 103, no. 1 (2014): 36, 40–41, 43–44; Dale C. Mayer, *Lou Henry Hoover: A Prototype for First Ladies*, Presidential Wives Series (New York: Nova, 2004), 323; Frederick B. Jonassen, "'Kiss the Book . . . You're President. . . :' So Help Me God' and Kissing the Book in the Presidential Oath of Office," *William and Mary Bill of Rights Journal* 20, no. 3 (2012): 897; Henry J. Cadbury, "'Individual Faithfulness' Letter from the Past—212," *Friends Journal* 10, no. 22 (1964): 525; Friends Meeting of Washington DC, "FMW Handbook: History of FMW," 2015, http://quakersdc.org/Handbook_History.

6. Phillips, "Friendly Patriotism," 3, 5, 10, 17, 27, 32, 43, 158–60; Thomas D. Hamm, *Liberal Quakerism in America in the Long Nineteenth Century, 1790–1920* (Leiden: Brill, 2020), 31–33; Kirby, *Men of Business and Politics*, 13–14, 25, 57; Alfred Edward Pease, ed., *The Diaries of Edward Pease: The Father of English Railways* (Cambridge: Cambridge University Press, 2013), 151, 153, 163, 201, 300, 305–6; Rufus M. Jones, *The Later Periods of Quakerism* (London: Macmillan, 1921), 786; Sandra Holton, "John Bright, Radical Politics, and the Ethos of Quakerism," *Albion: A Quarterly Journal Concerned with British Studies* 34, no. 4 (2002): 595–96, 600; Sandra Stanley Holton, *Quaker Women: Personal Life, Memory and Radicalism in the Lives of Women Friends, 1780–1930* (New York: Routledge, 2007), 65–67, 70–71, 74; Cash, *Statesman*, 11, 14, 57; Donald Read, *Cobden and Bright: A Victorian Political Partnership* (New York: St. Martin's Press, 1968), 82; George Macaulay Trevelyan, *The Life of*

John Bright (London: Constable, 1913), 102–3; Mary P. E. Nitobe, "13) Bombing on Chinhow and Meeting of Pacific Relations," in *Nitobe Inazo Kenkyuu [Inazo Nitobe Research]*, ed. Toukyou Joshi Daigaku Nitobe Inazo Kenkyuukai (Tokyo: Shunjusha, 1969), 510; E. Digby Baltzell, *Puritan Boston and Quaker Philadelphia: Two Protestant Ethics and the Spirit of Class Authority and Leadership* (New York: The Free Press, 1979), 92; The Yearly Meeting of Friends Held in Philadelphia, "Civil Government (The Old Discipline)," Quaker Heritage Press, July 7, 2013, http://www.qhpress.org/texts/obod/civil.html; Thomas C. Kennedy, *British Quakerism, 1860–1920: The Transformation of a Religious Community* (New York: Oxford University Press, 2001), 261–64, 294–95, 300; Elizabeth Isichei, *Victorian Quakers* (London: Oxford University Press, 1970), 189–90; Steven Dale Davison, "Quakers and Capitalism: A History of Paradoxes," in *Quakers, Politics, and Economics*, vol. 5, *Quakers and the Disciplines*, ed. David R. Ross and Michael T. Snarr (Longmeadow, MA: Full Media Services, 2018), 20, 22–23.

7. Holton, "Radical," 594; Cash, *Statesman*, xiii, 61; Smith, *Life and Speeches*, 1881, 1:125; Mills, *John Bright and the Quakers*, 2:41; Jones, *Later Periods*, 630, 634.

8. In 1845–49, blight caused mass starvation and disease in Ireland. Roughly one million died and one million emigrated. Cash, *Statesman*, xx, 8–11, 43, 46, 118; Mills, *John Bright and the Quakers*, 1935, 1:265; Read, *Cobden and Bright*, 22–23, 51, 73.

9. Read, *Cobden and Bright*, 82, 134, 201; Cash, *Statesman*, 72, 196, 207, 209–10; Gregg, "Called," 20, 22–23; F. Stanley Van Eps, "John Bright, Advocate of Peace," *Advocate of Peace* [1894–1920] 73, no. 11 (1911): 252.

10. Holton, "Radical," 598; Cash, *Statesman*, xviii, 145, 177.

11. George Barnett Smith, *The Life and Speeches of the Right Honourable John Bright, M.P.*, vols. 1–2 (London: Hodder and Stoughton, 1882), 219–21.

12. Gregg, "Called," 18; Cash, *Statesman*, xviii, 60, 86–88, 140, 164, 222–27, 233, 250; Jones, *Later Periods*, 647.

13. Cash, *Statesman*, xiii, xiv, xviii.

14. Nitobe received his coming-of-age name, Inazo, at age seven. George Oshiro, "The End: 1929–1933," in *Nitobe Inazô: Japan's Bridge Across the Pacific*, ed. John F. Howes (Boulder, CO: Westview, 1995), 262; John F. Howes and George Oshiro, "Who Was Nitobe?," in Howes, *Nitobe Inazô*, 3–5; John F. Howes, "Foreword," in *Nitobe Inazō: The Twilight Years* (Tokyo: Kyo Bun Kwan [Christian Literature Society of Japan], 1985), vii–viii; Oshiro, "End," 262–63; Nitobe, *Zenshuu*, 1970, 15:516–18, 545, 548, 550–52; Nitobe, *Zenshuu*, 1969, 16:325; Nitobe, *Zenshuu*, 1969, 10:154–55; Nitobe, *Zenshuu*, 1987, 23:442; Eiichirō Uchikawa, *Nitobe Inazō: The Twilight Years* (Tokyo: Kyo Bun Kwan [Christian Literature Society of Japan], 1985), 55–56, 66, 68, 81.

15. Nitobe, *Zenshuu*, 1970, 15:332, 345; Nitobe, *Zenshuu*, 1987, 23:442, 600–601; Tadamasa Fukiura, "Oorando Shotou no Kizoku Mondai wo Kaiketsushita Nitobe Inazo [Inazo Nitobe, Who Resolved the Åland Islands Question]," Tokuteihieirikatsudouhoujin Sekai no Kokki Kokka Kenkyuu Kyoukai [Research Institute of National Flags and Anthems of the World], February 28, 2019, http://kokkiken.or.jp/archives/323; Uchikawa, *Twilight*, 31; Thomas W. Burkman, "The Geneva Spirit," in Howes, *Nitobe Inazô*, 180, 183, 187–89; United Nations Office at Geneva, "Intellectual Cooperation and International Bureaux Section, 1919–1946 (Sub-Fonds)," United Nations Geneva Archives, accessed August 24, 2020, https://biblio-archive.unog.ch/detail.aspx?ID=408; Agneta Karlsson, "Sub-National Island Jurisdictions as Configurations of Jurisdictional Powers and Economic Capacity: Nordic Experiences from Åland, Faroes and

Greenland," *Island Studies Journal* 4, no. 2 (2009): 144; Nitobe, *Zenshuu*, 1969, 10:309–10.

16. Nitobe, *Zenshuu*, 1987, 23:266, 275, 280, 639; Nitobe, *Zenshuu*, 1969, 16:57; Mark Metzler, *Lever of Empire: The International Gold Standard and the Crisis of Liberalism in Prewar Japan* (Berkeley: University of California Press, 2006), 183, 192–95; Eckhardt Fuchs, Tokushi Kasahara, and Sven Saaler, *A New Modern History of East Asia* (Göttingen: V&R Unipress, 2017), 223–24; Uchikawa, *Twilight*, 13–14, 26–30.

17. Nitobe, *Zenshuu*, 1970, 15:240–41, 250; Fuchs, Kasahara, and Saaler, *Modern History of East Asia*, 222–23; Nitobe, *Zenshuu*, 1969, 16:454; Oshiro, "End," 253–58, 262–63; Walter LaFeber, *The Clash: U.S.-Japanese Relations Throughout History* (New York: W. W. Norton, 1998), 166, 169.

18. Donald A. Jordan, *China's Trial by Fire: The Shanghai War of 1932* (Ann Arbor: University of Michigan Press, 2001), i, xii, 20, 26, 28–29, 34–43, 46–48; Uchikawa, *Twilight*, 105–20.

19. Uchikawa, *Twilight*, 36–37, 52–61, 65–67, 73–83, 87–88, 101, 126–28, 140–43, 147–50, 161–64; Oshiro, "End," 267; LaFeber, *Clash*, 171; Howes, "Foreword," viii; Nitobe, *Zenshuu*, 1969, 16:216.

20. George H. Nash, "The 'Great Humanitarian': Herbert Hoover, the Relief of Belgium, and the Reconstruction of Europe After World War I," *Tocqueville Review* 38, no. 2 (2017): 62; George H. Nash, *The Life of Herbert Hoover: The Humanitarian, 1914–1917* (New York: W. W. Norton, 1988), ix; Patrick G. O'Brien and Philip T. Rosen, "Hoover and the Historians: The Resurrection of a President, Part I," *Annals of Iowa* 46, no. 1 (1981): 25–42; Patrick G. O'Brien and Philip T. Rosen, "Hoover and the Historians: The Resurrection of a President, Part II," *Annals of Iowa* 46, no. 2 (1981): 83–99; Hoover, *Years*, 13, 21, 99; Leuchtenburg, *Hoover*, 6; G. Jeansonne, *The Life of Herbert Hoover: Fighting Quaker,* *1928–1933* (New York: Palgrave Macmillan, 2012), 6.

21. Hoover, *Years*, 115, 141–48, 153; Leuchtenburg, *Hoover*, 24.

22. Hoover, *Years*, 15; Leuchtenburg, *Hoover*, 30; US Embassy Brussels Office of Public Diplomacy, "Hoover's Humanitarian Vision," Remembering Herbert Hoover, August 23, 2011, https://web.archive.org/web/20110823182920/http://www.rememberinghoover.be/Humanitarian_Vision.htm; George H. Nash, "An American Epic: Herbert Hoover and Belgian Relief in World War I," *Prologue* 21, no. 1 (1989).

23. George H. Nash, "Herbert Clark Hoover (1874–1964)," in *Notable American Philanthropists: Biographies of Giving and Volunteering*, ed. Robert T. Grimm Jr. (Westport, CT: Greenwood, 2002), 153; Hoover, *Years*, 270–71, 324, 425–27; Elizabeth Gray Vining, *Friend of Life: The Biography of Rufus M. Jones* (Philadelphia: J. P. Lippincott, 1958), 168, 171–72, 175, 179, 183; Rufus M. Jones, *A Service of Love in War Time: American Friends Relief Work in Europe, 1917–1919* (New York: Macmillan, 1920), xiii, 260; Nash, "Great Humanitarian," 66.

24. Herbert Hoover, *The Memoirs of Herbert Hoover, 1920–1933: The Cabinet and the Presidency* (New York: Macmillan, 1952), 25, 62, 115–18; Leuchtenburg, *Hoover*, 68; Melvyn P. Leffler, "Herbert Hoover, the 'New Era,' and American Foreign Policy, 1921–1929," in *Safeguarding Democratic Capitalism: U.S. Foreign Policy and National Security, 1920–2015* (Princeton, NJ: Princeton University Press, 2017), 61–62.

25. Hoover, *Cabinet*, 192, 207; United States Senate, "U.S. Senate: Charles Curtis, 31st Vice President (1929–1933)," United States Senate, accessed August 31, 2020, https://www.senate.gov/about/officers-staff/vice-president/VP_Charles_Curtis.htm; Kansas Historical Society, "Charles Curtis," Kansaspedia: Kansas Historical Society, March 2015,

https://www.kshs.org/kansapedia/charles-curtis/12029; Leuchtenburg, *Hoover*, 21; Hoover, *Years*, 171; Hoover, *Cabinet*, 43; "Interview with Former President Hoover," *NBC News* (New York: NBC Universal, November 6, 1955), NBC Learn, https://archives.nbclearn.com/portal/site/k-12/browse/?cuecard=2900.

26. R. Gordon Hoxie, "Herbert Hoover: Multi-National Man," *Presidential Studies Quarterly* 7, no. 1 (1977): 51; Hoover, *Cabinet*, 210–15, 226–36, 318; Leuchtenburg, *Hoover*, 83.

27. Charles Rappleye, *Herbert Hoover in the White House: The Ordeal of the Presidency*, repr. ed. (New York: Simon and Schuster, 2017), 148, 247, 262, 304; Leuchtenburg, *Hoover*, 104.

28. Roger Lambert, "Hoover and the Red Cross in the Arkansas Drought of 1930," *The Arkansas Historical Quarterly* 29, no. 1 (1970): 1, 5, 9, 16–17; Rappleye, *White House*, 242–44; Vining, *Friend of Life*, 226.

29. US Embassy Brussels Office of Public Diplomacy, "Humanitarian Vision"; Leuchtenburg, *Hoover*, 161; "Editor Gets Post with Hoover Unit; Neil Macneil, Retired Times Executive, Is Appointed Editorial Director," *New York Times*, September 16, 1954, https://www.nytimes.com/1954/09/16/archives/editor-gets-post-with-hoover-unit-neil-macneil-retired-times.html; "Colonizer William Penn and Engineer Herbert Hoover: How Their Businesses Affected Their Philanthropy and Statesmanship," in *Quakers, Business, and Industry*, vol. 4, *Quakers and the Disciplines*, ed. Stephen W. Angell and Pink Dandelion (Longmeadow, MA: Full Media Services, 2017), 201–3; Nash, "Great Humanitarian," 63; "Herbert Hoover Is Dead; Ex-President, 90, Served Country in Varied Fields; Flags Lowered; Leader at Beginning of the Depression Rewon Esteem," *New York Times*, October 21, 1964, https://www.nytimes.com/1964/10/21/archives/herbert-hoover-is-dead-expresident-90-served-country-in-varied.html.

30. Phillips, "Friendly Patriotism," 21; Kirby, *Men of Business and Politics*, 21, 55–57; Mills, *John Bright and the Quakers*, 1:407, 416, 433, 480; Arthur Tilney Bassett, *The Life of Rt. Hon. John Edward Ellis, M.P.* (London: Macmillan, 1914), 81; S. E. Robson, *Joshua Rowntree* (London: George Allen & Unwin, 1916), 58, 76–77; Rebecca Wynter, "Conscription, Conscience and Controversy: The Friends' Ambulance Unit and the 'Middle Course' in the First World War," *Quaker Studies* 21, no. 2 (2016): 218–20; Elizabeth Balmer Baker and P. J. Noel Baker, *J. Allen Baker, Member of Parliament: A Memoir* (London: Swarthmore Press, 1927), 132, 232–33; "The Nobel Peace Prize 1959," Quakers in the World, accessed October 30, 2019, https://www.nobelprize.org/prizes/peace/1959/noel-baker/biographical; Marit Fosse and John Fox, *Nansen: Explorer and Humanitarian* (Lanham, MD: Rowman & Littlefield, 2015), 32–35, 57. See also Nicola Sleapwood and Thomas D. Hamm, "Quakers and the Social Order, 1830–1937," chapter 9 in this volume.

31. Elizabeth Crawford, *The Women's Suffrage Movement: A Reference Guide, 1866–1928* (London: UCL Press, 1999), 116–17; Holton, *Quaker Women*, 2–3, 64; Ann Dingsdale, "'Generous and Lofty Sympathies': The Kensington Society, the 1866 Women's Suffrage Petition and the Development of Mid-Victorian Feminism" (PhD diss., University of Greenwich, 1995), 136–38; Joanna Dales, *The Quaker Renaissance and Liberal Quakerism in Britain, 1895–1930: Seeking a Real Religion* (Leiden: Brill, 2020), 57; Helen Victoria Smith, "Elizabeth Taylor Cadbury (1858–1951): Religion, Maternalism and Social Reform in Birmingham, 1888–1914" (PhD diss., University of Birmingham, 2012), vi, 16–20, 106–7, 109, 112, 114–16,

126–27, 208–9; Kennedy, *British Quakerism*, 171–79, 230, 364–65; Robson, *Joshua Rowntree*, 96–101.

32. Isichei, *Victorian Quakers*, 205; Kennedy, *British Quakerism*, 246; Holton, *Quaker Women*, 70–71.

33. Kirby, *Men of Business and Politics*, 57; Isichei, *Victorian Quakers*, 145; Nitobe, *Zenshuu*, 1969, 10:51–52; Baker and Noel Baker, *Baker*, 93.

34. Nitobe, *Zenshuu*, 1969, 16:56; Lee Arne Makela, "Immigration Act of 1924," in *Asian Americans: An Encyclopedia of Social, Cultural, Economic, and Political History*, ed. Xiaojian Zhao and Edward J. W. Park (Santa Barbara, CA: ABC-CLIO, 2013), 1:535, 537; Oshiro, "End," 261; Herbert Hoover, *Public Papers of the Presidents of the United States: Herbert Hoover: Containing the Public Messages, Speeches, and Statements of the President, March 4 to December 31, 1929* (Washington, DC: United States Government Printing Office, 1974), 57, 59–61; Herbert Hoover, *Public Papers of the Presidents of the United States: Herbert Hoover: Containing the Public Messages, Speeches, and Statements of the President, January 1 to December 31, 1930* (Washington, DC: United States Government Printing Office, 1976), 539–40.

35. Herbert Hoover, *The Ordeal of Woodrow Wilson* (Washington, DC: Woodrow Wilson Center Press, 1992), 282–84, 290–93, 298–99; Stephanie Midori Komashin, "How Ecology, Economics, and Ethics Brought Winstanley and Nitobe to Quakerism," *Quaker Studies* 22, no. 1 (June 2017): 42–44; Nitobe, *Zenshuu*, 1987, 23:377; Nitobe, *Zenshuu*, 1969, 16:424–25; Nitobe, *Zenshuu*, 1970, 15:240–43, 246.

36. Herbert Hoover, *Public Papers of the Presidents of the United States: Herbert Hoover: Containing the Public Messages, Speeches, and Statements of the President, January 1, 1932 to March 4, 1933* (Washington, DC: United States Government Printing Office, 1977), 1199; Nitobe, *Zenshuu*, 1987, 23:364–66; Nitobe, *Zenshuu*, 1969, 16:389, 401, 417.

37. Nitobe, *Zenshuu*, 1987, 23:244.

38. Translation the author's. Nitobe, *Zenshuu*, 1969, 10:29, 34; Inazo Nitobe, "Ijin Gunzou [Dynamic Portraits of Eminent Figures]," in *Zuisouroku* [Thoughts and Essays], *Zuikanroku* [Impressions and Essays], *Ijin Gunzou* [Dynamic Portraits of Eminent Figures], vol. 5, *Nitobe Inazo Zenshuu* [The Complete Works of Inazo Nitobe] (Tokyo: Kyo Bun Kwan [Christian Literature Society of Japan], 1969), 350.

39. Smith, *Life and Speeches*, 1881, 1:viii; Uchikawa, *Twilight*, 44; Rappleye, *White House*, 36.

40. Frederick B. Tolles, "Quakerism and Politics," https://quaker.org/legacy/pamphlets/ward1956.pdf, 20, 23; John Bright, "Introductory Words by the Right Hon. John Bright," quoted in John Dymond, *War: Its Causes, Consequences, Lawfulness, Etc.* (Leominster, UK: The Orphan's Printing Press, 1896), vii; Gregg, "Called," 19, 23.

CHAPTER 13

1. See Thomas C. Kennedy, *British Quakerism 1860–1920: The Transformation of a Religious Community* (Oxford: Oxford University Press, 2001); Brian D. Phillips, "Apocalypse Without Tears: Hubris and Folly Among Late Victorian and Edwardian British Friends," in *Towards Tragedy / Reclaiming Hope: Literature, Theology and Sociology in Conversation*, ed. Pink Dandelion et al. (Aldershot, UK: Ashgate, 2004), 57–76; Chuck Fager, *Remaking Friends: How Progressive Friends Changed Quakerism and Helped Save America* (Durham, NC: Kimo Press, 2014); Douglas Gwyn, *A Gathering of Spirits: The Friends General Conferences, 1896–1950* (Philadelphia: Friends General Conference, 2018), chap. 1–3.

2. Rufus M. Jones, *The Trail of Life in the Middle Years* (New York: Macmillan, 1934), 222; Kennedy, *British Quakerism*, 316–17; Phillips, "Apocalypse Without Tears," 74.

3. John Ormerod Greenwood, *Quaker Encounters*, vol. 3, *Whispers of Truth* (York, UK: William Sessions, 1978), 215–17; Roger Wilson, "The Best Things in ye Worst of Times," in *Quakerism: A Way of Life; In Homage to Sigrid Leliesen Lund*, ed. Hans Eirik Aarek (Stavanger, Norway: Kvekerforlaget, 1982), 145–46; Kennedy, *British Quakerism*, 404–5.

4. Walter C. Woodward, "World Conference of All Friends," *American Friend*, September 9, 1920; *All-Friends Conference . . . Guide and Souvenir* (London: Friends Bookshop, 1920).

5. The directory of delegates in the *Official Report* is organized by nation, and the American delegates are not broken down by yearly meetings. Only addresses are given. A good range of Friends General Conference and Five Years Meeting Friends can be noted. Conservative Friends in attendance are harder to detect.

6. Woodward, "World Conference of All Friends."

7. As quoted in a digest of the spoken lecture appearing in *The Friend* (Philadelphia), September 9, 1920. The fuller printed version under the same title was published that year by the Swarthmore Press, London. Some of Jones's ideas on conscience developed during his year of study at Harvard University in 1900 with the personalist philosopher George Herbert Palmer.

8. The basic conviction of personalism is that the person is the image of God. Persons are formed in dialogue and community with others; communities in turn mediate between the individual person and the wider society for social change. For more on personalism, see Rufus Burrow, *Personalism: A Critical Introduction* (St. Louis, MO: Chalice Press, 1999); Gary Dorrien, *The Making of American Liberal Religion*, vol. 2, *Idealism, Realism, and Modernity* (Louisville, KY: Westminster John Knox, 2003). For more about personalist influence on early twentieth-century Friends, see Douglas Gwyn, *Personality and Place: The Life and Times of Pendle Hill* (Philadelphia: Plain Press, 2014).

9. *All Friends Conference, London, August 1920: Official Report* (London: Friends Bookshop, 1920), 31–34; Walter C. Woodward, "Fruits of the Conference," *American Friend*, September 23, 1920. For more on British Quaker socialists of this period, see Tony Adams, *A Far-Seeing Vision: The Quaker Socialist Society (1898–1924)* (Bedford, UK: QSS, 1993).

10. *Official Report*, 38–50.

11. Ibid., 83–93.

12. Ibid., 94–100, 126–31. Equivocal responses to the war among FGC Friends may be seen in Gwyn, *Gathering of Spirits*, chap. 3 and 4.

13. Wilson, "Best Things," 145. London Yearly Meeting approved a strong statement on economic relations in 1918, with eight "Foundations of a True Social Order." The last of these reads, "The ownership of material things, such as land and capital should be so regulated as best to minister to the need and development of man." But the document was directed toward Quaker ethics, not government policy. For the full text, see Britain Yearly Meeting, *Quaker Faith and Practice* (London: Britain Yearly Meeting, 1995), 23.16. For more on Hodgkin, an unjustly forgotten Friend, see Herbert G. Wood, *Henry T. Hodgkin: A Memoir* (London: Student Christian Movement Press, 1937).

14. *Official Report*, 132, 160. For more on the Brintons and Pendle Hill, see Gwyn, *Personality and Place*; and Anthony Manousos, *Howard and Anna Brinton: Re-inventors of Quakerism in the Twentieth Century* (Philadelphia: FGC Quaker Bridge, 2013).

15. *Official Report*, 173.
16. Ibid., 199–210.
17. *Friends and War: A New Statement of the Quaker Position* (London: Continuation Committee of the Conference of All Friends, 1920), 22.
18. Greenwood, *Whispers of Truth*, 359; Walter C. Woodward, "When Friend Meets Friend," *American Friend*, September 30, 1920 (emphasis in original).
19. See, for example, *Official Report*, 34, 177; Leigh Eric Schmidt, *Restless Souls: The Making of American Spirituality* (San Francisco: HarperCollins, 2005), chap. 3.
20. Woodward, "World Conference of All Friends"; T. A. Jenkins, *Friends' Intelligencer*, August 28, 1920.
21. See Thomas D. Hamm, *The Transformation of American Quakerism: Orthodox Friends, 1800–1907* (Bloomington: Indiana University Press, 1988), chap. 4 and 5 (on revivalism and Holiness among evangelical Friends). Carole Spencer, in *Holiness: The Soul of Quakerism* (Milton Keynes, UK: Paternoster, 2007), makes the case that the Holiness movement among Friends reclaimed the perfectionist theology of early Quakers. For a helpful summary of these liberal Quaker trends, see Thomas D. Hamm, *The Quakers in America* (New York: Columbia University Press, 2003), 56–63. See also Timothy Burdick, "Neo-Evangelical Identity Within the American Religious Society of Friends (Quakers): Oregon Yearly Meeting, 1919–1947" (PhD diss., University of Birmingham, 2013), and Timothy Burdick and Pink Dandelion, "Global Quakerism 1920–2015," in *The Cambridge Companion to Quakerism*, ed. Stephen W. Angell and Pink Dandelion (Cambridge: Cambridge University Press, 2018).
22. Conference announcement (undated). Thomas had carped at Hoover since the war years regarding the latter's control of US funds for relief in Europe. For more, see Gregory A. Barnes, *A Centennial History of the American Friends Service Committee* (Philadelphia: Friends Press, 2016), 65–73.
23. Conference announcement (undated). Indeed, the centennial of the Great Separation among American Friends had passed in 1927 and 1928 without celebration but with expressions of loss. See Stephen W. Angell, "The Dog That Did Not Bark: Yearly Meeting Reunifications in North America: The Case of Canada's Yearly Meetings," in *An Early Assessment: U.S. Quakerism in the 20th Century; Papers from the Quaker History Roundtable, June 8–11, 2017*, ed. Chuck Fager (Durham, NC: Kimo Press, 2017), 59–81.
24. Edward Janney, unpublished memoir, 141, in the O. Edward Janney Papers, RG5/072, Friends Historical Library, Swarthmore College. In a similar vein, Edward Mott of Oregon Yearly Meeting reported that the Young Friends Movement in the East organized monthly occasions for social dancing, something "unthinkable from the standpoint of true rectitude . . . a trend that is beyond reason." See Mott, *Sixty Years of Gospel Ministry* (Portland, OR, 1948), 113.
25. American All-Friends Conference "Announcement" and "Brochure" in archives of Friends Collection, Lilly Library, Earlham College. Edward Grubb, in "Personal Greetings from Abroad," *American Friend*, September 19, 1929.
26. *Friends' Intelligencer*, September 21 and 28, 1929. More detailed accounting of attendance by yearly meeting affiliation was not available.
27. Mott, *Sixty Years of Gospel Ministry*, 95–96, 116.
28. As quoted in *Friends' Intelligencer*, September 11, 1920; as quoted in *American Friend*, September 19, 1929.
29. *American Friend*, September 19, 1929.
30. *American Friend*, September 26, 1929. For the progressive movement's dilemmas on race, see Michael McGerr, *A Fierce Discontent: The Rise and Fall of the Progressive Movement in America* (Oxford: Oxford University Press, 2003), chap. 6.

McGerr quotes Theodore Roosevelt commenting in a letter on "the terrible problem offered by the presence of the negro on this continent." See also a range of comments on race in addresses to Friends General Conferences in the same period in Gwyn, *Gathering of Spirits*, chap. 4 and 5.

31. *American Friend*, September 26, 1929.

32. Summaries from *American Friend*, September 26, 1929.

33. John William Graham, "London at Oskaloosa," *Friends' Intelligencer*, September 21, 1929. See Gwyn, *Gathering of Spirits*, 45.

34. Opening editorial, *American Friend*, September 19, 1929.

35. "The American All-Friends Conference—and After," *Friends' Intelligencer*, September 28, 1929; "American Friends Gather at Oskaloosa," *The Friend*, September 26, 1929.

36. Besides the academic speakers already noted, Wilbur Thomas had been both a Friends pastor and a professor at Earlham College. John William Graham had taught at Manchester University in England. For Quaker responses to Hoover's candidacy in 1928, see Isaac May, "Quakers, Herbert Hoover and the 1928 Election," in Fager, *Early Assessment*, 204–16. For more on AFSC's development in this period, see Barnes, *Centennial History*, chap. 4 and 5.

37. Greenwood, *Whispers of Truth*, 360; Walter C. Woodward, *American Friend*, February 6, 1936.

38. For the developing relationship of Friends General Conference with the World Council of Churches (WCC), see Gwyn, *Gathering of Spirits*, chap. 6 and 7. Though the WCC was not formally constituted until after the war, elements of the nascent body aided hundreds of Jews in escaping to Switzerland. For more on this formative period, see *World Council of Churches Online: World War II Era Records*, Brill.com.

39. *The Friend* (London), September 10, 1937. Since London Yearly Meeting had sided with Orthodox Friends after the Great Separation of American Friends in 1827–28, they traditionally referred to Hicksite Friends as "the other branch." But with liberal renewal well established on both sides of the Atlantic, this usage was now archaic.

40. Report on the conference in *The Friend* (London), September 24, 1937; *Friends World Conference, Official Report* (Philadelphia: AFSC, 1937); Herbert Hadley, *Quakers Worldwide: A History of the Friends World Committee for Consultation* (York, UK: Friends World Committee for Consultation, in association with William Sessions, 1991), 12. For more on Quaker missions, see Stephen W. Angell, "Quakers and Missions, 1861–1937," chapter 10 in this volume.

41. Rufus Jones to Violet Holdsworth, July 1937, quoted in Elizabeth Gray Vining, *Friend for Life: The Biography of Rufus M. Jones* (Philadelphia: J. B. Lippincott, 1958), 269; "The Conference Week," in *Official Report*.

42. Rufus Jones, "Conference Broadcast Message," in *Official Report*.

43. Rufus Jones, opening address, *Friends' Intelligencer*, October 9, 1937 (emphasis in original). Christian realism was a reaction against the religious idealism and moral optimism of earlier liberal Christian renewal. Jones had also responded to Christian realism in Rufus M. Jones, *Re-thinking Religious Liberalism* (Boston: Beacon, 1935).

44. *Friends' Intelligencer*, September 25, 1937. For more on Rachel Davis DuBois and her pioneering work in racial dialogue, see her autobiography, *All This and Something More: Pioneering in Intercultural Education* (Bryn Mawr, PA: Dorrance, 1984). Excerpts from her writings can be found in Leonard Kenworthy, ed., *Nine Contemporary Quaker Women Speak* (Kennett Square, PA: Quaker Publications, 1989), 21. See also her input into Friends General Conferences in this period in Gwyn, *Gathering of Spirits*.

45. Rufus Jones, "The Friends World Conference: An Evaluation," *The Friend* (London), September 24, 1937 (emphasis in original).

46. Walter C. Woodward, "Now It Can Be Said: Quakerism a World Movement," *American Friend*, September 30, 1937; Kati Lotz (one of thirteen delegates from German Yearly Meeting), "An Impression of the Friends World Conference," *Friends' Intelligencer*, October 9, 1937.

47. Elbert Russell and L. Hollingsworth Wood, "Impressions of the Friends World Conference," *Friends' Intelligencer*, October 2, 1937.

48. *Friends' Intelligencer*, September 25, 1937.

49. Greenwood, *Whispers of Truth*, 360. For more on the history of FWCC, see Hadley, *Quakers Worldwide*.

50. Clarence Pickett, *American Friend*, May 7, 1942.

AFTERWORD

1. Rufus M. Jones, *Finding the Trail of Life* (London: Allen & Unwin, 1926), 19, 44.

2. Except where otherwise noted, this paragraph and the one that succeeds it are based on Elizabeth Gray Vining, *Friend of Life: The Biography of Rufus M. Jones* (Philadelphia: J. B. Lippincott, 1958). Jones's life is also discussed in David Harrington Watt, "Philadelphia, Rufus Jones, and the Reinvention of Quakerism," in *Religion in Philadelphia*, ed. Elizabeth Hayes Alvarez (Philadelphia: Temple University Press, 2016), 218–24; and David Harrington Watt, "Eugenicists, Quakers, and Rufus Jones, 1893–1938," *Quaker Religious Thought* 135 (September 2020): 14–26.

3. Emma Jones Lapsansky-Werner, "Mary Hoxie Jones," in *Historical Dictionary of the Friends (Quakers)*, ed. Margery Post Abbott et al. (Lanham, MD: Scarecrow Press, 2012), 184; "Collection Overview," Rufus M. Jones Papers, Quaker & Special Collections, Haverford College, Haverford, PA, accessed February 10, 2021, http://archives.tricolib.brynmawr.edu/resources/hcmc-1130.

4. Elizabeth Cazden, "Rufus Matthews Jones," in Abbott et al., *Historical Dictionary of the Friends (Quakers)*, 185; Horace G. Alexander to Rufus Jones, October 15, 1940, Rufus M. Jones Papers, Quaker & Special Collections, Haverford College, Haverford, PA.

5. Peter Guldbrandsen to Rufus M. Jones, September 19, 1935, Rufus M. Jones Papers, Quaker & Special Collections, Haverford College, Haverford, PA. For other discussions of the controversies in which Jones was embroiled, see Vining, *Friend of Life*, 143–45, 243; and Thomas D. Hamm, *The Transformation of American Quakerism: Orthodox Friends, 1800–1907* (Bloomington: Indiana University Press, 1988), 162, 164–67.

6. Emphases added.

7. Rufus M. Jones, *The Later Periods of Quakerism*, 2 vols. (London: Macmillan, 1921), viii.

8. Vining, *Friend of Life*, 111; Jones, *Later Periods*, viii. The men's names were Allen C. Thomas, William Charles Braithwaite, and Norman Penney.

9. W. H. Frere, review of *The Later Periods of Quakerism* by Rufus Jones, *English Historical Review* 37, no. 148 (1922): 596; Jones, *Later Periods*, xiii.

10. W. W. Fenn, review of *The Later Periods of Quakerism* by Rufus Jones, *American Historical Review* 28, no. 2 (1923): 311; Edward Grubb, review of *The Later Periods of Quakerism* by Rufus Jones, *Bulletin of Friends' Historical Society of Philadelphia* 11, no. 1 (1922): 41–43; Frere, review of *Later Periods*, 596.

11. For a superb analysis of the series, see Alice Southern, "The Rowntree History Series and the Growth of Liberal Quakerism," *Quaker Studies* 16, no. 1 (2011): 1–73.

12. Jones, *Later Periods*, 618, 620, 597, 909. Jones's ideas about race are explored in Stephen W. Angell, "Howard Thurman and Quakers," *Quaker Theology* 16, no. 9 (2009): 31–38.

13. Pink Dandelion, "Introduction," in *The Creation of Quaker Theory: Insider Perspectives*, ed. Pink Dandelion (Aldershot, UK: Ashgate, 2004), 3.

14. Jones, *Later Periods*, xiii.

15. Ibid., xiii, 156–66, 314–76, 713–56, 833, 930–32, 965, 982, 985–86.

16. Southern, "Rowntree History Series," 38–40. Jones, *Later Periods*, praises some aspects: see xii–xiv, 437, 814, 891, 900, and 931.

17. Michel-Rolph Trouillot, *Silencing the Past: Power and the Production of History* (Boston: Beacon Press, 1995), and Joan Wallach Scott, *Gender and the Politics of History*, 2nd ed. (New York: Columbia University Press, 1999), are classic explorations of this issue. For a splendid analysis of what sorts of stories tend to get silenced in books that focus on a single religious denomination, see Keith Harper, ed., *American Denominational History: Perspectives on the Past, Prospects for the Future* (Tuscaloosa: University of Alabama Press, 2008). It is difficult to make confident pronouncements about how much the sixteen writers who wrote chapters for this book have in common with one another. They received their training in a variety of fields, including English, religious studies, law, and history. Many of the authors are members of the Society of Friends. Slightly more than half of them are men. Most are White. One of the authors lives in Japan; another lives in Canada. Two live in the United Kingdom. The rest live in the United States.

18. World Office of the Friends World Committee for Consultation, "About FWCC," accessed February 10, 2021, http://fwcc.world/about-fwcc.

19. Pink Dandelion and Stephen Angell, "Introduction," in *The Cambridge Companion to Quakerism*, ed. Stephen W. Angell and Pink Dandelion (Cambridge: Cambridge University Press, 2018), 4–5.

SELECTED BIBLIOGRAPHY

Abbott, Margery Post, Mary Ellen Chijioke, Pink Dandelion, and John W. Oliver Jr. *Historical Dictionary of the Friends (Quakers)*. Lanham, MD: Scarecrow Press, 2003.

Adams, Katherine, and Michael Keene. *Alice Paul and the American Suffrage Campaign*. Urbana: University of Illinois Press, 2008.

Adams, Tony. *A Far-Seeing Vision: The Quaker Socialist Society (1898–1924)*. Bedford, UK: Quaker Socialist Society, 1993.

Anderson, Jervis. *Bayard Rustin: Troubles I've Seen: A Biography*. Berkeley: University of California Press, 1998.

Angell, Stephen W. "Quaker Women in Kenya and Human Rights Issues." In *Freedom's Distant Shores: American Protestants and Post-Colonial Alliances with Africa*, edited by R. Drew Smith. Waco, TX: Baylor University Press, 2006.

Angell, Stephen W., and Pink Dandelion, eds. *The Cambridge Companion to Quakerism*. Cambridge: Cambridge University Press, 2018.

———, eds. *The Oxford Handbook of Quaker Studies*. Oxford: Oxford University Press, 2013.

Austin, Allan W. *Quaker Brotherhood: Interracial Activism and the American Friends Service Committee, 1917–1950*. Urbana: University of Illinois Press, 2012.

Bacon, Margaret Hope. "New Light on Sarah Mapps Douglass and Her Reconciliation with Friends." *Quaker History* 90, no. 1 (2001): 28–49.

———. *Valiant Friend: The Life of Lucretia Mott*. New York: Walker, 1980.

Barbour, Hugh, Christopher Densmore, Elizabeth H. Moger, Nancy C. Sorel, Alson D. Van Wagner, and Arthur J. Worrall. *Quaker Crosscurrents: Three Hundred Years of Friends in New York Yearly Meeting*. Syracuse, NY: Syracuse University Press and New York Yearly Meeting, 1995.

Barbour, Hugh, and J. William Frost. *The Quakers*. 2nd ed. Richmond, IN: Friends United Press, 1994.

Barnes, Gregory Allen. *A Centennial History of the American Friends Service Committee*. Philadelphia: Friends Press, 2016.

Beebe, Ralph K. *A Garden of the Lord: A History of Oregon Yearly Meeting* of Friends Church. Newberg, OR: Barclay Press, 1968.

Benjamin, Philip S. *The Philadelphia Quakers in the Industrial Age, 1865–1920*. Philadelphia: Temple University Press, 1976.

Birkel, Michael. *Quakers Reading Mystics*. Quaker Studies. Leiden: Brill, 2018.

Braithwaite, Joseph Bevan, ed. *Memoirs of Joseph John Gurney*. 2 vols. Norwich, UK: Fletcher and Alexander, 1854.

Braithwaite, William C. *The Beginnings of Quakerism*. London: Macmillan, 1912.

———. *The Second Period of Quakerism*. London: Macmillan, 1919.

Brandt, Nat, and Yanna Kroyt Brandt. *In the Shadow of the Civil War: Passmore Williamson and the Rescue of Jane Johnson*. Columbia: University of South Carolina Press, 2007.

Braude, Ann. *Radical Spirits: Spiritualism and Women's Rights in Nineteenth-Century America*. 2nd ed. Bloomington: Indiana University Press, 2001.

Brekus, Catherine A. *Strangers and Pilgrims: Female Preaching in America, 1740–1845*. Chapel Hill: University of North Carolina Press, 1998.

Brock, Peter, ed. *Liberty and Conscience: A Documentary History of the Experiences of Conscientious Objectors in America Through the Civil War*. Oxford: Oxford University Press, 2002.

———. *Pioneers of a Peaceable Kingdom: The Quaker Peace Testimony from the Colonial Era to the First World War*. Princeton, NJ: Princeton University Press, 1968.

Bronner, Edwin B. "'The Other Branch': London Yearly Meeting and the Hicksites, 1827–1912. London: Friends Historical Society, 1975.

Brown, Clare R. "To Faithfully Do Our Part: The Contribution of Joseph Sturge to the Anti-Slavery Movement in Britain and America with Special Reference to the Principles Which Motivated His Work." PhD diss., University of Bristol, 2015.

Brown, Heloise. *"The Truest Form of Patriotism": Pacifist Feminism in Britain, 1870–1902*. Manchester: Manchester University Press, 2003.

Burdick, Timothy J. "Neo-Evangelical Identity Within American Religious Society of Friends (Quakers): Oregon Yearly Meeting, 1919–1947." PhD diss., University of Birmingham, 2013.

Burton, Nicholas, and Richard Turnbull. *Quakers, Business and Corporate Responsibility*. Cham, Switzerland: Springer, 2019.

Cadbury, Deborah. *Chocolate Wars: The 150-Year Rivalry Between the World's Greatest Chocolate Makers*. New York: Public Affairs, 2010.

Carey, Brycchan, and Geoffrey Plank, eds. *Quakers and Abolition*. Urbana: University of Illinois Press, 2014.

Carter, Max L. "Elizabeth Kirkbride Gurney's Correspondence with Abraham Lincoln: The Quaker Dilemma." *Pennsylvania Magazine of History and Biography* 133 (October 2009): 389–96.

Cherry, Charles L. *A Quiet Haven: Quakers, Moral Treatment, and Asylum Reform*. Rutherford, NJ: Fairleigh Dickinson University Press, 1989.

Cho, Mijin. "British Quaker Women and Peace, 1880s to 1920s." PhD diss., University of Birmingham, 2010.

Coffin, Levi. *Reminiscences of Levi Coffin, the Reputed President of the*

Underground Railroad. Cincinnati: Robert Clarke, 1880.

Cooper, Wilmer A. *A Living Faith: An Historical and Comparative Study of Quaker Beliefs*. 2nd ed. Richmond, IN: Friends United Press, 2006.

Crothers, A. Glenn. *Quakers Living in the Lion's Mouth: The Society of Friends in Northern Virginia, 1730–1865*. Gainesville: University Press of Florida, 2012.

Dales, Joanna C. *The Quaker Renaissance and Liberal Quakerism in Britain, 1895–1930: Seeking a Real Religion*. Leiden: Brill, 2020.

Dandelion, Pink. *The Cultivation of Conformity: Towards a General Theory of Internal Secularisation*. London: Routledge, 2019.

———. "Guarded Domesticity and Engagement with 'the World': The Separate Spheres of Quaker Quietism." *Common Knowledge* 16, no. 1 (2010): 95–109.

D'Antonio, Patricia. *Founding Friends: Families, Staff, and Patients at the Friends Asylum in Early Nineteenth-Century Philadelphia*. Bethlehem, PA: Lehigh University Press, 2006.

Davie, Martin. *British Quaker Theology Since 1895*. Lewiston, NY: Edwin Mellen, 1997.

D'Emilio, John. *Lost Prophet: The Life and Times of Bayard Rustin*. New York: Free Press, 2003.

Densmore, Christopher, Carole Faulkner, Nancy Hewitt, and Beverley Palmer Wilson. *Lucretia Mott Speaks: The Essential Speeches and Sermons*. Urbana: University of Illinois Press, 2017.

DeVol, Charles E. *Fruit That Remains: The Story of the Friends Mission in China and Taiwan*. Canton, OH: Evangelical Friends Church Eastern Region, 1988.

Digby, Anne. *Madness, Morality, and Medicine: A Study of the York Retreat, 1796–1914*. Cambridge: Cambridge University Press, 1985.

Dorrien, Gary. *The Making of American Liberal Theology*. 3 vols. Louisville, KY: Westminster John Knox Press, 2002–2005.

Fager, Chuck. *Angels of Progress: A Documentary History of the Progressive Friends, 1822–1940*. Durham, NC: Kimo Press, 2014.

———. *An Early Assessment: U.S. Quakerism in the 20th Century; Papers from the Quaker History Roundtable, June 8–11, 2017*. Durham, NC: Kimo Press, 2017.

———. *Remaking Friends: How Progressive Friends Changed Quakerism and Helped Save America*. Durham, NC: Kimo Press, 2014.

Falcetta, Alessandro. *The Daily Discoveries of a Bible Scholar and Manuscript Hunter: A Biography of James Rendel Harris (1852–1941)*. London: T&T Clark, 2018.

Farrant, Ann. *Amelia Opie, The Quaker Celebrity*. Hindringham, UK: JJG, 2014.

Faulkner, Carol. *Lucretia Mott's Heresy: Abolition and Women's Rights in Nineteenth-Century America*. Philadelphia: University of Pennsylvania Press, 2011.

Forbush, Bliss. *Elias Hicks, Quaker Liberal*. New York: Columbia University Press, 1956.

Frost, J. William. "'Our Deeds Carry Our Message': The Early History of the American Friends Service Committee." *Quaker History* 81, no. 1 (1992): 1–51.

Gould, Mitchell Santine. "Friends of the New York Seaport: Antebellum Quaker Commerce, Culture, and Concerns." *Quaker History* 108, no. 1 (2019): 25–41.

Graber, Jennifer. *The Gods of Indian Country: Religion and the Struggle for the American West*. New York: Oxford University Press, 2018.

Greene, Dana, ed. *Lucretia Mott: Her Complete Speeches and Sermons*. New York: Edwin Mellen, 1980.

Greenwood, John Ormerod. *Quaker Encounters*. 3 vols. York, UK: William Sessions, 1977–78.

Grellet, Stephen. *Memoirs of the Life and Labours of Stephen Grellet*. Edited by Benjamin Seebohm. 2 vols. London: A. W. Bennett, 1862.

Grubb, Edward. *Authority and the Light Within*. London: James Clarke, 1908.

———. *The Historic and Inward Christ*. Swarthmore Lecture, 1914. Bishopsgate, UK: Headley, 1914.

———. *The Meaning of the Cross: A Study of the Atonement*. London: Allen & Unwin, 1922.

———. *The Religion of Experience: An Examination of Some of the Difficulties of Christian Faith*. London: Headley, [1918].

Gurney, Joseph John. *Observations on the Distinguishing Views and Practices of the Society of Friends*. London: John and Arthur Arch, 1834.

Gwyn, Douglas. *A Gathering of Spirits: The Friends General Conferences 1896–1950*. Philadelphia: Friends General Conference, 2018.

———. *Personality and Place: The Life and Times of Pendle Hill*. Philadelphia: Plain Press, 2014.

Hadley, Herbert. *Quakers Worldwide: A History of the Friends World Committee for Consultation*. York, UK: Friends World Committee for Consultation, in association with William Sessions, 1991.

Hamm, Thomas D. *Earlham College: A History, 1847–1997*. Bloomington: Indiana University Press, 1997.

———. *God's Government Begun: The Society for Universal Inquiry and Reform, 1842–1846*. Bloomington: Indiana University Press, 1995.

———. *Liberal Quakerism in America in the Long Nineteenth Century, 1790–1920*. Quaker Studies. Leiden: Brill, 2020.

———. *The Transformation of American Quakerism: Orthodox Friends 1800–1907*. Bloomington: Indiana University Press, 1988.

Healey, Robynne Rogers. *From Quaker to Upper Canadian: Faith and Community Among Yonge Street Friends, 1801–1850*. Montreal: McGill-Queen's University Press, 2006.

———. *Quakerism in the Atlantic World, 1690–1830*. University Park: Pennsylvania State University Press, 2021.

Hedstrom, Matthew S. "Rufus Jones and Mysticism for the Masses." *Cross Currents* 54, no. 2 (2004): 31–44.

Hewison, Hope Hay. *Hedge of Wild Almonds: South Africa, the "Pro-Boers" and the Quaker Conscience, 1890–1910*. Portsmouth, NH: Heinemann, 1989.

Hewitt, Nancy A. *Radical Friend: Amy Kirby Post and Her Activist Worlds*. Chapel Hill: University of North Carolina Press, 2018.

Hickey, Damon D. *Sojourners No More: The Quakers in the New South*. Greensboro: North Carolina Friends Historical Society, 1997.

Hilty, Hiram H. *Friends in Cuba*. Richmond, IN: Friends United Press, 1977.

———. *Toward Freedom for All: North Carolina Quakers and Slavery*. Richmond, IN: Friends United Press, 1984.

Holcomb, Julie L. *Moral Commerce: Quakers and the Transatlantic*

Boycott of the Slave Labor Economy. Ithaca, NY: Cornell University Press, 2016.

Holton, Sandra S. *Quaker Women: Personal Life, Memory and Radicalism in the Lives of Women Friends, 1780–1930.* New York: Routledge, 2007.

Ingle, H. Larry. *Quakers in Conflict: The Hicksite Reformation.* Knoxville: University of Tennessee Press, 1986.

Isichei, Elizabeth. *Victorian Quakers.* Oxford: Oxford University Press, 1970.

Jones, Rufus M. *The Later Periods of Quakerism.* 2 vols. London: Macmillan, 1921.

———. *A Service of Love in Wartime: American Friends Relief Work in Europe, 1917–1919.* New York: Macmillan, 1920.

Jordan, Ryan P. *Slavery and the Meetinghouse: The Quakers and the Abolitionist Dilemma, 1820–1865.* Bloomington: Indiana University Press, 2007.

Kashatus, William C. *Abraham Lincoln, the Quakers, and the Civil War.* Santa Barbara, CA: Praeger, 2014.

Kennedy, Thomas C. *British Quakerism, 1860–1920: The Transformation of a Religious Community.* Oxford: Oxford University Press, 2001.

———. *A History of Southland College: The Society of Friends and Black Education in Arkansas.* Fayetteville: University of Arkansas Press, 2009.

Kershner, Jon R. *Quakers and Mysticism: Comparative and Syncretic Approaches to Spirituality.* New York: Palgrave Macmillan, 2019.

Krippner, James, and David Harrington Watt. "Henry Cadbury, the Peace Testimony, and the First World War." *Quaker Religious Thought* 133 (2019): 5–13.

Lapsansky, Emma J., and Anne Verplanck. *Quaker Aesthetics: Reflections on a Quaker Ethic in American Design and Consumption, 1720–1920.* Philadelphia: University of Pennsylvania Press, 2003.

Lapsansky-Werner, Emma J., and Margaret Hope Bacon. *Back to Africa: Benjamin Coates and the Colonization Movement in America, 1848–1880.* University Park: Pennsylvania State University Press, 2005.

Lerner, Gerda. *The Grimké Sisters from South Carolina: Pioneers for Woman's Rights and Abolition.* New York: Schocken, 1967.

Le Shana, David C. *Quakers in California: The Effects of 19th Century Revivalism on Western Quakerism.* Newberg, OR: Barclay Press, 1969.

Littleboy, William. *The Appeal of Quakerism to the Non-mystic.* London: Friends' Book Centre, 1916.

Manousos, Anthony. *Howard and Anna Brinton: Re-inventors of Quakerism in the Twentieth Century.* Philadelphia: FGC Quaker Bridge, 2013.

May, Isaac Barnes. "The Blessed Channel of Work: Gender, Power and the Union of the Women's Foreign Missionary Societies in the Religious Society of Friends." *Quaker History* 107, no. 1 (2018): 27–53.

———. "Opening the Shutters: Gurneyite Quakerism and the Struggle for Women's Equality in the Meeting for Business, 1859 to 1930." *Quaker Studies* 18, no. 2 (2013): 170–90.

McDaniel, Donna, and Vanessa Julye. *Fit for Freedom, Not for Friendship: Quakers, African Americans, and the Myth of Racial Justice.* Philadelphia: Quaker Press of Friends General Conference, 2009.

McMahon, Elisabeth. "A 'Spiritual Pilgrim': The Life of Rasoah Mutuha, an East African Quaker." *Quaker History* 95, no. 1 (2006): 44–56.

Mendl, Wolf. *Prophets and Reconcilers: Reflections on the Quaker Peace Testimony*. London: Friends Home Service Committee, 1974.

Mendlesohn, Farah. *Quaker Relief Work in the Spanish Civil War*. Lampeter, UK: Edwin Mellen, 2002.

Milligan, Edward H. *Biographical Dictionary of British Quakers in Commerce and Industry 1775–1920*. York, UK: William Sessions, 2007.

———. *The Past Is Prologue: 100 Years of Quaker Overseas Work, 1868–1968*. London: Friends Service Council, 1968.

Minear, Mark. *Richmond 1887: A Quaker Drama Unfolds*. Richmond, IN: Friends United Press, 1987.

Mingins, Rosemary. *The Beacon Controversy and Challenges to British Quaker Tradition in the Early Nineteenth Century: Some Responses to the Evangelical Revival by Friends in Manchester and Kendal*. Lampeter, UK: Edwin Mellen, 2004.

Moke, Paul. "Quakers in the Coalfields: Economic Justice and the American Friends Service Committee, 1920–Present." In *Quakers, Politics, and Economics*, edited by David R. Ross and Michael T. Snarr, 120–43. Philadelphia: Friends Association for Higher Education, 2018.

Mombo, Esther. "A Historical and Cultural Analysis of the Position of Abaluyia Women in Quaker Christianity: 1902–1979." PhD diss., University of Edinburgh, 1998.

Moore, John M., ed. *Friends in the Delaware Valley*. Haverford, PA: Friends Historical Association, 1981.

Ngesa, Stanley Chagala. "Maragoli Tradition Absorbs Quaker Christianity." MA thesis, Earlham School of Religion, 2020.

———. "Quaker Christianity in Kenya." *Friends Journal* (October 1, 2019).

Nixon, E. Anna. *A Century of Planting: A History of the American Friends Mission in India*. Canton, OH: Evangelical Friends Church Eastern Region, 1985.

O'Donnell, Elizabeth A. "Woman's Rights and Woman's Duties: Quaker Women in the Nineteenth Century, with Special Reference to Newcastle Monthly Meeting of Women Friends." PhD diss., University of Sunderland, 1999.

Oliver, John W., ed. *J. Walter Malone: The Autobiography of an Evangelical Quaker*. Lanham, MD: University Press of America, 1993.

Oliver, John W., and Emma J. Lapsansky-Werner, eds. *Stone Man Preacher: J. Walter Malone*. Canton, OH: Oliver House, 2016.

Oliver, John W., Jr., Charles L. Cherry, and Caroline L. Cherry, eds. *Founded by Friends: The Quaker Heritage of Fifteen American Colleges and Universities*. Lanham, MD: Scarecrow Press, 2007.

Palmer, Beverly Wilson, et al., eds. *Selected Letters of Lucretia Coffin Mott*. Urbana: University of Illinois Press, 2002.

Phillips, Brian. "Friendly Patriotism: British Quakerism and the Imperial Nation 1890–1910." PhD diss., University of Cambridge, 1989.

Pringle, Cyrus G. *The Record of a Quaker Conscience*. New York: Macmillan, 1918.

Punshon, John. *Portrait in Grey*. Rev. ed. London: Quaker Home Service, 1984.

Rappleye, Charles. *Herbert Hoover in the White House: The Ordeal of the*

Presidency. New York: Simon and Schuster, 2016.

Rasmussen, Ane Marie Bak. *A History of the Quaker Movement in Africa*. New York: I. B. Tauris, 1995.

Roberts, Sian. "A 'Position of Particular Responsibility': Quaker Women and Transnational Humanitarian Relief, 1914–1924." *Quaker Studies* 21, no. 2 (2016): 235–55.

Rock, Hugh. "Rufus Jones Never Did Establish That Quakerism Is a Mystical Religion." *Quaker Studies* 21, no. 1 (2016): 49–66.

Rumball, Hannah F. "The Relinquishment of Plain Dress: British Quaker Women's Abandonment of Plain Quaker Attire, 1860–1914." PhD diss., University of Brighton, 2016.

Schmidt, Leigh Eric. *Restless Souls: The Making of American Spirituality*. San Francisco: HarperCollins, 2005.

Sleapwood, Nicola. "The Birmingham Quaker Community, 1800–1900." In *Quakers, Business, and Industry*, ed. by Stephen W. Angell and Pink Dandelion, 213–41. Longmeadow, MA: Full Media Services and Friends Association for Higher Education, 2017.

Smith, Gary Scott. *Religion in the Oval Office: The Religious Lives of American Presidents*. New York: Oxford University Press, 2015.

Smith, Hannah Whitall. *The Christian's Secret of a Happy Life*. London: Willard Tract Repository, 1875.

———. *My Spiritual Autobiography: Or, How I Discovered the Unselfishness of God*. New York: Fleming H. Revell, 1903.

Smith, Helen V. "Elizabeth Taylor Cadbury (1858–1951): Religion, Maternalism, and Social Reform in Birmingham 1888–1914." PhD diss., University of Birmingham, 2012.

Southern, Alice. "The Rowntree History Series and the Growth of Liberal Quakerism." *Quaker Studies* 16, no. 1 (2011): 7–73.

Spencer, Carole Dale. "Evangelism, Feminism, and Social Reform: The Quaker Woman Minister and the Holiness Revival." *Quaker History* 80, no. 1 (1991): 25.

———. *Holiness: The Soul of Quakerism*. Milton Keynes, UK: Paternoster, 2007.

Stansell, Ron. *Missions by the Spirit: Learning from Quaker Exemplars*. Newberg, OR: Barclay Press, 2009.

Stephen, Caroline Emelia. *Light Arising*. Cambridge: W. Heffer & Sons, 1908.

———. *Quaker Strongholds*. 3rd ed. London: Edward Hicks, 1891 [1890].

Sykes, Marjorie. *An Indian Tapestry: Quaker Threads in the History of India, Pakistan, and Bangladesh*. York, UK: William Sessions, 1997.

Thomas, Lamont D. *Paul Cuffe: Black Entrepreneur and Pan-Africanist*. Urbana: University of Illinois Press, 1988.

Thomas, Nancy J. *A Long Walk, a Gradual Ascent: The Story of the Bolivian Friends Church in Its Context of Conflict*. Eugene, OR: Wipf and Stock, 2019.

Thomas, Samuel S. "Gender and Religion on the Mission Station: Roxie Reeve and the Friends' African Mission." *Quaker History* 88, no. 2 (1999): 24–46.

Thurman, Howard. *With Head and Heart: The Autobiography of Howard Thurman*. San Diego, CA: Harcourt Brace Jovanovich, 1979.

Trueblood, D. Elton. "The Paradox of the Quaker Ministry." *Quaker Religious Thought* 8, no. 1 (1962): 8.

Vining, Elizabeth Gray. *Friend of Life: The Biography of Rufus M. Jones.* Philadelphia: J. B. Lippincott, 1958.

Wagenknecht, Edward. *John Greenleaf Whittier: A Portrait in Paradox.* New York: Oxford University Press, 1967.

Watt, David Harrington. "Eugenicists, Quakers, and Rufus Jones, 1893–1938." *Quaker Religious Thought* 135 (September 2020): 14–26.

———. "Philadelphia, Rufus Jones, and the Reinvention of Quakerism." In *Religion in Philadelphia*, edited by Elizabeth Hayes Alvarez, 218–24. Philadelphia: Temple University Press, 2016.

Weaver, Harold D., Jr., Paul Kriese, and Stephen W. Angell, eds. *Black Fire: African American Quakers on Spirituality and Human Rights.* Philadelphia: Quaker Press of Friends General Conference, 2011.

Wellman, Judith. *The Road to Seneca Falls: Elizabeth Cady Stanton and the First Woman's Rights Convention.* Urbana: University of Illinois Press, 2004.

Whittier, John Greenleaf, ed. *The Poetical Works in Four Volumes.* Boston: Houghton Mifflin, 1892.

Wilbur, John. *Journal of the Life of John Wilbur.* Providence, RI: G. H. Whitney, 1859.

———. *A Narrative and Exposition of the Late Proceedings of New England Yearly Meeting.* New York: Piercy & Reed, 1845.

Wilson, Roger C. *Manchester, Manchester and Manchester Again: From "Sound Doctrine" to "a Free Ministry"—the Theological Travail of London Yearly Meeting Throughout the Nineteenth Century.* Based on Wilson's Presidential Address of 1988. London: Friends Historical Society, 1990.

Wood, Herbert G. *Henry T. Hodgkin: A Memoir.* London: Student Christian Movement Press, 1937.

Wynter, Rebecca. "Conscription, Conscience and Controversy: The Friends' Ambulance Unit and the 'Middle Course' in the First World War." *Quaker Studies* 21, no. 2 (2016): 213–33.

CONTRIBUTORS

STEPHEN W. ANGELL is the Leatherock Professor of Quaker Studies at the Earlham School of Religion. He is an associate editor of *Quaker Studies* and *Quaker Theology*. His books include *The Cambridge Companion to Quakerism* (with Pink Dandelion); *The Oxford Handbook of Quaker Studies* (with Pink Dandelion); and *Black Fire: African American Quakers on Spirituality and Human Rights* (with Harold D. Weaver Jr. and Paul Kriese). With Pink Dandelion, he is editor in chief of the Brill series in Quaker Studies.

JOANNA CLARE DALES earned a PhD at Cambridge University for her thesis on "The Novel as Domestic Conduct-Book, Richardson to Jane Austen." She taught in the English departments of the University of Glasgow, the University of Leeds, and the Open University. Dales earned a second PhD at the University of Birmingham in 2016 for the thesis "John William Graham (1859–1932), Quaker Apostle of Progress," and, enabled by the Carroll Scholarship, she spent a year in residence at Pendle Hill, the Quaker study center in Pennsylvania.

PINK DANDELION directs the work of the Centre for Research in Quaker Studies at Woodbrooke and is Professor of Quaker Studies at the University of Birmingham and a Research Fellow at Lancaster University. He edits *Quaker Studies* and convenes the Quaker Studies Research Association. His books include *The Cultivation of Conformity: Towards a General Theory of Internal Secularisation*; *Early Quakers and Their Theological Thought, 1647–1723* (with Stephen Angell); and *The Oxford Handbook of Quaker Studies* (with Stephen Angell). With Stephen Angell, he is editor in chief of the Brill series in Quaker Studies.

RICHARD KENT EVANS is Visiting Assistant Professor of Quaker Studies at Haverford College and is the program coordinator for the Political Theology Network. He is the author of *MOVE: An American Religion*, as well as a number of book chapters and articles on Quaker history, African American religions, and the history of madness. Evans received his PhD in North American Religions from Temple University in 2018.

DOUGLAS GWYN is an independent scholar. He has contributed articles to the *Journal of the Friends Historical Society* and *Quaker Studies*. He has also contributed book chapters to *The Creation of Quaker Theory: Insider Perspectives*, *The Oxford Handbook of Quaker Studies*, and *Early Quakers and Their Theological Thought, 1647–1723*.

THOMAS D. HAMM is Professor of History and Quaker Scholar in Residence at Earlham College, where he holds the Trueblood Chair in Christian Thought and has been on the faculty since 1987. His books include *The Quakers in America*; *Quaker Writings: An Anthology, 1650–1920*; and *Liberal Quakerism in America in the Long Nineteenth Century, 1790–1920*.

ROBYNNE ROGERS HEALEY is Professor of History and the codirector of the Gender Studies Institute at Trinity Western University in British Columbia, Canada. She is associate editor (history) of the Brill series in Quaker Studies and convenes the Conference of Quaker Historians and Archivists. Her publications include *Quakerism in the Atlantic World, 1690–1830*; *From Quaker to Upper Canadian: Faith and Community Among Yonge Street Friends, 1801–1850*; and *Quaker Studies: An Overview, the Current State of the Field* (with C. Wess Daniels and Jon R. Kershner); as well as many articles and chapters in the field of Quaker history, especially concerning eighteenth-century topics and the evolution of the peace testimony.

JULIE L. HOLCOMB is Associate Professor in Museum Studies at Baylor University. She is the author of *Moral Commerce: Quakers and the Transatlantic Boycott of the Slave Labor Economy* and the editor of *Southern Sons, Northern Soldiers: The Civil War Letters of the Remley Brothers, 22nd Iowa*

Infantry. In addition to her books, Holcomb has published widely in a variety of academic and popular venues. She serves as editor of *Quaker History*, the peer-reviewed journal published by the Friends Historical Association. She received her PhD in History from the University of Texas at Arlington.

SYLVESTER A. JOHNSON is Assistant Vice Provost for the Humanities and Executive Director of the Tech for Humanity initiative at Virginia Tech. He is the founding director of Virginia Tech's Center for Humanities, which intersects with Tech for Humanity by supporting human-centered research and humanistic approaches to the guidance of technology. Johnson's research has examined religion, race, and empire in the Atlantic world; religion and sexuality; national security practices; and the impact of intelligent machines and human enhancement on human identity and race governance. In addition to cofacilitating a national working group on religion and US empire, Johnson led an artificial intelligence project that developed a successful proof-of-concept machine-learning application to ingest and analyze a humanities text. He is the author of *The Myth of Ham in Nineteenth-Century American Christianity* and *African American Religions, 1500–2000* and coeditor (with Steven Weitzman) of *The FBI and Religion: Faith and National Security Before and After 9/11*.

STEPHANIE MIDORI KOMASHIN is a doctoral candidate in Religion and Indian Philosophy at Hokkaido University and a Specially Appointed Lecturer at Hokkaido University of Education, Asahikawa, in Japan. A recipient of the Japanese Government (MEXT) Scholarship, she holds an MDiv from Princeton Theological Seminary. Her publications include "How Ecology, Economics, and Ethics Brought Winstanley and Nitobe to Quakerism," in *Quakers and Mysticism: Comparative and Syncretic Approaches to Spirituality*; "Quakers in Asia-Pacific," in *The Cambridge Companion to Quakerism*; "Miyabe Kingo no Joseikan" (Kingo Miyabe's View of Women), in *Kirisutokyou-Gaku (Studium Christianitatis)*; and, with Andrew Komasinski, "How Relational Selfhood Rearranges the Debate Between Feminists and Confucians," in *Feminist Encounters with Confucius*.

EMMA JONES LAPSANSKY is Emeritus Professor of History and Curator of the Quaker Collection at Haverford College. After a yearlong break in her undergraduate education to work in the civil rights movement in Mississippi with the Delta Ministry of the National Council of Churches, she received her PhD in American Civilization from the University of Pennsylvania. Her research interests include Quaker history and African American history—and, in particular, the intersection between the two—as well as Pennsylvania history, the American West, and various aspects of American social and material-culture history. Her recent publications include *Quaker Aesthetics* (with Anne Verplanck); and *Back to Africa: Benjamin Coates and the Colonization Movement in America, 1848–1880* (with Margaret Hope Bacon). With Gary Nash and Clayborne Carson, Lapsansky has authored *The Struggle for Freedom*, a college text on African American history, the third edition of which appeared in 2018.

ISAAC BARNES MAY is an Assistant Professor of American Studies at the University of Virginia. He holds a PhD in Religious Studies from that institution and a Master of Theological Studies from Harvard Divinity School. May was a contributor to *The Cambridge Companion to Quakerism*. He writes on law, religion, and the religious left.

NICOLA SLEAPWOOD is a PhD candidate in Theology and Religion at the University of Birmingham. With her doctoral project, supported by the Quakers and Business Group, she seeks to establish reasons behind Quaker business decline over the course of the nineteenth and twentieth centuries. Her publications include a chapter on the Birmingham Quaker business community in the nineteenth century in *Quakers, Business, and Industry: Quakers and the Disciplines*, volume 4, and "Albright & Wilson and Change in the Quaker Business Environment During World War I," in *Quaker Studies* (2019). Sleapwood holds an MA in Medieval Studies from the University of York.

CAROLE DALE SPENCER is Adjunct Professor of Spiritual Formation at Portland Seminary of George Fox University. She was formerly Associate Professor of Christian Spirituality at Earlham School of Religion. Spencer is the author of *Holiness: The Soul of Quakerism* and has contributed numerous book chapters and articles on Quaker history and theology, including, most recently, "James Nayler and Jacob Boehme's *The Way to Christ*" and "Hannah Whitall Smith's Highway of Holiness," in *Quakers and Mysticism: Comparative and Syncretic Approaches to Spirituality*.

RANDALL L. TAYLOR worked at NASA's Jet Propulsion Laboratory in procurement and project management for thirty-seven years. He holds a JD from UCLA School of Law, and he served as articles editor for *UCLA-Alaska Law Review*. He has published extensively in law reviews and in technical journals, particularly *IEEE*, on topics related to engineering and management of space exploration projects and missions.

DAVID HARRINGTON WATT is the Douglas and Dorothy Steere Professor of Quaker Studies at Haverford College. In collaboration with Laura Levitt and Tracy Fessenden, he edits the North American Religions series for NYU Press. Books in the series explore such topics as lived religion, popular religious movements, religion and social power, religion and cultural reproduction, and the relationship between secular and religious practices. Watt's publications include *Antifundamentalism in Modern America*; *Fundamentalism: Perspectives on a Contested History* (with Simon Wood); and *Bible-Carrying Christians: Conservative Protestants and Social Power*. His current research focuses on twentieth-century Quakers' interpretations of the peace testimony and on Quakers' responses to the Holocaust.

INDEX

Aarek, Hans Eirik, 15
AASS (American Anti-Slavery Society), 40, 43, 47–49, 104
Abel, William, 192
abolitionism, 37–57
   American Civil War, 54–55
   free produce movement, 43–45
   Hicksites, 37–38, 50–52, 62–65, 104, 151
   overview, 39–43
   previous studies, 13–16
   Underground Railroad, 45–47
   and Whittier, 158–59
   Wilburites, 50
   women's rights, 47–49
   worldly entanglement, 24–25
absolute pacifism, 9, 12, 214, 221–22, 224–25, 248, 256
   See also peace testimony
abstention from slave-labor products, 29, 43–45, 52, 54, 63
ACS (American Colonization Society), 23, 39
active service, 214, 221, 224, 227
adult schools, 8, 92, 106, 138, 176
Advocate of Peace, The, 227–28
Africa
   African American settlement in, 23
   British imperial expansion, 215–16
   and empire, 20
   Global South, 191, 278
   mission work, 8, 16, 72, 89, 103, 157, 172, 192–94, 196–97, 202–5, 206, 209–10
   religion and commerce, 29–30
   social order, 174
   See also South Africa
African Americans, 22–24, 34–35, 45–47, 53, 55–56, 166, 232, 273
   See also abolitionism; race/racism
AFSC. *See* American Friends Service Committee (AFSC)
agnosticism, 139, 147, 162
Aids to Reflection (Coleridge), 129
Aiken, Guy, 15
Åland Islands Question, 238
Alaska, 14, 72
Alexander, Horace, 195
Allen, Richard, 45
Allen, William, 23
All-Friends Conferences, 248–67
   London (1920), 2–3, 7, 34, 230–31, 249–54
   Oskaloosa (1929), 256–61
   Philadelphia (1937), 261-66
   See also Friends World Conference
alternative service, 12, 181, 214, 221–30
   See also conscientious objection; peace testimony
American All-Friends Conference, 256–61
American Anti-Slavery Society (AASS), 40, 43, 47–49, 104

American churches, 100, 119–20, 226, 255
American Civil War, 26, 31, 38–39, 54–57, 81, 215, 227, 236–37, 248
American Colonization Society (ACS), 23, 39
American Free Produce Association, 43, 44
American Friend, The, 70, 156, 167, 187, 189, 255, 259–60, 265–66
American Friends
  All-Friends Conference, London, 255
  All-Friends Conference, Oskaloosa, 256–57
  education, 108
  enlistment in World War I, 214
  Friends World Conference, Philadelphia, 262
  Holiness movement, 154–57
  Inward Light, 77
  liberal Quakerism, 128
  mission work, 72–73, 82, 197, 202–11
  modernizing world, 65–69
  paid ministry, 101, 279
  peace testimony, 214–15, 217, 227–29, 248–49, 252
  religious madness debate, 122–23
  response to revivalism, 92
  slavery, 63
  social order, 174, 182–89
American Friends Board of Foreign Missions, 197, 209
American Friends Service Committee (AFSC), 71, 73–74
  All-Friends Conference, Oskaloosa, 256–57, 259
  alternative service, 228–30
  development of, 248–49
  Friends World Conference, Philadelphia, 262
  and Hoover, 33
  and Jones, 270
  Oregon Yearly Meeting, 15
  overview, 8–9
  peace testimony, 213–14
  Pendle Hill, 170
  relief work, 243
  Social Gospel, 188
  work of Friends during and after World War II, 264
American Historical Review, 273
American Indian boarding schools, 27
Amugamwa, Benson, 210
Anglicans/Anglicanism, 100, 116, 132, 144, 153, 175–76, 194, 201–2, 233
Anglo-Boer War, 28–29, 218–20
Anglo-Egyptian War, 245
anti-abolitionist mob violence, 42
anti-colonization efforts, 39
antislavery activism. *See* abolitionism
Anti-Slavery Friends, 53–54
antiwar statements. *See* peace testimony
Apology for the True Christian Divinity (Barclay), 8, 154, 194
Appeal of Quakerism to the Non-mystic, The (Littleboy), 169
Appeal to the Colored Citizens of the World (Walker), 39, 45
Ashton, Philip, 177
Asia, 20, 29, 89, 174, 191, 208, 215–16
assimilation, 9–10, 27–29
Association of Evangelical Friends, 6
Association of Friends for Advocating the Cause of the Slave, 43
Association of Medical Superintendents of American Institutions for the Insane, 115, 124
asylums, 113–24
  See also individual asylums
Australia, 20, 33, 59, 222–23, 249, 252
Austria, 15, 262
Ayllón, Juan, 192–93
Aymara peoples of Bolivia, 72, 192–93, 200
Azusa Pacific University, 102

Baird, Esther, 195, 197, 204
Baker, Joseph Allen, 235, 244–45
Baker, Lorenzo, 203
Balkill, Helen, 67
Ballot Act of 1872, 237
Baltimore, Maryland, 88, 183
Baltimore Monthly Meeting, 234
Baltimore Yearly Meeting, 7, 87, 186, 228
Bancroft, Joseph, 184–85
Banes, Cuba, 203

Bangor Quarterly Meeting, 82
Barbadoes, James, 40
Barclay, Robert, 8, 59, 73, 92, 95–96, 120, 146–47, 154, 156, 194
Barclay College, 102
Barlow, John Emmott, 244, 250–51
Barnard, Hannah, 60–61
Barr, Daisy Douglas Brushwiller, 34–35, 186
"Basis of Quaker Optimism, The" (Jones), 263–64
Bassett, William, 42–43
Baxter, Richard, 143
Beaconites, 3–4, 13, 131
Bean, Hannah E., 67, 78, 82
Bean, Joel, 60, 67, 82, 84, 91, 155–56
Bear Creek, Iowa, 89–90
Bear Creek Meeting, 82
Bebbington, David, 163
Beecher, Catharine, 47
Bell, William, 80–81
Benezet, Anthony, 21–22, 43
Benjamin, Philip, 183
Bennett, Edward Trusted, 137
Berea Bible Institute, 192
Berlin Conference, 216
Bethlehem Steel, 30
Bethlem (Bedlam) Hospital, 114, 121
Bevan, Stacy E., 82
Bible Association of Friends, Philadelphia, 66
Bible study, 4–5, 49, 61, 101–2, 153–54, 162
biblical authority, 7, 66–67, 76, 131–34, 136, 139, 154, 171, 258, 275
bibliolatry, 136
Bigland, Alfred, 179–80
Bill to Reform Banks, 240
Binford, Raymond, 259
biography, 14–15
Birmingham, England, 25, 132, 144
Birmingham Central, 233
Black abolitionists, 39–40, 42, 45–47
Black American settlers, 23
Black Laws, 53
Black South Africans, 28–29
blood as necessary for redemption, 140, 189
Bloomingdale Insane Asylum, 115, 121, 123
Blount, Mattie, 192

Board of Trade, 178, 233
Boer War. *See* Anglo-Boer War
Bolivia, 72, 103, 191, 192, 200, 212
Bond, Archibald A., 210
Bond, John S., 82
Bonus Army, 31, 243
book(s) of discipline, 87, 182, 235
Borneo War, 236
Boxers, 204
boycotts. *See* abstention from slave-labor products
Brahmo Samaj, 198
Braithwaite, Anna Lloyd, 66
Braithwaite, Joseph Bevan, 60, 70–71, 135, 137, 140–43, 145–46, 153–54, 157, 168
Braithwaite, Joseph Bevan Jr., 138
Braithwaite, William Charles, 13, 143, 167–68, 171
Branson, Anna, 259
Breed, Ebenezer, 184
Bretton Woods agreements, 266
Brigham, Amariah, 113, 119–20, 123
Bright, Elizabeth Priestman, 235
Bright, Jacob, 243
Bright, John, 11, 28, 175–77, 233–38, 243–47, 274
Bright, John Albert, 243
Bright, Margaret Elizabeth Leatham, 235
Bright, William Leatham, 243
Brinton, Anna Cox, 171, 253
Brinton, Howard, 158, 170–71, 253
Britain, social order, 10, 174–82
Britain Yearly Meeting. *See* London/London Yearly Meeting
British Empire, 20–21
British Foreign Office, 29
British Friend, The, 91, 125, 140, 156, 245
British Friends
  abolitionists, 39, 48, 62, 65, 200
  and the AFSC, 230
  All-Friends Conference, London, 249–52
  Beaconites, 3–4
  and Bright, 235–38
  education, 108
  enlistment, 214
  ethical principles to Quaker involvement with empire, 25–29

female ministers, 96
Friends Service Council (FSC), 261
and Gurney, 153
liberal Quakerism, 7, 8–9, 128–32, 137–38
mission work, 28, 72, 194–95, 201
modernizing world, 65–69, 71
paid ministry, 279
pastoral Friends, 106–8
peace testimony, 215–21, 224–25
in politics, 11
previous studies, 13
psychiatric treatment, 114
Quaker Renaissance, 167–70
responses to revival movement, 91–92
social class, 110
Test Act of 1673, 232
theological challenges, 139
World War I, 221–25, 248–49
British Friends Mission, 198, 202
British India Society, 63
British Ladies' Society for Promoting the Reformation of Female Prisoner, 65
Broad Church theology, 131–32, 139
Brock, Peter, 217
Brooklyn, New York, 88
Brown, Charles Brockden, 68
Brown, Clare, 14
Brown, Heloise, 219
Buchanan, James, 41
Buckingham Female Anti-Slavery Society, 45
Budge, Frances Anne, 152
Buffum, Arnold, 40, 53
Bundelkhand, India, 197
Burdick, Timothy, 15
Bureau of Indian Affairs, 234, 242
Burma War, 236
Burrows, George Man, 117
Burundi, Africa, 8, 103
Bush, Julia, 14
business activity/businessmen, 30, 175–82, 184
Butler, Esther, 197
Butler, John, 91
Butler, Smedley Darlington, 31–32, 35
Butler, Thomas, 31
Bweyenda, Dorika, 205, 206

cacao in Portuguese colonies, 29–30
Cadbury, Dorothy, 175
Cadbury, Elizabeth Bartram, 269, 272
Cadbury, Elizabeth Taylor, 14, 244, 251
Cadbury, George, 30, 107, 144, 168, 178, 180
Cadbury, Henry J., 16, 102, 170, 228, 252, 260
Cadbury family, 29–30, 31, 178–79
Cala, Francisco, 203
Calcutta, India, 194–95, 198
Calhoun, John C., 41
California, 8, 14, 156, 192–93, 234
Calvin, John, 133
Cambridge Companion to Quakerism, The, 16
Cambridge Platonists, 147
Campbellite revival, 82
Canada, 14, 15, 16, 59, 87, 89, 220, 223, 237, 249, 258
capitalism, 25, 61, 63–64, 70, 180, 187–90, 222–23, 253
Capron, Effingham, 40
Caribbean, 31
Carlisle Indian Industrial School, 27
Carlyle, Thomas, 233
Cash, Bill, 238
Catholics, 115, 117, 143, 158, 194
Caton, Mary Anne, 69
Ceadel, Martin, 216
Central America, 8, 16, 31, 242, 278
Central Philadelphia Monthly Meeting, 234
Central Yearly Meetings, 6, 8
Chaco War, 200
Chamberlain, Joseph, 179
Chandler, Elizabeth Margaret, 39
Channing, William Ellery, 104, 133
Charles II, King, 9, 213
Cherry, Charles L., 114, 117
Chester County, Pennsylvania, 40–41
Chester County Anti-Slavery Society, 50–51
Chiarugi, Vincenzo, 117–18
Children of Peace, 16
Chilson, Arthur, 194, 196–97, 209–10
Chilson, Edna, 194
China, 8, 31, 33, 72, 191, 197, 199–200, 203–4, 208, 216, 239, 249
Cho, Mijin, 13–14
Cho, Nancy, 69

Christianity and War, 218, 219
Christian mysticism, 125, 165
Christian spirituality, 256
Christian's Secret of a Happy Life, The (Smith), 86, 161–62
Christian Worker, The, 167
Churchill, Winston, 230
Church Missionary Society, 199
Church of England, 95, 232
Church of God, 161, 194
Cincinnati, Ohio, 45–46
CIS (Council for International Service), 248–49, 261
civic participation, 9–11
civilian relief. *See* relief work
Civilization Act, 59
Clark, Dougan, 75–76, 85, 88, 92, 99, 101, 156, 158
Clark, Roger, 180
Clarke, James Freeman, 109
Clarkson Anti-Slavery Society, 44
Clay, Henry, 53
Cleveland Bible Institute, 8, 102, 166, 193–94
Clinton County, Ohio, 79
Clothier, Caleb, 43
Clothier, Esther Clark, 244
Clothier Hall, Swarthmore, 263
clothing, 69
  See also plainness and simplicity
Coates, Benjamin, 23
Coates, Lindley, 41
Cobden, Richard, 236
Cobden-Chevalier Treaty of 1860, 237
Coffin, Charles F., 80, 84, 91
Coffin, Elijah, 53
Coffin, Emma Cook, 100
Coffin, Levi, 45–47, 53, 55, 274
Coffin, Rhoda M., 78, 80, 82, 91
Coleridge, Samuel Tayler, 128–29
college and seminary education, 101–3
colonization, 19–24, 29–30, 39, 53, 215–18, 238, 278
Comanches, 27
Committee of American Residents in London, 240
Committee on General Meetings, 92
Committee on Requited Labor, 43

Commons League, 237
competitive capitalism, 187
Comstock, Elizabeth L., 78, 91
Concert of Europe, 216
Confederate States of America (the South), 236–37
Conference on International Arbitration, 27–28, 217
congregational ecclesiology, 3, 16
Congregational Friends, 16, 39, 47, 50, 52, 62–63, 104, 134, 152
Connecticut, 115, 119
conscience clause, 181, 224, 244
conscientious objection, 12, 200, 213–14, 221–31, 237, 249, 256, 321n30
  See also peace testimony
conscription, 12, 180–81, 200, 204–5, 222–25, 248, 256
conservatism, 37–38, 54
conservative-liberal divide, 206–7, 210
Conservatives, 4–5, 7, 16, 45, 89–90, 215, 256, 258
  See also Wilburites
consulates, 261
contagion, 84, 137, 275
conversion and sanctification, 85–86, 90–91, 136, 152, 154
Cooke, Frances, 144
Coolidge, Calvin, 245
Cooper, Wilmer, 16
Corcoran, Abigail, 64
Corn Laws of 1815, 236, 245
corporate spirituality, 150, 172, 279
Cosand, Joseph and Sarah Ann, 193, 198–99
cosmopolitan Quakers, 255–56, 261, 264, 266–67
cotton famine, 237
Council for International Service (CIS), 248–49, 261
Court Dress, 245
Coutant, Sarah, 269
Cox, Anna Shipley. *See* Brinton, Anna Cox
Creative Worship (Brinton), 170
Crewdson, Isaac, 3–4
Crimean War, 26, 71, 216, 236
Crothers, A. Glenn, 14
Cuba, 8, 28, 32, 103, 203, 262, 265

Cuffe, Paul, 22–24
cultural Quakers, 21–22, 31
cultural separatism, 150
Curtis, Charles, 242
Czechoslovakia, 262

Dallas County, Iowa, 82
Darwin, Charles, 131, 141
Darwinism, 139, 216
Davidson, Adam, 199–200
Davidson, Alfred, 199–200
Davidson, Henry, 207–9
Davidson, Mary Jane, 205
Davidson, Robert, 199–200, 207–9
Davidson, Warburton, 199–200, 204
Davidson, William, 199–200
Davie, Martin, 13
Davis, Merle, 210
Dawley, Alan, 184
debtors, 48
Declaration from the Harmless and Innocent people of God, Called Quakers, 213–14, 227
Declaration of Sentiments, 40, 49
Delaware, 21, 47, 62
Delaware Valley, 14, 21
Dell, Frank, 258
Democratic Party, 32–33
Denmark, 15, 249
Dennis, William C., 189
denominationalism, 5, 10, 203
denomination-wide directives, 64–65
Derbyshire, 221
Description of the Retreat (Tuke), 114
Des Moines, Iowa, 184
Devonshire House, 249–51
devotional literature, 154, 156, 158, 161–62, 165, 169, 271
diplomacy, 23, 26–27
direct revelation, 4, 75–76
disciplines, 64
disunion, 42
diverse origins of Quaker missions, 192–95
diversity, creation of modern Quaker, 275–80
diversity of Quakerism, 174, 182–83
"Divinity School Address" (Emerson), 133
Doherty, Robert, 15

Dominican Republic, 32
Dorland, Arthur, 220
D'Ortez, Mariano and Cecilia, 194
doubt, 131–32
Douglas, John Henry, 80–81, 85–86, 100
Douglass, Frederick, 37
Douglass, Sarah Mapps, 22
Driver, Samuel Rolles, 141
Dublin Yearly Meeting, 91–92, 107
DuBois, Rachel Davis, 34, 264–65
Duchy of Lancaster, 233, 246
Duke Divinity School, 102
Duncan, David, 137
Durham, 233
Dutch East India Company, 20
dynastic Quakerism, 12

Earle, Pliny, 113, 123
Earlham College, 75, 78–79, 93, 102, 156, 193
Earlham School of Religion, 108, 111
early Friends
    attitudes toward ministry, 95–97
    English Empire, 21–22
    and the HMC, 138
    Holiness movement, 155–57
    Inward Light, 133, 145–47
    justification and sanctification, 77
    liberal Quakerism, 130
    Manchester Conference, 142–43
    modernist-fundamentalism conflict, 256
    mysticism, 165, 271
    persecution experienced by, 250
    sanctification, 136
    and Wilburites, 49–50
East Africa, 16, 72, 196–97, 204–5, 209–10
Eastern yearly meetings, 255
East Fallowfield, Pennsylvania, 50–51
ecstatic expressions, 209
Edgerton, Joseph, 50
Edgerton, Walter, 53
education
    adult school movement, 92, 176
    All-Friends Conference, London, 253
    All-Friends Conference, Oskaloosa, 259
    British Friends, 108
    of girls and women, 194, 196–97
    and ministry, 95, 101–3
    renewal movement, 79

Education Act of 1902, 244
egalitarianism, 96, 196–97
Egypt, 216, 237, 246
Eighteenth Amendment, 187
Elder, William, 37
Elkinton, Anna Griscom, 262
Elkinton, Mary Patterson, 72, 193, 234
Elkinton, Passmore, 256, 261, 262
Ellis, Edith, 225
Ellis, Edward, 243–44
Ellis, Sarah Stickney, 68
Ellis, William, 198
Ellwood, Thomas, 125
emancipation, 38, 53, 56, 63, 159
    See also slavery
Emancipation Proclamation, 56, 237
Emergency Relief and Construction Act, 243
Emerson, Ralph Waldo, 125, 128–29, 133–35, 145, 160–61
emotionalism, 139
empire(s), 18–36, 179
    and abolitionism, 24–25
    African American Quakers, 22–24
    assimilation and expansion in Quaker religion, 27–29
    contested ideals in the imperial frame, 25–27
    defined, 19–21
    early Quakers and English empire, 21–22
    fighting Quakers, 31–33
    Herbert Hoover and the "American Century," 33–36
    in *The Later Periods*, 278
    missions and, 202–5
    religion and commerce on the world stage, 29–30
employers' conference, 181–82
English East India Company, 20
English Empire, 21–22
English Historical Review, 273
Enlightenment, 128, 150, 151
enlistment, 12, 38, 54–55, 180, 214, 221–27, 248
    See also peace testimony
equality, 11, 39–40, 45, 53, 109, 194, 196
Erie Canal, 61

Essays and Addresses (Rowntree), 168
Essays and Reviews (Shea and Whitla), 131–32, 137
Essays on the Evidences, Doctrines, and Practical Operations of Christianity (Gurney), 153
Essays on the Habitual Exercise of Love to God (Gurney), 154
ethical principles, 25–27
Europe, 240–43, 255, 261–62
European corporations, 29
European empires, 8, 15, 21–22, 26
European–Native American relations, 26
evangelical Christianity, 129, 273
Evangelical Friend, The, 167
evangelical Friends, 6, 66, 218, 257
    and Gurney, 153
    Jones's *The Later Periods*, 276
    liberal Quakerism, 135–37
    modernist-fundamentalist conflict, 183, 255–56
    pastoral system, 103
    previous studies, 15
    programmed, 94
    Quaker Renaissance, 167
    unity, 130–31
    See also mission work
Evangelical Friends Alliance. See Evangelical Friends Church International
Evangelical Friends Church International, 6, 189
evangelicalism, 6, 70–71, 76–77, 79, 128, 132–33, 139, 147, 150, 153–54, 166, 169, 171–72, 175–76, 203, 235, 275, 277, 279
evangelicals, 6, 76, 77, 79, 85, 135–37, 138, 175, 255, 275
evangelism, Christian, 171, 179
Evans, Edward, 253
exclusivist framework of conversion, 205–6
executive secretary positions, 111
exemption clause, 223–24
extraction, 19–20, 24, 28

Factory Acts, 176
Fager, Chuck, 16
Falcetta, Alessandro, 14

Fallowfield Preparative Meeting, 51
Falret, Jean-Pierre, 117
Farmington Quarterly Meeting, 41–42, 44
Fast Friends, 154
FAU (Friends Ambulance Unit), 12, 180, 181, 214, 224, 244
Faulkner, Carol, 14
Fell, Margaret, 59, 96
Fellowship of Reconciliation, 171, 204, 222, 226, 249
Female Vigilant Association, 46
Fénelon, François, 158
Fenn, W. W., 273
Ferris, Benjamin, 58–62
FFMA (Friends Foreign Mission Association), 8, 195
FGC (Friends General Conference), 2, 7, 15, 105, 111, 215, 225–26
FGC Friends, 258, 260–61
fighting Quakers, 31–33
Finland, 238
Finney, Charles Grandison, 135
First Day schools, 4–5, 106
Fistler, Delia, 195, 197
Five Years Meeting (FYM), 2, 6–7, 13, 15, 70, 100, 157, 189, 207, 215, 226–27, 255, 256–58
Ford, Isabella, 13–14
Fort Sumter, South Carolina, 54
Fosdick, Harry Emerson, 15, 165
"Foundations of a True Social Order," 181–82
Fox, George
  antireform argument, 51–52
  autobiographical writing, 150–51
  conscientious objector, 213
  Dell on, 258–59
  divisions among Hicksites, 59
  female ministers, 96
  Inward Light, 133, 145–47
  James on, 112, 124–25
  liberal Quakerism, 129–30
  ministry, 95, 100, 144
  mission work, 200–201
  mysticism, 164, 271
  and Nitobe, 233–34
  as outlaw, 9
  perfection doctrine, 154

reform movements, 38
religious madness debate, 120
Frame, Esther, 87, 89, 98, 101
Frame, Nathan, 87, 98
France, 15, 21, 25, 115, 117, 230, 237, 242, 249
Franco-Prussian War, 216
Frankel, Mark, 14
freedmen, 38, 55–56, 81
Freedmen's Bureau, 55
free produce movement, 25, 38, 39–40, 43–45, 50, 54, 63
Free Quakers, 31
Free Silver, 187
free trade, 176, 179–80, 237–38
French and Indian War, 22
French imperialism, 26
French Protestants, 202
Frere, W. H., 273
Friend, The, 8, 41, 54, 56, 67, 81, 90, 235, 261
Friend-in-residence, 111
Friends Ambulance Unit (FAU), 12, 180, 181, 214, 224, 244
Friends and War, 254
Friends Asylum (Friends Hospital), 121
Friends at Their Own Fireside (Ellis), 68
Friends Bible Institute, 103
Friends Bible Institute and Training School, 106
Friends Central Bureau, 105
Friends church, 4, 99–100, 103, 137, 171–72, 194
Friends Foreign Mission Association (FFMA), 8, 195
Friends General Conference (FGC), 2, 7, 15, 105, 111, 215, 225–26
Friends Historical Society, 17, 143
Friends Hospital, 114, 121–23
Friends Industrial Mission, 72
Friends' Intelligencer, 185–86, 189
Friends Missionary Advocate, 206
Friends' Review, 67, 91, 93, 122, 167, 187
Friends Service Council in Britain (FSC), 213, 224–25, 244, 261–62, 264
Friends Social Union (FSU), 178, 180–81
Friends' South African War Victims' Fund, 219–20
Friends Theological College, 103

Friends United Meeting (FUM), 70, 103, 109–10
Friends University, 257
Friends War Victims Relief Committee, 214, 216, 224
Friends World Committee for Consultation (FWCC), 3, 7, 74, 266
Friends World Conference, Philadelphia (1937), 261–67
frontier Friends, 66
Frost, Gideon, 185
Frost, J. William, 15, 69
Froude, James Anthony, 131
Fry, Elizabeth Gurney, 60, 64–65, 121, 205–6, 274
Fry, Isabel, 13–14
Fry, Joan Mary, 144, 251
Fry, Margery, 14
Fry, Ruth, 14
Fry family, 29–30
FSC (Friends Service Council in Britain), 213, 224–25, 244, 261–62, 264
FSU (Friends Social Union), 178, 180–81
FUM (Friends United Meeting), 70, 103, 109–10
fundamentalism, 98, 171–72, 183, 189, 256
Fussell, Edwin, 51
FWCC (Friends World Committee for Consultation), 3, 7, 74, 266
FYM (Five Years Meeting), 2, 6–7, 13, 15, 70, 100, 157, 189, 207, 215, 226–27, 255, 256–58

gag rule, 40–41
Galton, Samuel Sr. and Jr., 25–26
Gandhi, Mohandas, 195, 208
Ganguly, J. N. C., 251–52
Garrett, Thomas, 46–47
Garrison, William Lloyd, 37–38, 39–43, 47–48, 159
Gaynor, Lucy, 197
gender egalitarianism, 96
gender equality, 37–38, 45, 196–97
gender in mission work, 192, 196–97
general meeting movement, 84–86
Genesee Yearly Meeting, 44, 52
Genius of Universal Emancipation, 39, 63
George, David Lloyd, 30
George, Lloyd, 178

German Crimes and Our Civil Remedy (Sefton-Jones), 222
Germany, 15, 115–16, 117, 216, 242, 248, 251, 261–62, 264
Gibara, Cuba, 203
Gibbons, James S., 52
Gibson, William, 96–97
Gifford Lectures, 112
Gilboa Methodist Church, 83
Girsberger, Freda, 205
Glens Falls, New York, 88
global peace conferences. *See* All-Friends Conferences
global Quakerism and mission work, 7–9, 89
Global South, 191, 278
good works, 50, 151
Gospel of Divine Help, The (Worsdell), 140
government. *See* laws of nations
Graham, John William
  All-Friends Conference, Oskaloosa, 257, 260
  British imperialism, 28
  Inward Light, 146
  liberal Quakerism, 135–36, 137–38
  London Yearly Meeting, 249
  Manchester Conference, 141
  ministry, 144
  mysticism, 129–30
  previous studies, 14
  theological challenges, 139–40
Grant, Ulysses S., 11, 26–28
Great Britain, 28, 167–69, 202–5, 273
Great Depression, 36, 188–89, 242–43
Great Plains, 27
Great Revival, 84
Great Separation, 3, 15, 134, 262, 273–74, 328n23, 330n39
Green Street Meeting, Philadelphia, 62
Greenwood, John Ormerod, 195
Grellet, Stephen, 152–53, 205–6
Grimké, Angelina and Sarah, 47
Grubb, Edward, 129–31, 136, 138, 139, 146–47, 168
Grubb, Isabel, 257–58
Grundy, Martha Paxson, 183
Guatemala, 103, 191, 192, 197
Guide to True Peace, A, 158

Guislain, Joseph, 117
Gunn, Lewis C., 44
Gurney, Eliza, 56
Gurney, Joseph John, 60
    authority of scripture, 3–4
    Conservative Friends, 90
    Jones's *The Later Periods*, 274
    Orthodox Friends, 134
    overview, 76–77, 153–54
    paid ministers, 97
    peacemaking tour, 65–66
    reform movements, 49
Gurneyites, 76–78, 153–54
    British Friends, 108
    Gurney-Wilbur conflict, 50
    Holiness movement, 154–57
    internal improvements, 67
    Jones's *The Later Periods*, 273–74
    liberal Quakerism, 134–36
    mission work, 8
    paid ministry, 94
    pastoral system, 97–103
    reform movements, 39
    renewal movement, 78–79
    revival movement, 87–93
    revivals and missions, 80–82
    separations/schisms, 4–7, 215
    silent worship, 159
    status and social class, 110
    See also Richmond Conference
Guyon, Jeanne, 158
Guy's Hospital, 114

Haines, Margaret, 199
Haiti, 32, 35
Hallaran, William, 117
Hamm, Thomas D., 15–16, 51–52, 98, 100, 135, 275, 276, 277
Hampton, Virginia, 56
Handbook of International Organization, 238
Harding, Warren G., 241
Harris, Frederick Leverton, 179–80
Harris, J. Rendel, 14, 141, 144–45, 147, 169
Harris, J. Theodore, 178
Hartford Retreat, 115, 119
Hartshorne, Henry, 187–88
Harvey, Cyrus W., 87–88
Harvey, T. Edmund, 14, 181, 244

Haslam, John, 121
Haudenosaunee people, 24
Haverford College, 34, 54–55, 69, 78–79, 93, 107–8, 164–65, 262, 269
Haviland Bible Training School, 102
Hawaiian Islands, 82
Hawley-Smoot Tariff Act, 242
Hayes, Rutherford B., 237
Heath, Carl, 261, 266
Hedstrom, Matthew, 15, 165
Helena, Arkansas, 55
Herald of Peace, 84–85
heresy, 60, 137, 151, 162–63
Herrera, Rosaura, 192
Heyrick, Elizabeth, 39, 63
Hicks, Edward, 63–64
Hicks, Elias, 3, 59–62, 64, 65–67, 70, 103–4, 134, 150–52, 161, 186, 187
Hicksite Caln Quarterly Meeting, 40–41
Hicksite Friends of Genesee Yearly Meeting, 44, 52
Hicksites, 150–53
    abolitionism, 37–38, 50–52, 62–65, 104, 151
    approaches to spirituality, 157
    changing nature of ministry, 111
    and the FGC, 225–26
    freedmen aid, 55
    free produce movement, 44
    Hicksite-Orthodox split, 42
    Jones's *The Later Periods*, 273–74
    laws of nations, 186
    liberal Quakerism, 134–35, 254
    ministerial training, 108
    modernist strain, 188
    and Mott, 135
    Native American nations, 26–27
    overview, 50–53
    paid ministry, 279
    philanthropy, 185
    professional ministry, 103–5
    programmed and unprogrammed Friends, 94–95
    reform movements, 39
    revivalism, 76
    schism between Hicksite and Orthodox Quakers, 97
    separations/schisms, 3–7, 71, 215
    Social Gospel, 183

Hicksites *(continued)*
   Society for Universal Inquiry and
      Reform, 187
   status and social class, 110
   transcendentalism, 160–61
   and Whittier, 159
   and Wilbur, 154
   women, 64
higher education, 11, 79
High Point, North Carolina, 184
Hindus, 159, 208
Hine, J. G., 92
hireling ministry, 79, 81–82, 95–96, 100, 104–5, 157
Hirohito (emperor), 193
HMC (Home Mission Committee), 92, 137–38, 141
Hobbs, Barnabas C., 91
Hobbs, Mary Mendenhall, 136
Ho-Chunk nation, 27
Hodgkin, Edward, 252
Hodgkin, Henry T., 170–71, 200–202, 204, 207, 249, 253
Hodgkin, Thomas, 28–29, 141
Hodgson, Mary Jane, 137
Holdsworth, Violet Hodgkin, 147, 263
Hole, Adelaide, 194
Hole, Edgar, 194
Holguin, Cuba, 203
Holiness movement, 4–6, 13, 85–88, 92, 98–99, 136, 150, 154–58, 166–67, 169, 171, 193–95, 215, 255
Holton, Sandra Stanley, 13–14, 236
"Holy Experiment" (Penn), 232
Holy Spirit, 50, 77, 86, 101, 135–36, 151, 153, 198, 201–2, 209
Holy Spirit Church, 209
Holy Spirit in Puritan Faith and Experience, The (Nuttall), 143
home mission, 8, 106–7, 138
Home Mission Committee (HMC), 92, 137–38, 141
Home Rule for Ireland, 238
Honduras, 103
Hooton, Elizabeth, 59
Hoover, Herbert, 11, 31, 33–36, 233–34, 240–43, 245–47, 256
Hoover, Huldah Minthorn, 234

Hoover, J. Edgar, 32
Hoover, John Y., 234
Hoover, Lou Henry, 234
Hopper, Isaac T., 52
Hoshangabad, India, 195
Hotchkiss, Willis, 72, 194
House of Peers, Japan, 233, 239
Howarth, Samuel, 229
Howes, John F., 240
Hoyt, Fred, 210
Huanggutun Incident, 239
Hubbard, Richard J., 80
Hu Ching-I, 204
Hull, William, 226, 259
humanitarianism, 15, 33–34, 79, 160, 179, 230, 231, 240–43
Hunn, John, 47
Hunt, Jane, 25, 48
Hunt, Richard, 25

identity, challenges to, 60–62
idolatry, 205, 207
Ijin Gunzou (Dynamic Portraits of Eminent Figures) (Nitobe), 246
Immediate, Not Gradual Abolition (Heyrick), 39
immediatist abolitionism, 24, 40, 62
Immigration Act of 1924, 245
imperialism, 25–29, 33–36, 202–5, 215–20, 278
   See also empire(s)
Imperial Reserves, 239
India, 63, 72, 82, 191, 194–95, 197, 198, 208, 216, 237, 249, 265
Indiana/Indiana Yearly Meeting, 6, 16, 34–35, 46, 62, 80–82
   general meetings, 84
   modernist-fundamentalist conflict, 255
   overview, 53–54
   pacifism, 215
   paid ministry, 98
   prosperity, 184
   recorded ministers, 105
   revival movement, 86
   See also Richmond Conference
Indigenous peoples, 8, 20, 21, 26, 174
   See also Native Americans
individualism, 129–30, 173, 258–60

Industrial and Social Order Council, 182
Infant Asylum, 185
Inge, William Ralph "Dean," 144
Ingle, H. Larry, 15
insanity, 112–27
Inskip, John S., 85
intermarriage, 116–17, 177
interspirituality, 170–72
intervisitation, 64, 128
Inward Light, 59–60, 148
　and Bean, 91
　and the Bible, 132
　as debated issue, 157
　and Emerson, 160
　and Gurney, 76–77, 153
　Hicksites, 62, 150
　Holiness revivalism, 86
　liberal Quakerism, 129–31, 133–35, 143–44, 145–47
　and Mott, 151
　Quaker Renaissance, 168
Iowa/Iowa Yearly Meeting, 67, 82, 89–91, 98, 184, 203, 234, 255, 256–61
Ireland/Irish Friends, 21–22, 60, 107, 157, 185, 237–38, 249
Irish Home Rule, 177
Irish Potato Famine, 185
Isichei, Elizabeth, 13, 106
"Issue, The" (Bean), 91
Italy, 115, 242, 264
Iwate Production Cooperative Central Committee, 240

Jackson, Arthur, 260–61
Jacobi, Carl Wigand Maximilian, 117, 120–21
Jamaica, 8, 72, 203, 237–38, 249
Jamaica Yearly Meeting, 252
James, William, 112, 124–26, 162, 164–65, 170
Janney, Edward, 257
Janney, Samuel, 27
Japan, 8, 72, 191, 193, 198–99, 205–6, 233–35, 245–46, 249, 264, 265
　See also Nitobe, Inazo
Jay, Allen, 90, 93
Jenkins, Thomas, 255
Jerusalem, 196, 208
Jews Relief Act, 237

Johnson, Jane, 46
Johnson, Oliver, 52
John Woolman School, 108
Jones, Eli, 23, 54, 196–97, 208, 270
Jones, James Parnell, 54–55
Jones, Jane, 82–83
Jones, Mary Hoxie, 269, 272
Jones, Peace, 269
Jones, Rufus, 6, 13, 15, 60, 92–93, 268–80
　All-Friends Conference, London, 250–51, 253–54, 255
　All-Friends Conference, Oskaloosa, 257
　American Friends Service Committee, 71, 229–30
　"Basis of Quaker Optimism, The," 263
　on Bright, 236–37
　and Emerson, 133
　Friends World Conference, Philadelphia, 263–66
　and Harris, 169
　and Hoover, 241
　Inward Light, 145
　and James, 125–26
　Later Periods, The, 271–80
　liberal Quakerism, 136–37
　and the Malones, 167
　mysticism, 129–30, 164–66
　and nationalism, 208
　paid ministry, 103
　peace testimony, 227
　punitive God, 139
　Quaker education, 259
　Quaker Renaissance, 167–68
　race-relations issues, 34
　revivals, 84
　Richmond Declaration, 135
　Social Gospel, 188
　summer schools, 107
　and Thomas, 256
　World War I, 248
　See also American Friend, The
Jones, Sybil, 23, 54, 70, 80, 196, 208, 270, 274
Jones, Sylvester and May Mather, 203
Jones, Thomas, 259
journal-keeping, 150–52, 154, 155–56, 159–60, 165, 167
Journal of John Woolman (Whittier), 159–60

357

Journal of John Wilbur, 154
justification, 67, 77–78, 86–87, 91, 136

Kaffer War, 236
Kaifu, Chuzo, 193
Kaimosi, Kenya, 72, 103, 194, 209–10
Kansas/Kansas Yearly Meeting, 6, 88, 91, 98, 207, 209, 215, 255, 257
Kelley, Abby, 48
Kellogg-Briand Pact, 239
Kelly, Thomas, 165
Kennedy, Thomas, 12, 13, 144, 175, 176, 178, 180–81, 218–19, 225
Kennett Monthly Meeting, 53
Kent, Stephen A., 125
Kenya, 8, 16, 72, 103, 191, 192–94, 196–97, 206, 209–10, 223, 265, 278
Kershner, Jon, 15
Keswick Movement, 163, 169
Kett, Anna, 13
Kida, Bunji and Toshi, 193
Kimber, Emmor, 43
Kimber, Thomas, 91
Kimberley, John, 181
King Philip's War, 21
King's African Rifles, 204–5, 223
Kiowas, 27
Knight, Rachel, 252
Krippner, Jim, 16
Ku Klux Klan (KKK), 34–35, 186

labor movement, 162, 181, 217
Labour Party, 30
Ladies' Peace Auxiliary, 219
Lake Mohonk Conference, 27–28, 217
Later Periods of Quakerism, The (Jones), 268, 271–80
Latin America, 89, 172, 174, 191, 216, 242
laws of nations, 186–87
Lay, Benjamin, 22
Laymen's Foreign Missions Inquiry, 208–9, 270
League of Nations, 231, 238–39, 244–45, 251
Leatham, Edward Aldam, 243
Leatham, William Henry, 243
Lebanon, 8, 72
Lenape people, 233

"Letter to a Member of the Society of Friends" (Bassett), 43
"Letter to the Kings of the Indians" (Penn), 21
Liberal Party government, 29–30
Liberal Protestants, 109
liberal Quakerism, 6–7, 218, 221, 275–80
  All-Friends Conference, Oskaloosa, 258
  in America, 132–37
  British Friends, 92, 137–38
  Broad Church theology, 131–32, 139
  Inward Light, 145–47
  James on, 112
  Manchester Conference, 140–45
  mysticism and modernism, 164–65
  pastoral system, 108–11
  previous studies, 14, 128–48
  programmed and unprogrammed Friends, 94
  Quaker Renaissance, 167–70
  religious madness, 124–26
  theological challenges, 139–40
  and Whittier, 160
liberal Quaker renewal, 249, 250, 255–56
liberal reform peace movement, 222
Liberal Unionists, 179
Liberator, The, 39, 159
Liberia, 23–24
Liberty Party, 54
"Lifestories" (Oliver), 166
Light Within. *See* Inward Light
Lincoln, Abraham, 38–39, 54–56, 237
literacy, 8, 10, 73, 106, 176
  See also adult schools
literature, 67–68
Littleboy, Wilfrid, 17, 169–70
Liverpool and Birkenhead Women's Peace and Arbitration Society, 219
Llandudno, Wales, 248, 252
LMS (London Missionary Society), 201–2
Local Peace Association, 219
Logan, James, 21
London *Globe*, 122
London/London Yearly Meeting
  antislavery activism, 200
  and Clark, 76
  and the FAU, 224

"Foundations of a True Social Order,"
    181–82
  and the FSC, 225
  Hicksites, 135–36
  ministry, 96–97, 107
  mission work, 194, 201
  and peace, 249
  peace testimony, 218–21
  and politics, 235
  Quaker identity, 60
  recorded ministers, 95, 108
  responses to revival movement, 91–92
  Richmond Conference, 157
  Richmond Declaration, 168
  social class, 110
  Social Order Committee, 173–74
  "Testimony of Peace," 222
  War and Social Order Committee
    (WSOC), 180
  and Wilbur, 77
  See also All-Friends Conferences
London Missionary Society (LMS),
    201–2
London Naval Treaty, 242
Longoria, Ramon, 16
López Matias, Ramón, 116
Lotz, Kati, 265
Luhya people, 194, 197, 206, 210
Lundy, Benjamin, 39, 63
Lung'aho, Daudi and Maraga, 194
Lunn, Pam, 14, 179
Luther, Martin, 109
Lyell, Charles, 141
Lynn, Massachusetts, 184
Lytton Report, 239, 245

MacDonald, George, 139–40
Madagascar, 8, 82, 191, 201–2, 204, 249, 265
Madhya Pradesh, 195
Malone, Emma Brown, 8, 70, 166–67
Malone, J. Walter, 8, 166–67, 184
Malone College, 102
Malone University, 166
Manasseh, Pamela, 182
Manchester, England, 137
Manchester Conference, 71, 110, 131–32,
    140–42, 168, 169, 178
Manchuria, 239, 246

Manual of Psychological Medicine (Tuke),
    123–24, 126
Maragoli people, 194, 196, 204–6, 223–24
marriage, 10, 48–49, 87, 116–17, 175–76, 177,
    197
Marriott, Charles, 44–45, 52
Martin, Zenas, 203
Martineau, Harriet, 131
Martinez, Emma Philips, 203
Maryland, 62, 65, 88
Massachusetts, 14, 20, 22–23, 47, 162, 184
materialism, 147–48
Mathews, Shailer, 102
Matsuyama Incident, 239
Maurice, Frederick Denison, 132, 177
McClintock, Mary Ann, 48
McClintock, Thomas, 63
McCrummell, James, 40
McKinley, William, 28
McLaren, Alexander, 132
McLean Asylum, 115
Meeting for Sufferings, 42–43, 53, 219, 221,
    225
meetinghouses, 50–51, 88–89, 100
Meetings of Ministry and Counsel, 104
Meiji era, 193
Meiji Restoration, 238
Mendenhall, Nereus, 91, 136
Mendl, Wolf, 9
Mendlesohn, Farah, 15
mental health and illness, 10, 113, 114–26,
    270–71
Message and Mission of Quakerism, The
    (Hodgkin and Braithwaite), 171
"Message to Friends and Fellow Seekers,"
    231
Metcalfe, Rachel, 8, 195
Methodists/Methodism, 4, 66–67, 70,
    82–83, 113, 117, 123, 154–56, 192, 202
metropole-periphery axis, 19–20, 26
Mexican Border War, 226
Mexican War, 26
Mexico, 8, 31, 72, 226, 262
Michigan, 52–53, 55
Middle East, 70, 196, 215–16
Middletown, Pennsylvania, 183
Midwest, 4, 70, 94, 167, 172
Miles, Laban J., 234

militarism, opposition to, 216–20, 222, 252
  See also peace testimony
Military Service Act, 222–24, 244
Miller, William, 123
Milligan, Edward, 2, 17, 176
Mingins, Rosemary, 13
ministry
  changing nature of, 111
  early Friends attitudes toward, 95–97
  hireling ministry, 79, 81–82, 95–96, 100, 104–5, 157
  paid ministry, 94, 97–99, 101–7, 109, 111, 138, 167, 279
  pastoral system, 97–103
  programmed and unprogrammed Friends, 94–95
  recorded ministers, 9, 78–79, 95, 97, 104–105, 107–108, 109, 111
  renewal movement, 79
  revival movement, 84–85, 87
  social order, 177
  traveling ministry, 155
  women in, 89, 96, 100–103
  and Woodbroke, 144
Ministry of Finance, 240
Minthorn, Henry John, 234
Missionary Life, A (Budge), 152
mission work, 191–212
  in Africa, 8, 16, 72, 89, 103, 157, 172, 192–94, 196–97, 202–5, 206, 209–10
  American Friends, 72–73, 82, 197, 202–11
  British Friends, 28, 72, 194–95, 201
  diverse origins of, 192–95
  and empire, 202–5
  evangelical spirituality, 157
  gender in, 196–97
  Global Quakerism, 7–9, 13
  Gurneyites, 80–82
  home mission, 8, 137–38, 141
  modernizing world, 72–73, 265–66
  and nationalism, 206–10
  non-Christian culture, 205–6
  pastoral system, 103
  Quaker distinctives in, 198–200
  revival movement, 89
  theological basis of, 200–202
  women, 192–97
Mississippi, 48

Mississippi River Valley, 33, 56, 75, 242
Mizuno, Rentarou, 239
model villages, 178
Moderate Friends, 5, 91–93
modernism, 6, 164–66, 171–72
modernist-fundamentalist conflict, 165, 255–56
modernists, 5–6, 102–3, 170
modernization, 61, 63, 65–69, 71, 73
modern Quaker diversity, creation of, 275–80
Molinos, Miguel, 158
Mombo, Esther, 16, 197, 210
Monterey, California, 234
Moody, Dwight L., 166
Mooresville, Indiana, 82
More, Henry, 147
Morrow, Emma, 192
Mott, Edward, 258, 260
Mott, James, 24–25, 43, 63
Mott, Lucretia Coffin
  and abolitionism, 37–38, 40, 42–43
  American Civil War, 54
  biography of, 14
  as dissenter, 188
  liberal Quakerism, 134–35
  paid ministry, 104
  as sectarian, 151–52
  and the Seneca Falls Convention, 24–25
  transcendentalism, 161
  women's rights, 48–49
Mount Street Meetinghouse, 140–41
Mukand Naik, Bal, 198–99
Mulobi, Jonathan, 210
Murray, Effie, 197
music, 68, 88–89, 99, 155
Mutua, Rasoa, 194, 197
mysticism, 124–26, 129–30, 133, 144–46, 158–61, 163–66, 169–71, 270–71, 273–77

NAACP (National Association for the Advancement of Colored People), 34–35
Nanjing, China, 197, 203–7
Nash, George, 241
National Christian Council of China, 202
National Defense Act, 228

National Holiness Association, 156
National Institute of Health and Veterans
    Administration, 242
nationalism, 206–10
National Peace Conference, 226
national security state, 31–33
National Urban League, 34
Native Americans, 11, 21, 22, 24, 26–28, 59,
    186, 201, 234, 273
natural religion, 131
"Nature and Authority of Conscience,
    The" (Rowntree), 250
Nature of Quakerism, The (Brinton), 170
Nayler, James, 59
Neall, Daniel, 43
NEASS (New England Anti-Slavery
    Society), 39–40
Nemesis of Faith, The (Froude), 131
neoevangelicalism, 6, 255, 267
Netherlands, 15, 262
New Castle, Indiana, 34, 184
New England Anti-Slavery Society
    (NEASS), 39–40
New England/New England Yearly
    Meeting, 7, 15, 21, 56, 77, 92–93, 154
  free produce movement, 45
  Gurney-Wilbur conflict, 50
  Quaker identity, 61–62
  silent worship, 159
  Unitarians, 61, 63, 79, 109, 133, 161
New England Non-Resistance Society, 43
New Jersey, 14, 21, 65, 232
Newman, Henry Stanley, 28, 202–3
Newport, Elizabeth, 54
Newport, Indiana, 46
New York Infirmary for Women and
    Children, 185
New York/New York Yearly Meeting, 7, 14
  and abolitionism, 24, 40–42
  freedmen aid, 56
  free produce movement, 44–45
  meetinghouses, 88
  and peace, 249
  psychiatric treatment, 115
  Quaker identity, 60–62
  separations/schisms, 52
  social order, 183
  Underground Railroad, 46

women's rights, 48
Workingmen's Party movement, 187
New York Society for the Relief of the
    Ruptured and Crippled, 185
New Zealand, 249
"Next Steps in the International
    Cooperation of Friends," 262
Ngesa, Stanley Chagala, 206, 223
Nichols, Elizabeth Pease, 71
Nicholson, Timothy, 90–93
Nicholson, William, 91
Nickalls, John L., 17
Niebuhr, Reinhold, 264
Nitobe, Inazo, 72, 193, 199, 233–35, 238–40,
    244–47
Nobel Peace Prize, 33, 213, 264
Noel-Baker, Philip John, 244
non-Christians, 198, 205–6, 208
noncombatant service, 12, 224, 228,
    321n30
non-Quakers, 29, 68
  abolitionism, 38, 104
  and business community, 184–85
  clothing, 69
  First Day school movement, 106
  intermarriage, 177
  justification and sanctification, 77
  ministering women, 89
  and pacifism, 213
  peace testimony, 222
  public relations campaign, 277–78
  radical innovations, 82
  reform movements, 49–50
  social class, 110
  theorists of the mind, 115, 117–18
  and Whittier, 159
nonresistance, 38, 52, 235
nonviolence. *See* peace testimony
Norris, William, 61
North America, social order in, 182–89
North Carolina, 14, 46, 88, 90, 184, 188
Norway, 15, 59, 249
Nuttall, Geoffrey F., 143

O'Brien, Mary, 178
*Observations on the Distinguishing Views
    and Practices of the Society of Friends*
    (Gurney), 153

Observations on the Influence of Religion (Brigham), 119–20
O'Donnell, Elizabeth, 13–14
Official Report, 251
Ohio Friends Mission, 198
Ohio/Ohio Yearly Meetings, 4, 6, 16
    antislavery petitions, 41
    free produce movement, 45
    Gurney-Wilbur conflict, 50
    Indiana Yearly Meeting, 84
    Inward Light, 134
    meetinghouses, 88–89
    mission work, 195, 204
    Ohio Friends in Nanjing, 203, 207
    pacifism, 215
    Richmond Declaration of Faith, 157
    separations/schisms, 52–53, 62
    Wilburites, 77
Ohio Valley, 65, 67, 187
Oliver, John, 166
Omaha nation, 27
Opie, Amelia, 68
Opium Wars, 216
Oregon/Oregon Yearly Meeting, 6, 8, 14, 15, 215, 255, 256, 258
Origin of Species by Means of Natural Selection (Darwin), 131
Orthodox Chicago Friends Meeting, 184
Orthodox Friends
    abolitionism, 24, 63
    Anti-Slavery Friends, 54
    freedmen aid, 55
    free produce movement, 44–45
    Friends World Conference, Philadelphia, 262
    Gurneyites and Wilburites, 77
    Jones's *The Later Periods*, 273–74
    liberal Quakerism, 134, 135
    liberal Quaker renewal, 255
    ministerial training, 108
    mission work, 29
    Native Americans, 26–27
    overview, 49–50
    paid ministry, 103–4, 279
    philanthropy, 185–86
    previous studies, 15
    reform movements, 38
    revivalism, 160
    schism between Hicksite and Orthodox Quakers, 95
    separations/schisms, 3–4, 62, 150
    Social Gospel, 188–89
    social order, 183
    See also Richmond Conference; Richmond Declaration
Osborn, Charles, 50, 53
Oskaloosa, Iowa, 256–61
"Our Testimony of Peace," 221–22
Owen, Robert Dale, 187

pacifism. *See* peace testimony
Packer, Ian, 179
paid ministry, 94, 97–99, 101–7, 109, 111, 138, 167, 279
Palestine, 8, 70, 223
Palfreeman, Linda, 224
Palmer, A. Mitchell, 32–33
Paraguay, 200
Parker, John J., 35
Parker, Margaret, 210
Parliament, 11, 114, 175–79, 181, 224, 232, 236–37, 245
Parliament of Nations, 226
pastoral Friends, 94–111, 184, 189, 255
    attitudes toward ministry, 95–97
    British Friends, 106–8
    changing nature of ministry, 111
    Gurneyites, 97–103
    Hicksite views on professional ministry, 103–5
    liberal Quakerism, 108–10
    meetinghouses, 88–89
paternalism, 181, 210
patriotism, 179, 221–24, 230
Paul (apostle), 96, 101
Paul, Alice, 60, 71
Pawnee nation, 27
peace conferences. *See* All-Friends Conferences
peace policy, Grant's, 11, 26–27, 28
Peace Society. *See* Society for the Promotion of Permanent and Universal Peace
peace testimony, 213–31

after World War I, 230–31
All-Friends Conference, London, 251, 252, 254
antislavery activism, 38
British Friends, 28–29, 167
Chaco War, 200
Dell on, 258–59
FAU's work, 180
laws of nations, 186
and Nitobe, 233–34
and politics, 234
prelude to World War I, 215–21
social action, 182
social order 175
World War I, 221–30, 248–49
Pearsall, Robert, 163
Pease, Alfred Edward, 243
Pease, Arthur, 243
Pease, Henry, 243
Pease, Henry Fell, 243
Pease, Herbert Pike, 243
Pease, Joseph, 11, 175–76, 232–34, 237, 243, 245
Pease, Joseph Albert, 243–44
Pease, Joseph Whitwell, 177, 243
Peckover, Priscilla, 219
Pemba, Africa, 28, 191, 200, 202–5
Pendle Hill, 108, 170–71, 253, 270
Penn, William, 21, 26–27, 28, 59, 65, 152, 232–34
Penney, Norman, 143
Pennington, Levi, 259
Pennock, Abraham, 44
Pennock, Joseph, 51
Penn School, 56
Pennsylvania Abolition Society, 37, 46
Pennsylvania Anti-Slavery Society, 46
Pennsylvania Hospital, 116
Pennsylvania/Pennsylvania Yearly Meeting, 14, 20, 21–22, 27, 52–53, 62, 104, 183–84, 232
Pentecostals, 6, 161, 209
People's Hall, 51
perfectionism, 136, 154
Permanent Court of Arbitration, 217
Permanent International Court of Justice, 245

personal conscience, 221, 224, 227, 231
personalism, 15, 250, 254, 255, 328n8
petition campaigns, 40–42, 47–48
Philadelphia Female Anti-Slavery Society (PFASS), 40, 44
Philadelphia/Philadelphia Yearly Meeting
and abolitionism, 37, 40–46
African Americans in, 22–23
American Civil War, 54–56
Bureau of Indian Affairs, 242
Conservative Friends, 90
free produce movement, 44–45
Friends World Conference, 261–67
Gurney-Wilbur conflict, 50
and Jones, 15
and Mott, 151
peace testimony, 217
Pendle Hill, 170–71
and Penn, 152
and politics, 235
professional ministry, 105
psychiatric treatment, 114
separations/schisms, 4
silent worship, 159
social order, 183
Social Order Committee, 173–74
"Some Particular Advices," 227–28
Underground Railroad, 46
Wilburites, 77
Workingmen's Party movement, 187
philanthropy, 23, 30, 35, 77, 176, 180, 185–86, 188
Philippines, 28
Phillips, Brian, 10–11, 13, 175–81
Phillips, Sian, 14
Pickering College, 223
Pickett, Clarence, 188, 254, 261, 262, 266–67
Pinel, Philippe, 114–16, 117, 121
Pittsburgh Courier, 35
Pius VII (pope), 152
plainness and simplicity
British Friends, 65
and capitalism, 63–64
Gurneyites and Wilburites, 153–54
modernizing world, 65–69
as Quaker witness, 10–12
and reform, 177

363

INDEX

plainness and simplicity *(continued)*
    renewal movement, 78
    revivalism, 87–89
    separations/schisms, 3
    social order, 175
    at work, 245
Plains Native Americans, 27
"Plea for a Peaceable Spirit, A," 220
Plummer, Jonathan W., 185
politics, Quakers in, 31–36, 177, 232–47
    Bright, 235–38
    Hoover, 240–43
    Nitobe, 238–40, 244–47
    politicians in concert, 243–47
polities, 19–21
polygyny, 196–97
popular media, 68–69
popular reform movements, 39, 50–51
Portugal, 29–30
Post, Amy Kirby, 15, 161
Post, Isaac, 161
postwar reconstruction work, 230
Pound, Roscoe, 110
poverty, 185–86, 188
    See also relief work
Poverty (Rowntree), 178
Powicke, F. J., 147
pragmatism, 9
prayer meetings, 80–84
premillennialism, 172, 189
Prichard, James Cowles, 113, 118–19
Priestman, Arthur, 178–80
Priestman-Bright-Clark kinship circle, 13, 244
Principles of Psychology (James), 125
prisoners-of-war commission, 244
prison reform, 38, 49
professionalization of ministry, 94, 99, 101, 108, 109, 138
    See also paid ministry
programmed and unprogrammed Friends, 8–9, 94–95, 98–99, 103–5, 107, 111, 156, 172, 279
Progressive Friends, 16, 39, 47, 50, 52, 62–63, 104, 134, 152
Prohibition, 186–87
prophetic action, 9
prophetic ministry, 138

prosperity, 183–84, 248
protectionism, 179
Protectionist, 53
prudence and moderation, 184
    See also plainness and simplicity
psychiatry, 112–27
    liberal Quakerism, 124–26
    Quaker theories of the mind, 113–17
    religious madness debate, 117–24
Puerto Padre, Cuba, 203
Pugh, Sarah, 37, 48
Purdy, Alexander C., 102
Purvis, Robert, 40, 46

Quaker Emergency and War Victims Committee, 244
Quakerism Past and Present (Rowntree), 176–77
Quaker Renaissance, 144, 147, 167–70
Quakers in America, The (Hamm), 15
Quakers in Canada, The (Dorland), 220
"Quaker Solution to the War Problem, The" (Hull), 226
Quaker Spirituality (Steere), 149
Quaker Strongholds (Stephen), 163
Qualification of Women Act of 1907, 244
Quietism, 76, 134, 150, 152, 153–54, 155, 158, 168, 235, 274

"Race Problem, The" (Ganguly), 251–52
race/racism
    All-Friends Conference, London, 251–52
    All-Friends Conference, Oskaloosa, 259
    definite views on, 186
    and the Malones, 166
    race-relations issues, 34–35
    racial capitalism, 26
    racial empire, 22–24
    racial equality, 39–40, 45, 53
    racial hierarchies, 27–28, 202–3
    racial justice, 264–66
    women's rights, 49
    See also abolitionism
Ramallah, 196, 208, 223–24
Randazzo, Christy, 15
"Rare Specimen of a Quaker Preacher, A" (Johnson), 52

Rawlings, Henry, 139
Reasonable Faith, A, 128, 131, 139
reconciliatory action, 9
Reconstruction Finance Corporation, 243
recorded ministers, 9, 78–79, 95, 97, 104–5, 107–8, 109, 111
Red Cross, 230, 243
Rees, Deborah, 194
Rees, Emory, 194, 197
Reeve, Roxie, 196–97
Reform Act of 1832, 175, 232
Reform Act of 1867, 237
reform movements, 37–57
    abolitionism, 39–43
    American Civil War, 54–57
    free produce, 43–45
    Hicksites, 151
    ministry, 78–79
    separations/schisms, 49–54
    Underground Railroad, 45–47
    women's rights, 47–49
    See also social order, 1830–1937
rejection of pastoral systems, 108–11
relief work
    alternative service, 221, 223–24
    conference statements, 254
    in Europe, 240–43
    European consulates, 261
    and Hoover, 240–43
    modernizing world, 71
    peace testimony, 216
    previous studies, 15
    in South Africa, 219–20
    See also humanitarianism; mission work
Religious Fanaticism (Strachey), 163
religious madness, 112–27
    debate, 117–24
    liberal Quakerism, 124–26
    Quaker theories of the mind, 113–17
Reminiscences, 55
renewal Friends, 3–7, 67, 78–79, 84, 90–91, 155
Republican Party, 35
Requited Labor Convention, 43, 44
resistance to slavery by enslaved people, 45–46
responses to revival movement, 89–93
reunification movement, 7
revivalism, 12, 76, 80–82, 91, 98–99, 101–2, 135, 159–61, 168, 277
revival meetings, 16, 155, 234
revival movement, 76, 82–93
Rhoads, James E., 184
Rhoads, Samuel, 44
Rhode Island, 21, 232, 269
Richardson, George, 8
Richmond, Indiana, 53, 80, 88
Richmond Conference (1887), 5–6, 70–71, 157, 199
Richmond Conference (1947), 266.
Richmond Declaration, 6, 70–71, 135–36, 137, 139, 157, 168, 199, 207, 275
Robert Falconer (MacDonald), 139
Roberts, Arthur, 15
Roberts, Joseph Jenkins, 23
Robinson, Ellen, 219
Rochdale Preparative Meeting, 233
Rock, Hugh, 129
Rockefeller, John D. Jr., 103, 270
Rogers, Mary H., 89
Romantics, 129
Roosevelt, Franklin D., 240
Ross, Isabel, 264
Rowntree, Arnold Stephenson, 178–79, 181, 244
Rowntree, John Stephenson, 28–29, 69, 138, 176–77
Rowntree, John Wilhelm, 107, 142-45
    evangelical teachings, 136
    and James, 125
    Jones's *The Later Periods*, 274
    Manchester Conference of 1895, 178
    modernizing world, 71
    peace testimony, 29
    Quaker education, 259
    Quaker Renaissance, 167–68
Rowntree, Joseph, 30, 60, 139, 143, 176
Rowntree, Joshua, 243–44
Rowntree, Seebohm, 30, 145, 178
Rowntree family, 29–30, 31, 178–79
Rowntree History Series, 1, 13, 125, 142–43, 268, 271
Roy, Ram Mohun, 198
Roxas, Joseph, 116
Royal African Company, 20
Ruggles, David, 46

INDEX

Rules of Discipline, 235
rural/urban Quakers, 61, 183–84, 185
Rush, Benjamin, 116
Rush County, Indiana, 82–83, 184
Rushmore, Jane P., 105
Russell, David, 15
Russell, Elbert, 6, 88–89, 93, 102, 188, 265
Rustin, Bayard, 34, 60

Sacramental Test Act, 175
sacraments, 61, 70, 120, 135, 153, 157, 198–99, 202
Salomons, David, 237
Salpêtrière Hospital, Paris, 115, 117, 121
salvation, 10, 61, 76, 77–78, 104, 136, 140, 198, 205, 209
sanctification, 67, 77–78, 85–87, 90–91, 98, 136, 152, 154–57
San Jose, California, 156
São Tomé, 29–30
Sapporo Band, 233
Sartor Resartus, 233
Saturday Review, 156
Scarborough Summer School, 144
schisms. *See* separations/schisms
Schmidt, Leigh Eric, 171, 254
Schrauwers, Albert, 16
Scramble for Africa, 216
Sea Islands, South Carolina, 56
Second Day Morning Meeting, 96–97
second-experience sanctification, 76, 85
Second Great Awakening, 39, 59
Second Moroccan Crisis, 221
sectarians/sectarianism, 10–13, 87, 151, 153, 157, 161, 171
Sefton-Jones, Herbert, 222
Selective Service Act, 228–29
self-reliance, 133–34
seminaries, 101–2, 107–8, 111, 168
Seneca Falls Convention, 24–25, 48
separations/schisms
    and the AFSC, 71, 229
    and diversity, 174
    Great Separation, 134, 274
    Gurneyites and Wilburites, 153
    Jones on, 274
    justification and sanctification, 77
    modernist-fundamentalist conflict, 255

multiple Quakerisms, 2–7
overview, 49–54
peace testimony, 214
prelude to World War I, 215
responses to revival movement, 89–93
unity, 130–31
settler colonialism, 20, 26
settlers, 19–21, 23
Shanghai War of 1932, 239
Sharon Temple, 16
Sharpless, Isaac, 217–18
Shaw, Amy, 223
Shillitoe, Thomas, 66
Shipley, Murray, 80
Sichuan, 199–200, 202, 203–4, 205, 207
silent worship, 4, 80, 91, 94, 98, 105, 109–10, 130, 150, 155, 156, 157, 159, 163, 168–69
simplicity. *See* plainness and simplicity
Sino-Japanese War, 199
slavery
    definite views on, 186
    diversity of Quakerism, 183
    and empire, 20
    and Gurney, 66
    Hicksites, 61–63
    mission work, 200
    and pacifism, 215
    Portuguese colonies, 29–30
    separations/schisms, 134
    and Whittier, 159
    See also abolitionism
Smiley, Albert, 27, 28, 217
Smith, Ada, 272
Smith, Archibald, 259
Smith, Florence, 192
Smith, Gerrit, 24, 44
Smith, Hannah Whitall, 15, 86, 161–63, 274
Smith, Helen, 14
Smith, Joseph H., 99
Smith, Ruth Esther, 192, 197
social activism/action, 66, 130, 169, 170, 182
social Christianity, 15
social class, 110–11
Social Gospel, 165, 183, 187–88, 193
Socialist Quaker Society (SQS), 178
socialist Quakers/socialism, 174, 177, 178–79, 180, 182, 187–89, 217, 251, 255

Social Law in the Spiritual World (Jones), 165, 250
social order, 1830–1937, 173–89
  Britain, 174–82
  North America, 182–89
social reform, 38, 49–50, 165, 178–80, 182
Society for the Promotion of Permanent and Universal Peace, 216
Society for Universal Inquiry and Reform, 70, 187
"Society of Friends and the Problem, The" (Howarth), 229
Socknat, Thomas P., 220
"Some Particular Advices for Friends and A Statement of Loyalty for Others," 227–28
Soul Winner, The, 167
South Africa, 20, 218–20, 252, 263
Southall, Joseph Edward, 12
South America, 8, 16, 157, 172, 242, 278
South Asia, 20
Southern, Alice, 143
Southland, Arkansas, 81
South Manchuria Railway, 239
Soviet Russia, 188
Spain, 21
Spanish-American War, 28, 203, 218
Spencer, Carole, 15, 136, 196–97, 270–71, 276
Spielhofer, Sheila, 15
Spiritualism, 15, 123, 161, 163
spoken ministry, 138
Springfield, Pennsylvania, 185
Spurgeon, Charles Haddon, 139
SQS (Socialist Quaker Society), 178
Stanley, Lenna, 197
Stanton, Elizabeth Cady, 24, 48–49
Stanton, Henry, 24, 48
Stanton, Joseph, 24
Steere, Douglas, 165
Stephen, Caroline, 14, 28–29, 144, 145–47, 163–64, 218, 274
Still, William, 37, 46
Stimson, Henry, 245–46
St. Luke's Hospital, 114
Stockton and Darlington Railway Bill, 234
store movement, 56

Studies in Mystical Religion (Jones), 126
Sturge, Joseph, 14
Sturge, Matilda, 142–43
subconscious, 146
Suez Canal, 216
summer school movement, 142–44
Swanwick conference (1911), 221
Swarthmore College, 108, 250, 262–63
Swayne, Noah Haynes, 232
Sweden, 15, 262, 265
Switzerland, 262
Sykes, Marjorie, 195
Syria, 8, 249, 265

Talbot, Caroline E., 89, 92
Tanaka, Giichi, 239
Tappan, Lewis, 40, 44, 48
Tatum, Lawrie, 27, 31
Tauler, Johannes, 144
Taylor, Amy Murrell, 56
Taylor, Frederick Winslow, 30–31, 33
Taylor, George W., 37–38, 44–45
Taylor Society, 30
Te-chen Wu, 239
technology, modern, 61, 68, 72–73
temperance, 10, 38, 49, 50, 52, 76, 97
Test Act of 1673, 232
testimony against war. *See* peace testimony
Thatcher, Albert G., 227–28
Theology of Holiness (Clark), 156
theorists of the mind, 112–28
Thomas, John J., 186–87
Thomas, Nancy, 16
Thomas, Samuel, 196
Thomas, Wilbur, 256–57, 259
Thompson, Jeremiah, 61
Thompson, Silvanus P., 140–41
Thoreau, Henry, 161
Thorp, Margaret, 222
Thurman, Howard, 15, 34, 165
Tierney, Agnes, 259, 261
Tokyo, Japan, 193, 199
Tokyo Medical Services Users' Cooperative, 240
Tolles, Frederick B., 160, 247
Tomlinson, A. J., 161
Toshi Kida, 193
trade unions, 177–79

Training School for Christian Workers, 102, 192
transcendentalism, 61, 133, 151, 160–61
traveling ministry, 87, 97, 155
Treatise on Insanity (Pinel), 115–16
Treatise on Insanity (Prichard), 119
Trevino, Maria de los Santos, 203
Trine, Ralph Waldo, 125
Trueblood, D. Elton, 101, 111
Trueblood, Willard, 210, 259–60
true church, 9–10, 13, 79
Tubman, Harriet, 47
Tuke, Daniel Hack, 123–24, 126
Tuke, Henry, 114
Tuke, Samuel, 114, 118–19, 122
Tuke, William, 114
Tuke family, 113
Tyzack, Charles, 202

Uchimura, Kanzo, 193
Underground Railroad, 39, 45–47, 234
Underhill, Evelyn, 144
Union, 54–56, 237
unionist movements, 177–79, 181, 187
Unitarians/Unitarianism, 63, 68, 79, 109, 133, 151, 161
United Fruit Company, 203
United Nations, 244, 266
universalism, 74, 163
University of Chicago Divinity School, 102
University of Edinburgh, 112, 262
unmarried women, 196–97
Unselfishness of God and How I Discovered It, The (Smith), 162
Updegraff, David B., 5, 67, 85–88, 91, 98, 101, 136, 156
urban Quakers. *See* rural/urban Quakers
Urundi, 209, 210
US Congress, 23, 26, 32, 40–42, 59
US Embassy Brussels Office of Public Diplomacy, 243
US Food Administration, 241

Valiant Sixty, 200–201
Varieties of Religious Experience (James), 124–25, 164
Victoria, Queen, 177, 243, 245
Victorian age, 13, 121, 131, 163

vigilance committees, 46
Vigilant Association, 46
Vining, Elizabeth Gray, 149, 165, 193
Virginia, 14, 20, 56, 65
Virginia Company of London, 21
Voysey, Charles, 137

Wakefield, Edward, 114
Walker, David, 39, 45
Wall, Garrett, 41
Walnut Ridge Meeting, 82–84
war, opposition to. *See* peace testimony
War and Social Order Committee (WSOC), 173–74, 180–82
War Department, 229
Washington, DC, 41, 56
water baptism, 5–6, 67, 156, 198–99
Weld, Theodore, 40
Welsh mining communities, 182
Wesleyan Holiness, 172
Wesleyans, 156, 161
West Africa, 20, 23
West China, 202, 204
West Coast of the United States, 172
Western Freedmen's Aid Society, 55
Western Yearly Meetings, 6, 89–90, 98, 255
West Milton, Ohio, 88–89
Westport, Massachusetts, 22–23
Wharton, Joseph, 26, 184
Wharton, William, 30
White, Josiah, 61
White, William, 183
Whitman, Walt, 125, 160, 161, 254
Whitney, Mary Caroline Braithwaite, 193
Whitney, William Cogswell, 193
Whitson, Elizabeth, 41
Whitson, Moses, 41
Whitson, Thomas, 41
Whittier, California, 192
Whittier, John Greenleaf, 37–40, 46, 68, 81, 133, 140, 158–60, 274
"Why I Am a Friend" (Bean), 156
Wichita, Kansas, 257
Wilbur, Henry, 105
Wilbur, John, 3–4, 49–50, 62, 77–78, 134, 154, 274
Wilburites, 4–5, 39, 49–50, 76–78, 90, 98, 134, 153–54, 157, 159, 185, 215, 273–74

Willets, Samuel, 185
William Penn College, 257
Williams, Rowland, 132
Williams, Walter R., 201, 207–8
Williamson, Passmore, 37, 46
Willson, David, 16
Wilmington, Delaware, 47, 187
Wilson, Albert, 222
Wilson, Francesca, 14
Wilson, John William, 179–81, 244
Wilson, Lloyd Lee, 16
Wilson, Woodrow, 32, 225, 241
Winchester, Indiana, 82
Winona Lake Peace Conference of Young Friends, 226, 229
Woman Learning in Silence, The (Fox), 96
Woman's Christian Temperance Union, 162
women
  abolitionism, 45
  antiwar activism, 219
  asylums, 121
  and labor, 176
  and the Malones, 166
  in ministry, 89, 96, 100–103
  mission work, 192–97
  philanthropy, 185
  previous studies, 13–16
  in public office, 232, 244
  social order, 175
  spiritual guidelines, 64
  Underground Railroad, 46
  women's rights, 24, 38, 47–49, 161, 162
Women's Foreign Missionary Association of Philadelphia Yearly Meeting, 193
Women's Peace Army, 222–23
Women's Speaking Justified (Fell), 96
Wood, Carolena, 253
Wood, Herbert George, 132, 146–47, 266
Wood, James, 91
Wood, L. Hollingsworth, 34, 226, 265–66
Woodbrooke Settlement, 108, 132, 142–44, 168–70, 181, 270
Woodward, Luke, 99
Woodward, Samuel, 123
Woodward, Walter C., 6, 187, 250–51, 254–55, 260, 262, 266–67
Woolman, John, 21–22, 43–44, 125, 159–60, 170, 253
Wooton, Daniel, 55
Workingmen's Party movement, 187
Working Women's Protective Union, 185
World Council of Churches, 262, 264
World's Anti-Slavery Convention, 48
World War I, 12, 33, 167, 175, 180–82, 192, 204–5, 213–31, 234, 240–41, 248–49
Worsdell, Edward, 136, 140
Wright, Martha Coffin, 48
WSOC (War and Social Order Committee), 173–74, 180–82
Wynter, Rebecca, 224

York Asylum/Retreat, 113, 114, 116–17, 118, 121, 122
Young Friends Movement, 221, 329n24

www.ingramcontent.com/pod-product-compliance
Lightning Source LLC
Chambersburg PA
CBHW022026290426
44109CB00014B/768